Rebecca S. Katz

The Georgian Regime Crisis of 2003-2004

A Case Study in Post-Soviet Media Representation of Politics, Crime and Corruption

SOVIET AND POST-SOVIET POLITICS AND SOCIETY

ISSN 1614-3515

Recent volumes

Rebecca S. Katz

THE GEORGIAN REGIME CRISIS OF 2003-2004

A Case Study in Post-Soviet Media Representation of Politics, Crime and Corruption

ibidem-Verlag
Stuttgart

Bibliografische Information der Deutschen Nationalbibliothek
Die Deutsche Nationalbibliothek verzeichnet diese Publikation in der
Deutschen Nationalbibliografie; detaillierte bibliografische Daten sind im
Internet über http://dnb.d-nb.de abrufbar.

Bibliographic information published by the Deutsche Nationalbibliothek
Die Deutsche Nationalbibliothek lists this publication in the Deutsche Nationalbibliografie;
detailed bibliographic data are available in the Internet at http://dnb.d-nb.de.

Editorial Assistance: Elena Sivuda

Cover picture: Tbilisi residents listen to political speeches in the fall of
2003. The overlaying photo captures a spiral outdoor staircase representing Georgia's ongoing struggle to improve their lives. © Rebecca
S. Katz

A CIP catalogue record for this book is available from:
Die Deutsche Bibliothek
http://dnb.ddb.de

∞

Gedruckt auf alterungsbeständigem, säurefreien Papier
Printed on acid-free paper

ISSN: 1614-3515

ISBN: 3-89821-413-3

© *ibidem*-Verlag
Stuttgart 2006
Alle Rechte vorbehalten

To Shelley White

Contents

Abbreviations

ABA	American Bar Association
AES	American Electric Services
BPG	(Caucasian) Brand Protection Group
BPI	Bribe Payers Index
BTC	Baku-Tbilisi-Ceyhan (oil pipeline)
CBPG	Caucasian Brand Protection Group
CEC	Central Election Commission
CEU	Central European University
CIA	Central Intelligence Agency
CIS	Commonwealth of Independent States
CoE	Council of Europe
CPI	Corruption Perceptions Index
EBSCO	Elton B. Stevens Company Information Services
FATF	Financial Action Task Force
FIAE	Foundation for International Arts and Education
FSU	Former Soviet Union
GAZPROM	*Gazovaya promyshlennost'* (Gas Industry)
GEL	Georgia Lari (ISO Georgian currency code)
GESI	Georgia Energy Security Initiative
GIOGIE	Georgian International Oil, Bas, and Energy (conference)
GYLA	The Georgian Young Lawyer's Association
IAW	In Accordance With
IDP	Internally Displaced Peoples
IFES	International Federation of Election Systems
IMF	International Monetary Fund
IOM	International Office of Migration
IREX	International Research and Exchange Board
IRI	International Republican Institute
ISFED	International Society for Fair Elections and Democracy

KGB	*Komitet gosudarstvennoi bezopasnosti* (Committee for State Security)
MP	Member of Parliament
NAFTA	North American Free Trade Association
NDI	National Democratic Institute
NGO	non-governmental organization
ODIHR	Office for Democratic Institutions and Human Rights
OSCE	Organization for Security and Cooperation in Europe
OSI	Open Society Institute
PACE	Parliamentary Assembly of the Council of Europe
PMMG	Public Movement "Multinational Georgia"
RAO EES	*Rossiiskoe [otkrytoe] aktsionernoe obshchestvo [energetiki i elektrifikatsii] "Edinaya energeticheskaya sistema"* (Russian [Open] Stock Company [of Energy and Electrification] "Unified Energy Systems")
SCAD	Southern Caucasus Anti-Drug Program
SOCAR	State Oil Company of *Azerbaijan*
SPSS	Statistical Package for the Social Sciences
TBC	Transbalkan Pipeline Company
UDC	United Georgian Energy Distribution Company
UNDP	United Nations Development Program
USAID	United States Agency for International Development
USSR	Union of Soviet Socialist Republics
WTO	World Trade Organization

List of Tables

List of Illustrations

Introduction

Theory development in criminology limits itself to an analysis of tip of the iceberg issues such as time-limited delinquency or a similar shortsighted focus on explaining crime within rich and powerful Western Nation States. Such a narrow focus only serves our own short-term interests and fails to analyze and offer solutions to the world's most significant crime problems corruption and corporate crime.

Moreover, since 9/11 and the subsequent invasions of Afghanistan and Iraq, and the corporate criminal behavior of Enron and WorldCom it has become necessary for criminologists to become more interdisciplinary with theory aimed at explaining international crimes. Thus by conducting a sociological analysis of the political, social, and economic structures within a post-communist state, as reflected through major newspapers' social construction of real events, this book will provide a foundation for an interdisciplinary perspective on crime and corruption. Utilization of this narrative analysis of Georgian-English newspaper will lead toward the development of a new theory of international crime taking into account variations in crime across persons, times and places. Such a theory may explain crime by examining variations in social structural forces at the international, national, and local level providing a more complete picture of the interconnections among all these levels. Developing a broad theoretical model might explain both institutional and individual crime among Western democratic post-capitalist nation states and among non-western newly democratic nation states across the developing world. While I will not develop a comprehensive theory here, this narrative analysis provides substantive grounded theoretical and empirical evidence to begin constructing such a theory.

Scholars and a multitude of non-governmental organizations reveal that millions of global citizens live in poverty, amidst civil and ethnic conflicts or wars best characterized as a part of the state-making process and at worst clearly reflective of organized criminal enterprises.[1] Moreover, many of these nations' people live in places where corruption stands as the most common type of crime. Recently Laub and Sampson argued that the inception of criminal behavior and changes in criminal behavior over time remain embedded within historical and other contextual features of social life. No significant sociological or criminological work examines the effects of revolutions, wars, economic depressions, or natural disasters on crime across the globe, particularly within newly democratic developing countries or third world countries.[2] Recently Charles Tilly provided a theoretical model to explain collective violence and while laudable, the theory fails to provide an explanation encompassing corruption, non-violent government or corporate crime.[3] Other omissions include criminologists' failure to take into account the unique histories of different places as well as neglecting the effects of the socio-political economy on collective living.

These diverse forms of life in different places and spaces across the globe are so disparate and unique from American or Western conceptualizations it necessitates transforming our thinking about what defines crime. Although Western critical criminological and postmodern paradigms offer an opportunity to expand our academic thinking and become inclusive of the rest of the worlds' crime problems, they only offer the inception of a new idea. This idea necessitates an examination of our privileged positions and the ways in which that blinds us to seeing the world as it is rather than as we believe it exists.

Exploration of this privilege reveals that the discipline of criminology maintains an andocentric and Eurocentric perspective almost exclusively examining white male delinquency. Moreover, extant criminological theories rarely mention capitalism, democracy, civil rights, or human rights in the foreground of their theories but rather take those uniquely Western historical and

---

1   Charles Tilly, "War Making and State Making as Organized Crime." in Peter B. Evans et al., eds., *Bringing the State Back In* (Cambridge: Cambridge University Press, 1985).

2   John Laub and Robert Sampson, *Shared Beginnings, Divergent Lives* (Cambridge , MA, and London: Harvard University Press, 2003), 33-34.

3   Charles Tilly, *The Politics of Collective Violence Cambridge Studies in Contentious Politics* (Cambridge: Cambridge University Press, 2003).

institutional structures for granted.[4] Furthermore, as Carrington and Hogg explain, the discipline often courts political favor with the governmental powers thus stifling the intellectual rigor and detachment that is both necessary and sufficient to examine the effects of current institutional arrangements.[5] For example, only recently have some authors begun to ask how economic globalization affects international and national crime rates. Economic globalization is the birth-child of Western hegemonic powers that united transnational corporations with powerful rich governments resulting in not so subtle bullying of smaller, poorer, and less powerful nation states.

The political and economic domination of the poor by the rich cogently demonstrated in Green and Ward's book notes that "being asked for a bribe is the second common form of criminal victimization, after consumer fraud, outside the industrialized world."[6] The "grand corruption" of political elites reaches monetary heights up to four billion dollars annually. Similarly, few criminologists have opted to expose the truth about the extent to which the American Government has illegally pursued organizations or nation-states that threaten the existing status quo from Universities such as the Berkeley School of Criminology to the Black Panthers to individuals like Martin Luther King and nations like Chile or Iraq. Secondly, it is important to understand the variegations in these issues as they differ for women and different ethnic groups across place and time.[7] Specifically, some nation states never experienced the first wave of feminism or the equivalent of a civil rights movement for their ethnic minority peoples. Moreover, many nations exploited by early forms of European and American imperialism and colonialism continue to experience negative effects within their economy and civil society leading to increased crime.

I lived and worked in the Republic of Georgia for an academic year and while I had resided abroad before this experience, here I observed a lived

---

4   Penny Green and Tony Ward, *State Crime, Governments, Violence and Corruption* (London and Sterling, VI: Pluto Press, 2004).

5   Kerry Carrington and Russell Hogg, *Critical Criminology* (Devon, UK: Willan Publishing, 2002), 1.

6   Green and Ward, *State Crime, Governments, Violence and Corruption*, 1.

7   Rebecca S. Katz, "Genocide: The Ultimate Racial Profiling." *Journal of Law and Social Challenges* 5 (2003):65-92; Peggy C. Giordano, Stephen A. Cernkovich, & Jennifer L. Rudolph, "Gender, Crime, and Desistance: Toward a Theory of Cognitive Transformation." *American Journal of Sociology* 107 (2002):990-1064.

experience that forever changed my worldview. Objectivity while observing from the inside becomes a subjective and transformative experience. My observations, my experiences' and the Georgian-English newspapers I collected and analyzed here build the foundation for a human rights sociopolitical criminological theory of crime. Such a theory will offer a new way to understand and perhaps reduce crime, corruption, and economic and political inequality that plagues most of the world's people. As an outsider living inside the Georgian culture, I offer this narrative analysis of politics, crime, and corruption as socially constructed by a variety of Georgian English newspapers and journalists. Limitations of the research include the exclusion of an analysis of Georgian language newspapers.

Before beginning the analysis, readers require an overview of this nation's political, social, and economic history including Georgia's ethnic make-up and extraneous global pressures.

II   The History of Georgia in the Caucasus

For over fifty thousand years, a variety of tribal people occupied the geographic space in the Caucasus Region south of Russia and north of Turkey and Armenia. Georgia's east coast faces the Black Sea and its western border lies next to the Caspian Sea and *Azerbaijan*. For most of its history, Georgia survived in two halves, only briefly united in the eleventh century, and once again in the early twentieth century before Russian imperialism and then communism subsumed it. The western half of Georgia consists of several ancient regions referred to as *Colchis, Lazica, Absagia, Imeretia, Egrisi* or more recently *Abkhazeti* or *Imeretia*. During its classical period, the name of Eastern Georgia was Iberia and later became referred to as *Kartli* (in English, Georgia).[8] Georgia is a very small country about half the size of Portugal. As of 2003, four million three hundred and thirty three thousand people live in Georgia.[9]

The Georgian language, commonly referred to as a Caucasian language, developed into a variety of different dialects over four thousand years ago. Suny cites the work of ancient historians who report that dozens of dialects (*Svan, Mingrelian,* and *Laz*) and seventy unique Georgian tribes thrived in this area. These tribes included the *Karts*, the *Megrelo-chans*, the *Svans*, *Kashkia, Mushki* and the *Tibal* with respective Georgian language dialects.

Interestingly, Soviet scholars reported that a Georgian national consciousness began to develop as far back as the first century B.C. as communal societies transformed into tribal alliances and military democracies.[10] This nationalism was born amidst Georgians' incipient struggle with on-going foreign conquest. Georgia was once a part of the Hitte Empire, the Persian Empire (having a more pervasive influence than other empires), the Greek Em-

---

8   Ronald Gregor Suny, *The Making of the Georgian Nation* (Bloomington: Indiana University Press, 1994).
9   UNICEF Innocenti Research Centre, "Social Monitor 2004 Economic growth and child poverty in the CEE/CIS and the Baltic States." *United Nations' Children's Fund Innocenti Social Monitor* (2004).
10   Suny, *The Making of the Georgian Nation*, 7.

pire, the Roman Empire, and the Byzantine Empire. Georgia was also conquered by the Arabs, the Seljuk Turks, the Mongols and the Ottoman Turks (as well as Iranian and Daghestani invasions from the East), and finally the Russians in the late eighteenth century.

Although the current capital city of *Tbilisi was* an Islamic city for four hundred years until 1121, the state of *Kartli-Iberia* (Georgia) adopted Christianity in the fourth century when the pagan monarch King Mirian converted after receiving a visit from a former Christian slave from Turkey called *Nino*. She is now the major Saint in the Georgian Eastern Orthodox church. In the eleventh century, Georgia united under King *Bagrat* the III for six brief years and became for the first time, *Sakartvelo*, or Georgia, a political and ecclesiastical unit.[11] From the eighth through the eighteenth centuries competing princes and principalities of varying degrees of wealth ruled Georgia. However, most Georgians lived out their lives as poor agrarian peasants. Similar to its Russian neighbors to the north, it became frozen in time in a sort of middle age for a thousand years. Nevertheless, even in its early history Georgia grew into an artistic oasis. The State Museum in *Tbilisi* contains numerous artifacts of fine metal works from elaborately sculpted knives and swords to fine jewelry with delicately shaped and intricate designs emulating a variety of different shapes or animals. In this rich Georgian culture poetry, symphonies and plays became staple cultural products and remain so today even though most Georgians cannot afford to enjoy such luxuries. Georgia remains so poor today that only one floor of the state museum stands open to the public. Nonetheless, on every other building across *Tbilisi* commemorative plaques set facing the streets reminding passer bys that a famous artist, writer, or actor once lived in this building. Typically, streets names memorialize artists, not politicians.

In addition to their rich cultural repertoire Georgians also boast a powerful intellectual tradition. Specifically, by the late nineteenth century Marxist fervor began to grow in Georgia even before becoming visible in Russia. Russian educated Georgian intellectuals returned to Georgia with hopes of freeing Georgians from Russian imperialism and from the Armenian bourgeoisie who they perceived as their oppressors in the new factories. These

---

11   *Ibid.*, 33.

first Marxists in Georgia were Mensheviks not Bolsheviks, meaning that they were Social Democrats, highly nationalistic, and preferred the election of party representatives as opposed to the centralized version of party control preferred by the Leninists. As the revolution took shape in 1917, the Mensheviks called for a less radical revolution by first developing a bourgeoisie-democracy and later a workers' democracy. Small groups of factory workers joined forces with the intellectuals to foment the Menshevik's cause. Subsequently, the publication of an underground newspaper began and workers' organized strikes emanating from the *Tbilisi* Religious Seminary.

At that time, Joseph Stalin was one of these radical student leaders at the Seminary. Stalin (not his real name) was a Georgian born in the city of *Gori*, where a Soviet era museum still exists and is open to the public in his honor. There you will find no discussion of Stalin's purges and no evidence of his dictatorship. There is no discussion of his ruthlessness and no mention of him as an authoritarian or genocidal government official. Rather he is only praised there as a formidable and respected leader of the Soviet Union. Stepping inside and partaking in traditional tour resembles a time travel experience. It is as if the Soviet Union remained alive and well. Unfortunately, Georgian school-children continue to go to the museum and thus get a very white washed and nationalistic version of Joseph Stalin. On December twenty-first the Communist party in Gori celebrated the anniversary of his birth calling upon other Georgians to "stop calumny against Stalin."[12] Even the writer offers no explanation as to why some people might criticize the man who murdered untold numbers of people during his tenure as Communist Party leader. However, during the incipient stages of the Communist Revolution Stalin was a seminary student who fought against Russian imperialist control from within an oppressive academic administration.

Conflicts ensued between the Russians supporting the Czar and the Georgian Social Democrats as well as between Armenians and Azeris and the Czar's troops and Georgian workers. In 1905, the October Manifesto was declared limiting the power of the Czar. This declaration was symbolic at best and by 1906, Georgia's Social Democratic movement ended at the hands of the Czarist Russian government. Thus even early in the Communist Revolu-

---

12   N.N., "Stalin Anniversary." *Georgia Today* (19-25 December 2003):5.

tion Georgians were at the forefront of hopes for a socialist democracy, unfortunately, Russian imperialism prevented its development.

Suny argues that in the years prior to the First World War a fervent debate ensued regarding the question of nationalism. On the one hand, Stalin and his Bolshevik camp favored assimilation of ethnic minorities across a centralized state structure throughout the Transcaucasia area. By contrast, the Menshevik camp favored protection for all forms of national culture and a decentralized state structure. As the threat of Turkish invasion neared in 1914, Suny argues that each *Transcaucasia* ethnic group viewed the threat differently. Specifically, the Armenians, wanted to ensure their own victory and freedom in what was at the time Turkish Armenia. The Georgians and Azeri's (or Tartars) were both opposed to involvement in World War One. The Georgians were afraid of the Turks and the *Adjarans* (also Georgians), mostly Islamic, supported Turkey in the war. However, the Azeri's believed a war would only weaken Turkey who they saw as their brothers both then and now (ethnically and linguistically). Nevertheless, even after the Russians became victorious over the invading Turks in the Caucasus, Georgians and other *Transcaucasia* peoples continued to feel oppressed by the Czarist government. The Mensheviks continued to fight for Georgian autonomy and were noteworthy in their attempt to secure a more Marxist vision of the future. Interestingly, while post-Soviet Georgia pays homage to many of its writers, poets, and artists by naming streets after these cultural icons, there is no honor for the early Menshevik Revolutionaries, their underground newspapers, or the Social Democratic revolutionaries who fought for Georgian autonomy and freedom and against a centralized imperialistic and then Leninist version of Communism. Although the Mensheviks eventually lost control to the Bolsheviks, in the beginning of the revolution both groups remained dominated by Georgians. Perhaps an avoidance of this historical truth and the fact the Joseph Stalin and his primary henchman of the purges, Beria, were both Georgians, is more difficult to digest than the more sanitized version of history that the Georgians were simply victims of Russian Bolshevik Communism for seventy years. However, when the Mensheviks still welded some power early on, they were also guilty of committing murder against peasant opposition forces who they perceived as a threat to Menshevik power.

Georgians' slightly whitewashed version of history remains fueled by the current absence of any general historical education within the post-Soviet Georgian State University system, although by the spring of 2005 the curriculum and organization of the University was in transition. Georgian college students receive no general education and no de-communistized history of the Georgian nation. University students only study their unique discipline or major. However, a Fulbright Scholar teaching in Georgia during the late Soviet period (1990) explained that Georgian foreign language education in public school and the university was exceptional. It began and continued from age six to sixteen.[13] Evidence of this is apparent today as many well-educated Georgians speak at least one foreign language in addition to Russian and Georgian. In 1990, Reilly describes a superior humanities education in public school that caters to the interests of students regardless of abilities and describes the soviet educators' subjective determination of grades based on oral examinations as refreshing. However, the post-soviet Georgian higher education system is characterized by subjective grading and oral examination processes that have become fraught with corruption or repetitive re-testing, straining the time of already underpaid professors.[14] While I never observed corruption first-hand in the University where I worked, rumors abounded that bribery in exchange for grades was common. Yet even in the midst of high levels of poverty, unemployment and corruption, as reflected in the white washed version of Stalin's leadership, Georgian nationalism and ethnic pride remain powerful forces illuminated by patriotic fervor even if based on a distorted version of history and a naïve or overly optimistic hope for the future.

Georgian nationalism flourished during the early Soviet years in the arts and theater with only episodic attempts at social control from Moscow. Surprisingly, as Stalin's authority became institutionalized and centralized in Moscow, Beria initiated and maintained his own little fiefdom in Georgia and

---

13   David H. Reilly, "Education in the Republic of Georgia, S.S.R: Comparisons with America." *Education* 112:2 (1991):242-247.

14   Aili Piano and Arch Puddington, eds., *Freedom in the World 2004: The Annual Survey of Political Rights and Civil Liberties. Freedom House* (Lanham, MD: Rowman & Littlefield, 2004).

managed to create a great deal more political freedom from Moscow than most other Stalin era Soviet Republics were able to muster.[15]

Initially, the Mensheviks led the Transcaucasia Commissariat consisting of present day Armenia, *Azerbaijan*, and Georgia and then the Democratic Federative Republic of Transcaucasia. However, both of these were short-lived. During World War I, the Turks advanced, the Russians withdrew and the existing differences between the Armenians, Azeri's, and Georgians resulted in each group taking control of specific territories and forming their own political units. Georgia declared its independence in 1918, established a Georgian national flag, later re-adopting it when Georgia achieved independence from the Soviet Union in 1991. At the same time, the Georgians accepted aid from the Germans in order to garner protection against the advancing Turks. This agreement was short-lived and soon the British replaced the Germans as Georgian allies. Both Britain and other Western powers provided military arms to Georgia to resist Bolshevik Russia. However, western assistance was also short-lived because they became more concerned about getting involved in a military quagmire with Russia than supporting Georgia's fledgling independence. First Armenia and *Azerbaijan* fell to the Russian Bolsheviks and finally Georgia. Georgia's independence lasted only three years until 1921 when the Russian Red Army Bolsheviks marched into *Tbilisi* and the Mensheviks fled. While there were many efforts by Georgians over the next thirty years to assert some degree of independence and autonomy from Moscow, Georgia remained ruled by the Moscow Communist Party leaders with the exception of Beria's brief control during the latter part of Stalin's dictatorship.

Other scholars argue that Georgia's struggle with nationalistic fervor began only after Stalin's demise and continues to this day. Georgian nationalism thrived throughout my Civic Education Project Fellowship period during the academic year 2003-2004. Suny argues that while the rest of the Soviet Union recovered from the influence of the Stalin years, he believes Georgia remains unchanged. This mirrors my experience, in that for the most part Georgian political and social institutions are fraught with inefficiency and corruption remains prolific. Nonetheless, as with other parts of the former Soviet

---

15   Suny, *The Making of the Georgian Nation*.

Union, Georgia became less agrarian and more industrialized during the Communist era with fifty three and one half percent of the work force becoming industrial workers while by 1979 only sixteen percent were collective farmers.[16]

In 1972, *Eduard Shevardnadze* left his position as the Minister of Internal Affairs of the Soviet Union and became the leader of the Georgian Communist Party. Interestingly, he became the party secretary to combat corruption, Georgian nationalism and ethnocentricity, elitism, the illegal economy, and the poor performance of the legitimate economy. Even more fascinating is that thirty years later corruption and poor economic performance were the same factors that led to his demise. However, during the Soviet period, Suny argues that *Shevardnadze* successfully reformed the collective farming districts, improved the economy and eliminated some corruption within the administration.

During the latter years of the Soviet period, *Shevardnadze* authorized the arrest of a *Tbilisi* State University Professor, Zviad *Gamsakhurdia*, a Nationalist, who professed a variety of claims about stolen Georgian freedom, history, and monuments. Later *Gamsakhurdia's* popularity resulted in his election as the first democratically elected Georgian President, a man who was partially responsible for the subsequent civil and ethnic wars following the end of the Soviet period. *Shevardnadze's* communist era reforms had minimal deleterious effects on the growing Georgian ethnic nationalism that emanated from fear and hatred of Russian Soviet and communist assimilationist policies. Nonetheless, *Shevardnadze's S*oviet era reformist perspectives resulted in Gorbachev's appointment of him as Foreign Minister of the USSR in 1985. *Mikhail Gorbachev* and *Shevardnadze* together attempted to improve the economy, end the USSR's isolation, and introduced a socialist democracy. In the process, they unknowingly began to undermine the authority of the communist party leading to the proliferation of a variety of soviet republics' sovereign ambitions and the concurrent growth of nationalism across the Soviet Union. In the end, these factors lead to the disintegration of the Soviet Union. While the initiation of reforms occurred across the Soviet Union, many Georgians continued to argue for the re-assertion of Georgian na-

---

16   *Ibid.*, 297.

tionalist history and identity. The elite of the Georgian party also began to exclude and oppress Georgian minorities including the "Russians, *Ossetians, Abkhaz, Ajars, Azerbaijanis,* and others'.[17] This systemic discrimination was also partly responsible for Georgia's ethnic and civil wars.

The resulting ethnic and civic nationalism, led the *Abkhaz* Communists to demand secession from the western *Abkhazeti* region of Georgia. It is important to note that *Abkhazia* achieved autonomy in 1921 from the Moscow Communists, allegedly because the *Abkhazians* suffered the loss of their own native leaders during the re-organization by the Georgian majority culture. Subsequently in 1932, the *Abkhaz* republic was demoted from a Soviet Socialist Republic to an autonomous Republic of Georgia. They too suffered the loss of their native leaders during Stalin's era. Therefore, *Abkhazians* felt powerless by this state of affairs. Those sentiments continued into the late 1980's. Thus when *Gorbachev's* liberalization program began, *Abkhaz* separatist ideology once again grew more powerful. Similar dynamics led to separatist and nationalist independent movements across the Soviet Union.

On March 25, 1989, Georgians began holding independence rallies against the Soviet Regime. Subsequently, the Georgian Supreme Soviet declared itself independent following a national referendum. Simultaneously the *Abkhazians* and *Ossetians* began to assert their desire for separation from Georgia. The minority ethnic groups wanted to remain part of Russia, and simultaneously Russia wanted to maintain a strong influence in the Caucasus region and so their interests coincided.[18] Another factor involved in *Ossetian* and *Abkhazian* separatist movements included the popular sentiments fomented by the ideology of the Georgian nationalist and separatist leader, *Zviad Gamsakhurdia. Gamsakhurdia* later became the leader of the Nationalist Democratic Party. On April 19th 1989, following the *Abkhazians* declaration of their desire for deportation from Georgia, Georgians demonstrated in *Tbilisi. Subsequently,* Russian soldiers marched into *Tbilisi* as ordered by the Georgian communist party leader. In the end, nineteen Georgians died as the Russian soldiers used shotguns and toxic gas to repress the demonstrations. Georgians still honor their memory annually as a way of acknowledging their

---

17   *Ibid.,* 318.

independent spirit in the face of Russian domination. This day is referred to as Bloody Sunday. Following Bloody Sunday, *Gamsakhurdia's* nationalistic leadership and the equally nationalistic *Abkhaz* separatist leader, *Vladislav Arbzinba*, with support from Russia, began a violent conflict. By July 1989, inter-ethnic clashes ensued in *Sukhumi* in the *Abkhazian* region where initially eleven Georgians, three *Abkhazians* and one Greek were killed and four hundred and forty-eight were wounded. By May 1990, a thirty-thousand strong rally in *Sukhumi Abkhazia* demanded the secession of *Abkhazia* from Georgia. Meanwhile, as the *Abkhazian* conflict brewed, from November 1989 through January 1990, *Osesstian* and Georgian hostilities began following South *Ossetia's* adoption of a resolution to turn itself into an autonomous region. In October 1990 a non-communist political party won the election to the Supreme Soviet of Georgia in the country's first multiparty election in communist history. These left wing parties of the Round Table-Free Georgia won control of the Georgian government and the ethno-nationalist, *Zviad Gamsakhurdia*, became elected President. This resulted in the formation of at least two separate Georgian militia groups within the *Abkhazian* region supporting the newly elected Georgian President. The two groups were the *Zaviadists* and the *Mkhedrioni*, labeled by one Georgian scholar as a coalition of liberals and "thugs" who were only criminals.[19] They participated in most of the fighting throughout the war between *Abkhazia* and Georgia. Both groups developed separate identities with distinct authoritarian leaders or warlords. According to political theorists, these dynamics were not unexpected, because the global historical precedent, of simultaneously erecting a democratic infrastructure and free market capitalism,[20] would eventually result in ethnic separatism and conflict.[21] Although the Soviet Union ceased to exist as of December 8th 1991, the ethnic violence in Georgia failed to subside. The resulting ethnic wars in *Ossetia* and in *Abkhazia* led to intense dis-

---

18   J. L. Black, *Vladimir Putin and the New World Order: Looking East, Looking West?* (Lanham, MD: Rowman & Littlefield, 2004).

19   Ghia Nodia, "Georgia's Identity Crisis." *The Journal of Democracy* 6:1 (1995):104-116.

20   Jason Castillo, "The Dilemma of Simultaneity: Russia and Georgia in the Midst of Transformation." *World Affairs* 160:1 (1997):34-42.

21   Maxine Molyneux, "Gendered Transitions in Eastern in Eastern Europe." *Feminist Studies* 21:3 (1995).

pleasure with the new Georgian President. Many were killed and almost two hundred thousand people were forced to leave their homes under the threat of violence from *Abkhazia,* becoming internally displaced peoples. This ethnic conflict eventually led to the civil war aimed at overthrowing President *Gamsakhurdia.*

Violence continued throughout the early 1990's as *Gamsakhurdia* and his nationalistic followers battled for control of the central government and a Georgian only ethnic state. [22] The *Tbilisi* revolution or what some Georgians call the "two week civil war" (22 December 1991 through 6 January) took place primarily around a three block area surrounding the Parliament in *Tbilisi* as the *Zaviadists,* or supporters of *Gamsakhurdia* fought against a new government. This *Tbilisi* Revolution led to the departure of President *Gamsakhurdia* and the appointment of a new military council with acting Prime Minister, Mr. *Sigua Ioseliani.* In January, the new anti-*Gamsakhurdia* coalition invited *Shevardnadze* to return to Georgia. Subsequently, he won appointment as the Chairman of the State Council. In October 1992, *Shevardnadze* became the Parliamentary Chairman with ninety-six percent of the vote. As the war in *Abkhazia* continued two hundred thousand to two hundred and fifty thousand Georgians were forcibly removed from their homes while some escaped. Additionally, at least ten thousand departed South *Ossetia* under similar conditions. These internally displaced peoples lost their homes, possessions, jobs, and sometimes-family members, in what some have called ethnic cleansing. Additionally, eighty thousand *Ossetians* immigrated from Georgia to Russia.[23] Finally, in January 1992, Georgians restored the former 1921 Constitution.

In March of 1992, *Eduard Shevardnadze* returned to Georgia to head the new State Council, and Georgians hoped he would save the country from extinction and on-going war. Initially, *Shevardnadze* fought against renewed attempts at a counter-coup orchestrated by the former President as well as against threats from *Abkhazian* rebels. In July of 1992, *Abkhazia* restored its autonomy through re-authorizing its 1925 Constitution preserving their rela-

---

22   Lincoln Allison and Nana Kukhianidze, "Letter From: Georgia. An Everyday Story of Ethnic Cleansing." *New Statesmen and Society* 2 (1995):12-13.
23   Charles King, "Potemkin Democracy: Four Myths about Post-Soviet Georgia." *The National Interest* 64 (Summer 2001):93-104.

tionship with Russia. Subsequently, in October *Shevardnadze won* election as Speaker of the Parliament. In July of 1993 a cease-fire between *Abkhazia* and Georgia was signed. Subsequently, in early August of 1991, eleven *Abkhazian* hostages and the *Abkhazian* leader, *Arbzinba,* were captured by *Zaviadist* militia. Claimsmaking and counter-claims by Georgian and *Abkhazians* transpired each of whom blamed the other. Initially *Shevard-nadze* tried to peacefully negotiate to garner the release of the hostages. As the deadline for release of the hostages expired Georgia moved three thousand troops to *Abkhazia* to rescue them. This intensified the fighting between the *Abkhazians* irregulars and Georgians regulars that continued even after August 1992 when Russian peacekeepers arrived in *Abkhazia. Meanwhile* confrontations continued between Georgians and *Ossetians* over similar calls for an independent Ossetian republic. By the end of 1993, *Gamsakhurdia* was dead, murdered by suspects still unknown to authorities. Only recently, Georgians began to honor his memory following the election of their new President in 2004.

Readers should note that prior to the disintegration of the Soviet Union and preceding the ethnic conflicts in the region, ethnic intermarriage between *Abkhazians* and Georgians was common. These interethnic families also fled their homes under duress during the ethnic war, becoming Internally Displaced Persons IDPS. Most of these IDPs currently continue to live in the capital city inside dilapidated high-rise buildings or old hotels. One in particularly, the Hotel Iveria, formerly a Soviet era luxury hotel, now stands in disrepair in stark contrast to its previous life in downtown *Tbilisi.*

A small group of IDPs who visited one of my classes, reported having many *Abkhazian* friends and neighbors prior to the war but suddenly as interpolitical ethnic rhetoric increased, friends became enemies. By April 1994 Georgia and *Abkhazia* had become two separate states. Eventually, South *Ossetia also became an independent republic.* Both states remain separate today although they remain internationally unrecognized.[24] Most of the two hundred thousand IDPs continue to live in the same collection centers. Therefore, a whole cohort of children have grown up in these allegedly "temporary homes". They typically attend separate schools from other children, and their families generally live under worse conditions then even the average poverty-stricken capital city resident.

In 1995, the Parliament adopted a new Constitution with a Presidential system. *Shevardnadze* was elected President with seventy-four percent of the vote. In 1997, Parliament adopted a number of laws implementing further constitutional provisions, including civil, criminal, and tax codes. The establishment of civil and criminal judicial systems occurred simultaneously as local self government and administrative units also were created. In 1998, Georgia held its first certification exams for common court judges, with a passing rate of only nineteen percent. As the result of these historical machinations, Georgia became a fledgling but yet unstable democracy.

The most notable part of Georgia's long history of victimization and colonization by foreign powers is that Georgians have maintained a vibrant and rich culture characterized by flourishing art, theater, music, classic literary poetry and novels as well as a variety of culinary delights. Although Georgia was at one time one of the richest Soviet republics, referred to as the Soviet Rivera with Communist party members visiting the Black sea regions to the north in *Abkhazia* as well as to the South in *Adjara*, post-Soviet Georgia remains characterized by war, industrial collapse, unemployment, poor pensions and no social security. These factors have led to increased corruption and economic inequality.[25] For example, currently sixty-five percent of the population lives under the poverty level. Furthermore, there is some indication that both poverty and criminal victimization disproportionately affects women, particularly ethnic minority women.[26] Although many ethnic minority peoples immigrated after the fall of the Soviet Union, as of 2000,

---

24   Nodia, "Georgia's Identity Crisis;" Allison and Kukhiandize, "Letter From: Georgia;" King, "Potemkin Democracy;" Dov Lynch, "Separatist States and Post Soviet Conflicts." *International Affairs* 78:4 (2002):821-848.

25   Nora Dudwick, Elizabeth Gomart, Alexander Marc, and Kathleen Kuehnast, *When Things Fall Apart Qualitative Studies of Poverty in the Former Soviet Union*. (Washington, DC: The World Bank, 2003); Alena Ledeneva, "Commonwealth of Independent States." in Peter Eigen, ed., *Global Corruption Report 2003* (Berlin: Transparency International, 2003).

26   Karl E. Meyer, "Icebergs in the Caucasus." *World Policy Journal* 18:2 (2001):89-92; Castillo, "The Dilemma of Simultaneity;" King, "Potemkin Democracy."

about thirty percent of Georgia's population are ethnic minority group members.[27]

As indicated above, ethnic nationalism flourished throughout the Caucasus after the demise of the former Soviet Union and much of the conflict that can followed can be attributed to Stalin's forced resettlement policies. [28] These conflicts included one between *Azerbaijan* and Armenia, a second within Ingushetia, and a third between *Chechnya* and North *Ossetia*. Stalin's former re-settlement policies in the Soviet Republics included the 1918-20 forced movement of the *Cossacks*, a Mountain Caucasus people, along with the *Ossetians*. Another Caucasus people, the *Ingush,* also were forcibly re-settled, once in 1944 and again in 1957. Soldatova explains that the rhetoric for these forced movements was the rehabilitation of repressed peoples. However, the movements were clearly forms of overt xenophobia and later resulted in intensifying ethnic nationalistic sentiments and interethnic war. Not until the end of the 1950's, were many of these individuals permitted to return to their homes. In concert with these forced movements, the resulting wars were also exacerbated by a variety of competing economic and political sovereign objectives within many of the former soviet republics as well as the ambitions of the Northern Caucasus peoples to unify under either "the banner of Islam or the under the Eastern Orthodox Christian church." These dynamics coupled with the repression of all religious groups during the Soviet period including closing or destroying churches, synagogues, and mosques lead towards the eruption of violence across the FSU. These early forms of repression contributed to the development of ethnic nationalism as exemplified by later Georgian constitutional amendments prohibiting anyone but a Georgian from holding public office.[29] In the end, fifteen separate sovereign republics emerged out the ashes of the Former Soviet Union. Five other states continue to exist that remain internationally unrecognized (six until May 2004) and two of them are in Georgia (it was three). This includes *South Ossetia* and *Abkhazia. Outside of Georgia* these contested sovereign nations include

---

27   Stephen Jones, "Democracy from Below? Interest Groups in Georgian Society."
      Slavic Review 59:1 (2000):42-74.

28   G.U. Soldatova, "The Former Checheno-Ingushetia." *Russia Social Science Review*
      34:6 (1993):52-73.

29   Soldatova, "The Former Checheno-Ingushetia."

Chechnya that continues to seek its independence from Russia, a second in Moldova called the *Pridnestrovyan Moldavian* Republic and finally *Nagorno-Karabakh* Republic in *Azerbaijan* that developed following a war between *Armenians* and *Azeri's* in the early 1990's. [30] Across the former Soviet Union, ethnic nationalism remains a powerful force and may continue to be a factor in the political inefficiency, high levels of economic inequality, and corruption that remain powerful institutionalized forces in Georgia. These constraints exacerbate Georgia's continuing struggle with poverty as exemplified by their 2002 gross domestic product per capita (purchasing power parity) of seven hundred and thirty one dollars. [31]

As the result of the Georgian government's lack of control over the implementation of its laws and its excessive corruption, citizens have little faith or trust in their government and are ambivalent about their civic involvement. However, the U.S. government, the European Union, the United Nations and a variety of non-governmental agencies provide financial aid to Georgia with the stated goal of improving civil society. While on the one hand this is a necessity in newly democratic countries, one scholar argues that an overabundance of such civil assistance further weakens the ability of the state to implement and control its infrastructures and thus regain the faith and trust of its citizens. [32] Jones argues that when pluralism flourishes beyond a certain tipping point, it facilitates a weaker civil society and results in corrupt relationships between the government and other third party interest groups. Similarly, a plethora of non-government organizations in Georgia may be negatively affecting the Georgian struggle to become a more stable democracy with a strong and independent civil society. [33] Jones also hypothesizes that International Monetary Fund's loans to the country appear to act as a destabilizing force by preventing internal government mechanisms and entrepreneurship to begin to interact in the same manner as they developed among western capitalist democracies. This political instability is reflected in

---

30   Lynch, "Separatist States and Post Soviet Conflicts."
31   Fabian Bornhorst and Simon Commander, *Integration and the well-being of children in transition economies.* Innocenti Working Paper 98 (Florence: UNICEF Innocenti Research Centre, United Nations' Children's Fund Innocenti Social Monitor, 2004).
32   Jones, "Democracy from Below?"
33   *Ibid.*

the two failed assassination attempts against the former Georgian President, Edward *Shevardnadze*, one in 1995 and another in 1998. Throughout the mid and late 1990's political purges, bomb attacks and political murders characterized the Georgian government.

Other current social problems in Georgia include organized crime and prostitution. For example, in the independent southwestern corner of Georgia called *Adjara*, illegal trafficking in women remains common and allegedly managed by their government leader, referred to as a warlord by some, *Aslan Abashidze*.[34] Trafficking and prostitution remain linked and the extant research on both reveals that poor economic conditions are often the primary force in women's lives pushing them to choose a life of prostitution over other more conventional but less profitable roles.[35] Corruption remains interwoven in the fabric of trafficking in women, arms, and drugs across all of Georgia's borders as it does in many developing nations. Moreover as mentioned previously, across Georgia as well as many other former Soviet Block countries, corruption remains institutionalized. This corruption fuels organized transnational crime involvement in trafficking. Of course, corruption is also a part of the legacy from the Soviet period. Additionally, it also remains a means of economic survival in the context of rising economic inequality, joblessness, poverty and on-going violence and political upheaval.[36] Georgia's vagaries of corruption include election fraud as well as police extortion of citizens and violence committed against jail detainees. It also includes tax evasion and business fraud.[37] Georgians acknowledge these problems and according to a recent survey hold the government responsible. Moreover, less than one third of Georgians have faith in the parliament or the President.[38]

I observed two instances of corruption or official bribery while traveling in various areas across Georgia. On the way through the Armenian-Georgian border our paid *Martshrutka* (a public mini-van) driver who was transporting

---

34   King, "Potemkin Democracy."
35   Rebecca S. Katz, "Prostitution." in Lawrence Salinger ed., *Encyclopedia of White-Collar and Corporate Crime* (Croton-on-Hudson, NY: Golson Books Sage Publications, 2004).
36   Alison Jamieson, "Transnational Organized Crime: A European Perspective." *Studies in Conflict and Terrorism* 24 (2001):377-387; King, "Potemkin Democracy."
37   *Ibid.*
38   Ledeneva, "Commonwealth of Independent States."

students and faculty from a student conference in *Yerevan* was stopped for extended period of time by the Georgian border guards. The guards conversed with the driver for approximately one hour apparently making a deal to share the profits of his illegally transported Armenian cognac. During the second instance, a police officer pulled over my tour guide's driver, and without writing a ticket for illegal driving, demanded five laris. While it might be easy for some readers to feel morally outraged by such behavior, it is simply a means by which many Georgians are trying to survive during economically difficult times. The frequency and prevalence of such institutionalized forms of bribery becomes apparent in an article discussing a convoy of Daimler Chrysler trucks traveling through *Tbilisi* on its way from Brussels to Afghanistan carrying humanitarian aid.[39] This convoy route was referred to as the "New Silk Road" or the Transport Corridor between Europe-Caucasus and Asia.[40] While the description of this particular road focused on its utilization for humanitarian assistance, in general the poor condition of Georgian roads and the corruption of the international border guards and "bribe seeking police" normally make such travel difficult and sadly tragic. Traveling by car through Georgia illustrates the level of the persistent poverty of Georgian citizens.

Other tragedies confronting Georgians include Infant mortality, a powerful indicator of poverty. Georgia's infant mortality rate stands at twenty-four per one thousand live births. Another measure illustrative of economic inequality is the Gini Income Coefficient. Georgia's coefficient currently lies at .454.[41] Such extensive political and economic domination of the poor by the rich are noted by Green and Ward who explain that "being asked for a bribe is the second common form of criminal victimization, after consumer fraud, outside the industrialized world."[42] The "grand corruption" of political elites reaches monetary heights up to four billion dollars annually. Moreover, a number of Western countries also have a significant problem with public cor-

---

39   Sopho Gorgodze, "TRACECA test drive reaches Georgia." *The Messenger* (18 September 2003):1.
40   Nino Patsuria, "Via est. Vita." *Georgia Today* (19-25 September 2003):1.
41   UNICEF Innocenti Research Centre, "Social Monitor 2004 Economic growth and child poverty in the CEE/CIS and the Baltic States."
42   Penny Green and Tony Ward, *State Crime, Governments, Violence and Corruption* (London and Sterling, VI: Pluto Press, 2004).

ruption even though it remains underreported in the traditional corporate owned media. For example, a recent United States Senate bill presenting itself as support funds for American soldiers in Iraq contained a Halliburton (Vice President Dick Cheney's former company) no-bid contract with the federal government for energy revitalization in Iraq. Halliburton currently remains under federal investigation for illegal price fixing. This illustrates one example of corruption at the highest level. In the United States, the Department of Justice is required to report all types of public corruption.

This mandate has existed since 1976 and necessitates that the Department of Justice to report to congress annually on public corruption. The Department of Justice provides this data through the Public Integrity Section of the Criminal Division who describe federal efforts to combat public corruption. This includes the Elections Crime Branch created in 1980 to supervise the Department of Justice efforts in combating ballot fraud and campaign finance offenses. These two areas remain understudied by criminologists.[43] Across the U.S. in 2002, four-hundred and twenty-nine convictions for corruption of federal officials occurred and after including state and local convictions as well, one thousand and eleven convictions for corruption or bribery took place. While there were two and half times more murder convictions across the U.S. than convictions for public corruption in 2002, there were more convictions for public corruption than for the combined violent convictions for assault, sexual abuse, and kidnapping. Among violent offenders, only murder and robbery convictions exceeded corruption convictions.[44] Greed and a long history of subsidized capitalism may explain corruption in the United States. However, it appears that Georgia's rapid transition from a state run economy to a market economy, the unstable condition of their polity and gross levels of poverty, and economic inequality led to the development of their own version of institutionalized corruption. This form of corruption appears to be more pervasive than corruption in the West. Telling the story of Georgia's socio-political and economic events in 2003 and 2004 through this

---

43   U.S. Department of Justice, *Report to Congress on the Activities and Operations of the Public Integrity Section for 2002* (Washington, DC: Public Integrity Section, Criminal Division, U.S. Department of Justice, 2002).

narrative analysis of Georgian newspapers may better explain Georgian social and political culture and may help us to better understand and prevent
bribery and corruption in the future.

44   U.S. Department of Justice, *Bureau of Justice Statistics. Compendium of Federal Justice Statistics.* (Washington D.C.: Office of Justice Programs, 2002), NCJ 205368.

III   Narrative Analysis of Georgian English-language Newspapers

III.1   Methodology

While Georgia remains a very poor country, a middle class does exist although most of these people live in the capital city of *Tbilisi*. Thus class privilege is available to few Georgians especially in the rural regions where poverty is more pervasive and the absence of electricity, gas, paved roads and access to news is limited if not completely absent. This pervasive economic inequality exists across Georgia and among many other post-Soviet or post-colonial nations around the globe. These dynamics reflect weaknesses in a variety of civil and cultural institutions.[45] While the modernization and privatization of the media has become fairly well established, these institutions remain weak and continue to deteriorate constraining the ability of the news media to provide accurate information to the majority of Georgian citizens. Moreover, the rapid transformation of post-soviet societies into commercial and capitalist economic systems in conjunction with the end of the state's commitment to the welfare of its citizens negatively affects a variety of social structures and institutions including the mass media. In other words, the media's transformation from public to private ownership has not translated into the absence of government interference or its affiliation with political parties. Furthermore, a number of television stations remain owned and managed by the state. In the context of intense political struggles, media reform and independence from the state has become more difficult to achieve. Professional, unbiased, and ethical media institutions remain underdeveloped in many parts of the FSU as evidenced by the presence of slander and misinformation. For example, in Russia, the media is accustomed to slandering oppositional political parties and manipulating the competition or more recently be-

---

45   Bohdan Johan and Malgorzata Moleda-Zdziech, "Central and Eastern Cultural Policies, Media Reform and Development of Media Markets in the Mid-Nineties." *Leisure Studies* 17 (1998):69-93.

ing controlled by the federal government. Moreover, media owners also consist of large industrial corporations and banks. The largest such corporation in Russia is *GAZPROM*, an oil company owning several dozen newspapers with considerable influence over TV stations (38% of *GAZPROM* remains owned by the state according to Transparency International).[46] Coman argues that corporate ownership of newspapers is partly the result of the inability to garner enough advertising to provide sufficient capital for support of ongoing production. In Russia, the control of media outlets remain in the hands of a few groups tied to political clans. Initial privatization of the mass media involved either a rapid transition with sales to individual oligarchs or a state sponsored mediated transition period. By extension within some post-soviet societies, Western influence continues to dominate media programming and in some cases, Westerners own the media. Another problem with the press in the former Soviet Union (FSU) remains the absence of professionally trained journalists. In Georgia, this results in college journalism students writing for major newspapers as a sort of internship experience. This also occurs because newspapers cannot afford to provide salaries to journalists.

While most post-soviet societies' constitutions guarantee freedom of speech and "implicitly or explicitly freedom of the press",[47] many FSU nations have few if any press laws. Even where press laws are in place, such legislation has been unable to eliminate the influence of political parties or the government. The Georgian constitution "recognizes and defends universally recognized human rights and freedoms as eternal and supreme values." These include, "freedom of speech, thought, conscience, religion and belief," "freedom to express one's opinion about these things and freedom from persecution for such expression," "freedom of intellectual creativity, intellectual property rights, and censorship is prohibited." "Every individual has the right to freely receive and disseminate information orally or in writing" and "the mass media is free." There is also a prohibition of the monopolization of mass media by the state or natural persons.[48] However, as this analysis will illustrate, the Georgian government periodically attempts to limit the free press, al-

---

46   Ledeneva, "Commonwealth of Independent States."
47   Mihai Coman, "Developments in Journalism Theory and Media 'Transition' in Central and Eastern Europe 1990-1999." *Journalism Studies* 1:1 (2000):36.
48   The Constitution of Georgia.

though it is clearly a violation of their constitution. Mihai Coman defines several traits of post-soviet journalists many of which are applicable in Georgia. This includes the domination of the field by young people who began working in the media after 1989 and lack any relevant training or academic background.

> They present themselves as an antithesis to the old guard and consequently promote an ideology of negation, a sentiment of necessary superiority based on the idea that those who have not worked in the communist media were not touched by the communist ideology and ......the idea of being on a mission that does not require any critical self evaluation or journalism education and training.

Furthermore, other problems with the media in post-soviet countries include:

a. "...[the media] consider themselves to be elite within society ....because of their background (most have university degrees) and because of the role they assume for themselves. Most...define themselves as representatives of the fourth estate...but their understanding of the role of the media is confused. Typically, the adversarial perspective is dominant with journalists considering that their role is to oppose power (no matter which party or group is in power), to criticize it and to uncover its abuses."

b. There is a "dispersion of professional organizations..."minimally "with two professional associations competing with each other for members and highly politically oriented."

c. While some countries have adopted ethical codes but even where these are evident there remains an absence of any "professional culture, common values, and norms of behavior."

d. Most journalists receive their knowledge about their work via "on-the job-training," even though Western nations have been financing the development of a variety of university based journalism education programs throughout the FSU.

e. There are two axes of development of the profession, "the role conception and the social position." Coman describes the role conception as
consisting of three roles, the militant who is preoccupied with shaping
public opinion, the announcer who focuses on infotainment and entertainment, and the artesian who is most respectful of the professional
journalist values.[49] On the second axis, there are the wealthy barons
and those who support practical journalism both vying for domination.
The barons are media moguls who often own multiple media outlets
and want political power. This leaves journalists attempting to create a
professional culture and a normative environment subject to political
abuse by the government or their own employers.

In light of these dynamics, the press remains highly influenced by the
state, although Coman reports that generally print media have more freedom
than the broadcast media. In Georgia, few people can afford a regular subscription to a newspaper and thus most people remain highly dependent on
Television news. Unfortunately, it is television that while less subject to economic pressure, remains more likely to be affected by judicial pressure, political pressure, and partisanship.[50] Equally problematic is that newspapers
often couch political issues as personal conflicts rather than conflicts within
the social structure or as problems with institutional or historical roots. This
increases the likelihood that most information will become less accurate and
more dramatic. Coman argues that these characteristics thus fail to mobilize
social movements as the press did early on in the precipitous fall of the Soviet Union. Finally, Coman states there is no empirical work that studies the
effects of post-communist media on the public and no theoretical framework
to examine media changes from Communism to post-communist societies.
Conan calls for such work in the future. This research attempts to meet Conan's call to action by conducting a narrative analysis of Georgian-English
newspapers from August 2003 through March 2004.

---

49   Coman, "Developments in Journalism Theory and Media "Transition."
50   *Ibid.*

III.2   July and August 2003

Georgians' access to information about their economy, government, and so-cial, and cultural life remains limited due their economic deprivation as well as the absence of a stable dependable and reliable news network in print, on television or on the internet. Print media or newspapers and magazines re-main primarily available to the middle class residents of the capital city who can afford such luxuries. Nonetheless, ownership of private property such as cars and mobile phones remain important signifiers of class status in Georgia as exemplified by one editorial reporting the prevalence of Georgians who enjoy such middle class comforts. Specifically, there are five hundred thou-sand mobile phone users in Georgia, one-hundred and twenty-thousand internet consumers, forty-five TV stations, seventeen radio stations, and one hundred and twenty-four newspapers. This writer argues that these middle class status symbols have influenced the development of international Non-government organizations (NGOs).[51] The plethora of NGOs' is purported to have a significant democratic influence on the neophyte civil society as well as on capitalist economic development in Georgia. While this relationship be-tween middle class and upper class Georgians and the development of the third sector is somewhat dubious, NGOs continue to make up the whole of Georgian civil society. The author of the above newspaper article continues to report: "Almost every strong political movement and leader has tried to ob-tain their own TV, radio stations and newspapers." Welding such influence may have a powerful affect on voters' choices come election time. The writer also implies that there are a variety of alliances between such media outlets and a number of NGOs. The implication is that an improvement in Georgia's access to the information highway could make governmental and political party information and NGO's more accessible to a greater number of Geor-gian citizens. This Ph.D. candidate further explains that in the year 2000, Georgia had only fifteen telephone lines per one hundred inhabitants com-pared to sixty-one telephone lines per one hundred inhabitants in Germany. In public schools, one computer exists for every six hundred students. I sus-

---

51   Gela Kvashiliava, "Political Implications of the Information and Communication." *Georgian Times* (25 August 2003):4.

pect that this may be a generous assessment as I taught one data analysis class for *Tbilisi* State University and they had three very old computers in one small office with only two functioning, no internet access, and significantly older versions of the Statistical Program for the Social Sciences. The most modern and up-to-date computer lab in the city among universities opened in the spring of 2004 at the Eurasian Foundation's Caucasus Center for Social Research. They maintained a computer laboratory with six personal computers including internet access and EBSCO full text on line library materials and the most recent edition of SPSS. They generously allowed me to teach my data analysis class in their laboratory for an entire semester. However, internet access remains widely available throughout the capital city for a minimal fee. The internet cafes usually seem full of young adolescent males playing video games. Several internet providers are available in the capital city for private household utilization, even though they are not affordable for most Georgians.

No Georgian computer companies produce software or hardware for computers or computer accessories. Usually economic globalization makes Hewlet Packard, Microsoft, and other Western computer products easily available, especially inside the capital city. However, these are affordable only to upper middle class Georgians or the Western ex-patriots living in Georgia working for international organizations. In the midst of this Western dominated economic system only powerful elites associated with specific political parties control the media and thus shape public opinion. Only two NGO's monitor the television networks and newspapers in Georgia and both indicate that newspaper journalists are typically young college students studying journalism who publish articles by paying the newspapers.[52] This remains true because few residents can afford to buy a paper, making the newspaper business extremely unprofitable. As a result, newspapers remain owned by business conglomerates who also own a number of other businesses. Another problem for newspapers is the absence of a uniform distribution network. Open bidding for small newspaper stand owners occurs every morning leading street sellers to purchase a certain limited (a dozen or less) number of papers to sell daily. Finally, newspapers usually cost their

---

52   Conversation with NGO representative in 2004.

company owners several times more to produce the product than the profit earned from sales.

In addition to the need for a independent unbiased media, *Kvashilava* explains that a variety of other improvements remain necessary before Georgia will resemble a truly democratic nation state. These include, a legitimate economic infrastructure, the creation of an easily accessible e-government for all citizens, the demise of the political parties' grip over control of newspapers and televisions, and a decrease in the number of criminal organizations with ties to political parties. Until then, the article states, criminal oligarchs will be to continue to manipulate the political situation and the media to their advantage gaining additional power.

In order to improve the media's ability to provide objective news, a four-day training seminar for Georgian TV journalists was recently held. The event sponsor was the Caucasus Foundation of the German Fund of Conrad Adenauer. The conference aimed at developing journalists' ethics. [53] This process consisted of helping writers learn how to avoid manipulation by political parties and to report the news without bias. Dr. Christian Trippe, an "expert" from the German International Media Company Deutsche Welle provided the training. In an interview, Trippe explained that even in Western Europe, specifically France and Germany, it took decades for the media to become free in practice even with the presence of a democratic government and a republican constitution. Dr. Trippe also addressed Georgians' growing concerns about the nation's economic dependence on Russia.

This on-going Georgian concern with Russia's imperialism is based upon their extant history and perhaps the denial of Georgian citizens' about their own role in the Bolshevik revolution. This led the interviewer to ask about the recent sale of Georgian Telecom to a Russian company. Readers should note that Russia also recently purchased a Georgian electric company from an American company. This sale leaves Russia in control of both Georgians' natural gas and electricity. Dr. Trippe offers a rather simplistic argument, that this is just another artifact of economic globalization without explicating the power differences between Georgia and Russia. Nor does the expert provide an analysis in the context of Russia's on-going 'Peacekeeping role' inside the Georgian Abkhazian conflict zone. The expert also fails to mention Russia's on-going relationship with the authoritarian and fraudulently elected President of *Adjara, Aslan Abashidze.* Nevertheless, Dr. Trippe's innocuous response to this question makes sense in light of the fact that *Deutsche Welle* (*DW*) recently expanded its broadcasting network in Georgia as exemplified by their ownership of seven TV stations under the United Television Network broadcasting including *DW*-TV in Georgia. They also own one radio station that broadcasts *DW* news and music in German and Russian. The Georgian nation's immaturity becomes apparent with regard to the effect of neo-colonial forms of economic globalization.

Similarly, this illustration of Georgia's youth also appears in another article discussing an on-going border dispute with *Azerbaijan.*[54] Since 1994, both countries have claimed territorial ownership of the 6th century *Davit Gareji* Monastery complex. The complex spans both nation-states covering over sixty miles of cave networks. However, Georgian and *Azeri* historians argue about the details of the inception of the Monastery's complex. Moreover, both countries aim to renovate and preserve the complex. Similar unresolved historical and territorial arguments exist about a variety of issues across the Caucasus region.

The Caucasus region has a rich and diverse history and includes a variety of unique and yet intersecting Eastern and Western cultures that spans over two thousand years. These multiple historical influences are similarly reflected in its wide expanse of geographical variations ranging from mountains with ski resorts to beaches and tropical fruit. Unfortunately, this diversity also includes vast amounts of poverty characterized by communities that continue to barter for goods rather than utilize a cash economy. Also prolific across the country are the contrasts of twenty-first century urban plight as well as ancient architecture from cave cities to Orthodox Christian churches dating back to the fifth century. Georgians claim that one Cathedral in the ancient

---

53.   Rusudan Kbilashvili, "Political Changes through Economic Exchange, German Expert Reports over the Interests of the U.S. and Russia in Georgia." *Georgian Times* (25 August 2001):6.

54   Mammad Baghirov, "Ancient Monasteries Cause Modern Border Disagreement." *Brosse Street Journal* (20 July 2003):1.

capital of *Mtskheta* is the grave cite of Jesus' burial robe. The church stands as a magnificent mixture of ancient pagan symbols intertwined with Eastern Orthodox Christian icons. Unfortunately, tourism remains an insignificant part of the Georgian economy with a $35, 047 Tourism Department budget, and only one Georgian Airline Company, a Turkish Airline Company, an Austrian Airline Company and one British Airline company flying in and out of the capital city several times a week. Georgia could create a magnificent tourism industry if the political will existed. This might significantly boost their GDP. Similarly, a frequent pun shared with newcomers by Georgians when pointing out the Ministry of Economy building in *Tbilisi* to ask: "What economy?"

Recent budget cuts in the Defense Ministry reflect these macro level economic problems. The cuts include a decrease in expenditures by four and one-half million U.S. dollars. Similarly, Border Guard funding cuts will include one million dollars while cuts within the Interior ministry will reach slightly over three million dollars for a total of almost nine million dollars. [55] However, rather than viewing these budgetary problems as threat to the welfare of the people, they are socially constructed as a threat to national security. Such framing of problems reflects the degree to which political parties rely on economic problems to inflame nationalist sentiment.

As mentioned previously, currently both civil and ethnic nationalism in Georgia remains the direct result of years of civil repression and forced movement of ethnic groups. Additionally, this type of thinking reflects the formerly incongruent policy of soviet style nationalism as well as seventy years of authoritarian Communist party rule dictated from Moscow. These types of political domination resulted in the civil war and the three ethnic conflicts that developed between 1990 and 1993 in *Ossetia*, *Abkhazia*, and *Adjara*. Recently, Georgian IDPS organized a hunger strike and demanded that President *Shevardnadze* increase his efforts to return them to their homes and remove the Russian peacekeepers. Many Georgians see that as an oxymoron since it they perceive that ethnic conflicts were encouraged by the Russians. Moreover, it is commonly believed that the Russians are peacekeepers only because the Western powers refused to recognize the geno-

---

55   N.N., "Cutting of Budget Expenditures will negatively Impact on Country's Security." *Georgian Times* (25 August 2003):2.

cidal nature of these ethnic conflicts. It may be more likely that the United States did not want to challenge Russian hegemony in the Caucasus too quickly following the fall of the Soviet Union.[56] A scheduled meeting between U.S. President George Bush and President *Putin* of Russia in September aimed to discuss the Georgian *Abkhazian* Conflict. The U.S. Ambassador to Georgia, Mr. Richard Miles, reportedly stated: "America does not wish the Russians to leave as peacekeepers". [57] This being said, it is important to note that the *Baku-Tbilisi-Ceyhan (BTC)* oil pipeline project, an oil pipeline stretching from *Azerbaijan* into Georgia and then into Turkey (scheduled for completion in 2005) involves British and American oil companies, not Russian oil companies. Moreover, the Americans have already taken over one former Russian military base outside *Tbilisi* following 9/11 and maintain a contingent of U.S. Marines who are allegedly providing equipment and training to Georgian armed forces.[58]

Even with Russian peacekeepers on the ground, it appears that the Russian Mafia provides more protection to the local population from random crime than the Russian military. Apparently, the Russian Mafia has imposed some form of order in *Abkhazia* over local criminal gangs to protect Hazelnut farmers who claim gangs continue to steal their harvest. Of course, this negatively affects their incomes.[59] In the process, gangs also physically assault farmers and ambush vehicles. While one paragraph explains that farmers' report local police make efforts to control the theft, another paragraph argues that police pay-offs "from top to bottom" allow these crimes to occur. During the Georgian-*Abkhazian* conflict, masked raiders also murdered local farmers and stole their harvests. Interestingly, even the police frequently wear masks when conducting arrests or raids. Thus, it becomes extremely difficult to differentiate the good guys from the bad guys. In one interview, a farmer explains that thieves stole his last two harvests. This farmer also reported that thieves tortured him and that the *Abkhazian* authorities ignored

---

56   Black, *Vladimir Putin and the New World Order.*
57   N.N., "Presidents of US and Russia will Discuss the Issue of the Georgian-Abkhazian Conflict." *Georgian Times* (25 August 2003):2.
58   *Ibid.*
59   Tamuni Shonia, "Abkhazia: Lucrative Farms Attract Mafia: Hazelnut Farmers in Disputed Region are grateful to Russia Mafia for imposing order on local criminal gangs." *Ibid.,* 10.

his victimization. It remains unclear if this means that the police failed to investigate or simply failed to arrest any suspects. Such informational ambiguity may leave Georgians feeling even more victimized by the *Abkhazians* and perhaps more likely to maintain their fifteen year old animosity with regard to the on-going plight of the IDPs. One local government administrator in the *Gali* region claims that their fight against the criminals in this area has been successful but he also explains that residents are partially responsible for bringing the area under control. However, it is unclear how local citizens are supposed to accomplish that goal. One local resident explained: "Some local criminal bosses came to *Gali* from all over Russia this year, they are called professional thieves. One of them, an influential crime boss, gathered some ninety minor gang leaders who formerly robbed local Georgian farmers and ordered them not to do it again. In order that they did not leave empty-handed he fixed a kind of levy, and left specific racketeers in charge of each piece of land. Thus in addition to paying *Abkhaz* taxes, now the protection fee exists. The writer reports that the good thing about all this is that it covers the entire population. This means that it is less likely that farmers will go bankrupt even though the racketeers remain in control. Another local resident agreed, and claimed that the farmers are now better off with the Moscow based criminals being in control of things, for example, she stated: "We pray for him." Finally, this woman stated: "Last year we were robbed four times...it's one thing when a thief steals something and makes off quietly, and quite another when unscrupulous bandits scare our kids, beating and humiliating us in front of them. Theft is common, but what we've had here in *Abkhazia*, and especially in the lower *Gali* region in recent years, is a completely different scale." The reporter concludes by explaining that after more than ten years, locals in *Gali* report that they would "vote for their new "protector" if he decided to run for the *Abkhaz* presidency."[60] Further, scholarly support for the political favor given to organized criminals is illustrated by Dov Lynch's research published in *International Affairs* reporting,

> Crime mingles with geopolitics in these conflicts in an unset-
> tling manner. Russian peacekeeping troops have become in-

---

60   *Ibid.*

volved in smuggling activities across the front lines in Georgia and *Moldova*. In the *Gali* district of *Abkhazia*, crime and smuggling have become a way of life for the vulnerable Georgians who have returned, the Georgian paramilitary groups that are active there, and the peacekeeping troops. The trade in hazelnuts and citrus fruits, and also petrol from the Russian Federation has blurred the lines between ethnic groups in the conflict, uniting them all in the search for profit.[61]

While this scholar does not provide a citation for his detailed observations, in a footnote he reports spending time in the *Abkhazian* region in 2000. Among the locals interviewed by the above journalist, it becomes apparent that the Soviet legacy of tolerance for and acceptance of powerful oligarchs, corruption, and crime remains. Furthermore, crime stands as a viable means of economic survival even among those assigned the task of maintaining law and order. Criminals and crime control agents are often the same people. Other support exists for this motivation to engage in crime as a method of economic survival. This is illustrated in a recently published survey of post-Soviet Russian residents, who report that their attraction to engage in crime far out-weights measures of low self-control's effect on crime involvement as well as the propensity to report the likelihood of doing more crime in the future.[62] Crime within post-soviet states may be quite functional. However, one dysfunctional type of crime that Georgia shares with a variety of post-communist and post-colonial nation states is voter fraud.

In a recent parliamentary debate, participants discussed proposed changes to the election code, and the possibility of mandating a computerized voting system for the parliamentary election scheduled for early November.[63] However, the estimated cost ranges between three and a half and four million US dollars. Promoters of the new system argued that it would save between one and one 1/2 half million U.S. dollars per election year if

61   Lynch, "Separatist States and Post Soviet Conflicts." 843.
62   Charles R. Tittle and Ekaterina V. Botchkovar, "Self-Control, Criminal Motivation and Deterrence: An Investigation Using Russian Respondents." *Criminology* 43:2 (2005):307-354.
63   Helen Kvanchilashvili, "Despite Potential, Computerized Voting Gains Little Support as election nears." *Brosse Street Journal* (20 July 2003):1.

adopted. Such improvements are necessary to further eliminate Georgia's continued problems in administering free and fair elections.

In other discussions of the forthcoming November elections, the newspaper reports that the "Georgian State Department" recently gathered information from experts on fair elections explaining that there are six types of election fraud most common in Georgia, these include:

a.   Voters are not listed on the voters' lists.

b.   Voters are listed several times with new and old addresses.

c.   Someone else might vote for a voter, if the registered voter fails to show up to vote.

d.   Voter lists include deceased persons or persons that have moved to another place and those who never existed.

e.   A voter has several false identification papers giving him or her an opportunity to vote several times.

f.   Results are often significantly altered.

A problem not identified above includes one mentioned in another article discussing poor voter registration procedures and the minimal participation of minorities in elections. Specifically, the Office of Security of the Council of Europe (OSCE) states that the participation of ethnic minorities is one of the main components of a democratic election and in the *Samtske-Javakheti* Region in southern Georgia where large populations of Armenians live, it remains questionable with regard to whether or not the electoral process really ensures that their voices are heard. [64] Thirty percent of the population of Georgia belongs to ethnic minority groups including Jews, Kurds, *Osesstians, Abkhazians, Armenians, Roma* (Gypsy), and some Russians.[65] However, it is unknown to what degree minority disenfranchisement remains problematic in Georgia. This is one of the most serious problems in developing and maintaining transparent and democratic elections. In 2004, the Freedom House rating for political freedom within Georgia remained four on a scale of one to seven with seven representing the most repressive govern-

---

64   N.N., "OSCE Supreme Commissar Visits Samtske Javakheti Region." *Georgian Times* (25 August 2003):8.

ment. Georgia's civil liberty rating in 2004 was also a four.[66] This scale ranges from one to seven with higher scores indicating fewer civil liberties or little freedom. Georgia's classification as a democratic nation remains disputable. Moreover, the OSCE mission includes facilitating public participation in identifying and appointing qualified people to hold the position of the Chairperson of the Central Election Commission (CEC). OSCE argues that this will facilitate a free, democratic and transparent election. The CEC is the organization responsible for voters' registrations lists as well as tabulating and announcing election results. The OSCE plans to recommend a variety of individuals for the position of CEC chair. They will provide this short list to the President from which he is expected to choose the Chairperson.[67] While some may argue this is western altruism, others might call this form of interference or neo-imperialism. Western organizations clearly convince themselves that this particular method will somehow manage to prevent or deter voter fraud.

Voter fraud is not the only significant organized crime problem in Georgia; another includes the problem of money laundering. In late August, the U.S. Treasury Department and the Georgia Finance Monitoring Office organized a seminar to share information on the apprehension of those who control of money laundering. Organizations involved in this seminar included the Banking Supervising Office of the National Bank of Georgia, the Insurance and Supervising Office, the Notary Chamber, the Auditor Council, and the Antimonopoly Office.[68] While omitted here the relationship between money laundering and corruption might be related to Georgia's difficulty in paying off its foreign debts. Specifically, the President of the Bank of Georgia, *Irakli Managadze* states: "The country is in default and fails to pay foreign debts under the schedule fixed by the Paris Club." [69] Apparently, if the government does not amend the 2003 budget, the International Monetary Fund and Paris

---

65   Jones, "Democracy from Below?"

66   Piano and Puddington, *Freedom in the World 2004.*

67   N.N., "OSCE Press Release: Organization for Security and Cooperation in Europe Mission to Georgia." *Georgian Times* (25 July 2003):21.

68   N.N., "Money Laundering and Geopolitical Results Seminar National Bank of Georgia." *Georgian Times* (25 August 2003):3.

69   N.N., "Press Scanner-Volume of Petroleum Smuggling down." *The Messenger* (7 October 2003):8.

Club may withdraw their financial support. Georgia's foreign debt stands at almost two billion dollars. The IMF has been pressuring the Georgian Parliament to decrease the 2004 budget by two hundred million GEL. However, the most recently proposed budget cut (as of August 2003) was for only one hundred and thirty million lari. The journalist argues that if the IMF suspends its funding to Georgia, other foreign investors may leave worsening the already troubled economy.[70] As mentioned above one factor involved in Georgia's economic problems remains the illicit economy and the laundering of this money. It seems intuitively evident that in order to resolve Georgia's money laundering problems, the government must first address and alleviate the foreign debt burden. However, to accomplish that requires eliminating or at least preventing public corruption. This is unlikely to be resolved soon because the Executive branch of the government blames the parliamentary branch for problems with the economy and vice versa. The writer seems convinced that if the President can persuade the IMF that the Parliament is responsible for the non-payment of loans, then the IMF will remain active in Georgia. Finally, the Georgian National Energy Regulatory Commission is considering raising the tariffs on energy by ten percent to correct the budgetary deficit. Yet the writer alludes to the possibility that increased tariffs might led to an increase in illegal smuggling of oil from *Baku Azerbaijan*. The advent of another transport corridor for illegal oil may also increase the smuggling of a variety of other illegal goods into Georgia. Approximately, one month later, another report reveals that the smuggling of petroleum products recently decreased by about fifteen percent after the Minister of State Security filed five criminal cases following a specific Presidential decree apparently urging such action. The article also indicates that most stolen or counterfeit fuel comes from *Azerbaijan* or Russia. It is unlikely that these limited arrests of a few smugglers will eliminate the shadow economy in Georgia or even have a minor impact on this method of providing goods to those who cannot afford such items legitimately. However, as in Western nations, even infrequent arrests of perpetrators often provide political clout to the current administration, ensuring its long term survival. Of course, journalism coverage

---

70   Maia Misheladze, "Weekly Economic Review Georgia on the Verge of Default." *Georgian Times* (25 August 2003):9.

of these legal maneuvers by the administration also provides support to the extant status quo. Frequently such claimsmaking by Georgian journalists results in taking the side of one political party against another or siding with the executive branch versus the legislative branch leaving unbiased and objective reporting absent from the public debate and front stage politics.

Another article discusses the on-going battle between the executive branch and the legislative branch by publishing a criticism from the Parliamentary Chairperson *Nino Burjanadze.* She reportedly chastised President *Shevardnadze* following his statement that the death penalty ban was a mistake. *Burjanadze* retorts that *Shevardnadze*'s comments reflect a rejection of democratic values and a poor understanding that the problem with crime is not the absence of the death penalty or the absence of criminal law, but that the real problem of crime is the minimal enforcement of the criminal law. *Shevardnadze's* comment and even her critique reveals the lack of understanding about how economic inequality and relative deprivation promotes crime. Critical examinations of criminal behavior repeatedly demonstrate that crime is often a means of economic survival. Moreover, neither side in the above argument demonstrates any awareness that the death penalty has minimal deterrent effects. This is evidenced by the 1999 OSCE recommendation that Georgia ban the death penalty.[71]

As mentioned previously, another major issue facing Georgia's fledgling democracy includes the on-going ideological sentiments rooted in ethnic nationalism. These powerful feelings flourish against the historical backdrop of over two hundred years of Russian Imperialism and numerous takeovers by hostile neighbors as far back as the fifth century. Perhaps these powerful emotions in addition to Georgia's vast economic woes have been the impetus motivating a significant numbers of Georgians to emigrate. While the last Soviet census was conducted in 1989, the Georgian State Department of Statistics published another census in 2002 reflecting that over a million people departed Georgia since the fall of the Soviet Union. While many of those exiting consisted of ethnic minority group members, others were Georgians who left as the result of on-going employment problems. Freedom House reports

---

71   N.N., "Parliamentary Chairperson Regretted over President's Statement about Death Penalty." *Georgian Times* (25 July 2003):3.

that eight percent of Georgians are ethnic Armenians, six percent Russians, six percent *Azeri*, three percent Ossetians, two percent Abkhazians, and five percent consist of other unidentified groups.[72] Ethnic nationalism is reflected in the fact although thirty percent of Georgian citizens are ethnic minority group members who speak other languages,, the Georgian constitution mandates that persons occupying official state positions must speak the Georgian language. One newspaper article attests to the problematic nature of the language issue as the Parliament considers a language bill that would mandate a five-year period for officials to learn Georgian or else lose their positions.[73] As mentioned above, this on-going struggle between the majority ethnic group and the minority groups is reflected in the geographic separation of ethnic minority enclaves from the remainder of the ethnically dominant Georgians. For example, the *Ninotsminda* region shares its border with Armenia and ninety eight and one half percent of the population remains ethnic Armenian, according to *Rafik Arzumanian*, the Chairman of the Regional administration in *Ninostminda*. Additionally, Armenians are ninety-two percent of the population in *Akhalkalaki* (both *Ninostminda* and *Akhalkalaki* are a part of the *Javakheti* region). Importantly, there is even a *Tbilisi* based Armenian language weekly newspaper called the *Vrastan* and the Editor of that paper is quoted as reporting that three years ago Georgian President *Eduard Shevardnadze* gave permission to Georgian residents of the region to use Russian in official state documents. An Armenian poet, George *Snkhchian*, from *Ninotsminda* was quoted as stating: "In the Soviet period, there were no qualified Georgian language teachers in Armenian schools in [those] regions." Therefore, the majority of those living in the area primarily speak Russian.[74] The chairperson of the NGO, *Multiethnic Georgia,* reports that there is no state program organized with a mission to teach Georgian to the non-Georgian population. However, he further explained that there is an OSCE and Georgian sponsored program that teaches Georgian to Armenians employed in state agencies in *Javakheti*. This insistence that ethnic minority peoples speak Georgian while perhaps utilitarian reflects the greater problem

---

72   Piano and Puddington, *Freedom in the World 2004.*
73   Tatul Hakobyan, "Ethnic Armenian Judges May Lose Jobs in Dispute over language." *Brosse Street Journal* (20 July 2003):1.
74   *Ibid.*

of ethnic discrimination against minority peoples in Georgia. These language mandates as well as a variety of other social, legal, economic, and political problems (mostly centered around unemployment) are reflected in the submission of forty three thousand and three hundred and ninety-six asylum requests filed by Georgians since 1990, according to an article citing *Tamuna Mardaleishvili*, press secretary for the International Organization for Immigration office (IOM) in *Tbilisi*. The IOM usually informs Georgians that their chances of receiving political asylum are slim. Illegal immigration is also problematic although one joint IOM and Czech Republic project assists illegal Georgian immigrants in returning to Georgia. Seeking political asylum in a nation characterized by poverty and corruption makes sense, however other motives may include the prevalent use of violence as a means of resolving high-level political power struggles.

For example, such struggles for control even occur between religious leaders. Specifically, a *Tbilisi* District Court recently rejected an appeal by an excommunicated Georgian Orthodox priest, *Basil Mkalashvili*, who was charged with organizing and committing violence against Jehovah's Witnesses and Baptists Evangelists. This may reflect another dimension of nationalism that contains religious as well as ethnic components. Similarly, *Mkalashvili* reportedly has supporters who threaten protests if he is arrested or detained. [75]

Another serious problem in central Georgia remains the living conditions of the IDPs. Many IDPs reside in dilapidated hotels, schools, and other poorly maintained buildings across the country. In August, a group of IDP's from *Abkhazia* seized a state administration building belonging to a company called *Metromsheni* in the *Gidani* district of *Tbilisi* and held the chief of the company hostage demanding that the building be made available as a residence for refugees. The IDPs threatened self-harm if they were not given the building as their new living quarters. Police allegedly surrounded the building and while they refrained from using any force, the article does not indicate how the problem was resolved or if it was resolved. [76]

---

75   Anna Chkadidze, "Mkalavishvili appeal rejected by court." *Ibid.,* 2.
76   N.N., "IDP Women from Abkhazia Threaten with Self Harm." *Georgian Times* (25 July 2003):4.

The headlining article in the August issue of *The Messenger* addresses the recent Central Election Commission ruling forbidding the media from discussing political issues, i.e., restricting free speech. Such a decision clearly violates their constitution and is contrary to the formation of a stable democracy.[77] The International Society for Fair Elections and Democracy (ISFED), a Georgian NGO, reported that the ruling "is a dangerous document that could negatively influence the pre-election campaign period and freedom of speech during the elections." The out-going CEC chair signed the ruling that clearly infringed upon the parliament's power to make laws. Furthermore, the ISFED also explained that the new ruling prevents the public from receiving accurate information about political candidates, prevents candidates from publicizing their campaign platforms' and keeps the media from providing other types of political information. The article further states that the delineation of these rights in the Declaration of Human Rights, the International Covenant on Civil and Political Rights, and the European Convention on Human Rights are necessary for all nation-states. The Georgian director of the ISFED also explained that the ruling specifically violated the nineteenth and twenty-fourth articles of the Georgian Constitution providing the right for the individual to freely receive and disseminate information and express his or her opinion, orally, in writing or any other form. Even in the event of war and or a state of emergency, the President has no right to limit freedom of the press or speech. Apparently the CEC ruling states:

> During an information program, it is prohibited to broadcast live or recorded interviews, statements or positions of a political party or candidate, if these interviews, statements or advocacies are related to the election process and or the expression of a voter's will. It is prohibited to broadcast any reporting that popularizes the slogan, photo materials, or title of any political party.[78]

Finally, ISFED explained that only parliamentary laws and the ethics of journalism should control this process, not rulings from the CEC. In a separate

---

77   Mary Makharashvili, "Freedom of Speech Under threat." *The Messenger* (27 August 2003):1.

78   *Ibid.*

discussion of the CEC ruling, a member of the government party explained that he believed the ruling was a good thing because the media remains easily manipulated by those with money and that both political parties and large financial groups (insinuating criminal organizations) support the television and newspaper companies.[79] Clearly, there is no historical or institutional memory of democracy in Georgia and no established norms valuing free speech. Rather the extant ideology remains that avoiding both conflict and critical thinking are more normative, especially if it maintains the political strength of the party in power. Such posturing between branches of the government and the news media remains an on-going battle in post-Soviet Georgia. In addition to these overt forms of political repression, Georgia's government also commits crimes of economic domination against the people.

The following is an example of the results of crimes of economic domination that appeared in an article discussing counterfeit products and smuggled consumer goods. In a recent series of working group meetings between Georgian media representatives and the Caucasian Brand Protection Group (CBPG) a variety of organized crimes were discussed, including counterfeiting and smuggling, in addition to consumers' rights and related laws.[80] One such meeting included the Head of the Georgian State Anti-Monopoly Service who indicated that the resolution of these kinds of offenses would fail without the participation of citizens. Since counterfeiting is a serious problem, the CBPG's established purpose aims to protect consumers from counterfeit products in the marketplace. The CBPG includes a number of major Georgian companies and international corporations primarily focused on protecting their product lines and profits (Georgian Glass and Mineral Water, JT international, Gillette, Nestle, Phillip Morris, Procter and Gamble, Schwarzkopf and Henkel, Tchibo and Unilver) not consumers. Therefore, the real objective was to strengthen the laws prohibiting, criminalizing and punishing those who produce or sell counterfeit products. The group reports that preventing and punishing such behavior will reduce corruption and crime. Obviously, such efforts remain primarily aimed at reducing harm to the economic elite or as the author put it "honest businessmen" and increasing state revenues

---

79   Mary Makharashvili, "CEC suppresses freedom of the Press." *Ibid.,* 5.
80   Anna Arzanova, "BPG enlists mass media in fighting counterfeiting." *Ibid.,* 3.

through sale taxes or tariffs. Such efforts will not protect the ordinary consumer. As if these cumulative economic, criminal and political problems were not enough to create massive unrest and ambivalence, another major social problem facing Georgia remains the absence of reliable electricity and gas for heating and lighting homes. For many Georgians both in the capital and in the outlying rural regions electricity and gas heat are available only periodically or are completely absent from daily life.[81] One reason electricity and gas scarcity continues to be problematic is that the Georgian gas supplier *Tbligazi,* failed to collect gas payments from *Tbilisi* customers or to make payments to the Russian gas supplier. The debt owed to the Russian company is in the range of over seven hundred thousand dollars. Similarly, the city of *Tbilisi* is required by contract to pay the Russian company monthly, even though this regularly fails to occur. The company's president states that he reminded the Georgian Government and City Hall of their arrears owed. City Hall replied by apologizing and asking the Russian company to continue to supply gas while promising to pay four hundred and thirty thousand dollars by early September.

Another illustration of these economic problems remains evident in the on-going contentious politics between the President's political party and their political opponents over a proposal to cut the federal budget. Opposition parties in the Parliament argue that they will only agree to cuts if the President agrees to fire the Minister of Finance.[82] The President replied that he had no plans to do so. The article suggests that the Finance Minister is a millionaire and a member of the Mafia. Such allegations and political machinations further illuminates the motives behind the CEC's recent attempt to eliminate coverage of politics from the newspaper thus silencing political opposition to *Shevardnadze's* administration. This demand for the minister's resignation occurred after the Finance Minister failed to show up for a recent cabinet meeting. His deputy, who did attend the meeting, accused the leader of the Georgian Railway of being responsible for the budget shortfalls by failing to transfer the funds to the state. Political accusations like this one and the struggle to assign culpability are daily events in Georgian politics. Political

---

81   N.N., "Itera threatens gas cuts." *Ibid.,* 3.
82   Natia Mamistvalovi, "Chrdileli points finger at Chkhaidze." *Ibid.,* 5.

battles continue in another article describing a television interview with the Chairperson of the Parliament. *Burjanadze* disclosed the recent unification of her party with the United Democratic Party, to become the *Burjanadze* Democrats. She welcomed other parties to join the alliance in opposition to *Shevardnadze's* government. *Burjanadze* argues that this new political block aims to resolve the problems of unpaid pensions and salaries, the absence of funding for the army and law enforcement and the budget shortfall of one hundred and thirty-five million GEL.[83] However, the President recently attempted to alleviate these budgetary problems by calling on the Ministry of Finance and Taxation to collect an additional two hundred and seven million GEL in taxes. The deputy minister of finance posits that this is not possible. It seems obvious, there are no jobs, there is little money circulating, people are unable to pay their bills or their taxes, so the taxes cannot fill the budget coiffeurs thus the government remains in debt and the people stay poor. Of course, other variables in the equation include the politicians and oligarchs who embezzle large sums of money that could be helpful if effectively doled out to larger groups of the population in the form of social welfare or even salaries for non-elite government employees. [84]

III.3 September and October 2003

As September begins and the election draws nearer, the newspapers continue to discuss the CEC ruling restricting the media. In this article, the CEC ruling covers an entire page. The CEC decision states that the commission has the authority to demand that TV and radio companies submit their airtime allocation coverage of political issues prior to airing. Additionally, TV and radio stations are required to submit their schedule of political advertisements for each political party as well as the schedule of tariffs paid by those parties for their allocated airtime beginning on September 13th. Further, the CEC is "entitled to oversee and control the airtime allocated for political parties and election contestants in the case this airtime is not used by the parties or con-

---

83   "No Prospects for the opposition's unification." *Ibid.*
84   Anna Arzanova, "Government's task Unrealistic, Monday on Mzera." *Ibid.*, 5.

testants." The TV, radio companies and newspaper outlets are prohibited from broadcasting agitating commentary on election contestants or their representatives or any recorded sentiments of the political contestants unless these prior government approval is granted. Additional limitations include prohibitions against broadcasting entertainment programs that include political candidates without prior government approval. State and local public officials are also prohibited from campaigning or advocating while participating in TV or radio programs or while they are conducting their official duties. Moreover, TV and radio companies are not permitted to broadcast any information about current officials running for office. First time violations will result in a warning and second violations will result in the removal of the TV or radio companies' accreditation. Following such action the CEC will then issue a decree with regard to the offending party (details are omitted). However, the decree may be appealed to the judicial system. The decree also prohibits coverage of electoral campaigns beginning fifty days prior to the November elections, at improper times, as well as any information programming that makes comments about the personal character of political candidates, and any media event when political party members are present. Finally, the CEC ruling also prohibits political parties and election contestants from making any statements that call for overthrowing the Constitutional order of Georgia or from advocating war or violence, or the incitement of ethnic, religious, or social unrest. The CEC may also file a complaint to the Constitutional Court in order to prohibit a particular political party's existence. A majority of CEC members may make this decision. One of several things may motivate such repressive behavior, either the CEC or its members do not understand the way a democracy functions, or they are genuinely motivated to eliminate unnecessary political fighting or violence due to the significant number of parties vying for political power. Fifty -two political parties or blocks have applied for registration for the election in November. Thirty-two of these parties consist of officially registered parties, while the remaining 20 (or twenty-two) were approved by a referendum of the people. However, the CEC may simply be attempting to execute what they believe to be their normative authority. This misuse of power remains a legacy of the Soviet era as well as an indicator of the substantive absence of civic education both historically and currently. However, an international factor may also explain this behavior, that is when other modern well respected or perhaps feared democratic governments begin to exercise executive power beyond what is constitutionally acceptable (the United States and the Patriot Act), other governments follow suit.

In an interview with a newspaper editor and several political party members with regard to this ruling, most agreed that the CEC effort is unconstitutional and reflects a form of censorship. Only the newspaper editor actually argued that restricting politicians was a good idea although he argued that it would have no effect on the new Rights Party and the National Movement party, insinuating that popular support for these parties remains widespread. Fortunately, in early September, the new members of the CEC took office and abolished the earlier resolution restricting mass media coverage of the election (state and privately owned). [85] Although the ruling was rescinded a variety of television stations and newspapers subsequently filed a lawsuit alleging not only that the new regulation violated the rights of the free press but also the rights of political parties. The suit was actually filed by the local election monitoring NGO, the Fair and Democratic Elections. The executive director explained: "Nobody can prohibit electoral campaigns in mass media...because news programs were senseless with out political reports."[86] A subsequent report also indicates that the *Tbilisi* District Court overturned the controversial ruling adopted by the Central Election Committee in August, as it violated the constitution (this occurred one day prior to the departure of the previous Central Election Commission members).[87] Even after the plaintiffs in the law suits settled the case, the incident provided fodder for on-going political jockeying for power between the party in power and *Mikhail Saakashvili's* (the former Minister of Justice) National Movement party.

During this political posturing President *Shevardnadze* denied allegations made by *Mikhail Saakashvili*, that he has been involved with criminals.[88] *Shevardnadze* claimed that he had been meeting with criminal gangs since

---

85   Ekaterine Gegia, "Pre-Election Media Restrictions Revoked." *Georgia Today* (5 September 2003):2.

86   *Ibid.*

87   N.N., "Former CEC heads out." *The Messenger* (4 September 2003):1.

the 1960s, in order to ensure that their political demands would remain un-met. However, he denies any alliance with them. He also acknowledges that although criminal clans have continued to increase in the area lately, he promises that law enforcement officials are making re-newed efforts to combat them. As *Saakashvili's* criticisms of the administration continue, the new political block, the *Burjanadze-Democrats* led by *Zurab Zhvania* and *Nino Burjanadze*, also critique *Shevardnadze's* administration.

In a TV interview, *Zhvania* stated that although he supported *Shevardnadze* for five to six years, he holds the administration responsible for creating two worlds, the law on paper, and the "terrible life in which our people live." He also accuses the administration of engaging in blackmail and dirty campaigning including defacing posters of the political opposition. While *Zhvania* may blame such behavior on adult political party members, it remains more likely that adolescent delinquents are the real perpetrators of such acts.[89] Other topics leading to political ping-pong include economic issues particularly taxes, wages, and income inequality.

Tax laws and tax collection are significant social problems in Georgia and remain embedded in corruption and bribery involving businesspeople and politicians, often the same person wearing two hats. Of course, this certainly remains true in American politics as well, as most U.S. Senators were millionaires prior to running for or holding public office. However, sometimes, political support comes from businessmen (journalists typically refer to all business people as businessmen reflecting the gender domination of the new capitalist class by men.) whose relatives become elected public officials and sponsor legislation providing benefits to their families.[90] Additionally, over the last year, six hundred modifications to the tax code occurred. Moreover, public attitudes about taxes indicated that the Georgians view taxes as a burden not an obligation with social and economic returns. Income taxes can be as much as sixty-eight percent of a person's gross salary, employer payroll taxes as high as twenty-eight percent of all payroll funds, and Value Added

---

88.   N.N., "President Called Accusations "Absurd." *Georgia Today* (5 September 2003):5.

89   Anna Arzanova, "Tuesday on Mzera. Zhvania defends his bloc." *The Messenger* (4 September 2003):5.

Taxes are as high as twenty percent for companies with more 24,000 GEL gross earnings. Consequently, one of the largest problems remains collecting these taxes. A 2002 report reveals that the Tax department considered over one hundred and five appeals worth a total value of 235,000 lari. The top ten taxpayers primarily include large businesses rather than business people in general. These businesses included the following large companies:

a. Georgian Railways (2.8 billion GEL)
b. *MAGTICOM* Limited, a telecom company (2.4 billion GEL)
c. JSC *BILAVIAMSHENI* a building company, (1.4 billion GEL)
d. *Geocell* a telecom company (1 billion GEL), Poti Port (7.3 million GEL)
e. Georgian Energy Wholesale Market (6 billion GEL)
f. JSC Hotel *Tbilisi* Marriott (5.7 Million GEL)
g. JSC *Saqartvelos Eleqtrokavshir* Telecomunications Center Branch (5.7 million GEL)
h. Georgian-Austrian Joint Venture *Metechi* Hotel (4.9 million GEL)

The Chief of the Tax department also disclosed that the power companies owe a great deal of money in back taxes to the government.[91] He reports that almost thirty-seven percent of the shortage of government funds comes from unpaid taxes by the utilities sector. In 2002, these companies paid only five percent of their due taxes and only one percent in 2003. One company, *Sakenergo-200* owes an additional ten million in back taxes that accumulated over the last seven months while the total owed the government is eighty-seven million GEL. Another company, *Tbilisressi,* owes over eighty-nine million GEL. Unfortunately, the laws that privatized the former state utilities, prohibits the government from enforcing the tax laws through the seizure of assets. Initially, this was designed to assist the growth of newly privatized industries and to prevent the re-establishment of a central state run economy. However, most of these companies are still operating under Presidential decrees originally designed to assist them only in the incipient stages of privati-

---

90   Helen Kvanchilashvili, "Troubled Tax System vexes businesses." *Brosse Street Journal* (29 September 2003):1.
91   Lase Zautashvili, "Difficulties in Tax collection system. Report for the Governmental Session." *The Georgian Times* (1 September 2003):9.

zation. The Chief of the Tax department also alleges that a variety of businesses continue to fail to pay their VAT. Moreover, taxes and social security withdrawals from employees' salaries often go unpaid by employers. The director also indicated that part of the problem includes both the malfeasance of tax collectors (and clearly taxpayers) and their immunity from criminal and administrative punishment. This absence of funds from the VAT and social taxes amounts to two billion dollars. He also alleges that government agency heads often fail to pay their income taxes and that the law does not punish individuals who evade taxes (This writer could not find in the administrative code or criminal code any references to income tax evasion). Together these problems result in loss of one hundred and seventy million GEL annually. State and private power companies, automobile plants, and a Metallurgic company also owe back taxes that range from nine to almost ninety million GEL. He further explains that managers of state agencies who are responsible for budgets are also partially responsible for the state's financial problems. It remains unclear if he is suggesting that his office be given the power to fire these officials, to make recommendations for investigation or if he is just referring to the problem of corrupt officials. Land taxes are also in the arrears to the tune of two hundred million lari. While these figures draw a bleak picture, there were some administrative sanctions implemented in 2003. Specifically, the twenty-one enforcement actions were made against nine-hundred and eighty-nine taxpayers after conducting tax audits. The amount owed by these tax evaders amounted to almost two million GEL. Unfortunately, such investigations and enforcement processes are quite time consuming. For example, the Chief of the Tax Department identified one of the problems as the rapidly changing addresses of such companies, the bankruptcy of the companies, disagreements about the amount owed as well as court appeals to fight re-paying the debt to the state. Georgian law also allows taxpayers to file extensions or postponements. However, he claims that while one-hundred and sixty-four such agreements exist, none of the taxpayers actually met the requirements of the law to delay their payments. Usually they fail to pay as specified by the postponement schedule. Tax notifications explain to late taxpayers that they will have their property seized (liens). Such notices went to over five thousand taxpayers in 2003 and contained a procedure in place to register these notifications in priority of collection. Last year, notices were sent to almost three thousand five hundred taxpayers with property scheduled for seizure adding up to four hundred and sixty million GEL. This year the government has seized six-hundred and fifty three tax-payers' properties. Additionally, one-hundred and forty-three tax auctions have been held resulting in the collection of almost seventy million GEL. Thirty-nine more property seizures are planned. The failure to collect taxes, while partly due to the corruption on the part of businesses and tax collectors probably increases economic inequality, while economic inequality also increases the likelihood that the poor or working poor will also fail to pay their taxes.

The working poor probably fail to pay taxes because they are simply unable to do so. By extension, in another discussion about Georgia's high level of economic inequality, journalists cite official data indicating that the average monthly salary of a Georgian household is about forty-five GEL with total income from other source reaching about sixty GEL.[92] They report the monthly cost of living is one hundred and twenty-five GEL, although it is unclear how many individuals per household this includes. The article reports that many people survive by selling their clothing, family heirlooms, and homes. I visited at least two such places while living in Georgia. An open market (flea market) in *Tbilisi,* located near a shopping center, consists of many small booths or spaces occupied by women and or men selling off family jewelry, knick knacks, old soviet era coins and medals, books, and a variety of a sundry things in order to eek out a living.

It is not an exaggeration to state that economically, times were much better during the end of the Soviet era. For example, compared to 1990, there are seventeen fewer washing machines for every one-hundred families, seventeen fewer vacuum cleaners, eighteen fewer TV sets, and seventy-nine fewer radios. A walk down any residential neighborhood in the capital city illustrates some of this as on many apartment balconies hang clothes lines where family laundry dries in the air because few people can afford clothes dryers. Additionally, only one to two percent of the population controls forty

---

92   M. Alkhazashvili, "Gap between rich and poor vast." *The Messenger* (24 September 2003):3.

percent of the nations' wealth. The reporter alleges that those who achieved this wealth did so by manipulating vouchers, procuring illegal loans, pocketing foreign government loans, stealing people's savings, taking advantage of privatization, smuggling in the shadow economy, corruption and involvement in drug and human trafficking. Most Georgians live under the poverty level and the GDP has grown only 1.6 times between 1996 and 2002, while income increased by only 1.4 times, and budget revenues grew only 1.55 times. As the result of these conditions, last fall, *Zurab Zhvania* called for a change in the minimum wage to help Georgians keep up with the cost of living. These pervasive economic problems leave most Georgians reeling with hopeless and frustration.

One journalist reports that a recent budget proposal failed to pass parliament due to government's ineptitude thus undermining receipt of IMF and U.S. funding. The writer argues that this occurred only because the current administration has become more concerned about maintaining its foothold in the forthcoming elections than in ensuring the long-term future of Georgia.[93] A similar piece criticizes recent budget planning that allegedly overestimated tax collections and imports and ignored the issue of debt repayments already overdue. [94] In an attempt to alleviate corruption problem, the Georgian Transnational Crime and Corruption Center (Anti-Corruption Bureau) was created in 1999. By design, the office was to weld investigative and police powers of arrest in addition to advising the President. Unfortunately, the office has little power and currently only makes recommendations to the Prosecutor General's office and has no law enforcement authority.

In late September, I had the opportunity to attend a public presentation sponsored by the Anti-Corruption Bureau of Georgia held at *Tbilisi* State University. The Chairman of the Bureau, *Kakha Uglulava* spoke about the absence of real authority and power of his office.[95] The writer mentions that while the organizers promised the session would start on time "Georgian re-

---

93   *Idem*. "Political Interests sacrifice cooperation with IMF." *The Messenger* (4 September 2003):1.
94   *Idem*. "Budget Plan 2004 resembles unfulfilled past budgets." *Ibid*.
95   Sopho Gorgodze, "Breaking Bad Traditions Anti-Corruption Bureau seeks greater powers." *The Messenger* (1 October 2003):1.

ality prevailed and *Ugulava* found himself apologizing for being late."[96] Promptness is not a Georgian attribute but this self-identified stereotype allegedly reflects the ever-present traffic problem across the capital city. However, I never had any trouble being prompt and I always relied on public transportation. Therefore, this issue seems more likely to be related to the institutionalized inefficiency that characterizes much of the daily life in *Tbilisi*. Although clearly building additional road networks would be a good thing for the city. Regardless of the timeliness of the inception of the conference, the author describes the audience as far more frustrated by the continued absence of a crackdown on corrupt officials. She also explains that the most common outcome in corruption cases is that the guilty party resigns from his current position and then later runs for Parliament. She reports that the recent dismissal of the Chair of the State Department of Forestry followed revelations that he was "known for rampant corruption."[97] However, the author fails to explain what this really means in terms of evidence or suspicion. It seems as though the concept of a trial and the idea of being innocent until proven guilty by a court of law and a jury of one's peers is also not a part of Georgia's institutionalized or historical memory. Corruption Director *Ugulava* reportedly "explained that the bureau's limited powers make it difficult to 'break the tradition of Corruption which is in our blood'."[98] He argued that the main problem remains the Prosecutor General's office. He describes it as in desperate need of reform. However, the article does not provide readers with any specific information with regard to problems within the Prosecutor's office. Furthermore, the author failed to provide a description of the specific reforms needed. *Ugulava* reported that the Bureau needs permission to collect personal information on government officials including information from government tax and revenue departments. He also suggests that his office needs the authority to indict or charge wrongdoers with offenses just like the Ministry of Security and Ministry of the Interior. One advantage the anti-corruption office maintains is their monitoring team that collects information on campaign financing. However, the law only requires the presentation of this information after the elections, not before. Additionally, it is unclear if the

---

96   *Ibid.*
97   *Ibid.*, 3.

agency actually receives the information and if they do what they do with it following its receipt. Naively, the Director also allegedly claimed that the number of people offering bribes decreased recently. Furthermore, he argued that money laundering is not a problem in Georgia. What remains omitted from the article that my translator explained during the presentation, was that the agency collects all its information through anonymous phone tips. Clearly, this method of collecting data is not valid or reliable nor does it represent the most salient issues surrounding corruption problem. Nonetheless, a more reliable resource for such data remains available through transparency international's annual corruption reports. Their report contains information collected from household surveys from over 40,838 people across 47 countries. Their findings indicate that eighteen percent of those surveyed in Georgia reported that if they could eliminate corruption from one institution it would be within the judicial system.[99] While the World Bank provides assistance to private firms to transform the courts it appears that funds may be utilized to rebuild and re-model court buildings.[100] Across the capital city, I observed many such examples of remodeled offices, money used to improve front stage appearances although a more pragmatic choice might have been to use the funds to improve the efficiency or effectiveness of the insitution. No discussion follows with regard to how these funds are actually used to reform judicial procedures or improve civil rights. However, the chair of the Supreme Court of Georgia, *Lado Chanturia* stated, "Court reform is being successfully implemented in Georgia with the support of our foreign friends. We need the assistance of our foreign friends for years to come as court reform will not be completed until the entire court system meets International Standards."[101] Additionally, the writer fails to provide any discussion of the specific standards on which Georgia falls short.

In an attempt to improve the country's financial situation, a new economic regulatory law passed in November 2002 will go into effect in early

---

98   *Ibid.*, 3.
99   Transparency International Global Corruption Barometer 2003.
100   Mary Makharashvili, "A Visible kind of court reform." *The Messenger* (1 October 2003):1.
101   *Ibid.*

September.[102] The law requires all imported items to have a Georgian label affixed indicating the payment of the Value Added Tax (VAT). Fines will be administered for those who fail to comply with the law and these range from two hundred to five hundred GEL for a first offense, to between eighty hundred and fifteen hundred GEL for repeat offenses. The Georgian Anti-Monopoly Service is currently checking for such labels. However, some officials acknowledge the difficulty of ensuring the application of the law to small street venders or at *bazrobas*. I rarely found such labels on anything I purchased from a street vendor. However, vendors' report difficulties getting precise information from the Anti-Monopoly office on which products must have this adhesive label even though it seems apparent that the label is for all products. As mentioned previously, Georgian authorities have difficulty managing illegally imported products and thus collecting legitimate taxes and tariffs on such products. The Georgian Parliament also passed this law in order to provide Georgians with information about the product's legitimacy. However, in part these economic changes may be a response to the recent decision by the International Monetary Fund to suspend Georgia's assistance program.[103] For example, both the World Bank and other donor institutions continue to criticize Georgia's fiscal policy. A regional director of the World Bank in the Caucasus, D.M. Dousette Coirolo, reportedly stated: "I am very disappointed at your government's failure to fulfill the IMF's obligations over the course of three months." While this director claims that there remains no connection between the IMF and the World Bank, he acknowledges that the IMF suspension will lead to problems in the on-going implementation of World Bank programs. Nonetheless, he indicates that the World Bank will continue to provide loans for the development of small and medium businesses, funding for health care, poverty reduction programming as well as to find ways to stimulate economic growth. The cumulative amount of World

---

102   *Idem.* "Confusion remains over Georgian Labeling." *The Messenger* (18 September 2003):3
103   *Idem.* "World Bank Disappointed with Georgia." *The Messenger* (16 September 2003):1.

Bank and IMF loans provided to Georgia totals over six hundred and forty million U.S. dollars. Eleven different projects have reached completion. [104]

Besides these numerous economic problems and the debts owed the IMF and Paris Club, an editorial criticizes *Shevardnadze's* more recent efforts to develop a stronger relationship with Russia rather than the United States or NATO. The writer argues that this an unwise move that frustrates him and that many Georgians feel the same way.[105] The writer bases this supposition on an August statement made by *Shevardnadze*, [Georgia will] "become a part of a NATO, however, it will not happen soon." He made this statement at the graduation ceremony for the third Georgian army battalion trained by the U.S. Army. Although the writer in question may be over-reacting, he also re-ports that other political parties also have criticized *Shevardnadze's* admini-stration for giving Georgia a negative reputation in the West. These critics al-so blame his administration for giving false hope to Georgians that the United States would take care of the Georgian people and re-integrate *Abkhazia* into Georgia. However, the writer is also concerned about several other political parties including the Communist Party, the Political Union party, and *Abashidze's* Revival Union party. He writes that they are also motivated to ally Georgia with Russia and away from the west. Apparently, this angst is related to the writer fears that that if the forthcoming election is not fair, the administration will revert to an authoritarian style of governing. However, he believes if elections are held democratically, Georgia's western orientation will be solidified. This writer promoted political parties claiming to maintain a western orientation and these included *Mikhail Saakashvili* of the National Movement, the New Rights party lead by *David Gamkrelidze* and the *Burjanadze*-Democrats chaired by *Zurab Zhvania* and *Nino Burjanadze*.

Another writer endorses a favored politician, a PM running for re-election from the *Ambrolauri* region, *Niko Lekishvili,* who reportedly brought a variety of new businesses to the region. These included wine factories, min-ing, and a mineral water bottling factory. He also financed and reconstructed local schools and roads and assisted local farmers in reviving viticulture. The

104   Sopho Gorgodze, "TRACECA test drive reaches Georgia." *The Messenger* (18 September 2003):1.
105   N.N., "Foreign Policy to be decided from November 2." *The Messenger* (4September 2003):1.

writer presents this candidate as one of the few politicians running who is an acceptable candidate.[106] His evidence consists of the increase in the local birth rate and the decrease in out-migration. Obviously, touting his achievements may either provide hope to potential readers, or discourage them by leading them to believe that there are no other candidates like this one.

In his regularly scheduled Monday morning radio interview, President *Shevardnadze* recently asked other political parties to meet and discuss the forthcoming election to garner an agreement that they all will conduct themselves appropriately.[107] He also asked opposition parties to avoid being disrespectful toward his good will. Then he stated: "I was always ready to cooperate with the strong enemies and I do not consider the opposition as my enemies."[108] His confident words appear aimed at dismissing other parties' criticisms. The President asked all political parties to avoid using negative public relations campaigns, including his own party. He also asked the public to avoid finding all political ads so distasteful that they fail to participate in the election process. While on the surface, it appeared that he was initially trying to silence the opposition; he seemed to genuinely exhibit a modest desire to maintain a civil democratic process. However, the criticisms of *Shevardnadze's* administration continue, this time with regard to a recently authorized change in the number of parliamentary representatives. The change was not orchestrated by the President, over two hundred thousand Georgians signed a referendum to reduce the number of parliamentarians from two-hundred and thirty-five to one hundred and fifty. *Shevardnadze* argues that this recently passed legislation does not violate the constitution and will not affect the forthcoming election. While no explanations are offered for the recent change, it may be a part of an effort to reduce lengthy debate (a slippery slope in a democracy) or save money by paying fewer parliamentarians' salaries. Other issues discussed in the interview included the destruction of two electric towers and recent prison escapes.

Apparently, unidentified suspects sabotaged two electric towers and the President promised that the Minister of Affairs will investigate and arrest

---

106   N.N.,"Lekishvili faces little challenge." *Ibid.*
107   N.N., "Shevardnadze's Monday Morning Interview." *The Messenger (16* September 2003):1.
108   *Ibid.*

the perpetrators. He condemned the saboteurs, allegedly involved in similar incidents in the past. He called it a crime against the state and the people. In another part of the interview, *Shevardnadze* reports that the frequent escapes of prison inmates from Georgian penitentiaries are partly the result of having erroneously placed the prison system under the Ministry of Justice when there should be a separate Ministry of Corrections. Moreover, the funding for prisons must improve in order to hire additional correctional officers. The Minister of Justice resigned as the result of the recent escape of over one hundred and twenty-nine inmates from a maximum-security prison located in *Rustavi*. [109] The inmates killed one correctional officer and injured another in what the author called "the largest jailbreak in Georgian history". While the President called the transfer of the correctional system from the Ministry of Internal Affairs to the Ministry of Justice a mistake, the Minister of Internal affairs argues that if his office takes over this responsibility his department will require additional funding. The President does not mention the need for more funding but argues that poor leadership in the Ministry of Justice resulted in these and other prison escapes. Sixty-three of the over hundred escapees were subsequently apprehended. The Ministry of Justice informed the remaining escapees that if they returned by 15 September, no other charges would be filed against them. Another article indicates that the murder of a correctional officer facilitated the escape and that sixty-five inmates were later re-captured and eight turned themselves into authorities[110]. Following this incident the Minister of Justice resigned. However, on page seven a full-page story appears interviewing the prison's Public Relations officer, *Gocha Mukbaniani,* who talks about the recent escapes and discusses conditions in Georgia's prisons.[111] The public relations officer indicated that the prison is under-funded and cannot pay employees nor provide basic programming needs to the inmates. Correctional officers are paid thirty-three GEL a month or about fourteen dollars. Often guards hired come right off the street and sometimes are members of ethnic minority groups who do not speak Georgian or Russian. He describes the recent escape as possibly or-

---

109   N.N., "Minister of Justice resigns following record jailbreak." *Ibid.,* 4.
110   N.N., "Police Claims Capturing 79 Escapees from total 129. What's New." *Georgia Today* (19 September 2003):3.
111   N.N., "The Friday Interview-The Mediator." *Ibid.,* 7.

chestrated by the Department of the Interior aimed at sabotaging the Ministry of Justice in order to get the penitentiaries back under Interior control. The sentry guards shot at the escaping prisoners, but *Gocha* explains: "A guard won't kill a prisoner for 33 GEL a month."

> This remains true not because they have plenty of contact with them (including the illegal kind where a trader on the outside throws a bottle of vodka up to the sentry on one side and a prisoner throws money on the other). [It is] out of respect for life in general [rather] than for individuals. It's a tradition, not religion, that killing someone is a huge sin.[112]

Apparently, *Gocha* has minimal contact with the inmates and while he explained that it was because the inmates wanted so much, it appeared that his primary difficulty is telling them how little he can really do for them with funding remaining poor. He reports that the prison houses nine-hundred and eighty-six inmates with only twenty- three guards. In addition to the prison escape discussed in President *Shevardnadze's* Monday morning address, other positive issues surrounding crime included praising law enforcement's recent accomplishments. Specifically, the President touted the recent arrests of criminal organizations in *Svaneti* region. However, he omitted any discussion of the details of the crime of these organized groups. He also retorts that police arrests of [criminals] suspects in the Pankasi Gorge area is evidence of the improved capabilities of the police. He fails to use the word suspect, rather describing the suspects only as criminals as if the trials and convictions have already transpired. *Shevardnadze* also explains that the recent agreement with Russian gas and electric companies will provide both gas and electricity to Georgia since the American company departed before completing necessary renovations. He believes this was a good decision. However, he also reportedly indicated that Georgia would be better off if it had no scoundrels in it. In this interpretation, it is unclear if he is referring to the Americans or the Russians. Finally, he indicates that Russia will be importing two hundred and fifty to three hundred megawatts of energy in a few days that will improve electricity delivery in the capital.

---

112   *Ibid.*

The press positively describes the departure of the American electric company, American Electric Services, and the subsequent purchase by the Russian electric company, *RAO*. In this article, the press indicates that the Georgian government promises a forthcoming solution to *Tbilisi's* electricity problems.[113] However, the writer also explains that the new Russian company promised 24-hour electricity and that has not yet occurred. Two electric lines to *Tbilisi* remain badly damaged and thus receiving electricity from Russia regularly is impossible. These damaged lines include the *Alaverdi* line from Armenia and another called *Kavakasioni*. However, in a later article, the description of these lines appears to convey that while minimally operational, the real problem is the quality of the lines and *Tbilisi's* requirements for two-hundred and thirty to two hundred and forty megawatts daily. Poor line quality or the availability of only one hundred megawatts to a city of two million, translates into the inevitability that some *Tbilisi* city residents will not have power. This occurred in mid October, when four separate power plants shut down for about 1 and ½ hours.[114] Occasionally the *Tbilisi* power grid malfunctions also leading to the loss of electricity to the capital. The author claims that when AES operated in Georgia, the local "bosses" forced AES to buy electricity in Russia and then stole the electricity. These bosses are later referred to the as the "energy Mafiosi." While the author fails to explain how steeling electricity occurs, a later article refers to this theft as involving the removal of parts of the lines to sell on the black market. While the director of the Russian electric company promises a reduction in the electricity tariff for Georgia, he explains that this will change only if customers make payments for previously consumed electricity. *Tbilisi* residents make only seventy-five to eighty percent of their payments and residents in the regions frequently can only afford to pay for ten to fifteen percent. I lived in the capital city for the entire year and lost electricity periodically. Occasionally the electricity would go off for an hour or two, on a few occasions for the entire day, and more regularly for a ½-hour or so. Of course the length of time without electricity also varied by one's location within the city. In this editorial, the author explains that the State remains obliged to ensure that all Georgians receive electricity.

---

113   M. Alkhazashvili, "Why is Tbilisi still without electricity?" *The Messenger* (16 September 2003):1.

Georgian's view of this responsibility stands as both a relic from the Soviet Union and the more modern duty of the democratic state to regulate and ensure the proper functioning of public utilities. Legitimately, the government is responsible for the maintenance and care of the high voltage-lines and the two private companies explain that they will hold the state responsible if problems continue. The United Energy Distribution Company of Georgia delivers electricity to other regions outside the capital city. However, they are waiting for their license to be issued by the government regulatory Commission. One factor that may be involved in Georgian inefficiency in the supply of electricity might be related to the fact that an Irish company actually manages Georgia's state electricity. One could argue that this reflects globalization at its worst.

Energy problems across Georgia are pervasive. Even middle class Georgians may not have heat in the winter because gas is unaffordable. In visiting a variety of fellow academics' homes throughout the winter, many had no central heat but relied on small and outdated electric coil heaters. These college professors also sometimes worked in very cold conditions. Tbilisi State University provided no heat in the classrooms until well into the winter months. I spent many classroom evenings writing on the chalkboard wearing my gloves. Another friend explained that when he was in graduate school he wrote his dissertation at night with a flashlight while covered with a blanket setting on the floor. He said his children used to think the word for electricity was "oh!!!!" as every time the lights came back on, the adults in the family would happily express their relief with a sigh of "oh..!!!!." These on-going problems make for good political fodder as parties continue to make election promises about how they will improve the supply of electricity and or heat to Georgians. National movement party members argue for lower tariffs as well as a re-structuring of the energy system entailing fewer distributors, suppliers, and transmitters of electricity.[115] Interestingly, while this article reports that a Russian company bought Telasi the distribution company which provides electricity to Tbilisi, a previous article describes the arrangement as purchasing power from Russia not Russia's purchase of the distribution station. Clearly, the five W's of journaslism, what, when, where, who, and why

---

114   Misheladze, "Weekly Economic Review."

are often absent from Georgian newspaper reporting. A representative of the government party block argues that Georgia needs to repair old energy stations and build new ones. Further, the representative stated that while money has already been provided to accomplish this task, lack of professionalism and corruption interferes with making such changes. While he sings the praises of the regional network of electricity that includes Turkey and Russia, a representative of the *Burjanadze* Democrats calls for the punishment of those responsible for the electricity crisis. However, the Democrats agree that many existing hydroelectric stations require repair. The government official also argues that every village should have its own source of electricity and that Georgia not Russia should control the energy supply. The state run electric company called the *Sak-Energo* network controlled the generation, supply and distribution of electricity throughout Georgia until 1996 when Georgia restructured the system and new capitalists separately purchased and privatized a variety of companies, each one responsible for the following processes, generation, distribution and transmission. The result was sixty-six distribution companies. One of these, *Telasi,* previously provided the capital with electricity, until the American Company, AES, purchased it. Other business and foreign investors bought the remainder of the state electric companies. "The Ministry of Fuel and Energy regulates the newly privatized network and the Georgian Wholesale Electricity Market sets tariffs and does the accounting for the entire enterprise."[116] The corruption alleged earlier by one politician reportedly results from investment companies who overcharge as well as corrupt government officials, and citizens who steal electricity through illegal connections. Meter readings reflect that residents owe *Telasi* forty million U.S. dollars in back payments, while commercial businesses owe twenty-two million U.S. dollars. The government also owes the company five million U.S. dollars. Again, this is the reason AES agreed to sell its investment (seventy-five percent) to a Russian company, RAO EES, for twenty-three million dollars. A representative of an American Company administering the electricity distribution and transmission systems in the regions reports that Georgian politicians must stop overstepping its boundaries by trying to administer elec-

---

115   Tiko Nachkebia, "Candidates speak out about electricity." *The Brosse Street Journal* (29 October 2003):1-10.

tricity distribution and simply set policy. Furthermore, he explains that the government must become more fiscally responsible.

An article reprinted from the September twelvth edition of the Wall Street Journal written by Ian Berman, Vice President of the American Foreign Policy Council in Washington D.C. and Artem Agoulnik, the Program Associate at the council of Russia describe the energy problem.[117] The authors argue that *Shevardnadze's* acceptance of Russian natural gas and electricity jeopardizes Georgia's relationship with the West and that this reflects the President's plan to maintain his power. They also claim that while Georgia still desires membership in the EU and NATO, Moscow's influence may prevent it. The writers further explain that Georgia's new agreement with *Gazprom* (the Russian natural gas company) will ultimately allow the Russians to control the gas distribution to Georgia. Moreover, the Wall Street Journal article states: "The European Union's recent decision to appoint a special envoy to the South Caucasus is a sure sign that Europe is taking a keener interest in a region that will become a vital transit route for much of its energy within the next five years."[118] So the writers wonder if Georgia can remain an ally of the West without "heat and in the dark."[119]

In mid September, the American Councils for International Education sponsored a roundtable discussion about the forthcoming Georgian parliamentary elections.[120] The panel participants included Mark Mullen of the National Democratic Institute, *Zurab Chiaberashvili* of the International Society for Fair Elections and Democracy (ISFED), and Timothy Blauvelt, the Director of the American Councils of Education. The panel's objective focused on encouraging students and university graduates as well as public educators to motivate civic involvement in the electoral process. Mullen reported that Georgian elections have become increasingly worse over the last decade. He referred to the 1999 elections as the poorest in Georgia's recent history. He characterized them as fraudulent and exclusively focused on keeping the Labor Party out of parliament. However, he explained the result was the in-

---

116   *Ibid.,* 10.
117   Christina Tashkevich, "Wall Street Journal Article: concern over energy politics." *The Messenger* (16 September 2003):5.
118   *Ibid.,* 3.
119   *Ibid.*

creasing popularity of the Labor Party across Georgia. I attended this panel discussion and the article accurately represented the information presented including Mullen's concerns that the forthcoming parliamentary elections might also be fraudulent and that this would endanger the next Presidential election. However, Mullen also made it clear, and the article relays this, that if the elections are fair, a strong signal will be sent to the West that Georgia is ready to resolve some long-standing problems. Such a success will improve the West's perceptions of the Georgian government's legitimacy and willingness to become more democratic. Mullen also criticized political TV talk shows where competing candidates end up yelling at each other and thus only demonstrating their dislike for one another rather than informing potential voters. Mullen also provided a large chart to members of the audience relaying the voting records of specific parliamentarians. Mullen reports that politicians often lie to the public about their voting record. *Chiaberashvili* of the ISFED explained that his organization would observe and monitor the pre-election procedures as well as the actual parliamentary election. ISFED a parallel voter count that will be released on November third.

ISFED will station over three thousand observers across the country's election precincts to conduct parallel vote counts. This procedure is designed to provide a check of the accuracy of official tabulations in an attempt to ensure a free and transparent election process.[121] ISFED staff recently received election observation training from a Serbian NGO, the same NGO that compelled Slobodan Milosevic to resign from his office. Pre-election speculative banter continues in the newspapers as President *Shevardnadze's* party, the Citizens' Union of Georgia prepares its lists of candidates for Parliament. *Shevardnadze* appointed a friend to negotiate with opposition party leaders after former U.S. secretary of state James Baker recommended opening a dialogue with the opposition.[122] *Shevardnadze's* appointee, *Vazha Lorki-panidze*, remains viewed suspiciously as a manipulator who will simply try to silence the opposition. These two articles reflect that the CEU party is nomi-

120   Sopho Gorgodze, "Encouraging participation in Georgian Elections." *Ibid.,* 4.
121   Mary Makharashvili, "Fair Elections to conduct Parallel Vote Tabulation." *The Messenger* (18 September 2003):10.
122   Zaza Jgharkava, "Conjuring up Strategies." *Georgia Today* (19-25 September 2003):1.

nating a number of celebrities of the arts and theater as parliamentary candidates. Both writers argue that the party plans to use them as puppets. The other major issue always on Georgians' minds in addition to the forthcoming election, is the Abkhazian Georgian conflict.

Headlines in the Messenger continue to reflect the on-going resentment and tribulation between *Abkhazia* and Georgia.[123] The writer discusses a recently postponed negotiation that aimed to discuss a variety of issues with representatives from *Abkhazia*, Georgia, and the United Nations Observer Mission in Georgia. The agenda included the border dispute, the return of IDPs, and economic recovery. The Foreign Minister of *Abkhazia* reportedly indicated that this was part of a continuing dialogue and the Georgian Ministry of Extraordinary Affairs agrees. The chairperson of the pro-Georgian Supreme Council of *Abkhazia* threatened the *Abkhazian* delegation by stating: "If I find out that in this delegation there are individuals who took part in the genocide of our people-we will detain all of them."[124] In a later edition of *the* Messenger, the Chairman of the State Intelligence Department argued that the government would not be arresting anyone arriving for these talks.[125] The Minister of Extraordinary Affairs explained that the priorities for Georgia remain as follows: the determination of the status of *Abkhazia* within Georgia, the return of refugees and economic rehabilitation of the area. He also explained that the comment made by Chairman of the Georgian Supreme Council of *Abkhazia* in exile was a personal expression only and the government had no intention of arresting the Foreign Minister (or any other officials) of the unrecognized Republic of *Abkhazia*. Expressions of this hostility and resentment only rekindle Georgian and *Abkhazian* blame and pain that bubbles under the surface. Specifically, the International Republican Institute released the results of proportional random survey of Georgian people conducted in May from ten regions around the country concerning attitudes about the Georgian-*Abkhazian* conflict.[126] The respondents included fifteen

---

123   Allison Ekberg, "Georgian-Abkhaz talks postponed." *The Messenger* (24 September 2003):1.
124   *Ibid.*, 1.
125   N.N., "No arrests were to be made." *The Messenger* (25 September 2003):4.
126   Zulfugar Agayev, "Georgians favor re-opening railway with Abkhazia reports nationwide poll on wide variety of issues." *Brosse Street Journal* (29 September 2003):4.

hundred Georgian voters aged 18 and over. The IRI commissioned the survey from the Baltic's Survey Limited Group (The Gallop Organization) and the Institute of Polling and Marketing. Georgian respondents answered questions about the currently closed Georgian-*Abkhazian* railway line. The results indicated that seventy percent of respondents believed that it should be reopened. Interestingly, the Chairman, *Tamaz Nadareishvili*, of the *Tbilisi* based *Abkhazian* parliament in exile said that he doubted that this information was accurate as he claims he has the signatures of 1.5 million Georgians who opposed the opening of the railway until the all of the IDPs are able to return to their homes. The railway line has remained closed since the 1992-1993 Georgian-*Abkhazian* war. Armenia has been pressuring the Georgian government to open the line too as it is Armenians only link to Russia following their 1988-1994 war with Azerbaijan and the subsequent Azeri closing of the railroads connecting Russia and Armenia (Armenia forces still occupy the *Nagorno-Karabakh* area currently populated mostly by Armenians). Furthermore, seven other regions in former Azerbaijan populated predominantly by Azeri's also remain closed off from Russia. The following table illustrates Georgian's views on a variety of other social, economic, and political issues.

Table 1: Republican Institute Poll May 2003

Issue	Percentage
Peaceful resolution to Abkhazian and Ossetian Problems	80%
Willingness to use force to resolve Abkhazian and Ossetian Problem	14%
U.S. is Georgia's most important partner	59%
Biggest Threat is Russia	66%
Dissatisfied with the way democracy is developing	80%
Definitely voting on November 2	54%
Probably voting on November 2	19%
Definitely will not vote on November 2	11%
Motivation for voting is duty as citizen	51%
Motivation for voting is to fight fraud	26%
First institution most trusted in Georgia-Church	80%
Second Institution trusted most in Georgia-Media	73%
Top concerns in society are economic standard of living and territorial integrity	78%
Poor living conditions trouble me the most	49%
Unemployment troubles me the most	44%
Loss of territories troubles me the most	16%
Economic situation has worsened in the last 12 months	54%
What is the most valuable thing in your life-children	95%

In an unusual attempt to reframe *Abkhazian* issues and give Georgians more hope, a later article reassures readers that the IDP's will be returning to their homes in the near future. Specifically, an editorial lauds the UN delegation of Georgian and *Abkhazian* law enforcement personnel who are in the Former Yugoslavia to observe the process of IDPs returning to their homes.[127] The UN is sponsoring a civil police training and development program that will provide similar law enforcement officers to the Georgian *Abkhazian* border in advance of the expected or anticipated return of Georgian IDPS. These trained police officers will manage and facilitate the return of the displaced peoples. The issue of *Abkhazia* comes up again in another article reviewing Georgian politics of the previous week. Here the *Abkhazian* Deputy Security Minister accused the United States Military Train and Equip Program of being

---

127   Temur Tatishvili, "One more attempt to settle Abkhaz Conflict." *The Georgian Times* (20 October2003):4.

responsible for the murder of two *Abkhazians* in the *Gali* region last week.[128] He claimed that the perpetrators were dressed in U.S. military uniforms and that the whole purpose of Georgia's elimination of Russian bases is to re-place them with American bases and then invade *Abkhazia* returning it to Georgia. However, the author makes it clear that the Georgian government only wants a peaceful resolution to the Georgian-*Abkhazian* conflict. Con-versely, another *Abkhazian* politician reports that she is dubious that any real progress will develop and that the Yugoslavian conflict fails to resemble what happened in Georgia and thus no comparisons should be made. Further-more, she believes that Russia's involvement in the *Abkhazian*-Georgian conflict requires that they be included in any resolution of the issue, not any UN civil police force. The debate and anxiety about *Abkhazia* continues just as the forthcoming elections create additional fears among Georgians.

One article reports that the *Burjanadze* Democrats recently accused the government of planning to falsify the forthcoming elections.[129] Similarly, a second review indicates that the Labor Party claims that the Government is planning a terrorist attack in order to postpone the November elections.[130] It seems as though the deck is being stacked to prepare Georgians for the pos-sibility of fraud or violence perpetrated by the current party in power. Of course, the accusations also may create enough fear that voters will become psychologically and physically frightened of voting. Conversely, these asper-sions may also encourage voters to select an oppositional political party. A similar article covering television news stories appears in a section called "Monday on *Mzera*"[131] In an interview, *Zhvania* stated that President *Shevardnadze* is planning to declare a state of emergency and to post police at polling places. *Zhvania* exclaims that this would violate the election code. Although he agrees that the President maintains the authority to declare an emergency, he reminds listeners that such a status must not have any impact on the voting procedure.

---

128 Tamara Ninidze, "Reflections of the last week." *Ibid.,* 6.
129 N.N., "Opposition hopeful about fair elections." *The Messenger* (24 September 2003):5.
130 N.N., "Government plans terrorist attack." *Ibid.*
131 Anna Arzanova, "Zhvania speaks regarding the planned emergency situation. Mon-day on Mzera." *Ibid.*

In the same section, the third press scanner article from *Kourieri*, discusses the candidates competing for parliamentary seats from the *Vake* district, a middle class neighborhood in *Tbilisi*.[132] The candidates include a New Rights party candidate, *Levan Gachechiladze and a* Labor Party candidate, *Edisher Kvesitadze*. Both candidates are running against the new National Party candidate, *Maia Nadiradze*. This is a district once led by National Party leader *Mikhail Saakasvhili*. *Nadiradze* reportedly indicated that since *Saakashvili* did so much for the *Vake* district in repairing roofs and elevators, she should in fact win the election. However, my experience in *Vake* district elevators would not lead me to conclude that recent renovations occurred. Riding in an elevator in *Tbilisi* for this western women, particularly in the old soviet era apartment style building constructed in the Khrushchev era is at best a claustrophobic experience as well as somewhat unnerving horror ride (especially at night) when there is no lighting. Yet my Georgian friends and acquaintances, having grown up riding in these elevators were unshakable and courageous, or so I thought. Realistically, they were simply well accustomed to things that looked broken but worked well enough for regular utilization. My building, like many others had no elevator. Every day I climbed up the stairs to my fifth floor apartment just as thousands of Georgians probably did throughout the course of their daily lives. Nevertheless, any everyday event remains fodder for political contention in pre-election Georgia.

As political machinations continue to fill the pages of the English Georgian newspapers, the discussions also focused on the political parties vying for control of the parliament.[133] As mentioned above, the political party in power is apparently listing candidates who are celebrities in the arts, sports, and entertainment or people related to politicians currently holding office. Again, this writer also claims that these famous faces will become the puppets of the real politicians because the current Presidential Administration only wants a rubber stamp for his policies. As mentioned previously, the President's party, the Citizens' Union of Georgia, once contained many of his most current popular rivals. These include *Zurab Zhvania* who some argue betrayed *Shevardnadze* after he won election as the Parliament Chair by

---

132   Mary Makharashvili, "Governmental Block presents Levan Chrdileli for Vake Majoritarian Candidate." *Ibid.*

forming his own political party. Another includes *Saakashvili,* former Attorney General. After former U.S. Secretary of State James Baker, suggested *Shevardnadze* dialogue with other parties, the President invited a number of opposition party leaders to his office. He also appointed someone viewed as an ally to opposition parties, to mediate these dialogues. The author believes the President hoped that such a peace offering to political opponents would endear his party among potential voters.

Pre-election agreements among parties continue as the *Zhvania-Burjanadze* block gave eight seats to the Traditionalist party.[134] A traditionalist member, *Aleko Shalamberidze,* reports that his party could earn their alliance fifty-thousand to eighty thousand votes in the *Vani* and *Zestaponi* regions. However, he argues that the *Kvemo Kartli* region may be the most difficult place to garner votes as the dominant ethnic group in that area is Azeri. Furthermore, he alleges that the regional leader, an appointee of *Shevardnadze's,* continues to violate the rights of the residents there. *Shalamberidze* reportedly fails to understand why these residents continue to support *Shevardnadze's* party. He believes these citizens are treated very poorly by *Shevardnadze's* administration. However, it remains difficult to tell if these are accurate allegations, or if they are socially constructed stories aimed at changing voters' opinions before the election. As political claims and counterclaims continue, the Fair Elections NGO expresses concerns about preparations for the voting process. In a press conference, the NGO Fair Elections expressed their concerns that the six million GEL necessary to fund the November elections has yet to be provided to the Central Election Commission. [135] The new election code mandates the use of special ballot paper, "invisible ink," and ultra violate detectors each of which is designed to prohibit election fraud. It is necessary to purchase these devices abroad. A spokesperson for the NGO also reported that they remain concerned about the President's recent movement towards declaring a "state of emergency." They argue that if "this is announced this will intimidate the population, leading them to feel that the elections are tied to war and civil unrest, rather than as a means for

133   Zaza Jgharkava, "Conjuring up Strategies." *Georgia Today* (19 September 2003):1.
134   *Idem.* "Zhvania-Burjanadze Block gives Traditionalists 8 quote." *Ibid.,* 3.
135   Anna Arzanova, "Elections Remain without funding." *The Messenger* (25 September 2003):1.

Georgians to realize their constitutional rights to determine their own government."[136] Finally, their last concern revolves around the fact that chairpersons of the District Election Commissions are government appointees supportive of the President. Furthermore, these chairpersons maintain offices in the same buildings as Mayors. They believe this is problematic in that this makes voters potentially subject to intimidation by local authorities and increases the likelihood of voter fraud.

While ignoring this problem, another report reveals that the CEC appears to be taking some steps to prevent voter fraud as they are planning to computerize the voters' lists. Voters' lists have not been properly updated in ten years. The CEC also plans to purchase ultra violent scanners to ensure that nobody votes twice. The organization for Security and Cooperation in Europe is assisting the CEC to purchase the twenty-eight hundred scanners needed for the election. After voting, the placement of invisible ink on each voter's finger will allegedly prevent individuals from voting a second time.[137] Unfortunately, the article remains somewhat contradictory as at one point the writers' state that once voters' lists are posted at local voter precincts, if you're not listed, you can't vote in the parliamentary election in November. However, in a later paragraph, the article indicates that voters can check the voting list up through October 19th. Subsequently, they may request later modifications if their name is missing from the list. Unfortunately, no method exists to enable absentee voters to participate in the election process. Also problematic is that according to the members of the Georgian NGO, the International Society for Fair Elections and Democracy (ISFED), little information has been provided to voters to make them understand the proper procedures for checking voters' lists or for voting on Election Day. Therefore, ISFED plans to promote information through electronic and other media sources. Unfortunately, the only other issues that continue to appear regularly in the newspapers are allegations that Georgian politicians are corrupt and that gaining more economic resources remains their primary motivation for holding public office.

---

136 *Ibid.*
137 Kote Chkhartishvili and Nino Kopaleishvili, "CEC plans new computerized voter list, hand scanners to combat election fraud." *Brosse Street Journal* (29 September 2003):1.

In a recent meeting, politicians are described as power seekers. Specifically, *Shevardnadze* criticized wine producers who have become political rivals, arguing that they seek office only to serve their own financial interests. [138] However, the journalist complains that the real problem is not political but cultural as these wine making politicians are ruining the quality of Georgian wine. *Shevardnadze* also touted his administration's achievements, reporting that he has created one million jobs. Following a speech by the Highway Fund, the President responded that the only problem with Georgian roads remains the large number of loitering cows and other livestock. This understates the poor condition of Georgia's roads and highways. Even capital city streets are filled with potholes and cracks or remain unpaved. This article appears to be offering an almost comical view of *Shevardnadze* who appears out of touch with reality. Another candidate for a PM position also seems unrealistic in the assessment of his prospects of winning public office. This candidate is described as "Georgia's most wanted man," *Igor Giorgadze*. The Minister of Security reports that his arrest is forthcoming under charges of organizing the 1995 assassination attempt on President *Shevardnadze*. [139] In a separate article, *Giorgadze* is called "the number one terrorist in Georgia". [140] *Giorgadze* was running for a Parliamentary position in the *Samtredia* District until the CEC recently annulled his registration. Subsequently, in a Russian television interview, he reported believing that Georgia was on the verge of civil war and quoted a U.S. senator who called Georgia an abortive state. Further *Giorgadze* stated that Georgia must compromise on issues with *Ossetia* and *Abkhazia* and stop creating "clashes between Russia and the U.S." Interpol also suspects *Giorgadze* for the 1995 assassination attempt against *Shevardnadze*. However, in another newspaper *Giorgadze*, although still called Georgia's number "one terrorist," received a somewhat different description. [141] The writer explains that *Igor Giorgadze* tried to enter himself as a PM candidate in the Fatherland Political Block, but the Georgian Supreme Court affirmed the earlier decision of the CEC to block his registration. This

---

138   Mary Makharashvili, "Shevardnadze slams business people-politicians." *The Messenger* (25 September 2003):1.
139   *Idem.* "Khaburdzania on Igor Giorgadze." *Ibid.,* 4.
140   Christina Tashkevich, "Where is Giorgadze? Tuesday on Kourieri." *Ibid.,* 5.

journalist indicates that *Giorgadze* may have been tried and convicted in absentia, not for planning the assassination attempt on *Shevardnadze*, but rather for three murders of high-ranking politicians. Mysteriously, it is unclear if he was convicted or just charged. Later members of his party claim the trial violated the law, and therefore his conviction is invalid. Subsequently, the reporter identifies suspicions that *Giorgadze* worked with Russian special services when he allegedly committed these crimes. Once again, clarity is missing from the report so readers are left feeling at a minimum confused if not frustrated with their search for the truth. This inability of the media to provide an accurate rendition of facts may also be a relic from their Soviet history, but as the election draws nearer, the deleterious effects of Georgia's history resonate everywhere.

Even the ramifications of Stalin's policies of forced ethnic movements live on sixty years later. For example, in 1944 Stalin forcibly deported *Meskhetian* Turks to Central Asia from their homeland in the Southern region of Georgia.[142] Then in 1989, the *Meskhetian Turks* were forcibly removed from *Uzbekistan* to locations throughout Central Asia, Russia, Ukraine, and Turkey. As a result, the COE (Council of Europe) mandates that Georgia's admission to the COE will only transpire after the repatriation of the *Meskhetian Turks*. The Georgian government agreed to this condition twelve years ago. The deadline for the accomplishment of this goal was 2001. However, Georgian policy-makers have been reluctant to meet this obligation until after Georgians' IDPS exiled from *Abkhazia* return to their homes. The writer cites an article on Eurasianet by Dan Brennan who discussed Stalin's forcible removal of the 300,000 *Meskhetian Turks*. *The Messenger* author also explains that *Meskhetians* "continue to face problems with the governments of countries where they seek refuge. For example, the Russian government also refused to grant them any official status in the *Krasnodar* region.[143] While it seems possible for Georgians to have some degree of empathy for the *Meskhetian* Turks, it appears that their fear of their larger Turkish neighbors

---

141   Rusudan Kbilashvhili, "Ambassadors to Georgia prevented from "sightseeing" in the pre-election period?" *The Georgian Times* (20 October 2003):3.

142   N.N., "COE pushes Georgian on Meskhetian Repatriation." *Tshe Messenger* (1 October 2003):1, 4.

143   *Ibid.,* 4.

negates their ability to see the Turks as similar to their own Georgian IDPs. Meanwhile, the discussion about the status of Georgian IDPs continues.

After Presidents Putin and Bush met at Camp David in the U.S., the Chairs of the parliaments in the Caucasus countries met in Moscow with President Putin.[144] This unknown writer claims that Putin and Bush decided to cooperate in order to resolve the conflict over the *Abkhazian*-Georgian issue. *Nino Burjanadze* raised the issue of Russian's military presence in Georgia reminding the Russian President that the facilities should have already been closed. Visa requirements for Georgians to travel into Russia were also discussed. While *Azerbaijan* has a stronger link to Turkey, it is apparent that Armenia maintains a closer relationship with Russia than the other Caucasus nations. The author discusses Armenia's ties with Russia and mentions that scholars' agree, almost as if the statement aims to foster continuing rivalry between the Caucasus nations or perhaps fear.[145] Another writer describes the Moscow meeting between the Chair of the Georgian Parliament, *Nino Burjanadze,* the Russian Speaker of the *Duma* (Parliament) and the Russian Foreign Minister *Valery Loshinin as* shrouded in secrecy.[146] The writer also indicates that *Burjanadze's* running mate, *Zurab Zhvania* also has "suspicious ties" with some Russian politicians. Clearly, the media is facilitating the on-going development of mistrust and suspicion among the Georgian population of the continuing existence of secret liaisons with Russia. Concurrent with this visit to Moscow, a Russian delegation visited the *Pankasi* Gorge in Northern Georgia to provide humanitarian aid and to persuade *Chechen* refugees to return to *Chechnya*. The writer argues that this show of kindness is a form of subterfuge utilized in an attempt to transform Russia's image as a perpetrator of genocide against the *Chechens*. Allegedly, Russia blamed Georgia for the influx of *Chechen* refugees into the area, which the author calls "absurd."[147] In another article, the meeting was characterized as a plot to overthrow the current government.[148] This attempt to re-create or re-energize Georgian fears of Russian power is followed by accusa-

---

144   N.N., "It's Hard to blame yourself." *Ibid.,* 2.
145   Black, *Vladimir Putin and the New World Order: Looking East, Looking West?*
146   Ninidze, "Reflections of the Last Week: Weekly Political Review."
147   *Ibid.*

tions from a Georgian politician who also argues that another Georgian civil war is forthcoming.

A member of the government block, *Irina Sarishvili*, predicts that following the election the opposition party block that includes *Saakasvhili* and the *Burjanadze*-Democrats will claim that votes have been falsified. Subsequently, she explains that this block will attempt to de-stabilize the country. Moreover, *Sariashvili* claims that *Burjanadze* has been taking orders from Russian intelligent agents and that her party's employment of a Russian media image-company is indicative of where her real loyalties lie. However, the writer dismisses her accusations, concluding that slander has become an alternative to a real political platform but that there is little awareness that such claims resemble slander. In response, the National Security Secretary, *Tedo Japardize* reports that Irina *Sarishvili* has yet to provide any real evidence of this alleged secret plot or compromising conversation, *Burjanadze* had with President Putin.[149] Later, *Sarishvili* met for fifteen minutes with *Japaridze* but failed to reveal any details of the conversation. In a very paternalistic manner, the Security Secretary warned politicians to be careful in their meetings with foreign governments as it might take years for anyone to establish the kind of delicate relationship that *Shevardnadze* developed and maintains with Russia. In a related story, an American diplomat reportedly indicated that Russia is using the American government's anti-terrorist campaign to strengthen its position in the Caucasus and to "conquer" *Chechnya*. However, the author also writes that both Russia and the U.S. appear to be telling the Georgian government to basically "get it together" and try to solve some of its own problems itself, including suggesting that compromise over the *Abkhazian* issue has become necessary.

A compromise over the Georgian-Abkhazian problem might prevent the on-going economic deterioration of both countries. Specifically, one journalist argues that the *Abkhazian* economy maintains a GDP per person of five hundred and fifty USD while the Georgian GDP per person is eight hundred US-

---

148   N.N., "Russian Agents infiltrate Georgian politics: tactics for evading a plan." *The Messenger* (10 October 2003):2.

149   N.N., "Evidence against Burjanadze and Zhvania submitted." *Ibid.*, 5.

USD.[150] Similar to the out-migration of Georgians from Georgia proper, many *Abkhazians* also have emigrated since the war of 1992-93. Only nine of the formerly active twenty-nine tea factories *in Abkhazia* are currently active and many of the citrus plantations are in poor condition. Finally, the author argues that *Abkhazia* is receiving electric energy freely from the *Enguri* Hydroelectric Station and then illegally exporting it to Russia who then ships it back to Georgia. Thus in the end, these articles seem designed to provide some confirmation to Georgians that *Abkhazia* has become quite a pitiful and criminal place, and it remains in league with their enemy to the north, Russia.

Once again, in a discussion of the forthcoming parliamentary elections over twenty-four political parties continue to compete for the majority of votes in order to meet the seven percent threshold.[151] This includes nine political blocks and fifteen separate parties each vying for two-hundred and thirty-five seats. Individual constituencies will determine eighty-five of these seats while the remainder of the positions will go to those parties receiving at least seven percent of the vote. The writer argues that these elections will determine the political future of President *Shevardnadze* even though it is doubtful that he will run again in the forthcoming presidential elections scheduled for 2005. The author writes what I've heard Georgians say that this parliamentary election marks the beginning of the end of *Shevardnadze's* thirty year political career, first in Soviet Georgia and then in free Georgia. This author argues that three groups are leading the field in the parliamentary elections. These include, "For a New Georgia bloc" consisting of the government party in power, and the Citizen's Union of Georgia aligned with the National Democratic Party. The second group consists of the Socialists and the third group is *Mikhail Saakashvili's* National Movement. *Saakashvili* was formerly a member of *Shevardnadze's* party until he accused them of corruption. *Saakashvili* is also the chair of the *Tbilisi* city council or *sakrebulo*. Interestingly, the writer reveals that *Saakashvili* maintains his own Presidential ambitions.

In the press scanner section, a variety of different newspapers covered an incident that occurred recently in *Bolnisi* involving *Saakashvili's* Nationalist

---

150   M. Alkhazashvili, "Conflict has Left Abkhazia devastated." *The Messenger* (1October 1 2003):3.

151   Revaz Sakevarishvili, "Georgian Poll Scramble begins." *Ibid.*, 4.

Party campaign.[152] While it remains difficult to discern what actually transpired, a variety of other details provided across a number of different newspapers provides a basic picture of the events. Apparently, a group of people stoned the Labor party's offices while *Saakashvili* was in the city campaigning. Subsequently, *Sheveradnadze* called out law enforcement authorities. However, *Saakashvili* reported that local police threw stones not the protesters who he described as rallying to support the Nationalist Party and protesting against the government.[153] The prosecutor of the region, *Kvemo Kartli,* promised that he would investigate the incident in question thoroughly. *Saakashvili* also called President *Shevardnadze's* version of events "misinformation." Later in the week, another newspaper article disclosed additional information about the incident.[154] On September 26th, *Saakashvili* and a number of Nationalist Party members were traveling to a city called *Talaveri,* to visit a Nationalist Party candidate for parliament and to meet with voters. However, on the way a tractor attempted to run over *Saakashvili's* car on a bridge in the village of *Bolnisi.* Subsequently, as *Saakashvili* tried to meet with the local villagers, on both sides of the bridge, each group began throwing stones at one another and "punched each other in the face".[155] Thirty people were injured and later admitted to the hospital. This became referred to as "Bloody Friday" and brought back memories of the violence that characterized Georgia in its attempts to gain freedom and independence from Soviet Russia. *Saakashvili* blamed the President and his party for the incident and President *Sheveradnadze* blamed *Saakashvili,* accusing him of "arranging terrorist action in *Bolnisi* and hooliganism, opposing police officers, and organizing mass disorders."[156] Another version of the incident described it as a demonstration orchestrated by *Saakashvili's* Nationalist party followed by *Shevardnadze's* calling out of the military.[157] A member of the Armenian Dias-

---

152   Mary Makharashvili, "Industry will save Georgia on Bolnisi clash." *Ibid.,* 5.
153   Natia Mamistavalovi, "Saakashvili questioned on Bolnisi Events." *Ibid.*
154   Nino Patsuria, "Ethnic Feud for Election's Sake?" *Georgia Today* (3 October 2003):5.
155   *Ibid.,* 2.
156   *Ibid.*
157   "News in Brief-Armed forces mobilized in Bolnisi." *The Messenger* (6 October 2003):4.

pora in Georgia reported that it was the Governor, *Zurab Japaridze* who insulted Armenians at *Bolnisi* that began the altercation.

This type of ethnic discrimination against Armenians is described as problematic in *Bolnisi* and partly the result of Georgian ethnic nationalism in the area. Therefore, after the *Bolnisi* incident the PMMG (Public Movement Multinational Georgia) office met with seven representatives of other ethnic minority groups to discuss the problem. However, the writer reports that at the end of the PMMG board meeting, members endorsed an incumbent candidate who was allegedly involved in instigating the *Bolnisi* altercation. The writer blames the ethnic minority group members for this, claming that 'they' often vote for whoever currently has power. Although clearly, such a statement also smacks of ethnocentricity, as it may have been the other ethnic groups that endorsed the incumbent, not the ethnic Armenians.

In the wake of the *Bolnisi* incident, two U.S. delegations met with local officials and oppositional political party leaders to discuss the need for fair and democratic parliamentary elections. Senator John McCain, the head of the International Republican Institute with the head of the National Democratic Institute, Strobe Talbott, attended the meeting.[158] Americans also asked a number of questions about the *Bolnisi* incident and inquired about the election code. Previously during the former American Administration, *Shevardnadze* met with former Secretary Jim Baker who outlined a number of guidelines that Georgia should follow in implementing fair and democratic elections. The Baker agreement with *Shevardnadze* mandated that each political party should have representation at all levels of the election commission including the central election commission. [159] However, one political party, *Ertoba*, claims that the Revival Party and the Industrialists have prevented *Ertoba* members from being involved. The *Ertoba* party reports that police have also detained their party members in order to prevent them from organizing meetings with locals in the *Akhmeta* region. *Ertoba* also alleged that the government manipulated locals into attacking party members.

Following the meeting, a member of the Revival Party met with Senator McCain and handed him one thousand forged ballots from the previous 1999

---

158   Mary Makharashvili and Allison Ekberg, "U.S. delegations press fair elections." *The Messenger* (7 October 2003):1.

parliamentary elections. He asked McCain to deliver the ballots to President Bush. McCain suggested that the OSCE might be the appropriate office to receive these ballots. The Americans verbalized the need for curbing corruption as well as their hope that Georgia will find a way to avoid dependence on Russia for their energy needs. Chair of the Fair Elections NGO, *Zurab Chiaberashvili* explained to the U.S. delegation that supplying electricity is one of the major problems related to the falsification of elections results. *Chiaberashvili* also reported that the central problem is "organizing independent observations in such regions as *Kvemo Kartli* and *Adjara;* two regions where fair elections are rarely observed That is why we asked our guests to deploy foreign observers in these regions."[160] In another article, the NDI proposed that Georgian officials ensure that voters' lists be posted a significant period before the election to allow voters sufficient time to check for their names. They also encouraged Georgian officials to ensure the announcement of a precinct-by-precinct tabulation of votes. The delegation was impressed with the new computerized voting lists, the changes in the election laws and the new Central Election Commission. The delegation emphasized the importance of assigning objective observers in the regions populated primarily by minority group peoples or IDPs as well as in *Adjara*. In a related vein, this particular article reported the appearance of "credible photographic evidence" indicating that local police officials behaved inappropriately during the *Bolnisi* incident.[161] This kind of police discrimination and violence against minorities may translate into election misconduct with regard to minorities. Therefore, it is necessary to assign objective observers to areas where minorities live. Georgia's ethnocentric sentiments are also revealed in the Government's refusal to accept that Turkey committed genocide against the Armenian people during the First World War.[162] For example, the Georgian Special Services suspects that the Russians encouraged the Armenians in the *Javakheti* region to make up the genocide to disrupt the election. The writer also seems unaware of the historical fact of the genocide and argues that if the Georgian

---

159   Christina Tashkevich, "Ertoba faces attacks." *Ibid.,* 4.
160   *Ibid.,* 5.
161   *Ibid.*
162   Temur Tatishvili, "Why situation gets strained in Javakheti before Elections?" *The Messenger* (6 October 2003):4.

government acknowledges the genocide, it would place Georgian-Turkish relations in jeopardy. The head of the *Abkhazeti* legitimate government in exile, *Tamaz Nadareishvili,* also claims that the Armenians have no evidence of any genocide. *Nadareishvili* explains that it is the Armenians, who with the Russians, perpetrated genocide against the Georgians in the *Abkhazian-*Georgian war. Furthermore, she claims that they have evidence of this participation at the Prosecutor General's office. Another political leader in the pro-government block argues that some political parties pander to "this *Armenian Javakheti* movement". He also believes that doing so jeopardizes the peace in the *Caucasus.* The strength of ethnic nationalism within Georgia seems to grow stronger as perceptions persist that ethnic enemies surround them.

These perceptions of ethnic differences seem to become inseparable from the *Bolnisi* incident as it continues to be revisited. A subsequent discussion of the *Bolnisi* incident occurs in reference to another ethnic minority group in Georgia, the *Azeris.*[163] The author states that sixty percent of the voters in the cities of *Bolnisi, Gardabani,* and *Marneuli* within the *Kvemo Kartli* region are *Azeris.* In *Marneuli,* unemployment is high and residents rarely receive gas or electricity. Journalists interviewed locals who reported feeling so politically hopeless that they would not vote, while others disclosed that they planned to vote for the government block. A representative of the NGO called the Democratic Development Union of Georgian *Azeris* explained that the only pathway to the Parliament for the *Azeris* is to become involved in the government block. Otherwise, ethnic discrimination will prevent their political involvement. This individual explained that there while there were twenty-five seats allocated for the *Kvemo Kartli* region, only six *Azeris* currently hold parliamentary positions. Conversely, an *Azeri* MP stated that other parties are simply not receptive to resolving their problems. Azeri concerns surround the possibility that the election of any Nationalist candidates may make ethnic discrimination more prevalent. However, a candidate from the Nationalist party accuses officials from *Azerbaijan* of encouraging *Azeris* to vote for the

---

163   Anna Arzanova, "Monday on Mzera Clash between Mamaladze and Saakashvili." *The Messenger* (1 October 2003):5.

government party and simultaneously alleges that the Georgian government threatened local *Azeris* in order to garner their votes.

In a review of a talk show interview with *Mikhail Saakashvili*, a reporter asked *Saakashvili* why his campaign was "so aggressive". It remains unclear if the question aimed at supporting other parties' allegations of Nationalist verbal attacks on competing parties or if it was more concretely focused on *Saakashvili's* western style of campaigning, i.e., meeting people face to face. *Saakashvili* responded by explaining that he prefers to meet with people face to face. Eleven minutes into the interview, *Levan Mamaladze*, current MP incumbent in the *Bolnisi* district where the violence recently occurred, arrived on the set. Apparently, he was uninvited and came to the studio claiming that he and *Saakashvili* agreed to meet on the *Mzera* show. However, *Saakashvili* walked out of the studio, and according to the author called *Mamaladze* a scoundrel who needed to be in prison.[164] Apparently, another member of the National Party, also a candidate for MP in the *Bolnisi* district, telephoned the television station after the incident and accused *Mamaladze* of lying and being corrupt. Again, all these dynamics revolve around ethnic nationalism; readers should recall that most of the people living in *Mamaladze's* district are either Armenians or Azeris. *Mamaladze* appears to be trying to ensure his re-election from minority group constituents by claiming responsibility for facilitating Georgian language training for them during his last term in office. The television crew continued the interview later in *Saakashvili's* office when he retorted, "I want to explain our fundamental position, state officials and politicians do not deal with bandits, criminals and thieves in other countries in the world." He also exclaimed, "I am offended that our population must look at these bandits every day on TV."[165] Obviously, he is insinuating that his political competitor, *Mamaladze*, is a criminal. Hurling accusations of corruption and involvement in crime remains a common political ploy to debunk the competition.

Political corruption in Georgia partially explains the poor economic condition of the nation. For example, the Finance Minister's proposed 2004 budget will be unable to meet all the needs of the Georgian people. There is

---

164   *Ibid.*
165   *Ibid.*

simply not enough money entering the Georgian coffers to pay politicians or to take care of the general population, particularly pensioners.[166] Sadly, the pensioners are the people I saw on the streets of *Tbilisi* on a daily basis begging for money. These were senior citizens with no social or economic capital. While middle class Georgians could resolve this problem by living in extended family homes, senior citizens on the street were clearly less fortunate. Many people, foreigners, other women, and men, presumably middle class Georgians, frequently dropped change in the hands of these old Georgians.

Even these articles fail to capture the sense of hopelessness ordinary Georgians feel about their economic situation. However, the writer reveals that *Shevardnadze* has continuously rejected budget proposals on a variety of separate occasions. Unfortunately, the writer provides no explanation for the President's vetoes. Although readers may surmise that it is related to Georgia's on-going problems in repaying debts owed to the IMF and Paris club. Georgian officials' are hopeful that the IMF and Paris club will agree to re-schedule debt payments. A scheduled April meeting will discuss the possibility of a new payment plan.[167] Apparently, the 2004 draft budget necessitates 1.49 million GEL, two-hundred thousand more GEL than the 2003 budget. However, planned revenue is only 1.325 million GEL. Clearly, this is problematic especially in light of the Deputy Finance Minister's claim that seventy-five million GEL is to be allocated to pensioners and state employees' salary arrears. The debt owed to pensioners remains over eighty-five billion GEL. President *Sheveradnadze*, a senior citizen himself, reported, "The ministers are settling this problem step by step."[168] Moreover, the President claims that pension arrears only go back four months. Even more fascinating is that while the budget priority is poverty reduction, there are no allocations for forestry, roads, or the environment. Sixteen percent of the budget remains aimed at the social sphere, seventeen percent for healthcare, and twenty percent for education and forty-three million to the energy sector. This is not possible given the budgetary constraints without Western aid. One budgetary office official reports that he believes *Shevardnadze* will probably reject the

166   Zaza Jgharkava, "Soap Budget Again?" *Georgia Today* (3 October 2003):1.
167   M. Alkhazashvili, "2004 Budget meets empty Parliament." *The Messenger* (1 October 2003):2.
168   *Ibid.*, 1.

parliament's next budget proposal just as he has done previously in an attempt to silence voices of impeachment. According to another article, *Shevardnadze* reportedly already approved the parliament's budget proposal and returned it to the parliament for final review. However, this writer reports that only the new parliament elected in November will have the opportunity to approve it.[169] Nonetheless, a variety of Ministers continue to disagree about separate portions of the budget. The 2003 budget expenditures resulted in a deficit of one hundred and fifty million GEL, according to the author, due to poor administration. These economic problems are described further in an editorial in which the writer attacks the Finance Minister, for failing to provide allocated budgetary funds to the Ministry of Agriculture.[170] The journalist quotes the Finance Minister who reported that the goals of the state budget were unmet leaving funds unavailable. The writer also claims that the Minister has managed to keep funding coming in anyway and retorts that this is the only department in the nation that continues to function well. The price of wheat and of course the related possibility that bread, a Georgian food staple, will increase appears to be the primary concern here.

Bread is relatively inexpensive to purchase and thus occupies a central part of the daily diet of capital city dwellers. While I found the bread delicious and delightful wherever I purchased it, one writer argued that Georgian bakeries are producing bread of dubious quality.[171] Readers should note that bread shops are located on every street corner across the Capital city and this is where the writer argues that the most common legal violations occur, within the medium to small private bread making enterprises. Those were very much like the places where I purchased my bread. Two bread shops located near my apartment where I usually bought my bread made my palate happy. These diligent bread makers began working at dawn (I smelled the bread baking) and continued until dusk, standing on their feet, serving customers all day long. Each morning on my way to work, I said *"Gamarjoba"* (hello) to them and they responded warmly, *"Gamarjoba"*. While I rarely ob-

---

169   *Ibid.*, 4.
170   Maia Misheladze, "Weekly Economic Review." *The Georgian Times* (20 October 2003):16.
171   Mammad Baghirov, "Poor Regulation leaves bread quality in Georgia uncertain." *Brosse Street Journal* (29 September 2003):1.

served street vendors selling bread, many were available in the open market selling without licenses and thus not paying their taxes. The head of department on bread quality control in Georgia's Department of Standardization, Licensing and Rationing, *Omar Kvirkidze*, explains that inspectors find that most violations are short weight, raw bread, and high humidity of bread, particularly bread sold in the open market. The State Doctor General, *Nikoloz Shavdia,* indicated that people selling bread on the streets may not be healthy themselves and that it is illegal to sell bread on the streets, even though authorities do little to stop it. State inspectors can only inspect private enterprises with a court order. One parliamentarian, the Chair of the Committee on Health Care and Social Issues, *Zezva Ghugunishvili*, states that more strict controls over bread production should exist. Interestingly, while the article exclusively focuses on bread, there appears to be little or no regulation or monitoring of restaurants or any other eating establishments across the country. Nonetheless, my observations, and my stomach lead me to conclude that all the food, and I ate a lot of it over ten months, was superb. It certainly ranks higher than food from my home country of the United States. I can honestly say Georgian food rates as the best food I have ever eaten and I have traveled to many places in the Far East and in Western Europe. On the other hand, the PM argues that he is becoming concerned about the use chemical additives in bread. Understandably, he worries that modern preservatives might damage Georgia's heavenly tasting staple. I too hope Georgia can avoid the west's predilection for the factory production of bread. The Director of a *Tbilisi* Bread Making Plant number four, (the number is a likely left over from the Soviet era) *Malhaz Dolidze* reports that they don't use chemical additives in their production. However, *Dolidze* explained that many bakeries are located and operate in places poorly designed for producing foods, in basements for example where sanitary conditions are poor. This is a valid concern, the bakery underneath my apartment was located in a basement, a dark dirty looking room with a stone oven built into the ground. However, the bread was delicious. While the Chief Medical Officer of Sanitary Inspection reports that he attempts to control the sale of food on the street by using the 'ecology police', his office primarily monitors perishable goods such as milk, meat, and butter.

Concerns about bread primarily revolve around the fact that it is a food staple and that if quality becomes "protected" by western standards, many Georgians may be unable to afford it. Another concern is the availability of enough wheat to continue to produce the bread. Either problem could result in a disaster, particularly for poor Georgians. However, the minister managed to get fifty-thousand tons of American wheat imported into the country recently, which will help decrease the price of bread. The Agriculture Minister is working with parliament to drop the twelve percent tax on imports to ensure that the next American import of wheat enters Georgia relatively cheaply to continue to prevent bread prices from rising significantly in the spring. Ongoing fears about survival in conditions of poverty and indebtedness are surpassed only by Georgians' perceptions that the Russians may come to dominate them. Georgians resent the assignment of the Russians, rather than a United Nations task force as peacekeepers to manage the Georgian-Abkhazian cease-fire. This perceived slight becomes re-visited in stories like the following. Recently a Russian soldier was kidnapped from the Zugdidi area in the Samgrelo region bordering Abkhazia. A Georgian special services employee argued that the soldier became a bargaining chip exploited by competing oppositional political parties to create opposition to the government. Their secondary aim included destabilizing the region.[172]. Therefore, the soldier's victimization was exploited to garner the release of a previously kidnapped Georgian civilian. The Georgian was being held for a ransom of eighty-thousand GEL. The Mayor of the Abkhaz region of Gali where the kidnapping occurred reported that such crimes occur regularly. Further, the Mayor believes that these acts would not occur without support from the Russian peacekeepers. He also argued that it would have been easily resolved if the Russian peacekeepers simply asked the Abkhazians to free the Georgian in exchange for the Russia soldier. Instead, the writer reports that the Russian peacekeepers entered Sukhumi, stopped traffic with their armored vehicles, inspected vehicles, and entered Georgian family homes searching for the soldier. Moreover, the author claims that while Russian and Georgian journalists covered the story, Russian soldiers assaulted them. The

---

172   Gia Bakradze, "Kidnapped Russian Peacekeeper is Free." Georgia Today (3 October 2003):2.

Georgian speaker of the house discussed these events with Putin's special envoy to the *Abkhaz* conflict, *Valery Loschinin* in Moscow. *Loschinin* called the behavior of the Russian soldiers' "unjustifiable".[173] Similarly, a UN representative told the newspaper that under the international mandate the peace-keeping forces do not have authorization to search Georgian homes, only the Georgian Ministries can conduct such a search. The Georgian foreign ministry office also protested while the deputy foreign minister indicated that he had been in contact with the Russian peacekeepers throughout the incident. The commander of the Russian forces responded to complaints, claiming that his actions were within the limits of the mandate and said that as soon as the soldier returns, they will resume their normal activities. The kidnappers are called unidentified criminals. Later they released the soldier following a meeting with the kidnappers during which he demanded or pleaded for his son's release.[174] One writer editorializes claiming that similar Russian behavior has occurred previously and if it continues, Georgia will punish them. However, it is unclear how such a small powerless country could punish their larger richer and more powerful neighbor to the north.

Georgian suspicions and fears about Russia's role in Georgian politics and their role as peacekeepers in *Abkhazia* seems to remain an ever present festering abscess. For example, in one article an entire page is devoted to a vehement criticism of Russia's role as peacekeepers in Georgia.[175] This editorial discusses the Georgian veterans of the war currently staging a hunger strike to voice their opposition to the on-going stalemate with regard to *Abkhazia* and the presence of the Russian peacekeepers. Like many other Georgians, their most important objective remains the full re-integration of their country. In an attempt to criticize the *Burjanadze-Democrats,* a writer claims that one of their leaders referred to the peacekeepers as just border guards. Similarly, the writer also criticized the Georgian government by revealing a previous parliamentary resolution calling for the withdrawal of the

---

173   *Ibid.,* 3.
174   Temur Tatishvili, "Russian Soldiers Occupy Georgian Territory." *Georgian Times* (6 October 2003):1.
175   Ninidze, "Reflections of the Last Week: Weekly Political Review;" Khatuna Kviralashvili, "Who Needs Russian Peacekeepers' presence in Georgia? Withdrawal of Russian Troops from Abkhazia conflict comes to the top of the agenda again." *Ibid.,* 8.

Russian peacekeepers. The writer calls this a symbolic gesture because subsequently, President *Shevardnadze* extended the mandate for the Russian forces to remain in the area for an indefinite period. A *Burjanadze* Democrat party leader called this a "treacherous step."[176] The leader of the Movement for the New Georgia alliance also argued that when the executive branch failed to act upon the parliamentary resolution, they violated the constitution. However, the *Burjanadze* Democrat party official claims the parliament violated the constitution when they adopted the resolution. It remains unclear how either executive or legislative branches behavior might have actually violated the constitution in this instance. It is more likely that both officials are speaking metaphorically about the value of the constitution in a democratic nation-state, or they are simply casting blame to garner more votes and to avoid disclosing substantive party platform positions.

Developing, much less publicizing a political party platform remains absent from Georgian politics.[177] Although the government developed and began implementing a poverty reduction program, they provide no details and no other platform issues. Moreover, it is difficult to see how the poverty program may be perceived since Georgia's debt repayment problems have simultaneously resulted in cuts in foreign assistance. The Revival Party has proposed something called Free Economic Zones, presumably similar to free trade zones. These proposed zones might be a knee jerk response to *Abashidze's claims that* only the government should import oil, alcohol, cigarettes, and wheat. Virtually no other platform issues are mentioned with the exception of the Labor party's support for lowering taxes for small businesses in order to fuel economic growth. In addition, the New Rights Party proposes fining the government for each day they delay in delivering pensions. While creative, the implementation and effectiveness of such a system might be difficult. Thus while platform ideas are offered, they usually lack substantive development. Winning stands to be the most important goal of election competitors, not creating new policies or improving the lives of Georgian citizens. In such a context, when winning positions of power becomes the most important objective, election fraud becomes the means to the end.

---

176   *Ibid.*

Aslan Abashidze continues to promise the Council of Europe that *Adjara's* elections will be held freely and fairly, even though during previous elections, *Adjara's* voters' lists were delivered to the Central Election Commission late. He also told the Council of Europe that historically election observers in *Adjara* report that elections were fair and free. *Abashidze* also claims that Georgian accusations about his administration are forms of harassment. The writer refers to *Abashidze's* claims as false and argues that *Abashidze's* party continues to commit acts of aggression against rival parties. Finally, this journalist writes that *Abashidze* manipulates votes and terrorizes voters to ensure his party remains in power. Similarly, another article reveals that the previous census in *Adjara* omitted about ten percent of the population.[178] The author suggests that with two-hundred and eighty-thousand voters in *Adjara* this translates into premeditated voter fraud.

The parliamentary election continues as the most frequently discussed subject in the newspapers with two front-page articles discussing the funding problems associated with the elections. In a television interview with the U.S. Ambassador, Richard Miles on *Rustavi*-2, a writer reports that the United States is unhappy with Georgia's lack of progress in tackling the corruption issue. Moreover, the U.S. is reportedly displeased with Georgia's election preparations. Miles threatens that the U.S. may cut financial assistance if improvements do not follow.[179] However, humanitarian funding will not be affected. This includes support for winter heating, elections, and state security programming. The ambassador reported that the U.S. government and the international community have spent several million dollars on election preparation including support for six hundred to six hundred and fifty international election observers. Yet he concluded his remarks by saying that the U.S. stands motivated to facilitate Georgia's movement from socialism to a free market and a democracy. In addition to American observers a later article indicates that three thousand international observers will also be present monitoring the election process, including observers from Norway, the United

---

177   M. Alkhazashvili, "Parties drag on Economic Platforms." *The Messenger* (10 October 2003):3.
178   Anna Arzanova, "Adjara claims 280,000 voters." *Ibid.,* 5.
179   Natia Mamistvalovi, "U.S. Ambassador ties fair elections to U.S. funding."*The Messenger* (6 October 2003):1.

Kingdom, and Germany. These observers will also conduct a parallel count after voters leave the polling stations. In addition, they will monitor for any overt violations, including voter intimidation. One Georgian citizen reports that she became a volunteer after voting in 1999 and noticing that the army was bringing in voters by force. Election observers receive one day of training from the Society for Fair Elections and Democracy and must pass two examinations before becoming observers. Some observers will work in the central office and will receive phone calls or emails from observers in the field. Currently, observers are also assisting voters ensuring that their names are on the voters' lists within their districts.[180] The Organization for Security and Cooperation in Europe (OSCE) will also deploy twenty-one long-term and four hundred short-term observes from a variety of OSCE countries. The head of the OSCE mission stated: "We believe in principle that an election observation promotes transparency, it helps to build public confidence, and in the past in many, many countries it has had a positive and beneficial effect."[181] OSCE has maintained observers in Georgia since June and previously conducted two assessments. One assessment evaluated Georgia's preparations and conditions of the forthcoming election, and the second continues to monitor the Central Election Commission. The local director of the Caucasus Resource Center explained that without domestic and international observers, the election process would likely be unfair, just as it was in the previous elections held in *Adjara*. One senior citizen, a resident of a remote area, reported that he has seen violations in the past and he trusts the international observers not the domestic observers. Another *Tbilisi* resident added that she does not think observers are necessary but believes that the Georgian people should be more responsible for election and voting processes. Finally, the newspaper provides a list of what observers are looking for in terms of violations. These include those listed below in Table Two.

---

180   Ulviyya Hedarova, "Vote will be closely watched by 3,000 observers." *The Brosse Street Journal* (29 October 2003):4.

Table 2: Election Observers Mandates

Election Observers Mandates
1. Inaccurate voter lists
2. Voting on somebody else's behalf
3. Carousel or voting with the same ID card several times
4. Fan-voters are paid for signed blank ballots that are filled by others and returned the polling stations
5. Campaigning by the precinct commission and party members in favor of the candidates
6. Intimidation of the voters
7. Issuing extra ballots and envelopes to enable one voter to vote several times for a candidate
8. Giving the ballots to voters without proper identification
9. Election commissioner who deliberately damage the ballots.
10. Failing to sign and stamp the ballots thus making ballots uncountable.
11. Changing the election results.
12. The ill preparation of the precincts prior to elections.
13. Falsification with the mobile boxes by exaggerating the sick voter lists.
14. Erroneous distribution of the job functions among the commission members, without casting the lots.
15. Late submission of the election documents to the election precincts.
16. Failure to distribute voter identifications.
17. Presence of unauthorized individuals at the polling stations.
18. Pressure on the observers.

Although the CEC receives multiple sources of financial support, it may not be enough to facilitate the proper conduct of the forthcoming elections.[182] President *Shevardnadze* issued a decree ordering the finance ministry to allocate funds to the Central Election Commission, but the CEC reports that only two hundred thousand GEL out of a required six and one half million GEL has been distributed. Conversely, the finance Ministry claims that the CEC must first present a list of expenditures before they can provide all the funds, while the CEC claims that it has already submitted that list. The Chair of the CEC, *Nina Devdariani* reports that she will file a lawsuit against the Fi-

---

181   *Ibid.*
182   Mary Makharashvili, "Election Financing remains critical." *The Messenger* (6 October 2003):1.

nance Ministry if the money is not transferred. Finally, the ISFED is concerned that if this money remains unavailable the elections will not be free and fair.

In order to garner more votes, a variety of political parties are trying to attract popular candidates by inviting celebrities as well as the wealthy to join their party.[183] In accomplishing this goal, more funding will be available for both *Mikhail Saakashvili* and *Nino Burjanadze* who allegedly have their sights on becoming the next President when the Presidential elections occur in 2006. The writer also indicates that some places on party lists are for sale and these funds will finance party activities. While previously newspaper articles offered little or no information about political party platforms, it appears that when they are publicized, journalists' focus on only one or two parties.

The National Party's economic plan includes an economic safety net for the unemployed as well a social welfare program designed to provide housing for the homeless.[184] Although a spokesperson for the National Party claims that the modern world of technology and knowledge diffusion can make this happen, it is unclear how these factors will transform Georgian society. Following this ambiguous disclosure, a spokesperson for the National Party spoke with disgust about President *Shevardnadze* but the article provides no specific criticisms of the President.

Additional National Party objectives include the following; the stabilization of the energy supply, improving budgetary spending procedures, fighting excessive bureaucratic interference in business, simplifying the tax code, reforming law enforcement, making the police and the prosecutors office independent from the Chancellery and the President, de-politicizing decisions of prosecutors, creating a new anti-monopoly body independent of the government, reforming Customs to end corruption, improving the quality of transportation and communications and improving education and technology.[185] A Georgian ex-patriot speaking for the Nationalist Party also stated that every company should offer one percent of their profits to improve scholarships in higher education for the poor. Another party representative also reported that

---

183   *Ibid.*, 2.
184   M. Alkhazashvili, "National Movement envisions full employment and high technology." *Ibid.*, 3.
185   Christina Tashkevich, "National Movement puts Economic Plan on Sale." *Ibid.*, 3.

the Nationalists do not have any plans to nationalize industries in Georgia but they do call for "returning stolen property-for example in the energy sector."[186] It remains unclear if this means decreasing corruption or repairing ineffective and outdated electric plants, or the necessity of diverting Georgia's oil and gas resources. However, in another article the objective seems better described as an attempt to reduce production from the hydroelectric station in *Enguri* as well as from the *Tblisiresi* station. However, it remains unclear how reduced production will solve electricity problems if construction of new plants fails to occur or older plants remain in poor condition. They also plan to improve the financial situation of *Tbilsisgazi,* who continues to buy its gas from Russia. However, once again, no specific plan is described. Finally, the Nationalists also claim to want to decrease Georgia's dependence on Russia and Armenia for electricity.[187] As mentioned previously, since the disintegration of the Soviet Union, Georgians living in *Tbilisi* continue to have problems with heat and electricity during the winter months. However, journalists rarely write about the living conditions of the rural Georgians or peasant Georgians and their consistent absence of electricity, natural gas, and heat. Rather what seems to matter more, relative to newspaper reports, are the living conditions of the urban residents in the capital city. After all newspapers are nonexistent in the rural parts of Georgia as nobody can afford to purchase them. Most news in these parts of the country comes from word of mouth or the occasional state television broadcasts.[188]

Effective and functional provision of utilities to Georgian citizens is absent either due to the poverty of households or the corruption of officials at *Tbilisigazi.* Delivery of my natural gas bills and electric bills came to my home on separate slips of paper that were squeezed between the two sides of my double front door, a somewhat inefficient method, but creative considering the fact that myself and my neighbors in the Vake district were without mailboxes. Upon my initial arrival in Georgia in August of 2003, the natural gas lines were not functioning. Initially, I thought this was the result of poor func-

---

186   *Ibid.*
187   Natia Mamistvalovi, "Georgia's Winter Looks Dismal." *Ibid.,* 1, 4.
188   Flora Esbua, "Influence of Television News on Voters Decisions in Tbilisi and Rural Areas." Unpublished Graduate Student Manuscript. Tbilisi State University Faculty of Sociology, Civic Education Project, 2004.

tioning or disrepair. Later I found out that the lines had been shut-off because *Tbiligaz (Tbilisi* Gas) was unable to make payments to its Russian mother company, *Gazprom.* Those of us who had gas stoves and ovens needed to purchase a mobile gas-cooking device. It reminded me of an outdoor camping stove. This one burner sufficed to accomplish all the household cooking. As a guest at a Georgian friend's home, the woman of the house cooked a full meal for over eight people with just one such gas burner. I only saw the chef at the end of the evening. Later in my stay in Georgia, a new management company purchased *Tbiligaz.* They promised the safe and consistent delivery of natural gas. They also promised to repair the nineteen hundred and sixty kilometer *Tbilisi* gas line network bringing it into compliance with international standards. The company reported that sixty-five to seventy percent of the imported gas is lost due to leaks or technical flaws. The real losses may due to theft of the natural gas or corruption throughout the organization. Readers should note that the prosecutor threatened the former director of *Tbiligaz* with imprisonment under corruption charges. The new management reports that they will cease the door to door-to-door collection process but instead will require citizens to pay for gas in advance with a certificate system guaranteeing residents a certain amount of gas at specific intervals. Recently, *Gazprom* signed a twenty-five year agreement with the Georgian government to provide natural gas to Georgia. A reporter discussed on-going issues with the Russian company describing a recent meeting between the Partnership for Social Initiatives, the Director of the Caspian Energy Research Project, and a representative of NATO for Georgia.[189] The primary concerns voiced in the meeting revolved around energy security. The writer described *Gazprom* as a Russian monopoly threat to the local energy market. The other representatives present at the meeting did not oppose agreements with *Gazprom* but they argued that the agreements must conform to Georgia's interests and must not interfere with any future agreements made between Eastern and Western Energy companies. The article fails to suggest a solution to this problem but only describes the author's opposition to the twenty-five year agreement. It is difficult for a small country to have

---

189   Anna Arzanova, "A call to revisit Gazprom Deal." *The Messenger* (24 September 2003):1.

many choices with regard to energy especially when surrounded by larger and more powerful countries that control or manage those energy resources.

Geographically, Georgia lies very close to the Caspian Sea where U.S. and other western nations and their respective transnational oil and gas companies have powerful interests in exploiting the vast oil reserves located there. Georgia maintains a national interest in the region following the decision to complete an oil pipeline from the Caspian Sea through Georgia into Turkey. This is the *Baku-Tbilisi-Ceyhan* oil pipeline scheduled to become operational in a few years and expected to boost to Georgia's GDP. Currently another one of Georgia's problems with energy revolves around the availability of automobile gas. This may be partially resolved following the completion of the new *Baku-Tbilisi-Ceyhan* pipeline, scheduled to open in 2005. Unfortunately, only about five percent of the oil delivered through the pipeline will be belong to Georgia. Also problematic is that the oil pipeline route travels through the *Borjomi* Gorge where many of Georgia's vast water resources lie.[190] Therefore, pipeline leaks could endanger the water supply. Moreover, the pipeline will also pass near the village of *Dgvari* already devastated by poverty and mudslides. During the Soviet era, the government made unfulfilled commitments to homeowners that they would be re-located beginning back in the 1970's. As the result of these extant unresolved problems Georgia's current environmental Minister, *Nino Chkhobadze*, refused to grant a permit to British Petroleum to lay the pipeline in this region until pressured by President *Shevardnadze*. *Chkhobadze's* concerns were that leaks, damage to, or theft from the oil pipeline might contaminate the *Borjomi's* rivers, damage the nearby national forest, and create more mudslides in the area near *Dgvari*. A proposed resolution to the problem of oil theft by the Parliament aimed to deter theft and illegal transport of oil by placing it in the same category as drug transportation and money laundering.[191] [192] *Shevardnadze* also said he would publish a description of the bill for the public after parliament passed the law. However, this leaves the problems with regard to the *Dgvari*

---

190   Natalia Antalava, "Between Prosperity and Despair." *The Messenger* (10 October 2003):1.

191   N.N., "Import of Pipes for Baku-Tbilisi-Erzrum Starts in December." *Georgia Today* (3 October 2003):2.

192   N.N., "Toughening Punishment for Drug Crimes." *Ibid.*

mudslides and potential oil leaks unresolved.[193] *Dgvari* residents as well as several NGOs also expressed concerns about how the pipeline will affect the already weak geology in the area. The villagers report that they will not allow the construction to begin until they are re-settled even if it means lying on the ground in front of the machines. The pipeline is nine hundred meters away from *Dgvari*. It will carry one million barrels of oil from *Azeri* fields through Georgia to Turkey and subsequently to Western markets. Additionally a spokesperson for the NGO Bankwatch, that monitors international financial institutions reports that the pipeline plan is unconstitutional as it runs through the buffer zone for the national park. This spokesperson, *Manana Kochladze*, reports that criminal gangs often tap oil pipelines as do Georgians who are looking for a cheap source of energy and such activities could lead to serious leaks. However, BP argues that it will take protective measures through the *Borjomi* stretch of the pipeline to double the number of control devices and will install sensors to protect against illegal tapping. The writer criticizes *Shevardnadze's* lackadaisical attitude about these environmental problems while revealing that *Shevardnadze's* family has financial interests in a Georgian oil company that will benefit from the venture. The writer argues that this led to his request to exempt the company from paying its taxes in the *Ninosminda* oil depository.[194] This exemplifies corruption at the highest levels of government. However, this is not the only nation with a President whose interest in oil and making money supersedes his interest in public safety. Georgian newspapers reveal other types of corruption that controverts the public's best interest.

A few days later, an article reveals that the Anti-corruption office met with President *Shevardnadze* revealing the misappropriation of four million GEL in 2001-2002 by the Department of Tax and Customs.[195] Allegations were that seventeen low-level employees were involved in this crime. However, the writer insinuates that this is a symbolic pre-election bid to garner votes for the government block as evidenced by the implication of low-level employees. Only one high-level employee was accused and this was the

---

193   *Ibid.*, 6.
194   M. Alkhazashvili, "Shevardnadze lobbies Georgian Oil." *The Messenger* (10 October 2003):3.
195   *Idem.* "Elections put pressure on Corruption." *The Messenger* (9 October 2003):3.

Chair of the *Telavi* District Taxation Office. The author reflects that while the President often proselytizes that he favors punishment for corrupt officials, this is often just empty rhetoric.

Similarly, research by transparency international quotes President *Shevardnadze* who explains that

> so many people are involved in corruption, that there are not enough cells to hold them all. If we fail to eradicate the impunity syndrome, which has taken root throughout the country, in nearly every household in the conscience of nearly every citizen of Georgia, we will find it extremely difficult to advance and we will fail to meet many objectives.[196]

The global corruption report also indicates that although a Presidential decree in 2001 required the development of an anti-corruption council, "measures taken so far appear to have lacked substance." The establishment of a new tax fraud unit will allegedly curb the corruption problem but as the above information indicates this office appears to function poorly. Also problematic is that Parliamentarians remain exempt from any type of criminal prosecution. The elimination of systemic corruption requires a free press, and unfortunately, *Shevardnadze's* administration has attempted to repress the free press previously even though the constitutional court ruled such behavior unconstitutional. Specifically, the court recently heard such a case filed by the Georgian Young Lawyers' Association (GYLA). [197] The young Lawyer's Association filed a claim against the new law requiring journalists to publish "facts" and to get all stories approved in advance by the government. Further, this new law denies the press the right to make comments or predictions. Similar laws limiting press freedom also exist in *Adjara* and the GYLA filed claims against those as well. The court will announce its decision in late October. Media discussions about corruption and politics remain the primary focus of Georgian newspapers with scant attention devoted to what has become a main staple of news in the American press, violent crime.

---

196   Ledeneva. *Global Corruption Report 2003* , 169-170.
197   Mary Makharashvili, "Young Lawyers defend Constitution." *The Messenger* (9 October 2003):4.

Usually, the only type of violent crime discussed in Georgian newspapers consists of violence between political parties. For example, in October one reported revealed an attack on the Revival Party's headquarters in the city of *Chkhorotsku.*[198] Someone threw a hand grenade into the office and although no injuries followed, a Revival Party member said that this was a part of some "parties' pre-election campaign" activities.[199] Perhaps due to this incident or using this incident to control and limit the campaigning of government oppositional parties, the President decided to enforce a law requiring that all political parties to register in advance of any scheduled election campaigning. As described here, this law fails to reflect democracy in action. However, a later article reviewing *Shevardnadze's* Monday morning radio interview described the law differently.[200] *Shevardnadze* reports that the law regulates the conditions for organizing public gatherings both in the capital and in the regions. He explained, "This law was adopted by Parliament five years ago in compliance with constitutional requirements. The local government has a right to receive notification from the parties two days in advance and more so if they plan on blocking roads and halting traffic."[201] Moreover, he mentions that local officials may not have the personnel to handle such gatherings, thus this law will allow the federal military to assist in traffic control. Reportedly, this was also his justification for using the federal military to stop the violence in the previously described *Bolnisi* incident. The specific constitutional change referred to is clarified in a later article. The law was adopted in 1997 and is called, "Manifestations and Gatherings".[202] The law's objective was to prevent activities that would "destabilize" the country during pre-election periods. The adoption of the law occurred following President *Zviad Gamsakhurdia's* exit from office to control the activities of his party and supporters after the end of the civil war. Another author argues that this law violates Article twenty-five of the Georgian constitution adopted under *Shevardnadze* stating: "Everyone except those who are members of military forces, police, or security services has the right to hold street protests and

---

198   N.N., "News in Brief, Attack on Revival Party." *The Messenger* (6 October 2003):4.
199   *Ibid.*
200   N.N., "Shevardnadze's Monday Morning Interview." *The Messenger* (7 October 2003):1, 5.
201   *Ibid.,* 1.

demonstrations either at home or outdoors". The second part of the constitutional article indicates that the requirement to inform authorities is necessary only if the meeting or protest impedes the flow of automobile or pedestrian traffic. The 1997 law requires that political parties give local authorities a five-day advance notice about campaign activities and receive authorization to conduct street protests. In 2002, the Georgian Young Lawyers Association won a court battle in which sections of the 1997 were struck down as unconstitutional, although it is unclear what specific portions this references. The recently adopted Election Code also states that meetings of parties with the population during the pre-election period remain regulated by the CEC. However, no requirement exists for parties to notify the CEC of such meetings. The next week, *Shevardnadze* placed soldiers on alert in their barracks in anticipation of pre-election violence.[203] The Interior Minister allegedly received reports that oppositional "forces" were "keen to stir up destabilization nationwide". It seems that the government is attempting to pre-empt possible protests following the election, or that in the Georgian collective unconscious protests and demonstrations remain viewed synonymous with destabilization and violence, rather than symbolic of democracy and free speech.

Later in part of his Monday morning radio interview, *Shevardnadze* explains that he wants international observers to ensure that the elections are held fairly and democratically in order that the will of the Georgian people is followed. In an attempt to promote this party's agenda, the President praised the value of Georgia's teachers and suggested that they needed a salary increase. He also asked *Abkhazia* to refrain from celebrating their independence but rather to remember the bloodshed from the war and try to work with Georgia on a dialogue. The *Abkhazians* failed to comply as later in the week another journalist reported that the *Abkhazians* celebrated their tenth anniversary of independence from Georgia with parades in the street. The author claimed that that no Russian officials attended the celebration, but later reported that two Russian officials who supported *Abkhazian* separatists during the war were present.[204]

---

202   N.N., "President Revives unconstitutional law." *The Messenger* (9 October 2003):2.
203   Ninidze, "Reflections of the last week."
204   Arzanova, "Adjara claims 280,000 voters."

As the election drew closer, the CEC requested that Georgians help verify the accuracy of the voters' lists by checking to ensure their names were on the lists and asking them to notify the CEC of any errors.[205] However, one major problem remains that of absentee ballots. Specifically, while *Shevardnadze* has managed to create a space for officials in his administration to vote if they live outside of Georgia, absentee balloting remains unavailable to ordinary Georgians.[206] A legal advisor for the NGO Fair Elections, *Nugzar Kupreishvili,* explains that these problems may lead to other forms of voter fraud. A review of an article from the Georgian newspaper the *Kourieri (The Courier)* explains a number of potential election problems.[207] One problem includes the absence of authorized signatures of each member of the central election commission on voting ballots. A second problem includes the current requirement to keep the voting booth curtain open allegedly to prevent ballot box stuffing. Other types of problems reviewed here include pressuring people to change their vote, as well as the use of violence to intimidate voters, buying votes, and unfair media coverage. In order to avoid unfair or biased media coverage, last year representatives from political parties and the media signed an agreement with the assistance of an NGO called the Media Council.[208] The agreement required newspapers to adhere to high standards of impartiality, objectivity, and fairness while covering election campaigns. However, as the November second parliamentary election neared, the news is filled with "finger pointing and personal attacks among politicians....with no apparent effort made among the media to make the agreement work." One Georgian newspaper editor argued that the agreement would not work without including TV stations, as they are more typically the tool of the government, while newspapers cover the opposition. The agreement included a contingency statement that if the state TV began broadcasting abusive material about opposition candidates, the newspapers could rescind their agreement. Subsequently the editor of the Newspaper *Yeni Musavat* ended up do-

---

205   *Idem.* "CEC appeals for help." *The Messenger* (9 October 2003):1.
206   Sopho Gorgodze, "Georgia's numerous disenfranchised voters." *The Messenger* (10 October 2003):1.
207   *Idem.* "Friday on Kourieri-Carrousels, fans, marking: everything about elections." *The Messenger* (7 October 2003):4.
208   Ilgar Khudiyev, "Media election agreements fall apart in Azerbaijan, Georgia." *The Brosse Street Journal* (29 October 2003):5.

ing just that as government owned TV stations began broadcasting abusive material about the political opposition parties. One Representative of the Media Institute states that such agreements are difficult because so many media outlets have financial support from political parties. Interestingly, a representative of Imedi TV, a private TV station argues that such politically aligned newspapers are common all across the former Soviet Union. He also suggests that laws must be created that will require both politicians and media to be more accountable for what they say. He describes political ownership of media outlets as a form of corruption. Another less visible form of corruption involving public officials includes drug smuggling.

Internationally, drug smuggling remains a significant social problem that negatively affects most of the world's population. However, I would argue as other scholars have, that real problem of drug smuggling cannot be resolved by any supply reduction strategy, but rather by a demand reduction strategy. People use drugs as a method of suppressing their pain. In other words, it may be simpler to stay under the influence of mood altering chemicals than to face a life of hopelessness and few opportunities for economic advancement. Of course, across many countries the prevalence of alcohol and drug usually peaks in mid-adolescence followed by a precipitous decline. Apparently, Georgia's youth age fourteen to eighteen reportedly have a new drug of choice, a drug containing .5 kg of an opium poppy seed that costs two GEL and will allegedly get four people high when mixed with other chemicals (that are not named).[209] According to the Georgian Scientific Research Institute of Neurology, users also often accidentally over-dose and often end up spreading Hepatitis C and AIDS by sharing needles. The drugs allegedly come from Holland through South Ossetia. The writer claims that the drug itself is not illegal because the poppy seed has not been placed on the list of controlled substances in Georgia. While the Institute was prepared to meet with the Parliament recently to create an appropriate law making the substance illegal, so few MP's were present that the meeting failed to transpire. However, Adjara recently passed a law prohibiting this substance and made subsequent arrests. After attending a conference on Drug issues in the Ukraine,

---

209   Mary Makharashvili, "Poppy seeds-Georgia's newest drug of choice." The Messenger (8 October 2003):1.

the Georgian Minister of Health learned that organized crime groups (*Mafia*) are exploiting these loopholes in Georgia's laws to profit from the drug business. As a result, Georgian police are arresting suspects and selling the poppy seeds themselves then demanding bribes from the detainees before releasing them. Unfortunately, the journalist reports that while it is unknown how many poppy seed users currently exist in Georgia, the Health Department indicates that the number of people infected with AIDS and Hepatitis C is increasing daily. Health department officials also explained that on one day in September, among two-hundred and fifty-two people examined at the Institute, one-hundred and eighty of them were regular drug users. As mentioned previously, in a society characterized by poverty and unemployment, it is unremarkable that a large number of people find solace in drug abuse or that other groups profit from their misery. Moreover, in a nation with few legitimate opportunities, selling drugs becomes a method of financial survival. Given the fact that smuggling drugs, fuel, and illegal consumer products and bribery flourish in Georgia, money laundering becomes a necessary service also provided by organized criminal groups.

In a recent COE conference, participants describe Georgia as out of compliance with international money laundering regulations.[210] The Council of Europe demands that the Georgian government amend their Criminal Code and ratify the Strasbourg Convention on Money Laundering by 1 January 2004. The convention created the Financial Monitoring Service designed to monitor banks, insurance companies, and notary firms' compliance in maintaining comprehensive information about all clients' transactions. A former Georgian Bank President suggests that the laws and the FMS will be unable to prohibit money laundering in Georgia. A Georgia Today article reports that a team from the Council of Europe called the MONEYVAL, the Select Committee of Experts on the Evaluation of Anti-Money Laundering Measures, along with colleagues from the Financial Action Task Force (FATF) recently visited Georgia. They encouraged the Georgian government to adopt a comprehensive anti-money laundering preventative law that meets FATF standards. While Georgia signed the Convention on Laundering, Search, Seizure

---

210   M. Alkhazashvili, "Georgia needs effective measures to fight money laundering." *Ibid.,* 2.

and Confiscation of the Proceeds from Crime in April 2002, the law has not been ratified by the parliament. The Financial Monitoring Service of Georgia was created in July of 2003 when Parliament adopted the law "Concerning the Abolition of Illegal Incomes"; however, international organizations argue that the service fails to meet international standards, especially with regard to the precise procedure authorizing confiscation of assets. This Georgian law will go into effect in 2004 along with other additional regulations. Unfortunately, the article fails to explain those regulations in any detail. Interestingly, in an interview with the head of the financial monitoring service of Georgia, the issue is framed in the context of confiscating terrorist funds (defined by the U.S.) rather than other more salient issues facing Georgia that remain unrelated to terrorism. The MONEYVAL team more accurately characterizes Georgia's main problems as related to corruption, fraud, tax evasion, and smuggling in goods (tobacco, alcohol, and petroleum) not financing terrorism. Additionally, the shadow economy, which is cash based (80%), fuels money laundering. Further, there is no centralized reliable system or infrastructure designed to collect income or sales taxes more efficiently. Moreover, there remains no centralized system for the registration of activities subject to taxes. MONEYVAL also reported that Georgian authorities seem to be unaware of money-laundering problems in Georgia. MONEYVAL further identified the need for scientific studies to examine this problem in detail. MONEYVAL suggested that the government organize education seminars for authorities to assist them in improving their awareness of these issues as well providing training in the implementation and management of effective anti-money laundering systems. One such conference was held in October, organized and sponsored by the economic Crime Division of the Council of Europe in cooperation with the World Bank, IMF, and the National Bank of Georgia. Representatives from Georgia, Moldova, Armenia, and *Azerbaijan* participated in the conference. Each of these countries is a member of the MONEYVAL system. Unfortunately, one of the addresses by Council of Europe Secretary General focused on the fight against terrorism rather than the extant problems in Georgia.

This problem of criminal corruption in Georgia continues to make headlines as a journalist describes the NGO Transparency International (TI) 2003 annual report. Every year Transparency International publishes a Corruption Perceptions Index (CPI), a scale developed from querying experts on corruption reform. TI defines corruption as the misuse of public power for private benefit. Based upon the opinions of the experts, TI subsequently administers surveys across a number of nation states utilizing this perception index. Within each newly independent state for the period, 2000-2002 fifteen individuals were queried with regard to their perceptions of current levels of corruption. Nine of the individuals worked at a variety of international institutions. Aggregated perceptions for each newly independent state were complied. Each source perception was significantly correlated with the others at p<=.10. Both local citizens in each country and expatriates opinions were included. Scores ranged from 10 representing highly clean or non-corrupt governments to zero indicating a high level of corruption. Georgia's 2002 average score was a 2.4 with individual perception scores ranging from 1.7-2.8. Georgia ranked number eighty-five near the bottom of the list of one hundred and two countries. By 2003 Georgian's perceptions of corruption moved from a 2.4 to a much lower score of 1.8.[211] TI also develops a general ranking for all countries surveyed. Georgia's overall rank among the list of the most corrupt nations also worsened when they moved from eighteenth in 2002 to sixth in 2003.[212]. Deputy Coordinator for U.S. assistance, Thomas Adams, explains that Georgia's level of corruption resulted in the loss of over one-hundred-million GEL from the state budget. While it remains an excellent resource for indicators of corruption internationally, its recommendations for reducing or eliminating corruption remain rather tepid. TI reports that it is the obligation of all private businesses to fully comply with The Organization for Security and Development in Europe's Anti-Bribery Convention and stop bribing public officials. Peter Eigen, Chairperson of Transparency International asked donor countries and international financial institutions to stop "financially supporting corrupt governments and blacklist international companies caught paying bribes abroad."[213] Interestingly, Eigen also stated, that along

---

211   Johann Graff Lamsdorff, "Corruption Perceptions Index." in Peter Eigen, ed., *Global Corruption Report 2003* (Berlin: Transparency International, 2003).
212   Allison Ekberg, "No will to fight, Georgia sinks to new depths in Corruption." *The Messenger* (9 October 2003):1.
213   *Ibid.*, 5.

with other NGO's, they will continue to work to ensure that ordinary people share in the oil wealth of their countries. They plan to campaign for international and state owned oil companies to publish what they pay to governments in order to create a clearer picture of state revenues.[214] TI also developed another scale referred to as the Bribe Payers Index. This scale is based upon public surveys administered in over fifteen emerging capitalist economies around the world. Eight hundred and thirty-five surveys were collected from business people with regard to their views about the extent to which international companies pay bribes. The 2002 findings reveal that respondents believed those offering bribes were most likely to come from firms based in Russia, China, Taiwan, South Korea, Italy, Hong Kong, Malaysia, Japan, the U.S.A. and France. Eigen states that each of these nations has signed the OECD anti-Bribery convention but that "we are still awaiting the first prosecutions in the courts of the thirty-five signatory nations." Eigen further discloses: "Their bribes and incentives to corrupt public officials and politicians are undermining the prospects of sustainable development in poorer countries."[215] A more accurate representation of the truth is that the BPI surveys reveal companies from the U.S. are most likely to offer bribes to public officials in developing countries across the globe. Finally, the article reveals that Halliburton, also operating in Georgia, admitted publicly to paying 2.4 million U.S. dollars in bribes to Nigerian tax officials. It seems evident that one of Georgia's main facilitators of bribery may be the United States. The same nation providing large amounts of financial aid, advice, and demands, is a part of the problem. This extensive level of corruption continues to be mirrored in Georgia's high level of political violence.

Georgia's political violence seems to become worse as the parliamentary election approaches.[216] One journalist describes an assault against a member of the Central Election Commission. Several men attacked him near his home. Apparently, the attackers called him "betrayer of the homeland".This incident followed a CEC meeting that included the certification of voters without passports, and the printing of three million ballots on "special

---

214   *Ibid.*
215   *Ibid.*
216   Ketevan Charkhalashvili, "Broken Noses on Elections' Eve." *Georgia Today* (17 October 2003):1.

paper" designed to deter voting fraud. While it remains difficult to separate superficial accusations of corruption from the real thing simply based on media reports, clear evidence from scholarly sources reveals that across the FSU organized crime, corruption, and violence are frequent bedfellows.[217] Furthermore, organized crime has become synonymous with political party activities particularly as they compete against one another. For example, one violent incident that occurred in September was associated with political competition. The kidnapping of Governor of *Zugdidi* occurred and following a police chase, rescued after the capture of one of the two kidnapers.[218] However, the author reports that even after such offenders are appended, tried and convicted they remain involved in criminal activity from prison. They also are more likely than other inmates to escape from prison.

The Georgian Interior Ministry, responsible for dealing with crime, reports that most escapees from Georgian prisons are organized crime members, traditionally referred to in the FSU as "thieves-in-law."[219] The Interior Ministry explains that over two hundred and twelve Georgian thieves-in-law are currently operating in a variety of different cities across the Caucasus. .In the last year, police have arrested nineteen thieves in law, unfortunately only eight remain in police custody. Information is absent with regard to how many of these individuals have been tried, convicted, or sentenced. In an attempt to explain the apparent difficulties with trials, convictions and sentences, the Interior Minister explains that the "sentence Execution Department" is operating in a state of crisis. He explains that although convictions were obtained against all eight suspects, they continue to await final sentencing. However, the Minister may have also been trying to dissuade the journalist from inquiring further about Human Rights violations against these long-term detainees. An ongoing international criticism of the Ministry has been the use of excessive detention of criminal suspects prior to trial. The Minister also reveals that improving jail security will not solve this problem of planning and executing

217   CSKS Task Force Report. Center for Strategic and International Studies, "Russian Organized Crime and Corruption Putin's Challenge." *Global Organized Crime Project* (2000).

218   N.N., "Kidnapping and Release of Zugdidi Governor." *Georgia Today* (19 September 2003):3.

219   N.N., "What's new, Thieves-in-law and frequent escapes-biggest headache." *Georgia Today* (17 October 2003):4.

crime from jail. While not mentioned in the article, the reason that jail alone will fail to solve the organized crime problem relates to the fact that organized crime's livelihood remains based upon Georgian's demand for inexpensive consumer products. Such cheap goods are much more likely to be available from the shadow economy than within the legitimate economy. Thus, the illegitimate economy or shadow economy remains alive and well because it is necessary. Of course, the shadow economy cannot exist without its sibling, public corruption. Thus disentangling the web of poverty, corruption, organized crime, and the illegitimate economy appears impossible to resolve over the short run. Furthermore, the shadow economy or illegitimate economy is problematic across a variety of other CIS countries.[220] Eliminating it within only one country is simply not possible without addressing its existence across the FSU. An astounding sixty percent of the Georgian economy consists of the illegal sales and purchases.

However, naively, the student movement, *Kmara* (meaning Enough) expects corruption to end perhaps unrealistically with a simple change in government leadership or political power. They recently protested against the government in front of the parliament, accusing it of institutionalized corruption.[221] They laid funeral wreaths in front of the parliament building symbolizing the death of the state and argued that they would fight against any party in power if "no positive steps were taken towards the people" with regard to the forthcoming November parliamentary elections. *Zurab Zhvania* stated that the government should support an active youth movement. However, he also argued that these exploited youth were financed by a variety of unknown groups. Further, he reported that the supporters were taking advantage of the current political situation to "advance their own interests". Unfortunately, those specific interests were not identified. Recently, other negative press about *Kmara* included an alleged assault on several *Tbilisi* residents by members of the group. A Revival party member subsequently call the group "homosexuals" who were directed by *Mikhail Saakashvili*, along with the head of the United Democrats, who together want to destroy the Eastern Orthodox foundation of the country. Then he claimed that the movement's only goal

220   Caroline McGregor, "Building Anti-Laundering Systems." *Ibid.*, 8.
221   Gia Bakaradze, "Clashes with Youth Movement." *Georgia Today Ibid.*

was to popularize "homosexuality". It appears that no gay rights movement has evolved in the FSU, leaving attitudes about Gays and Lesbians resembling that of American's attitudes in the 1970's best described as uninformed. Clearly, one method of debunking a social movement is to characterize the group as evil or deviant. *Kmara*, however, has been quite active in attempting to bring attention to the extant corruption within the government, particularly within the current administration, which may have led to their characterization as "homosexual." *Kmara* has also spent some time throughout the year focusing on the corrupt leadership of *Aslan Abashidze*. *Abashidze's* party, the Revival Party, remains quite strong in *Adjara* and it seems commonly accepted that *Abashidze* epitomizes Georgian corruption. *Abashidze* is also perceived to be involved in a number of illegal financial enterprises. While usually public conversations about the corruption of government officials surfaces without any real data to back up the suppositions, the media did in one instance offer such evidence. In at least one article, a writer made a concerted effort to reveal the financial status of the political candidates currently vying for public office.

These financial disclosures about a variety of politicians and political blocks were revealed in an attempt to describe the various political blocks competing against *Shevardnadze's* party.[222] One political block includes the *Burjanadze*-Democrats, headed by the current Chair of the Parliament *Nino Burjanadze* with the Traditionalists, and the United Democrats (headed by *Zurab Zhvania*). This party block is described as having so few financial resources that they are unable to carry out any expensive pre-election campaigning. The cost of one billboard is one hundred and fifty dollars a month and a one-minute TV ad costs six hundred U.S. dollars. However, the individual party leaders appear to have sufficient personal funds to support some political advertisements. Readers should note that *Saakashvili* claims that he refuses to unite with the *Burjanadze-Zhvania* pair because one of their members, *David Salaridze*, the alleged financial backbone of the group is corrupt. According to the article, the least wealthy of the political party members are the Nationalist leaders. This includes *Mikhail Saakashvili*, current Chairperson of the *Tbilisi* City Assembly (*Tbilisi Sakrebulo*) and *Kote Kemularia*, a cur-

---

222   Zaza Jgharkava, "Opposition Financial Dossiers." *Ibid.,* 2.

rent parliamentary member. The remainder of this article discloses the salaries of a variety of politicians as well as the net worth of their respective homes and other properties in addition to the financial assets and incomes of family members (see Table 3).

Table 3: Property and Wealth of Politicians

Politician	Home	Bank	Salary	Other	Net Worth
Saakashvili	95,000 GEL	4,000 EUR	400 GEL		
Kemularia	70,000 GEL	9800 GEL	7900 GEL	1600 GEL	50,000 GEL
Spouse of *Saakashvili*			1000 U.S. Dollars		
Burjanadze		59,000 U.S. Dollars	18,448 GEL		
Zhvania		92000 GEL	11,531 GEL		180,000 GEL
Salaridze				9224 GEL	132,000 GEL
Gamkrelidze		37,250 US.Dollars	9360 GEL		596,000 GEL
New Rights Leader				9000 GEL	290,000 GEL

Saakashvili's wife works for an international agency and earns one thousand dollars a month, while *Kemularia*'s son owns property located in *Musket* worth fourteen thousand GEL and a piano worth four thousand GEL. A portion of *Kemularia*'s net worth includes ownership of thirty-three percent of a company called The *Kemularia*. *Nino Burjanadze*'s father is referred to as the Georgian Bread King, a rich man. However, the reporter claims that nobody knows anything about his current finances. *Zhvania*'s wife earns over ten thousand GEL a year as a coordinator of FUND Horizon. *Salaridze*'s daughter reportedly maintains a Georgian bank account containing ten thousand dollars. *David Gamkrelidze* owns nine hundred thousand shares of the *Aldagi* Insurance Company. His spouse owns a four hundred thousand GEL house, and forty percent of a local Human Resources Management Center. However, she only earns a little over three thousand GEL a year. Similarly, the New Rights Party leader owns shares in a company called Pulsara Limited and eighty thousand shares in Office Suite. His father also owns a one hundred and sixty thousand GEL home in *Tbilisi* and another fifty thousand GEL home in *Armazi*. He also has over eighteen thousand Euros in one bank account and thirty-one thousand dollars in another. Finally, he earns two thousand dollars a month from renting an apartment to Geocell Company. Clearly, many of these politicians have income from a variety of sources that allows them to live well beyond their regular salaries. While it was noteworthy that the newspaper provided such details, it is rare that this kind of information appears in print. However, even as these financial disclosures become publicized *Abashidze's* income and assets are omitted while his violent dictatorship continues to make news headlines.

In an interview with *Tsotne Bakuria*, a political party member of the Revival Block in the autonomous region of *Adjara, Bakuria* reports that his party has experienced what he calls thirty terrorist attacks. He implies that these assaults are the result of the false allegations of corruption in President *Abashidze's* decade long administration.[223] While the English in this article is difficult to wade through it is apparent that this politician is arguing that while people often drop out of the party (allegations are that this occurs following intimidation by *Abashidze*), for every member lost, one hundred more people join the party. He also argued that ninety percent of the votes in every *Adjaran* election go towards the party. While claims and counterclaims continue, the evidence of politically motivated violence across Georgia is immutable.

Later an ordinary street crime of robbery is revealed to have been a robbery perpetrated against the Polish Ambassador. Of course, this too then became fodder for political posturing.[224] However, one of the robbers' is described as a nineteen-year-old male, reflecting a classic textbook example of ordinary delinquency. The incident occurred in eastern Georgia in a village called *Ubadno* located by the sixth century Monastery complex, *Davit Gareja* near the Azeri border. The above male and two others were detained and charged with illegally possessing firearms. Four males reportedly robbed the Ambassador, stole his car and then later abandoned it. At no time does this

---

223   *Idem*. "Premature Deceased: Gelbakhiani, Bregadze, Javakhishvili...Who will be next?" *Ibid.,* 3.

224   Rusudan Kbilashvili, "Ambassadors to Georgia prevented from "sightseeing" in the pre-election period?" *The Georgian Times* (20 October 2003):3.

Georgian journalist refer to the males as suspects. Again revealing that due process remains virtually unknown in Georgia, at least by journalists. The author's editorial critique insinuates that it remains unsafe to travel in Georgia during the pre-election period without first notifying the Minister of Internal Affairs and having guards. Of course, considering the socio-economic status of international officials, a lucrative opportunity may have offered itself to these typical delinquents and they simply took advantage of it. However, the writer uses the incident to remind readers that the *Bolnisi* incident can occur again. Refreshing Georgian readers' minds about their own history becomes a methodology utilized by newspaper writers to re-produce Nationalist rhetoric. Subsequently, other journalists use this tactic typically by engaging Georgian's memory of former President *Gamsakhurdia*. This time his son was expoited in revitalizing nationalistic sentiments. *Giorgi Gamsakhurdia*, currently a *Tbilisi* police officer, was implicated in the unlawful search and harassment of a recently released incarcerated man, *Merab Chkapelia* and his family.[225] *Gamsakhurdia* and other officers were dressed in civilian clothes as they physically attacked family members of the former inmate. The family members were IDPS and reported that there was no reason for the police or *Gamsakhurdia* to single them out. Although the sequence of events is ambiguous, apparently *Giorgi Gamskhurdia* also threatened *Merab Chkhapelia with a weapon* outside a public restaurant and subsequently shot *Chkapelia* in the foot. This central plot remains rather mysterious but the writer may have omitted information intentionally simply to arouse suspicions or create more fear of political violence.

On election' day, voters will decide on a referendum to reduce the size of parliament from its current two-hundred and thirty-five members to one-hundred and fifty members. One journalist argues that the reason for such a reduction is the decline of the Georgian constituency.[226] Another reason motivating the change revolves around the retirement salaries currently paid former MP's that currently stands at about four hundred GEL a month following only four years of service. This costs Georgians about two and half million GEL a year as they support six hundred retired MPs. Two issues remain

---

225   Lali Javakhia, "Ex-President's Son Accused of violence against an IDP." *Ibid.*, 10.

problematic with regard to this forthcoming referendum. Firstly, politicians disagree about whether or not there is a current formula to determine how these one hundred and fifty MPS will represent constitutents. Thirdly, there is disagreement about when these changes will take affect. Some want the changes to occur immediately following the new Parliamentary election while others argue that the changes should not occur until the 2007 Parliamentary election. And while the Central Election Committee is required by law to advertise the referendum on the two state channels, no such public information has been made available. One MP claims that this is simply a stalling technique designed to avoid the new parliamentary vote that will be necessary if the citizens vote yes on the referendum. Changing the number of parliamentarians holding office will obviously affect some current power holders and these political elites want to maintain the status quo. The maintenance of the extant power structure remains related to the issue discussed above, the absence of any real political platforms, offered by any party.

One journalist criticizes this lack of accountability of political parties to clearly articulate platforms. The journalist writes that political parties fail to provide substance to their lofty goals, described only as tools designed to bedazzle citizens. [227] This writer contacted ten of the top political parties and asked them to summarize their platforms. However, only four responded by providing some information. Delineated platforms came from the New Rights Party, the Democratic Revival Party, the *Burjanadze* Democrats, the Party for a New Georgia and the Government block. The New Right plans to establish a real separation of powers creating more balance between all three branches of the government. They also promise to reduce taxes, improve tax collection and transform the illegitimate economy into the legitimate one. They also purport that they will improve budget planning and reduce government bureaucracy. They promise punishment for those who attack any religious minority group members. They also intend to create a dialogue between the Orthodox Church and the state. However, in another remarkable

---

226   Nino Kopaleishvili, "Referendum to reduce parliament could face legal challenges." *The Brosse Street Journal* (28 October 2003):3.

227   Natalia Topuria and Tinatin Gogoberishvili, "Four parties provide ambitious platforms but offer few details on paying for them." *The Brosse Street Journal* (29 October 2003):1, 10.

reflection of U.S. political culture, this party also promises to examine the special role of the Orthodox Church in protecting traditional family values. The party tells voters that they will take control of local schools, removing power from the federal government by returning control to the municipal authorities. Other goals included providing assistance to small and medium businesses, establishing new credit policies, and improving the tax system. Several of this party's goals are somewhat vague, including protecting private property and eliminating government pressure on businesses. Details of how these objectives would be accomplished were omitted.

The Democratic Revival Party platform goals include abolishing the private electric companies that they claim will result in reductions in the cost of electricity. They also promise to reduce the cost of water in *Tbilisi* by selling the previously privatized water supply. Additional platform issues included the promise to reduce small business taxes, and create free municipal hospitals, free health care for vulnerable people, increase government salaries, and pensions, and set-up unemployment compensation and economic assistance for larger families. The party also touts its own record claiming to have built eighteen factories, forty-six schools as well as supporting the construction of new churches.

The *Burjanadze*-Democrats generally promise a "decent country" and aim to support new industry both small and medium, defend privacy rights, reduce taxes, increase flexible investments (whatever that really means), improve traditional farming by providing new types of credit to farmers, pay off salaries owed to the people, raise pensions, and provide high quality education and health care. This party also plans to join NATO, claming that NATO membership will allow Georgia to regain control of *Abkhazia*. They also plan to become full members of the EU and strengthen ties with the United States while developing economic and trade relations with Russia. This journalist explains that the government block provided the least amount of information with regard to their platform saying that they would create new higher paying jobs, small and medium businesses and strengthen monetary policy and market institutions to improve the economy. They also promised to increase pensions, devote serious attention to IDP issues as well as better inform people of their rights, improve and reform the executive and judicial branches, and branches, and work towards better relations with Russia, Europe, and other major Atlantic organizations.

In an interview with the leader of the political party *Ertoba*, *Jumber Patiashvili* promises to bring Georgia out of its current socio-economic crisis by ending government corruption and improving the tax system.[228] He also states that Georgia currently only uses about twelve percent of their own natural resources and extorts that his party will change this. He insists that medical care must be free for the socially unprotected classes. He also referred to energy barons as the "*Engero-Mafia*" arguing that their exploitation of the Georgian people must end. Finally, he favors reducing the number of parliamentarians to one hundred and twenty deputies not just one-hundred and fifty. However, he fails to explain why he believes this would be an improvement. Again, while it is extremely important that the journalist provided this information to readers, most Georgians cannot afford newspapers. Moreover, it is dubious that such information could have or did reach Georgian TV viewers before the election.

The scuttlebutt on the streets of *Tbilisi* in late October was that the voters' lists remained inaccurate. Rumors included allegations that babies' names were on the lists as well as the deceased. One article also criticized the CEC for being so tardy in cleaning up the voters' lists as well as posting them for public scrutiny.[229] Back in February, the President issued a decree ordering the creation of new voters' lists, however apparently this process began recently. Only within the last week or so have both the International NGO IFES and USAID begun to display voters' lists on the Internet and of course, few Georgians have access to the Internet. A representative from IFES explained that among the over two million voters' names supplied by the Minister of the Interior, slightly over three hundred thousand of them were dead. *Burjanadze* asked the CEC why they failed to utilize the last census in compiling the lists. The head of the Council of Europe delegation, *Matyas Eoris* made similar inquiries. While the CEC chairperson, *Nana Devdariani* contends that she is doing everything in her power to ensure that the voters' lists are correct, she states inaccuracies could be as high as ten to fifteen per-

228   Zaza Jgharkava, "The Number of Deputies must be reduced to 120, not 150." *Georgia Today* (24 October 2003):3.

cent. In response to the request of *Burjanadze* and the COE delegation, she offers no explanation with regard to failure to use the more recent census to create the new voters' lists. She also fails to offer any explanation with regard to the high level of inaccuracy. The presence of these problems will undoubtedly influence the outcome of the election. Observers monitoring these processes will also be taking note of these difficulties when they make their final report.

The Council of Europe approved Georgia's membership in 1999 and their presence in Georgia is an attempt to ensure that Georgia's commitments made in that agreement are followed throughout the election period. The CoE and other international organizations' reports following the election will be submitted to the Parliamentary Assembly of the CoE. The quality of Georgia's election will significantly influence Georgia's future membership in the CoE.

Finally, five days before the election the Georgian parliament and finance ministry transferred six and a half million GEL to the Central Election Committee.[230] The Chairperson of the CEC previously indicated that if the money remained undelivered, a delay of the election might occur. The commissioner of the CEC even threatened to sue the Finance Ministry if funds were undelivered. Many Georgians feel hopeless about the probability that the elections will be held fairly and one citizen quoted by a journalist reports that whether or not the elections are financed properly is not the real issue, she reports that regardless the "elections will be falsified anyway". [231]

In late October, the Central Election Commission postponed the final completion of the voters' lists and explained that potential voters will be able to check the lists at their district by the end of October.[232] It remains unclear if the CEC is offering to correct mistakes since limited time remains before the actual election. The on-going shortsightedness of the CEC coupled with their obvious inefficiency makes any outcome suspicious. In a subsequent article from another news source, the political opposition continues to accuse the

229   Galina Gotua, "Georgia's status as Democracy in Question: COE." *Ibid.*, 2.
230   Eka Kadagishvili and Kote Chkhartishvili, "CEC told it will get 6.5 million GEL from government." *The Brosse Street Journal* (29 October 2003):5.
231   *Ibid.*

government and the CEC of falsifying the voters' lists to ensure the government's victory.[233] Journalists indicate that the political opposition plans to take to the streets if the elections are fraudulent. This writer indicates that the CEC delayed the release of the voters' registration lists intentionally to produce a fraudulent list. Additionally, voters' lists were only re-examined following *Nino Burjanadze's* request to do so. Meanwhile *Sheveradnadze* argues that claims about fraudulent voters' lists remain a charade aimed at delaying the vote. However, in a recent press conference the Interior Minister reported that the list held at his office is different from a previously issued list and accuses the CEC of falsifying the voters' list to orchestrate a win for the opposition parties not the government block. The Interior Minister, *Koba Narchemashvili*, also explained that he would ensure that law enforcement officers would prevent any planned effort by the political opposition to de-stabilize the country. The President added that he would not allow any political destabilization like the one that recently transpired in *Azerbaijan*. In response, *Burjanadze* retorted that if the Interior Minister really had proof of such a plan, why not make arrests now as such actions are clearly criminal and a violation of the constitution. In addition to these on-going accusations, political violence continued to characterize the pre-election environment. For example, a hand-made explosive device exploded in *Zestaphoni* at the home of a National Movement MP candidate, *Davit Mumladze*.[234] Additonally, gunshots were fired during this incident. *Mumladze* claims that members of the pro-government party instigated the violence. Subsequently, following protests against the violence in *Samtredia*, arrests were made of the protesters.[235] The Minister of Interior Affairs reported that the protest was criminal as they were trying to create instability across the nation as well as damage the railroad system. There is no indication that members of the National Unity party who organized the protest actually intended to anything other than sim-

---

232   N.N., "Deadline for Election List Checking Postponed." Rustavi-2 *online news* http://www.rustavi-2.com.ge/view.php?id=5633 (as of 27 October 2003).

233   Nino Patsuria, "Voter Calculation, Lobby Speculation, and Mounting Election Fever." *Georgia Today* (24 October 2003):2.

234   N.N., "Explosion in Zestaphoni." Rustavi-2 online news http://www.rustavi-2.com.ge/print.php?id=5635 (as of 27 October 2003).

235   N.N., "Criminal Case Against National Unity Leaders." Rustavi-2 online news http://www.rustavi-2.com.ge/view/php?id=5650 (as of 28 October 2003).

ply protest against the poor quality of the election lists and the previous violence. A report on October 31st reflects another incident of pre-election violence against a candidate from the New Rights party who alleged that he was assaulted on October 29th.[236] *Davit Gamkrelidze*, another leader of the party claimed that the attempt was an effort by political opponents to murder *Zviad Chokheli,* their MP candidate. The Interior Minister is investigating the incident as a crime. Similarly, another candidate for MP, from the United Democratic Revival Party, disappeared on one day and subsequently re-appeared the next day at his party's regional office. [237] This man, *Temur Gogsadze* was kidnapped and later physically assaulted. After the attack, the perpetrators threw him into the River *Kvirila*. Police are reportedly investigating the incident.

In another incident of political mayhem, *Saakashvili's* Nationalist party traveled to *Batumi* for a planned protest in front of the Supreme Council building in *Adjara*.[238] According to a Nationalist party spokesperson, three hundred supporters of the party gathered in support of the Nationalists. They alleged that some members of the block were injured during the rally. However, the *Adjaran* Interior Minister reported that this was unlikely because local police in the Republic of *Adjara* would prevent such an incident. It is evident that one side or another is distorting the truth to serve its own purposes. While both sides fight for votes and accuse the CEC of wrongdoing, the newspaper publishes the following poll of voter predilections.

The faculty of the Department of Sociology and Philosophy at *Illya Chavchavadze* State University of Language and Culture and a research group completed a pre-election poll of voters. The poll reflected that more people planned to vote for the *Burjanadze*-Democrats (19.4%) and National Movement Party (19.2%) while the Labor Party (16%) ranked third, the government for a new Georgia trailed in fourth place (9.1%), and the Revival Party was in last place (9%).[239] However, if you add the percentages reported

---

236   N.N., "Zviad Chokheli Comments on His Assault." Rustavi-2 online news http://www.rustavi-2.com.ge/view.php?id=5693 (as of 31 October 2003).

237   N.N., "Kidnapped Gogsadze Appeared." Rustavi-2 online news http://www.rustavi-2.com.ge/view/php?id=5677 (as of 20 October 2003).

238   N.N., "Street Clashes in Batumi." *Georgia Today* (24 October 2003):2.

239   N.N., "Pre-election polling." Rustavi-2 online news http://www.rustavi2.com.ge/print.php?id=5684 (as of 30 October 2003).

here, that only accounts for 72% of those polled. The remaining twenty-eight percent of respondents are missing from the newspaper report. Moreover, the article fails to provide any information with regard to how the sample was collected or if respondents were capital city residents or people from the out-lying regions. It is not surprising that in an era when the CEC is unable to get the voters' lists right, the newspapers or perhaps the researchers are unable to do science. Apparently, in one effort to pre-empt fraudulent voting, just two days prior to the election, the local NGO Fair Elections held a demonstration on *Rustaveli* Avenue. Demonstrators shouted the slogan: "We Demand Fair Elections."[240] Four hundred members of the NGO distributed pamphlets to Georgian citizens describing the correct voting procedures.

In addition to this public awareness campaign aimed at educating vot-ers, the last issue of Georgia Today in October also offered citizens a glim-mer of hope about the future of their country. The writer described *Tbilisi's* old airplane manufacturing plant that survived the Soviet period explaining that it will soon increase production activities thus offering more jobs.[241] This company, *Tbiliaviamsheni*, began building Soviet military aircraft during WW II following its relocation from Moscow. More recently, the company has con-tinued to build aircraft for the West as well as the East. In increasing their productivity, they will begin building a new Boeing 737 service center and thus require additional employees. In a second optimistic piece, discussion focused on describing a non-governmental organization called CARE Cauca-sus that assists rural communities in solving a variety of problems. Specifi-cally, CARE provides assistance in the development of micro-businesses. A second CARE program also helps IDPs start up new businesses. CARE works with local institutions under the umbrella of a USAID funded West Georgia Community Mobilization Initiative. In a section called "social" re-views, another NGO is described called Keselo. The organization is funded by a Dutch couple who explain that their organization will be restoring and renovating the ancient *Tusheti* Tower in *Omalo*. While the exact year of origin of the towers was omitted, the plan for its repair promotes Nationalistic sen-

---

240   N.N., "We Demand Fair Elections." Rustavi-2 online news.
       http://www.rustavi2.com.ge/print.php?id=5686 (as of 31 October 2003).
241   Nino Patsuria, "Tbilaviasmsheni Lifts Georgia to new Heights." *Georgia Today* (24 October 2003):5.

timent. The writer explains that the towers stand several meters high and were constructed following a Mongol invasion to be used as an early warning system to prevent future attacks. The village is located on the border of *Chechnya* and Russia's state of *Dagestan* where OSCE observers monitor movements of *Chechens* across the border.[242] Another article in this section also promotes Nationalistic sentiment by discussing the old town of *Telavi*, in the *Kakheti* region, referred to as one of the oldest and most beautiful towns in Georgia.[243] The town is located sixty kilometers east of *Tbilisi* and lies at the intersection of the mountains of *Gombori* and the river *Alazani*. The name of the town literally translates into Elms. Georgian ethnic nationalism remains closely connected to their Eastern Orthodox faith. This is illustrated in another article that discusses the discovery of a number of Georgian manuscripts and burial tombs in Israel dating back to the fifth century.[244] The writer claims that 'Georgian's possessed' forty monasteries in Israel between the 4th and 19th century until they were lost in the 19th century. Readers should recall that the Georgian Orthodox church is officially recognized in the Georgian Constitution. As mentioned previously, Georgian churches occupy nearly every street corner in *Tbilisi*. Even people passing churches while riding in taxis or busses cross themselves reflecting at least the symbolic strength of their faith or perhaps religious conviction. Therefore, this discovery of Georgian artifacts in Israel represents a powerful moment in the Georgian collective consciousness. In a recent expedition to photograph and recover some of these artifacts one particular inscription previously found mentioned *Elene*, the Queen of the *Kakhs*. It was found carved onto St. Nicolas' church even though it later turned up missing. Initially, the Georgians accused the Israeli Patriarch of being responsible for the disspearence of the artifact, however later the Israeli Patriarch provided support in restoring the inscription. An exhibit of the photographs of these Georgian artifacts came to *Tbilisi* last year and contained over four hundred pictures of thirty-six different monuments. These stories provide Georgians with a sense pride in their long and rich history infusing their national identity with a powerful religious consciousness,

---

242   Ketevan Charkhalashvili, "Dutchman Renovating Tusheti's Towers." *Ibid.,* 9.
243   *Idem.* "Telavi-Town of Elms." *Ibid.*
244   Nana Kobaidze, "120 Days in the Holy Land Who Destroys the monuments of the Georgian culture in the Holy Land." *The Georgian Times* (1 November 2003):17.

one could say, defining themselves as one of God's chosen people. Of course, the underlying theme reflects the Georgian hopes that they will eventually overcome all adversities, perhaps especially if the Nationalist party wins the forthcoming elections.

In a pro-*Shevardnadze* article in the International edition of the Georgian Times, a weekly political review claims that the Nationalist Party promises to metaphorically remove *Shevardnadze's* head before the election.[245] While, the writer insists that no post-Soviet election in Georgia has been free of violence, she insinuates that Nationalist Party meetings across Georgian provinces are continuing this trend but refers to these aggressive incidents as only"scuffles". She also states "This party has never managed to campaign in a peaceful atmosphere" and describes the *Bolnisi* incident as a "physical altercation initiated by *Saakashvili's* supporters and local authorities". The *Bolnisi* incident and others like it continue to be referred to as the western style of rallying that include shouting slogans like this one used in Batumi, "*Adjara* without *Abashidze*" in front of *Abashidze's* home. In response to this incident, *Abashidze's* government representatives attacked Nationalist movement members with truncheons. Another similar incident was blamed on the Nationalist party. In this case, a political party leader in *Zugdidi*, an opponent of the Nationalist party, died and the article accuses *Saakashvili of* "masterminding the murder". Subsequently, the victim's supporters threatened to "kill *Saakashvili*". Then later in *Zugdidi*, *Saakashvili* survived an attempt on his life as a car barreled toward him in an attempt to run him over. However, a group of local women managed to stop the car before *Saakashvili* run over. Additionally a member of the New Rights Party was shot while in *Tbilisi* and the writer blames *Saakashvili* although at the time he was as campaigning elsewhere. The shooting victim survived because he was wearing a bulletproof vest. There was some discussion about the perpetrators, with someone suggesting that *Saakashvili's* involvement with organized crime led to the shooting. Another asserted possibility was that the government planned to kill the shooting victim. Interestingly, the writer finally adds that the public does not take such events seriously, as many people believe that this kind of political violence is staged for public consumption. The writer argues that these performances are a normative part of political campaign tactics designed to sully rival parties' images and sway voters' opinions. Concurrent with these allegedly theatrical incidents, the nature of most political television advertisements involve little language but rather catchy tunes designed to capture voters' attention and thereby garner votes. I observed some of these commercials and they contained no dialogue no verbal promises only pictures of Georgian politicians shaking hands and smiling with other international and powerful politicians like Bush, Putin, and Tony Blair. Other types of campaign advertising are referred to as Black publicity aimed at destroying the images of politicians, like the campaign that accused *Nino Burjanadze* of being a Russian spy or the one that alleged that *Mikhail Saakashvili* and *Zurab Zhvania* were really Armenians. Even party slogans reflect that wining and losing elections is metaphorically about surviving or dieing as illustrated in this Nationalist slogan stating "Georgia without *Shevardnadze*." In a similar piece reviewing the political activities of the week, another writer characterizes all of Georgia's elections since the fall of the Soviet Union as "marked by fistfights and cursing".[246] Yet again, S*aakashvili's* western style of campaigning is portrayed as the primary culprit in pre-election violence in both *Batumi* and *Zugdidi*. Again, this author suggests that *Saakashvili* masterminded the murder of *Badri Zarandia*, a prominent politician whose supporters recently swarmed *Saakashvili's* car in *Zugdidi*.

President *Shevardnadze* joins in the campaign dance by singing his own praises. He discloses a forthcoming award that he will give to *Giorgi Chanturia*, the President of Georgian International Oil Corporation for his contributions to a number of regional oil pipeline projects. Speculation is that he will endorse this man as a candidate in the next presidential election scheduled for 2005. Other indications are that *Shevardnadze* might endorse his son as the next presidential candidate. *Shevardnadze's* former campaign manager, *Zurab Zhvania* also reportedly maintains presidential ambitions but the writer indicates that his popularity is currently low because of the accusa-

---

245   Kate Bojgua, "Reflection of the General Elections Tow Days Before the Election. Saakashvili promises to chop off the President's head-controversies of the pre-election advertising in Georgia." *The Georgian Times* (3 November 2003):3.

246   Ninidze, "Reflections of the Last Week: Weekly Political Review."

tions that he is really an Armenian. Another writer describes *Saakashvili* as a man with presidential ambitions. However, descriptions of both men, characterize them as poor politicians, an interesting label considering events that are about to unfold. Another writer subtlety argues that Western powers are welding greater influence in the region as evidenced by allegations of Western support for the suspected fraudulent presidential elections in *Azerbaijan*. The argument is that these interests are motivated by the West's desire for "oil in exchange for democracy". Therefore the hypothesis is that only a powerful oil mogul could garner enough Western support to win the next presidential vote, this is person is *Chanturia*. Most importantly, this issue of Western influence will be pivotal in the coming month particularly with regard to the alliance recently built between the *Burjanadze* Democrats and *Zhvania's* Democrats as well as *Saakashvili's* National Movement. However, one writer describes their unification as contentious because they continue to argue over one party member's position as the *Vake* district candidate for a PM, *David Salaridze*. The writer claims that *Saakasvhili* intensely dislikes *Salaridze* only because he was a political rival in the 1999 parliamentary election. However, in a previous article another writer reported that *Saakashvili* believes *Salardize* is corrupt.[247] Similarly, this writer expresses concerns about a negative outcome if Parliament ends up being more pro-Russian than pro-West. Moreover, if pro-Russian politicians win the elections, the writer argues that this would frighten many Georgians about continued interference and attempts at control from Moscow. The author even writes that while the Democrats promote their pro-Western aspirations, rumors continue to persist that they are covertly allied with Russia.

While debates about Georgia's western or eastern orientation remain in the headlines, another issue that usually escapes the attention of the newspapers is the status of Georgia's senior citizens. As I regularly walked the streets of *Tbilisi*, especially in the middle class neighborhoods where predominantly well off Georgians and foreigners live, a number of senior citizen are always present asking for money. Sometimes they hold icons of Jesus or Mary as they sit with a small bowl in their hands. Typically, many Georgians and foreigners drop ten or twenty *tetra* in the hands of these seniors. They

---

247   Jgharkava, "Opposition Financial Dossiers."

knew these people were trying to survive on a meager monthly pension of fourteen lari. Moreover, having visited well-educated colleagues and friends' homes where they continue to live without any central heat in the winter months, I expect these seniors were equally likely to live without heat during the winter. To promote attention to this issue a multi-NGO meeting was held at the *Tbilisi* Georgian NGO Horozonti where members of the Association of Century Human Being, called *Savane* tried to focus on the needs of poor and hungry Georgian seniors.[248] The head of *Savane* reported that he plans to request funding from the government to improve conditions for senior citizens. Mary Ellen Chatwin, Social Policy Advisor of Horozonti, discloses that currently there is no national policy on seniors, only a presidential decree that continues to be ignored. Tragically, while Western financial institutions provide large amounts of funds to Georgia, the poor continue to reap no apparent benefits. Moreover, Georgia is not alone, this problem persists throughout the world in many poor countries receiving IMF or World Bank funding.

In a review of economic conditions over the last week, the IMF's visit to *Tbilisi* is at the top of the list as they encouraged the government to increase the national budget, probably in part to re-pay IMF loans.[249] Additionally the writer accused the head of the IMF of demanding the privatization one of Georgia's banks, Agro-Business Bank. However, while officials denied that this was the case, an agreement was signed to accomplish this goal some time ago. Specifically the state bank will be privatized in 2005. In another case of western oil moguls getting richer off the backs of the poor, one writer discusses another gas pipeline project, the *Shahdeniz-Tbilisi-Erzerum*, or the South Caucasus pipeline. A signed and ratified agreement to complete this pipeline came into effect last year. The pipeline will deliver five percent of the gas carried from *Azerbaijan* to Georgia freely and Georgia will receive an additional discount on each cubic meter purchased. Allegations that Georgia is the apple of the West's eye are not surprising in the context of these two oil pipeline projects. In the midst of these oil pipeline projects the GEL has re-

---

248   Rusudan Kbilashvili, "I am hungry....I am cold ....and I am tired. Ageing Georgia's forgotten Development Issue discussed in the Horzonti Fund." *The Georgian Times* (3 November 2003):7.

249   Mays Misheladze, "Business Economics, Economic review of the last week." *Ibid.,* 10.

portedly grown stronger, purportedly due to the devaluation of the U.S. dollar and because of the continuing investment in the *Baku-Tbilisi-Ceyhan* oil pipeline project.

In an attempt by the Georgia Today editors to provide humor in anticipation of a tumultuous election day, one writer describes how election coverage morphs into the world of Georgian art and culture. Specifically, a set of new Georgian Chess figures sculpted and painted by *Giorgi Khutsishvili* were recently unveiled to the public.[250] The artist sculpted a variety of political figures from newspaper photos. The project sponsors included The Charity House staff called Catharsis who voted democratically to determine which politicians would become specific chess pieces. The White pieces are all Georgian politicians in the pro-government party while the King of the Black pieces is *Aslan Abashidze*, and the Queen is the Chairperson of the Parliament, *Nino Burjanadze*. The motif, Georgian politics is a chess game, a stage performance with pawns exploited to achieve political power. Similarly, another piece on the front page discusses an art fair exhibit that was held in front of the national library in late October during which more than twenty painters participated in a six-hour process of painting pre-election sentiments across the country.[251] The British Council sponsored this event. Perhaps in an attempt to counter this humor, one writer cautiously reports that sixty-two thousand Georgians have registered to vote within the Russian Federation. However, the Russian 2000 census reflects that over seven hundred thousand ethnic Georgians currently live in Russia, a fact ignored by Georgian journalists.[252] Finally, the co-leader of the *Burjanadze* Democrats, *Zurab Zhvania*, threatens that if the government falsifies the election results his block will support protests in the streets or perhaps even more dangerous activities.[253] He also predicted that government block would not be as successful at the polls as they expect and that the victory of the National Movement and the *Burjanadze* Democrats as well as the New Rights Party will then transform the government.

---

250   Maka Lomadze, "Fight for White." *Georgia Today* (31 October 2004):1.
251   Ketevan Charkhalashvili, "Painting Election Fairness." *Ibid.*
252   N.N., "62,000 Voters Registered in Russia." *Ibid.,* 3.
253   N.N., "Zhvania Imposes all the responsibility on the Government." *Ibid.*

On the last page of the *Georgia Today* edition published the day before the election a German national married to a Georgian woman is interviewed about his experiences as an OSCE election observer in 1999 as well as about the pre-election campaigning.[254] The just of his comments were that TV commercials about politicians running for office are void of any content while only insinuating that they will improve the economy. He also explained that the advertisements illustrate Georgian politicians shaking the hands of other international politicians. He disclosed that many Georgians have told him that they simply have no faith in the process anymore and that whether they vote or not, nothing will change.

III.4   November 2003

Georgians voted at the polls on Sunday November second. Subsequently the newspaper headlines reflected a weak demonstration of fair and free democratic processes.[255] International observers, while not commenting on whether or not the elections were held democratically, reported that the elections "fell short on a number of international standards". Both the International Election Observer Mission and the OSCE commented that problems included inaccurate voters' lists, and the absence of competence and objectivity among election administration officials. The most serous problem included the excessive control of the process as orchestrated by the ruling party. However, a U.S. state department spokesperson explained that calling the irregularities significant would be an overstatement.[256] The U.S. state department representative agreed with the OSCE who stated, "inaccuracies in the voters' list lessened voter confidence in an election process that may have disenfranchised a large number of otherwise eligible voters." A representative from the International Republican Institute, a Washington based organization, argued that

---

254   Maka Lomadze, "They are full of pictures and nice visuals, but the main thing is that Anna Arzanova, "Tuesday on Mzera. Zhvania defends his bloc." *The Messenger* (4 September 2003):5.they don't say what they actually will do." *Ibid.,* 12.

255   Nato Rostashvili, "Georgian glass of Democracy remains only half full." *Daily Georgian Times* (4 November 2003):1.

256   Allison Ekberg, "U.S. State Department backs OSCE statement." *The Messenger* (5 November 2003):1.

more substantial evidence will be forthcoming when the protocol form reflecting the vote tally, "a key to transparency" is published. Conversely, the IRI spokesperson explicated: "on the positive side, we also note that the OSCE recognized that certain aspects of the election demonstrated significant progress, notably the passage of the Unified Election Code and the transparency of the new Central Election Commission." Finally, the U.S. state department called on all parties and candidates to refrain from violence or the threat of violence as the tabulation of results continued. Observers also noted that inaccurate or manipulated voter lists have been problematic in Georgia since the first parliamentary election in 1999. This explains the Georgian's government endorsement and creation of an electronic database of registered voters. However, as noted previously, even as early as September, an audit of the new lists revealed serious flaws. The exclusion of whole city blocks from the database resulted in the utilization of handwritten voter lists across a variety of precincts. Also described as problematic included the insufficient training provided for election commissioners. Positive comments made by the observers included noting the diligent work of Election commissions in conducting accurate vote counting procedures. Furthermore, the new unified electoral code also was viewed positively. However, in a disparate version of events, exit polls illustrated two different sets of results.[257] One exit poll conducted by the Georgian Fair Election NGO reported that the political opposition won the race, while a second Georgian NGO (Trustworthy Elections and the Georgian Times Media Holding companies) argued that the government bloc won the race. Preliminary data published by the Central Election Committee indicated that the government bloc led (President *Shevardnadze's* party) at twenty-seven percent while *Saakashvili's* National Party was second at twenty-five percent followed by the Labor Party at eighteen percent, the Union for Democratic Revival at eleven percent, the *Burjanadze* Democrats at ten percent and the New Rights Party Bloc at nine percent. The Georgian Fair Elections NGO articulated that the Nationalist Party led at twenty-six percent, with the Party for the New Georgia garnering almost nineteen percent. The Labor Party collected seventeen percent of the

---

257   Lali Javakhia. "Exit polls showing mutually exclusive results." *Daily Georgian Times.* (4 November 2003):3.

vote with the *Burjanadze* Democrats at ten percent, the Revival Union at eight percent, New Rights at almost eight percent, and the Industry Saves Georgia, at five percent. The Fair Election Observers' parallel count illustrates a completely different outcome compared to the CEC count. The CEC's count reflected that the government block won with twenty-seven percent of the vote. The head of the Fair Election NGO *Zurab Chiaberashvili*, explained: "The elections were not fair and democratic." *Chiaberashvili* reported that one observer in *Ninostminda* was assaulted and hospitalized in critical condition the day before the election. Furthermore, he argued that more than twenty percent of the polling stations violated standardized voting procedures while fraudulent voting might have been as high as thirty-eight percent. His organization subsequently launched hundreds of appeals with the Central Election Commission. Another article claims the organization filed several lawsuits in a variety of regional courts accusing the government of producing fraudulent election results.[258] *Chiaberashvili* reported that the accuracy rate of the voting tabulations was about two percent, implying that votes in *Adjara* were fabricated. A later article indicated that opposition parties demanded the annulment of all the results because of the extent of the fraud.[259]

One IOM observer reported that while four hundred and fifty International observers from forty-three countries observed the elections, they characterized this election as worse than the previous parliamentary election.[260] Conversely, President *Shevardnadze* exclaimed in his regular radio broadcast that "these elections were rather free, fair and transparent than in previous elections in the Georgian history and the elections were held and this is most important." Once again, the President's perspective seems somewhat convoluted. His perspective belies the report of the Director of the International Security and Energy program, who observed that *Qutaisi* election ballots failed to be delivered until two o'clock in the afternoon preventing many people from voting. Voters in *Qutaisi* protested claiming that thousands of

---

258   N.N., "Nongovernmental organization filed cases at Different Regional Courts of Georgia." *The Georgian Times International Edition* (10 November 2003):6.
259   *Ibid.*

false ballots were dropped into four of the ballot boxes. The *Burjanadze's* Democrats also claim that at one polling station only three hundred three hundred voters were registered, while fifteen hundred marked ballots were removed from the voting boxes. Another member of the Georgia NGO fair election observers also explained that a variety of violent incidents transpired across Georgia each aimed at systematic organized voter intimidation. For example, while shots were fired at a Nationalist Party driver, he escaped unharmed. An OSCE observer told reporters that he had not seen this type of voting irregularity in any other nation.[261] A second International Observer commented that she watched people standing in line for hours to vote and some of them were never able to because their names were missing from the voting list. In a separate article, the President of the OSCE Parliamentary assembly stated: "We all yesterday witnessed some quite spectacular failures of the electoral administration."[262] In a meeting between *Nino Burjanadze* and the President of the OSCE Parliamentary Assembly, Bruce George, one observer disclosed that there were so many election violations in Georgia, it failed to mirror a democratic society.[263] Furthermore, she reported observing police at polling stations intimidating people. Interestingly, although claims of election violations are prolific, OSCE's offered an analysis of early results illustrating that the government bloc received only 23.9% of the vote, a loss of almost 20 percent since the 1999 parliamentary elections. The Daily Georgian Times quoted an election observer from the Georgian Young Lawyers Association who observed election processes in the autonomous region of *Adjara* and described the following election violations: [264]

---

260   Rusudan Kbilashvili, "Authorities are to Blame Georgia Failed to keep up with democracy with all the money we gave to help." *Georgian Times* (4 November 2003):1.

261   N.N., "OSCE observer refuses to leave Rustavi District Commission." Rustavi-2 online news http://www.rustavi-2.com.ge/view.php?id=5744 (as of 5 November 2003).

262   Tbilisi AFP, "OSCE condemns marred Georgian parliamentary poll." *Daily Georgian Times* (4 November 2003):6.

263   N.N., "OSCE Parliamentary Assembly President meets with Burjanadze." *The Messenger News in Brief* (5 November 2003):4.

264   N.N., "Fair Elections NGO Stands for the Protection of Observers' Rights." *The Daily Georgian Times* (7 November 7 2003):2.

a. Election commission members were keeping empty ballots under the registration journal.

b. One person going to vote was observed carrying several empty ballots in his pocket. The person appeared to be a local police officer.

c. One observer was attacked by several persons at the polling station while trying to maintain appropriate election observation procedures.

At some point, the observer notified the Fair Elections NGO who dispatched additional observers to verify his report. Shortly after this incident, the GYLA removed him as an observer. Later this observer was arrested in the city of *Kobuleti* for "distracting election procedures at the polling station," a criminal violation. Later the charge changed to hooliganism committed by using an object as a weapon (identified later as his backpack), as well as resisting police. The young man is being held for three months in pre-trial detention. Although observers remain prohibited from trying to stop election violations, it is unknown if his arrest reflects his behavior or if was an attempt to stop his reporting of election violations. Several different versions of the incident were described acrross a variety of newspaper reports primarily claims that he was behaving illegally.[265] The observer was later convicted and sentenced to three months in prison.

As promulgated by opposition parties' rhetoric and as feared by the government, threats of a forthcoming public protest against the government are forthcoming.[266] Political opponents of President *Shevardnadze* accused the government of rigging the vote and claim that their supporters are prepared to march on government offices in protest. Troops were placed on high alert by the government in anticipation of post-election civil unrest. Meanwhile, the Central Election Commission reported that only twenty percent of the total votes thus far counted indicate that the government block leads with 28.8 percent of the vote. They explain that the Nationalist movement is in second place at 23.5 percent. However, these figures contrast sharply with data released by a U.S. polling firm reporting that *Saakashvili's* nationalist

---

265   N.N., "Member of GYLA arrested in Adjara." *The Georgian Times International Edition* (10 November 2003):6.

266   Tbilisi AFP, "Initial Results give Pro-Government bloc lead in disputed Georgian Vote." *Daily Georgian Times* (4 November 2003):6.

party led with the pro-government party in second place. *Saakashvili* explains, "the government has lost," but once again the journalist reminds readers that that *Saakashvili* hopes to succeed *Shevardnadze* as President. *Saakashvili* is also quoted as stating: "Their support was at a miserable level and now they are trying to falsify the results using illegal means…I have addressed the people and called on them to defend their rights."[267] By all appearances, this article seems supportive of *Saakashvili's* call to protest, as readers are reminded about the inefficienct state of the economy, the feeble state of the country's electricity system and the governments' waning popularity. The writer also explains that some polling stations failed to open at all and as previous articles indicated, voters were unable to vote because their names were missing from the voter registration lists. Even *Saakashvili* told reporters that he could not vote as his name was missing from his precinct list. Nevertheless, the current Chairperson of the Central Election Commission reported that although the voting was badly organized, she believed that the elections should be considered valid…."I've seen worse elections," she stated. A noted Georgian political Scientist, *Ghia Nodia*, explained that such election results portend poorly for *Shevardnadze's* government. Moreover, the journalist notes that these problems could endanger western foreign aid.

In a detailed report of the election problems, one article reveals that over twenty persons broke into ballot boxes at one polling place and assaulted members of the election committee.[268] Similarly, at another polling location in *Rustavi,* Election officials illegally exchanged job positions. Additionally voters' registration lists' were not posted as required. Voting registrations lists were inaccurate, armed individuals appeared at some polling stations, and in other locations, members of oppositional parties broke into district election commission offices and pressured election chairpersons to manipulate the vote. While the Chairperson of the Central Election Committee used several different voters' lists in an attempt to ensure all voters were able to vote, posting different voters' lists across a variety of locations is inappro-

---

267   *Ibid.*
268   N.N., "Effort to Rig Exit Polls." Rustavi-2 on line news http://www.rustavi-2.com.ge/view.php?id=5707 (as of 2 November 2003); "Polling Station Assaulted in Rustavi." *Ibid.,* http://www.rustavi-2.com.ge/view.php?id=5702 (as of 2 November 2003).

priate.[269] The Chairperson explained that the new names originated from the computerized list created by the International Fund of Election Systems, while the first list was hand written and included previously omitted names. Journalists reported that she explained while marginal violations occurred, the voting procedures were not problematic. Apparently, the political opposition also tried to submit a voters' list but the Chairperson rejected it. Other allegations were that the Chairperson of the Central Election Commission ignored voters' lists containing supporters of opposition party members.[270] Three hours prior to the termination of voting, the Chairperson issued a statement informing voters that if their names were missing from voter registration lists that they should appeal to the District Election Commission to restore their voting rights.[271] Critics stated that such a change was pointless with only three hours remaining in the election. In a related story, the Minister of Security briefed the press informing Georgians that near the *Jvari* Monastery in *Mtskheta*, seventy-five hand shells, nine antitank shells, machine gun ammunition, and twenty-two kilograms of explosives were found.[272] The Minister believes that these weapons were a part of a planned coup to overthrow the President.

In describing another attempt to impede the democratic process, one reporter wrote that Russian Peacekeepers blocked several busses traveling from *Gali* to *Zugdidi* where passengers planned to vote outside their legal precinct.[273] This area is located in the autonomous region of *Abkhazia*. A *Rustavi* 2 headline revealed that the U.S. polling firm, Global Strategy Group, announced that *Saakashvili's* national movement received 20.8% of the votes, the government bloc for the new Georgia received 12.9%, Labor Party, 12.8%, *Burjanadze* Democrats, 7.6%, New Rights 6% and New Industry

---

269   N.N., "CEC Head Accused of Law Violation." *Ibid.,* http://www.rustavi-2.com.ge/view.php?id=5706 (as of 2 November 2003).

270   Ninidze, "Politics: Reflections of the last week."

271   N.N., "New Decision of CEC." *Ibid.,* http://www.rustavi-2.com.ge/view.php?id=5712 (as of 2 November 2003).

272   N.N., "Special Briefing at the Ministry of Security." *Rustiavi-2 on line news In Brief.* http://www.rustavi-2.com.ge/view.php?id=57 (as of 2 November 2003).

273   N.N., "Buses were Blocked at the Checkpoint Number 305 of the Russian Peacekeeping Forces." *Rustiavi-2 On Line News.* http://www.rustavi-2.com.ge/view.php?id=5709 (as of 2 November 2003).

2.8%.[274] In a subsequent article, the parallel count conducted by the Fair Election Georgian NGO revealed that, *Saakashvili's* National Movement received 26.6%, the government block 18.92%, the Labor Party 17.36, the *Burjanadze* Democrats 10.15%, the Democratic Revival Union 8.13%, the New Rights Party 7.99%, and the Industry will save Georgia 5.2%.[275] Conversely, the Central Election Commission's preliminary count reveals the following: Government block 31 %, the Nationalist Party 27%, the Labor Party 19%, the *Burjanadze* Democrats 12%, the New Rights, 11%.[276] Clearly, one or all of these sets of computations are incorrect or represent indicators of the presence of voting fraud.

On November fifth following the release of these initial disparate voting results, a large-scale demonstration began at Freedom Square in front of the *Tbilisi* City Hall. The primary organizers of the demonstration were the opposition party leaders.[277] These leaders exclaimed that the current party's time in office was over, and that the fraudulent results were unacceptable. *Mikhail Saakashvili* reportedly encouraged demonstrators to move peacefully to the Central Election Commission's office and continue protesting there. Police officers stood nearby to prevent violence. The *Burjanadze* Democrats explained that they would be joining the Nationalist party in peacefully demonstrating in another rally scheduled to begin on November eighth. Then both parties will call for new parliamentary elections and plan to accuse the government of usurping the election results.[278]

In another newspaper article, the *Burjanadze* Democrats were described as having previously joined forces with the Nationalist party back in November.[279] Accurately clarifying the time of the unification of these parties may lead voters to completely different conclusions about the parties' mo-

---

274   N.N., "Results of Exit Polls." *Ibid.,* http://www.rustavi-2.com.ge/view.php?id=5714 (as of 2 November 2003).

275   N.N., "Results of Parallel Count Conducted by Fair Elections NGO." *Ibid.,* http://www.rustavi-2.com.ge/view.php?id=5717 (as of 2 November 2003).

276   N.N., "Preliminary Results of CEC." *Ibid.,* http://www.rustavi-2.com.ge/view.php?id=5715 (as of 2 November 2003).

277   N.N., "Large-Scale Protest demonstration in front of Tbilisi City Assembly." *Ibid.,* http://www.rustavi-2.com.ge/view.php?id=5747 (as of 5 November 2003).

278   N.N., "Surprise Decision of the Burjanadze-Democrats." *Ibid.,* http://www.rustavi-2.com.ge/view.php?id=5771 (as of 7 November 2003).

279   Allison Ekberg, "Georgians take to the Streets." *The Messenger-Special Election Edition* (5 November 2003):1.

tives, unfortunately, the Georgian media are not able to provide any precision in such cases. At this time, the opposition leaders called on all Georgians to join the rallies in protest of voter fraud in the parliamentary election. In two other articles, *Saakashvili* reportedly shouted, "if they [*Shevardnadze*] wanted a revolution, they would get one."[280] While one writer describes the crowd that *Saakasvhili* spoke to as ten thousand strong, another article indicates that the crowd only numbered about two thousand.[281] Again separating fact from fiction remains a challenge that the newspaper writers and editors are unable to meet. *Saakashvili* called on the President and the government to acknowledge the real winners of the election, the Nationalist Party, or leave their positions. *Saakashvili* also retorted, "any opposition which does not join us will be considered to be on the side of the government." This rallying cry was once the standard response to opposition coming from the Communist party during the Soviet period. Of course, U.S. President George Bush has also relied on this rhetoric in garnering support for his war on terror. Such language makes a middle of the road perspective nearly impossible, which is exactly what the messengers usually want. Opposition politicians including both *Nino Burjandaze* as well as *Zurab Zhvania* spoke to Georgians at the Philharmonic Center on the evening of 4 November. *Zhvania* is quoted as stating: "We will give up our votes for nothing, and we shall defend the achievement of the Georgian people through peaceful means."[282] *Zhvania* also promised that the opposition would boycott the next Parliament if the correct results were not published. Following the speeches, supporters of the *Burjanadze*-Democrats first marched down *Rustaveli* Avenue to the front of the Parliament building where *Saakashvili* and supporters of the Nationalist party joined them. University students belonging to *Kmara* were also present. *Kmara* remains a staunch supporter of *Saakashvili* who has actively protested against the government since early 2003. Although the government mobilized law enforcement personnel and stationed them in front of the Parliament, police were described as making no attempt to interfere with or break up the demonstration. *Saakashvili, Burjanadze*, and *Jumber Patiashvili* (Unity Party) demanded that the government either present fair and accurate

---

280   Ninidze, "Politics reflections of the last week."
281   *Ibid.*

results of the election or face mass demonstrations across the country. *Saakashvili* told protesters that he had information that the government made a deal with *Adjara* to falsify the election results. Another article warns the government to be cautious in any attempt to arrest leaders of the opposition as such actions may create additional problems. In a negative report on the Nationalists, one journalist writes that prior to initial compilation of the election results, members of the Nationalist party attempted to illegally enter the *Gori* election office, allegedly to prevent voter fraud. Windows were broken during the incident and one member of the Nationalist Party was seriously injured. However, Nationalist party members accused policemen of causing the injury. Additionally, the writer insinuates that *Saakashvili* planned one of the previous attempts to assassinate President *Shevardnadze* arguing that Russian-oligarchs supported him. Obviously only a minority of Georgian journalists appear to have a negative perception of *Saakashvili*. Moreover, journalists are making it quite clear that the election issue is far from resolved. One writer reports *Zhvania*'s claim that a coup is forthcoming. *Zhvania* explained, "We do not intent to submit to a government....that falsifies the election results in its favor."[283]

On November 8th, the CEC announced the tentative election results minus 15 precincts.[284] This data reflected that the Democratic Revival Union, the party representing the government currently in power, won the election (after including votes from *Adjara*). They explained that 1, 559, 659 Georgians voted although eligible voters numbered 2,506, 388. Over thirty-five thousand votes were invalidated. After tabulating votes for each party and dividing by the total number of voters minus the invalid votes, again the percentages provided do not sum to one hundred percent. The error might be an editorial mistake or it could reflect that as the protestors have argued, the CEC has manipulated the results. The CEC released the following details: Democratic Revival Union, 21%, Government bloc for new Georgia, 21%, Nationalist Party, 19%, Labor Party, 12%, Burjanadze Democrats, 8%, New Rights, 7% and Industry will Save Georgia, 5%. Later the same day *Rustavi*-2

---

282   Ekberg, "Georgians take to the Streets."
283   Ninidze, "Politics reflections of the last week."
284   N.N., "Latest Data Released by CEC." *Rustavi-2 On Line News* http://www.rustavi-2.com.ge/view.php?id=5772 (as of 8 November 2003).

reported that the *Burjanadze* Democrats and their supporters met in the Philharmonic Concert Hall where they told the audience that as of November 7th they are boycotting the election results.[285] The audience and other supporters then moved from the Philharmonic to Freedom Square to join the leaders of the National Movement who continued to protest in front of the parliament building. *Rustavi-2*'s on line news service announced that the protest grew to include a group in front of the *Tbilisi* City Assembly located just a short distance down the street from the Parliament.[286] As mentioned previously this headline purports that citizens from different regions of the country as well as *Tbilisi* State University students from the "Student Committee of Protection of the Votes" were present.

As the protests continued, some writers reported that an unnamed NGO in Russia presented a plan to Putin for the "federalization of Georgia.[287] This allegation occurs in the context of several recent meetings between President *Shevardnadze* and President Putin. This information exacerbates Georgian mistrust and fear of the government's role in the voting irregularities and encourages support for the growing protest movement. Georgians appear to fear that violence will erupt at any moment as it did in 1989 during what has become known as the Bloody Sunday incident when Russian soldiers killed Georgian protestors. Other Georgians fear another civil war. As the protests continued, journalists tried to surmise the 'real reasons' for the movement. One writer proposes that there is a relationship between the protests and the sale of the American electricity company to the Russian company. This writer anticipates that the outcome will result in a Russian mandate to protect Georgians from themselves. The writer argues that the U.S. will not be able to assist Georgians in resisting Russian domination, just as they have been unable to provide safety in Afghanistan or Iraq. Again, these suppositions may only result in increasing Georgians' angst rather than sup-

---

285   N.N., "Burjanadze-Democrats meets their Supporters Tbilisi Ph"Foreign Press About Georgia ilharmonic Concert Hall." *Ibid.,* http://www.Rustavi2.com/ ge/print.php?id=5733 (as of 8 November 2003).

286   N.N., "Large Scale protest demonstration in front of Tbilisi City Assembly." *Ibid.*; "Foreign Press About Georgia http://www.rustavi-2.com.ge/view.php?id=5774 (as of 8 November 2003).

287   N.N., "Divide and Conquer-Such Discussions do not contribute to improving Georgian-Russian relations." *The Messenger. Special Election Edition* (5 November 2003):3.

porting free speech and the right to peacefully assembly. Subsequently, the Ministry of Georgian Affairs extended the current "state of emergency" until the new Parliament meets in its first session.[288] This state of emergency exists, reports the Deputy Minister, only because of the threats made by some politicians, the on-going protests, and the possibility that the outcome of these activities may de-stabilize the current government. Conversely, a separate article claims that the declaration of the state of emergency occurred several days before the polls opened. Moreover, the writer argues that government officials had been prepared for this possibility at least a month prior to the election.[289]

Two days later the leader of the pro-government party accused *Shevardnadze* of making a covert deal with the *Burjanadze* Democrats to permit them to hold parliamentary seats although they failed to reach the seven percent threshold.[290] *Burjanadze* tried to avoid responding to the accusation by simply stating that she will maintain her membership as an MP until the President removes her. Georgian college students studying abroad are reportedly equally frustrated with the recent fraudulent elections and a number of them wrote a letter to the Chairperson of the Central Election Commission asking her to annul the election results.[291] These students chastised the Student members of "Enough or *Kmara*" for associating themselves with the government opposition block and suggested they wait until next year when the regularly scheduled Presidential Election will result in S*hevardnadze's* political retirement. These non-*Kmara* students believe all these events have been staged and that *Zhvania* and *Saakashvili* are not real Georgians because they are financially supported by some other unnamed source. These students also expressed concerns about that the outcome of all the protests will result in violence. My observations, as the protests and demonstrations continued, were that Georgian perceptions across the country seemed to fall into several camps with one these reflected in the above students' percep-

288   N.N., "Ministry of Internal Affairs extends "state of emergency regime." *Ibid.,* 4.

289   N.N., "Kmara! Holds protest to protect votes."*Ibid.*

290   Tamara Melkadze, "Irina Sarishvili Chanturia withdraws from government-backed block." *Daily Georgian Times* (7 November 2003):1, 3.

291   Rusudan Kbilashvili, "Georgian Students vs. CEC "Why should we stand under the flag of irritating Saakashvili, Armenian Zhvania or the Liberty Institute supporting Jehovah's Witnesses?" *Daily Georgian Times* (7 November 2003):4.

tions. The other included the notion of waiting until *Shevardnadze's* term in office expires next year, then replace him with someone better. Another group seemed to view *Saakashvili* as a mythical hero who would rescue Georgia from itself and this seemed particularly prevalent among younger Georgians. The second perspective included Georgians frightened by the protests. They felt certain that the government would resort to violence to suppress the demonstrations. Finally, another common perception of Georgians seemed to be that this was a pre-planned protest and that this somehow made it seem artificial. However, what remained absent was any discussion of an alternate solution to deal with the fraudulent elections. Typically, discussions simply centered on the protest and the government's response with considerably fewer concerns about election fraud. Several days later, the theme of the protests transformed and the goal was no longer about voicing opposition to a fraudulent election but rather the overthrow of the current government or at the very least *Shevardnadze's* resignation.[292]

In response to the new objective, the Security Minister of Georgia told reporters that he would contain any attempted coup. Meanwhile in *Gori* the Nationalist movement (referred to here as the radical opposition) clashed with police resulting in one injured Nationalist party member. Moreover, *Saakashvili* was accused of killing a policeman during the incident. The story is that *Saakashvili* struck a police officer stationed nearby to maintain order. Allegedly, the police officer "felt insulted" and subsequently had a heart attack and died. The leader of the pro-*Shevardnadze* block accused *Saakashvili* of murder. *Saakashvili* dismissed the allegations, while acknowledging that the man died after the incident. While it remains unclear how relevant such an accident may or may not be with regard to *Saakashvili's* political future, clearly *Shevardnadze's* administration used the outcome to paint *Saakashvili* as a criminal. As the protests continued, some writers reflected on the general apathy of voters prior to the election and these same voters' lack of faith in *Saakashvili*.

In an interview with two women IDPs, one from *Abkhazia* and another from *Ossetia*, both reported having little faith in the political system and thus

---

292   Ninidze, "Politics: Reflections of the last week."

saw no reason to cast their ballots on November second. [293] One woman even explained that she tried to meet with *Saakashvili* on several occasions over the last four months but he would only agree to a meeting with her if she were a part of a group and if media representatives were present. She indicates that she cannot talk about everything she has lost in front of such a large group as it is simply too painful. Both women disclosed that they were living in poor conditions in the Hotels where they were placed over thirteen years ago. While the younger one does not want to return to *Ossetia* because she grew up here in *Tbilisi*, the older woman wants very much to return to *Abkhazia* where her sons who fought in the civil war remain buried. This issue is one of the most heart-wrenching subjects in Georgia, IDPs and their living conditions, clearly substandard for anyone living in a democratic country. However, this dilemma remains typical around the world. Globally the number of refugees and IDPS currently stands at seventeen million people. They live in squalid conditions and are often among the poorest people in the world. Ironically, the poorest people in Western democratic nation states also live in similarly substandard conditions.[294]

The Media continues to foment suspicion and mistrust in an article reporting a Russian TV station's misquote of the Secretary General of NATO who they indicated that Georgia would never be ready to become a full member of the alliance.[295] Russia's alleged statement about Georgia's future in NATO would not be an unusual dance to engage in given Georgia's current political instability. A similar article appeared in another major newspaper explicating: "Misinformation provided by Russian TV Station."[296] This more thorough piece makes it evident that the Secretary General was discussing all countries seeking membership in NATO when he explained that NATO's demands for all candidate countries are stringent. The paper then quotes someone they call a political expert, *Ramaz Klimiashvili*, who reports "NATO is a

---

293   Lali Javakhia, "IDPS and elections Why IDPs were excluded from the elections?" *The Georgian Times International Edition* (10 November 2003): 9.

294   United Nations High Commissioner for Refugees.

295   N.N., "NATO Secretary Gender deems it impossible for Georgia to join alliance in near future." Rustavi-2 On Line News
http://www.rustavi2.com.ge/print.php?id=5821(as of 13 November 2003).

296   Kate Bojgua, "Misinformation provided by Russian TV Station Georgia Has no Chance to Access the NATO." *Daily Georgian Times* (14 November 2003):1, 3.

is a high profile organization and nobody will allow us to access this institution with our shameful economy and elections!"[297] *Klimiashvili* adds that when *Shevardnadze* promised that Georgia would become a member of NATO by 2005, he was only politically posturing for his party's future. The same day a group of National Movement protesters broke through a police cordon around the city's administration building and began a hunger strike in the town of *Zugdidi* demanding the unconditional resignation of President *Shevardnadze* as well as punishment for those responsible for the fraudulent election.[298] Simultaneously, *Rustavi-2* reported that "several" members of the National Movement also began a hunger strike in front of the state Chancellery building in *Tbilisi* but the Police forced them to leave.[299] Police were accused of behaving aggressively towards journalists covering the incident although no further explanation is offered. *Saakashvili* continued to call upon Georgian citizens to join others in front of the Parliament in another rally beginning on November 14th to demonstrate against the fraudulent parliamentary election.[300] However, there is no mention here that *Saakashvili* has demanded the resignation of the President. Rather opposition leaders state that the rally will continue until the government offers a concrete solution to the problem. The next day a similar headline discussed the rally and made it clear that the primary demand of the opposition was President *Sheveradnadze's* resignation. *Saakashvili also stated that* was it was not necessary to discuss the matter any further.[301] The protest continued to gain momentum over the next several days as more people joined the demonstrators. Over the course of the next several days from my office on *Chavchavadze* Avenue, I observed several large groups of people waving the Nationalist Party flag and shouting slogans in Georgian marching down the main street in *Tbilisi* headed toward the Parliament building located just a few miles away. As mentioned previ-

---

297   *Ibid.*, 3.
298   N.N., "Nationals begin hunger vigil in Zugdidi." Rustavi-2 Online News http://www.rsutavi2.com.ge/print.php?id=5822 (as of 13 November 2003).
299   N.N., "Police used force against National Movement members in front of State Chancellery." *Ibid.*, http://www.rustavi2.com.ge/print.php?id=5819 (as of 13 November 2003).
300   N.N., "Saakashvili calls on public to take part in a massive rally." *Ibid.*, http://www.rustavi2.com.ge/print.php?id=5820 (as of 13 November 2003).
301   N.N., "Opposition holds grand rally." *Ibid.*, http://www.rustavi2.comget/print.php?id-5831 (as of 14 November 2003).

ously, Georgians either seemed to be very excited about the prospects for change or dreadfully concerned about another civil war. Similarly, President *Shevardnadze* expressed these concerns about the growing possibility of another war. Subsequently, he told the opposition leader, *Saakashvili* that he would sit down and talk with him in order to prevent such an event. However, *Shevardnadze* explained that *Saakashvili's* call for his resignation was unacceptable and radical.[302] *Sheveradnadze* also stated that he would include *Zhvania* and *Nino Burjanadze* in such a meeting. While *Zurab Zhvania* echoed the President's sentiments, no talks were scheduled. While these symbolic gestures for a dialogue from the government transpired, *Shevardnadze* placed law enforcement agencies and the military on alert. Subsequently, a variety of military personnel welding guns appeared in the city. Now I was becoming concerned, Civic Education Project personnel informed the Visiting Fellows that if violence ensued we would be transferred to another country, safe from harm.

Meanwhile in *Telavi*, National Movement demonstrations continued and protesters called for the resignation of the local administrator there, *Medea Mezrishvili*.[303] Subsequently, *Mezrishvili* resigned, however, the state Chancellery acknowledged that his resignation and the resignation of one other Governor were the result of issues unrelated to the election, specifically, budget mismanagement. As these resignations began, and the demands for *Shevardnadze's* retirement continued, the CEC met and abolished the accreditation of the broadcasting company *Rustavi-2*.[304] *Rustavi-2* was the sole television station responsible for consistently broadcasting the protests live for all Georgians. Needless-to-say a government agency in charge of voter's registration and voting tabulation does not have the authority to shut down a major news network, coincidently the same network responsible for calling attention to public protests by opposition party leaders. The report further delineates that the chair of the CEC, *Nana Devdariani* called for this reactionary move after *Kmara members* appeared on *Rustavi-2* and made powerful anti-

---

302   N.N., "President calls upon Opposition Leaders to Compromise." *Ibid.*, http://www.rustavi2.com.ge/print.php?id=5830 (as of 14 November 2003).
303   N.N., "Telavi Administration Head Resigned." *Ibid.*; "Foreign Press About Georgia http://www.rustavi2.com.ge/print.php?id=5834 (as of 14 November 2003).

CEC statements. Of course, opposition parties reported that they were against this CEC decision. The political culture and the current government perceive free speech, protests, and government criticism as illegitimate particularly when it is a critique of the status quo. *Rustavi-2* subsequently filed a civil case against the CEC. Interestingly, later the court refused to hear their case against the CEC because the CEC never made such a ruling. Shortly thereafter, *Rustavi-2* dropped the case.[305] It remains unclear if the CEC originally simply threatened to remove *Rustavi-2*'s accreditation or if such statements were made by other administrative officials. In either case, the misleading story could have lead to serious violence. Of course, the entire story may have been socially constructed in order to energize the opposition and protest movement.

Rumors began to circulate that the protests and the political opposition received funding from foreigners. One journalist began exploring this possibility in an effort to make sense of the political instability. The journalist revealed that George Soros' organization was funding the political activism of *Kmara* as the demonstrators began their sixth day of protests with the opposition parties.[306] A *Kmara* spokesperson did not refute that their organization received outside funding, but the spokesperson provided no specific details. The *Kmara* member also claimed that they had the support of many students at *Tbilisi* State University. However, another student leader reports that this is not accurate and that many students see *Kmara* as too partisan for their own tastes; that is too supportive of the Nationalists. Yet the *Kmara* student representative denied that they support any specific party rather that they are trying to change the current administration and that they demand release of the actual figures from the November election. However, the truth is that *Kmara*'s funding comes from the Liberty Institute, one of George Soros' organizations'. I discovered this one day when I visited the *Kmara* student headquarters. A student leader took me to their parent organization's office, the Liberty Institute. They explained that their funding came from Soros. *Koka*

---

304   N.N. "CEC vs. Rustavi-2." *Ibid.*, http://www.rustavi2.com.ge/print.php?id=5826 (as of 14 November 2003).

305   N.N., "Rustavi-2 removes appeal in court." *Ibid.*, http://www.rustavi2.com.ge/print.php?id=5855 (as of 18 November 2003).

Kvinikadze, head of the Youth Organization called the *Agordzineba*, told the newspaper reporter that only *Rustavi* 2's coverage of *Saakashvili* led to the growing crowds of demonstrators. Furthermore, he claimed that rallies were performances staged for the public. Moreover, he explained that most Georgian students were not involved in the protests. Apparently, the dominant view emerging here is that unless protests are spontaneous they are not genuine. While it is difficult to disentangle fiction from reality here, I initially believed that the planned nature of the protests was what primarily bothered some Georgians. However, later it seemed more likely that Georgians perceived that it was the pre-ordained objective to place power in the hands of one particular group of people after eliminating *Shevardnadze*. This was many Georgian's primary concern. This is revealed in *Kvinikadze's* next statement that *Saakashvili's* real motive for fighting against the government is so that he can become the next President. *Kvinikadze* expresses the concern of many Georgians who I knew, that these events could culminate in bloodshed. This writer also claims to have information that George Soros provided the *Kmara* group with two million dollars on October 10th to begin the demonstration. While some might see Soros as a good Samaritan who supports democratic development, others could more easily construct his image as a neo-imperialist, trying to control or manipulate events to his liking. This is an extremely important question to ask. When does aid become imperialism or rather how can we identify the boundaries of such assistance before it becomes transformed into imperialism? Similarly, much western assistance is provided in the name of promoting democracy or the free market. Yet both can clearly become forms of neo-imperialism. What remains most significant here is that sometimes such assistance can become interference or even more likely just an attempt to weld more control over a less powerful nation-state.

The above version of events provided by the *Daily Georgian Times* does not sing the praises of *Saakashvili* or the opposition movement, and fails to support the current administration. However, it does try to provide to some degree of critical coverage, an extremely important objective in a de-

---

306   Tamuna Melkadze, "This rally costs 2 million U.S. Dollars." *The Daily Georgian Times* (14 November 2003):1, 4.

mocracy. Another article also questions the motives of the Open Society Institute and George Soros in the growing protest after information reveals that
Georgia's Open Society Institute is filling a civil law suit against the Georgian
Government. The suit was filed against the administration for failing to release its previously paid VAT taxes, as the government is obliged to do for all
registered Georgian NGOs'.[307] Director of the Georgian OSI, *Kakha Lomaia*
reportedly told *the Messenger* that the government owes them six hundred
thousand U.S. dollars and that they are withholding the payment as a form of
political persecution. While previously supportive of George Soros' activities,
President *Shevardnadze* explained to journalists that George Soros is currently funding opposition groups in Georgia who are fighting against his administration. *Shevardnadze* argues that this is none of Soros' business. He
threatened to expel OSI from Georgia if they continued. *Lomaia* claims that it
would be unconstitutional for the President to expel a Georgian NGO. He explains that the OSI is a Georgian organization, staffed by Georgians. This
certainly reflects my experience as I provided several lectures at the OSI offices in *Tbilisi* as well as attended number of lectures and meetings at their
offices. However, it is undeniable that the Open Society Institute is funded by
and affiliated with George Soros. Richard Miles, the U.S. Ambassador to
Georgia, explained that he believed that Soros has accomplished a great
deal for post-Soviet states as they have continued to move toward democracy and market reforms. He also argued that Soros has become a "focal
point of [current Georgian tension] that tension" but that he "hope[s] this
would ease, as the situation becomes more normal."[308] A reprinted article
from the foreign press also stated that the demonstrations and the events
that followed have been a George Soros orchestrated and supported process.[309] In fact, OSI funding sent a *Tbilisi* political activist, *Giga Bokeria* to
Serbia to meet with members of the *Otpor* (Resistance) movement to learn
how they toppled the former Serbian President, *Slobodan Milosevic. Bokeria*,
one of the organizers of the current demonstrations, is the founder of the

307   Mary Makharashvili, "Soros Foundation Sues Georgian Authority Seeks VAT reim-
         bursement." *The Messenger* (19 November 2003):3.
308   *Ibid.*

Liberty Institute (another Soros supported organization) and as mentioned previously Liberty provides financial support to *Kmara*. OSI also paid *Otpor* activists to come to Georgia to provide a three-day seminar for *Kmara* students on how to hold peaceful demonstrations (and revolutions, according to the writer). Interestingly, the Eurasian Institute, a U.S. funded organization also funds the Liberty Institute. Historically, Soros and *Shevardnadze's* relationship predated his *role as* President. Specifically, *Shevardnadze* has known Soros since he was the Soviet Foreign Minister back in the 1980's. In 2000, *Shevardnadze* invited George Soros to Georgia to set up the Open Society Institute aimed at building democracy and civil society. Later in 2000, Soros met *Saakashvili* and praised his efforts as Justice Minister to fight corruption. Subsequently, *Saakashvili's* resigned from the post and Soros' relationship with the President began to deteriorate. Then in 2002, President *Shevardnadze* began complaining about Soros' interference in the political affairs of the country. The writer insinuates that it was shortly thereafter that a raid on the Liberty Institute perpetrated by a group of young people transpired. The result of the attack included the destruction of computers and assaults against several staff members. Following this incident Soros indicated that *Shevardnadze's* administration was not capable of holding democratic parliamentary elections in 2003. The writer quotes Soros: "It is necessary to mobilize civil society in order to assure free and fair elections because there are many forces that are determined to falsify or to prevent the elections being free and fair. This is what we did in Slovakia at the time of [Vladimir] *Meciar*, in Croatia at the time of [Franjo] *Tudjman* and in Yugoslavia at the time of *Milosevic.*"[310] MacKinnon reminds readers that while Soros previously received a warm welcome into post-Soviet societies following the fall of the USSR, more recently, both the Ukraine and Belarus have forced OSI to close. Masked gunman raided the Moscow OSI offices allegedly because of a real estate problem. MacKinnon reports that critics also blamed Soros' market interventions for the 1997 currency crisis in Southeast Asia. It seems that in some instances, Soros' philanthropy may do more harm than good. In

---

309 Mark MacKinnon, "Foreign Press About Georgia, Georgia Revolt Carried the Mark of Soros. From Wednesday's London Globe and Mail." *Daily Georgian Times* (27 November 2003):4.

310 *Ibid.*

1995, OSI provided the start up funds for *Rustavi-2*, whose recent coverage of the demonstrations continues to fuel public sentiment. Furthermore, *Rustavi-2* began a campaign of criticizing the President several years ago by producing a cartoon called "Our Yard" that portrays the President as a "crooked double dealer."[311] This may have led to the *Shevardnadze* administration's previous attempts to close *Rustavi-2* on two different occasions.

As the protests continued against the current administration, *Saakasvhili* insinuated that the government created the increase in bread prices in order to get people off the streets and away from the demonstration.[312] However, the author provides some limited evidence that bread prices were on the rise because of the simple artifact of supply and demand. However, she also insists that *Saakashvili* deceives the people by exploiting this story for his own ends. Another piece discusses the potential harm to foreign economic investments that this political "standoff" may cost.[313] *Shevardnadze* similarly argues that the businesspeople are most interested in the political stability of the country because such unrest hampers the development of the economy. One State Minister agrees explaining that imports have fallen since the beginning of November. Additionally, another minister reports that some freight carriers are re-routing goods to Russia to avoid Georgia. However, the head of the Parliament's budgetary office explained that economically Georgia was in trouble long before the protests. Furthermore, as mentioned previously the Federal budget has been in dire straights for some time because the government failed to collect taxes.

As the demonstrations in front of the Parliament continued, President *Shevardnadze* gave his traditional Monday morning radio broadcast. Subsequently, he held a longer briefing for Georgian and foreign journalists to reiterate that he will not resign before the end of his constitutional term in office.[314] He also announced that on November 18th the CEC is scheduled to

---

311   MacKinnon, "Foreign Press About Georgia."
312   Maia Misheladze, "Bread Price increased artificially to drive you back home - Saakasvhili says to protesters Top Nationalist manipulates bread price fluctuation." *The Daily Georgian Times* (14 November 2003):5.
313   Rusudan Kbilashvili, "Foreign Investors Hope Political Standoff doesn't effect Economy." *Ibid.*, 2.
314   N.N., "President must not Resign before the Ending of the Constitutional Term of Presidency." Rustavi-2 On-Line News http://www.rustavi2.com.ge/print.php?id =5838 (as of 17 November 2003).

release the final tabulation of the Parliamentary votes. Interestingly, *Shevard-nadze* thanked the head of the *Adjara* Autonomous Republic, *Aslan Abash-dize*, for his devotion to Georgia. It seems that the President genuinely seems out of touch with public opinion, particularly with regard to Georgian's negative perceptions about *Abashidze*. Following the President's address, the opposition parties announced that they would begin a new tactic as a part of the demonstration by cutting off access in and out of the capital city by blocking railways, subways, and major streets. Members of the student group *Kmara* will also participate the in the blockade preventing vehicles from enter-ing the major streets leading to the Parliament building. Reporters claim that Georgian Diaspora around the world began similar demonstrations in support of the opposition.[315] On November 18th *Saakashvili* informed demonstrators that *Shevardnadze* ordered military troops from *Adjara* to *Tbilisi*. The Presi-dent also asked the Mayor of *Tbilisi* to permit soldiers to maintain posts in the *Griboedov* Theater near the Parliament. However, the Theater Director re-fused to comply with the Mayor's request.[316] In revealing that the President's plan was to secretly post soldiers in the theater, *Saakashvili* infused the pro-testors with more determination. *Saakashvili* also claimed that these soldiers were the same units called out in *Batumi* during the October pre-election pe-riod who subsequently disrupted the peaceful demonstration of the National Movement. Throughout this period in November as the demonstrations con-tinued, I walked by the Parliament on several occasions and observed armed military or police forces posted nearby. They appeared to be waiting for fur-ther orders. *Saakashvili* exploited this by arguing that the assignment of mili-tary forces to *Tbilisi* occurred because local police refused to control the crowd. On November eighteenth, several thousands of protesters, this time supporters of *Shevardnadze* and *Aslan Abashidze*, arrived at the *Tbilisi* sports stadium, marched to the Philharmonic and then to the Parliament building with the stated goal of "preventing society from developing aggres-

---

315   N.N., "Georgian Diasporas Support Opposition's Demands." *Ibid.,* http://www. rustavi2.com.ge/print.php?id=5837 (as of 17 November 2003).
316   N.N. "Saakashvili's New Allegations against the President." *Ibid.,* http://www.rustavi2.com.ge/print.php?id=5851. (as of 18 November 2003).

sively."[317] This group said that they were protesting against "fascism and extremism" or more succinctly, they were protesting against the protesters.[318] As the counter protest movement began its activities, the government refused to grant permission to *Rustavi-2* journalists to attend the rally. As a result, a physical altercation between party members and journalists followed with each side claiming the other group initiated the confrontation. Later when Revival party pro-government supporters marched down *Rustaveli* Avenue to the Parliament building, the leader of the *Batumi* based party told his supporters to remain at the Parliament and stop *Saakashvili's* group from returning. Other political party members joined the pro-government protesters including "New Georgia" and "Industry Will Save Georgia." They criticized *Rustavi-2*, arguing that their reporting was biased favoring *Saakashvili's* party. During this counter protest, another Revival party representative, *Hamlet Chipashvili*, denied allegations that the government sent 10,000 troops from *Adjara* to *Tbilisi* to occupy the city. Meanwhile *Saakashvili* argued that nobody in the country would forgive the government if they brought soldiers into the city from *Adjara*. Again, while I observed soldiers assembled in one part of *Tbilisi* during the protests, I did not see any evidence that were more than fifty to one hundred soldiers, however, this was only in one specific area on one side of the Parliament, and I don't know if they were from *Adjara* or from Georgia.

The United States Deputy Assistant Secretary of State for European and Eurasian Affairs, Mr. Lynn Pascoe came to *Tbilisi* on or about the seventeenth or eighteenth of November, according to the U.S. Embassy, as part of a previously planned three-day tour of the Caucasus.[319] Pascoe held meetings with the President, the State Minister *Avtandil Jorbenadze* as well as with leaders of the opposition parties. After the meeting, *Saakashvili*, *Burjanadze*, and *Zhvania* each reported that the U.S. wanted Georgia to be able

317   Anna Arzanova, "Revival Supporters Protests Protesters." *The Messenger* (19 November 2003):1, 10; Sopho Gorgodze and Allison Ekberg, "Shevardnadze resigns in war of the roses. It takes a hero to keep the peace." *The Messenger* (24 November 2003):1, 9.

318   N.N., "Democratic Revival Union Against Fascism and Extremism." Rustavi-2 On Line News http://www.rustavi2.com.ge/print.php?id=5846 (as of 18 November 2003).

319   Mary Makharashvili, "U.S. Department of State official makes the rounds." *The Messenger* (19 November 2003):1, 5.

to resolve this problem peacefully. Additionally, *Zhvania* stated that Pascoe wanted to hear views from all the political opposition parties' and encouraged suggestions for viable solutions. However, another article also indicated that Pascoe demanded that the Georgian government begin an immediate investigation into all voting irregularities.[320] Pascoe and President *Shevardnadze* scheduled a meeting for the nineteenth with representatives of the Revival, Industrialists, and New Rights parties. Nonetheless, the protests continued and the chair of the CEC again began to make newspaper headlines.

A front-page headline reveals that the Fair Election NGO demanded *Nana Devdariani*, the CEC Chairperson fully disclose all the changes made in the election protocol just prior to the election.[321] The head of the NGO *Jerab Chiaberashvili*, explains that their parallel count of the votes at the precinct level remains incongruent from the official precinct counts provided to the respective districts. *Chiaberashvili* claims that his count reflects a greater total number of voters. Additionally, the numbers he received from the districts fail to coincide with the CEC count at the district level. Apparently, the CEC decided to reduce the number of ballots counted by refusing to count ballots that were marked as "protest ballots." These were ballots that indicated no party preference as well as ballots that were incorrectly marked.[322] This would affect the proportional method of electing parliamentarians i.e., the seven percent method of determining seats for party members. Thus, *Chiaberashvili* demanded that violators of the election code and those who tampered with the votes be criminally prosecuted. Subsequently, his NGO again appealed for a recount across several districts. The court has already ordered the *Mtatsminda* election district to complete a recount where *Chiaberashvili* claims that there were a variety of falsifications. He promises to continue to follow legal and civil remedies to ensure that these irregularities are resolved. He explained that while the simplest resolution might be through protest, he believes using the traditional civil method is more reliable.

---

320   Gorgodze and Ekberg, "Shevardnadze resigns in war of the roses."
321   Christina Tashkevich, "Fair Elections reports tampering with Protocols Promises to Continue Lawsuits." *The Messenger* (19 November 2003):1, 5.
322   Warren Hedges, "CEC decree overturned by court." *The Messenger* (19 November 2003):5.

It seems unclear if he meant for this to be a sarcastic remark or if he supports the current street demonstrations.

A variety of political parties also filed complaints about this CEC decision to omit counting protest or unmarked ballots. These parties include the Labor Party, the National Movement, and the *Burjanadze*-Democrats. Subsequently, the *Tbilisi* District Court ruled in the first complaint filed by the Labor party and abolished the CEC's decision to reduce the number of ballots counted.[323] *Chiaberishvili* also told reporters that other cases were filed against the CEC but he expects that the court may only return the cases to the lower level election commissions for review because the they are unable to annul specific election results. Another allegation from critics included the claim that it would not have been possible to complete voting tabulations as quickly as the government claimed.[324]

On November 21st the National Democratic Institute for International Affairs, a Washington D.C. based organization, issued an evaluative statement about Georgia's election. They indicated that the failure to release the official election results early on triggered the current political crisis. Further, the NDI asked *Shevardnadze* to demonstrate respect for the rights of Georgian citizens and "to act nonviolently."[325] Another article reviewed the details of NDI's statement more carefully.[326] Specifically, "international observers documented significant voter disenfranchisement on election day…, due to large scale problems with the voter registry." [They also noted] "Intimidation, ballot box stuffing, changing of tally sheets and major irregularities."[327] These violations occurred more frequently in *Adjara*, *Kvemo*, and *Kartli*. Current NDI chairperson, former US Secretary of State Madeline Albright, explained: "The consequences of a failed election process in Georgia could undermine peace and stability as well as deny the right of Georgians to freely choose those who would have the authority to govern in their name and in their interests." She also stated that the "Fair Elections (the Georgian NGO) projected results

---

323   *Ibid.*
324   Gorgodze and Ekberg, "Shevardnadze resigns in war of the roses."
325   N.N., "NDI statement surrounding Georgia's Parliamentary Elections." Rustavi-2 On Line News http://www.rustavi2.com.ge/print.php?id=5895 (as of 21 November 2003).
326   N.N., "NDI stands by parallel vote count." *The Messenger* (24 November 2003):9.
327   *Ibid.*

are a sound estimation of the will of those who cast ballots in November" while "NDI does not believe that preliminary official election results accurately reflect the will of those who were able to cast votes."[328]

Critics of the CEC include the Chair who discloses that she is not satisfied with her work or the work of the CEC. Of course, this is contrary to earlier reports indicating that she believed the elections were fair. Now, she discloses that there were many violations and falsifications. However, she also insists that incomparison to previous elections this one was an improvement.[329] While previous articles report that *Shevardnadze* issued a decree declaring a state of emergency even prior to the election, another journalist states that he declared one only recently and that it will expire within three days if not ratified by the Parliament.[330] However, *Mikhail Saakashvili* told reporters that he had spoken directly with representatives of the Georgian military who regardless of a declared state of emergency agreed to refuse to attack peaceful demonstrators.[331] While no earlier reports indicated that the President had ordered any arrests of oppositional leaders, *Saakashvili* made it sound as though he had in a recent TV broadcast. *Saakashvili retorted* that the President's order for his arrest as well as *Burjanadze's* and *Zhvania's*, was nonsense. He explained: "If even one of their members raises a weapon against their brothers and sisters demonstrating in front of the parliament house, they will receive a response from us and they will be strictly judged."[332] Of course, it is also possible that writers are not only confused about when or if any state of emergency was actually declared, but that they are also confusing the differences between threatening arrests and the declaration of a national emergency. This kind of confusion with regard to the facts will only result in increased public anxiety.

---

328   *Ibid.*
329   Anna Arzanova, "Nana Devdariani assesses CEC decision." *The Messenger Press Scanner* (24 November 2003):8.
330   Mary Makharashvili, "48 Hours: State of Emergency needs ratification, clarification." *The Messenger* (24 November 2003):1, 10.
331   *Ibid.*, 10.
332   *Ibid.*

On November 22nd activists from different parts of the Country flooded into *Tbilisi* to join the continuing protests.[333] The demonstrators continued their vigil even as the opening session of the Parliament approached. A constitutional mandate requires that the opening session begin approximately three weeks following the election. *Shevardnadze* and his administration promised it would proceed as scheduled. As the result of continuing commitment of the government to accept the election results as well as the opposition's desire refute the results, the opposition stated it would prevent the parliamentary session from transpiring. One journalist reported that the entrances to the Parliament building were blocked. However, it was unclear if the government facilitated the blockade or the opposition. Reporters also indicated that the demonstrators planned the largest rally for the opening session of the new Parliament. Simultaneously, the government continued to increase the presence of law enforcement personnel surrounding the parliament building. As the political crisis reached its zenith a number of the President's administrative officials began to resign from their posts.[334] On Sunday, the twenty-third of November the Secretary of the National Security Council, *Tedo Japaridze* resigned after expressing frustration with the President for misleading him about the current state of the country. *Japardize* explained that the elections were "marred by serious violations and irregularities" but that he believed that the new parliament should meet briefly if only to reschedule new parliamentary elections. Later on Sunday, *Shevardnadze's* aide on international issues, *Levan Aleksidze* resigned after stating that he believed that the president was responsible for ignoring election violations as committed by the CEC. After leaving the President's side, he reported that he would begin working for *Nino Burjanadze* as her aid. *Alekesidze* also explained that *Shevardnadze* exploited his relationship with *Abashidze* as 'he neglected the will of thousands of Georgian Citizens." Earlier in the week, the Director of the State television, *Zaza Zhengelia*, resigned as did his wife the Minister of Culture, *Sesili Gogberidze*. *Zhengelia* suggested that radicals sur-

---

333 N.N., "Opposition supporters bracing for a big rally on Freedom Square." Rustavi-2 On Line News http://www.rustavi2.com.ge/print.php?id=5896 (as of 22 November 2003).

334 Warren Hedges, "President's political allies jump ship." *The Messenger* (24 November 2003):10.

rounded *Shevardnadze* and these people failed to provide the President with accurate information about the country. He further stated, these radicals kept *Shevardnadze* "in a vacuum."[335] Meanwhile others who remained loyal to the President claimed that the United States was behind the opposition's protests and rallies. *Vakhtang Reheulishvili*, leader of the government block claimed that the International Federation of Election Systems (IFES) who provided technical equipment to computerize voter registration lists was responsible for the improper voters' lists. The IFES reported that it only used the voters' list provided to them by the CEC. The writer also argued that the members of the patronage system initiated by *Shevardnadze* and his cronies are fighting to retain their power. The President's representative to *Imereti, Temur Shashiashvili* addressed the U.S. ambassador on television Saturday night and also accused the U.S. of encouraging the opposition stating, "the U.S. has sold *Shevardnadze.*" In light of the fact that to sell something one must first own it or steal it, the statement insinuates that the United States maintains a long-term lease on the nation of Georgia itself. As mentioned previously, *Shevardnadze* told reporters that he believed foreign interests, as opposed to George Soros, secretly funded the opposition parties and their coup. The President asked his foreign colleagues to re-consider whom they supported.[336] This is reflected in a quote from the U.S. state department claiming that they felt "deeply disappointed in the conduct of the administration of Georgia's November second Parliamentary elections which failed to meet the commitments made by the Georgian leadership to the OSCE and to the United States."[337] This conduct specifically referenced "the delay in the vote count and the manipulation of results by the Central Election Commission". Moreover, the United States expressed concern that the Georgian government had ignored the will of the people.[338] The U.S. state department also made the following paternalistic statement,

> the United States concurs with the OSCE's assessment that inaccuracies in the voter list lessened voter confidence.

---

335   *Ibid.*
336   Gorgodze and Ekberg, "Shevardnadze resigns in war of the roses."
337   N.N., "United States 'deeply disappointed.'" *The Messenger* (24 November 2003):5.
338   *Ibid.*

Some progress was made in increasing transparency, although *Adjara* and *Kvemo Kartli* were clearly sources of massive fraud. The failure to provide an accurate, timely and transparent count of the vote overshadowed the progress made in some other areas...the parallel vote tally conducted by the National Democratic Institute and supported by reputable exit polls, which we believe to the best available gauge of the will of the voters, differs significantly from the results released by the CEC. These discrepancies reveal an extensive manipulation of the count.[339]

The U.S. state department asked (the article utilizes the world "demanded") the Georgian government to conduct a transparent investigation and hold accountable all those individuals responsible for the fraud. The U.S. explained that it continued to support Georgia's security and stability as well as their peace and democracy. The next day the State Department added: "It is closely monitoring the troubling and rapidly developing situation in and round the parliament building in *Tbilisi*, Georgia where there have been confrontations between supporters and opponents of the government" and asks all sides to try to find a compromise "acceptable to all and the interest of Georgia."[340]

On Saturday, representatives of two Army battalions of Georgia's Special Forces units approached leaders of the opposition with flowers, reflecting their support of the alliance against the government. The *Tbilisi* Police Chief announced that he would no longer obey *Shevardnadze*'s orders but that he would cooperate with "acting President of Georgia Nino *Burjanadze*." The Minister of Defense, *David Tevzadze*, similarly told reporters that the government would not actually enforce the President's decree of a state of emergency. However, he also explained the state of emergency might be necessary in order to establish a new leadership while maintaining public safety. The pivotal moment arrived and key players began to change sides as it became more apparent that the end of a long legacy approached.

On November 22nd opposition parties moved from the front of the Parliament into the building just as the President began to open the new ses-

---

339   *Ibid.*
340   *Ibid.*

sion.[341] The opposition's primary objective was to invite the former chair of the Parliament, *Nino Burjanadze*, to stand in as the only viable Chair of the new Parliament.[342] She stated that she was now the acting President of the country, in concert with the constitution. Simultaneously, the opposition occupied several other federal buildings and blocked the state Chancellery building hoping to prevent *Shevardnadze* from entering. *Saakashvili* led the protesters into the parliament (or broke in illegally) to prevent "a new Parliamentary chairperson from being elected." As the President began making his speech to open the Parliament reiterating that he would not resign, *Saakashvili* entered the parliament or as one journalist wrote "stormed in the session hall, rose in hand shouting 'Resign, Run from here!'"[343] Initially, the President, observing *Saakashvili* in the session, retorted: "No matter however they try to impede me I will get my message across to the Parliament." A group of protesters proceeded toward *Shevardnadze* and subsequently his bodyguards led him out of the building. Opposition supporters jumped over tables tossing bottles and papers into the air. Some Revival Party members also entered the parliament and were involved in minor physical altercations with Nationalist Party members. *Saakashvili* then declared the parliament invalid and announced that *Burjanadze* would enter shortly and hold a legitimate parliamentary session. While some government ministers claimed that there were weapons in the hands of the demonstrators, no further information was made available. No other allegations of the presence of armed individuals were made. Unfortunately, on the same evening of the coup, the *Messenger* indicated that they received reports that looting was occurring near the Parliament in a number of sales shops.[344] On the same day that Saakashvili led the coup, the Georgian Supreme Court annulled the November election.[345] The demonstrators, the opposition leaders, and the mass media's coverage of these events seemed to have led to an oppositional victory.

---

341   Temur Tatishvili, "President Shevardnadze Steps Down, 'I've made this decision to avoid bloodshed...'" *The Georgian Times International Edition* (24 November 2003):1-3.

342   Gorgodze and Ekberg, "Shevardnadze resigns in war of the roses."

343   Mary Makharashvili, "Parliament Legit? Analysts say not yet." *The Messenger* (24 November 2003):10.

344   Gorgodze and Ekberg, "Shevardnadze resigns in war of the roses."

345   Gia Bakradze, "Dismantling is Launched." *Georgia Today* (28 November-4 December 2003):1, 2.

Following the successful take over of the parliament, opposition leaders then entered the Chancellery building passing through law enforcement personnel with whom they allegedly exchanged hugs and kisses. During the take over, there were no reports of any theft or destruction of government property. Only Shevardnadze's chair was reportedly smashed and burned. The opposition's objective of seizing control of government offices and asserting that the new acting President was *Nino Burjanadze,* as specified by the constitution seemed to be successful. Although *Shevardnadze* still refused to resign. Protestors also placed Nationalist Party flags in *Shevardnadze's* office. *Saakashvili* announced the plan to seize regional administrative buildings. He stated that those refusing to join the opposition would 'removed by the people'. The next day *Saakashvili* called upon citizens to take control of the Interior Ministry as well as the state TV channel. As these events unfolded, journalists reported that *Shevardnadze* only labeled the opposition's efforts as an attempted coup d'etat.[346] Similarly, supporters of *Shevardnadze* argued that the official opening of the new parliament even though short-lived, lasting only ten minutes, somehow reflected the its legitimacy.[347] However, legal analysts explain that this is not accurate and that first a specially elected commission must certify the election. The President of the Georgian Young Lawyers Association, *Zaz Rukhadze,* also argued that the since the people have demanded *Shevardnadze's* resignation, he should comply. Furthermore, *Rukhadze* exclaimed that *Shevardnadze* should "do everything to prevent bloodshed in the country."[348] Later in the evening, *Saakashvili* stated: "*Burjanadze* will convene a special parliamentary session to prepare for the new general elections." Shortly thereafter, *Burjanadze* called on the existing government leadership to disobey the President's dubious call for a state of emergency. In the early morning hours, Russian President Putin sent his Foreign Minister to Georgia to meet with the President and opposition leaders. Putin stated that his intention was only to assist his neighbor and to avoid political destabilization. Putin stated that Russia had no intentions of interfering with Georgia's internal affairs. The US continued to call on all parties to refrain from violence. Additionally, *Shevardnadze* held a telephone

---

346   *Ibid.,* 10.
347   *Ibid.*

conversation with UN Secretary Kofi Annan, Russian President Putin, and US state Secretary Collin Powell. *Shevardnadze's* press department reported that these foreign officials were concerned about the confrontation and claimed that they all supported the President. However, the opposition reported that the converse was true. Subsequently on Sunday evening, November twenty-third President *Shevardnadze* tendered his resignation to *Zurab Zhvania* and *Mikhail Saakashvili.*[349] As he announced his resignation, the President stated that his real motives in leaving office were to avoid a civil war:

> I saw that these current developments would not end without bloodshed and if tomorrow I should be forced to the use the power I posses in such conditions, we would have been leading into bloodshed...I never betrayed my people, and now I declare that it is best that the President resign and prevent the flow of blood.[350]

The President reportedly thanked *Saakashvili* for his sincerity and indicated that he had grown accustomed to resigning and that now he could write about his experiences before his life ends. *Zhvania* reported that the President would not be leaving Georgia, because his country needed him in the transition. It is now official, the Speaker of the Parliament *Nino Burjanadze* will become acting President.

In reviewing the events as they transpired on the twenty-third, journalists also indicated that when the opposition groups entered the Parliament, there was no quorum of new Parliamentarians. Only one-hundred and eighteen Parliamentarians were present rather than one hundred and fifty-seven required. Furthermore, one journalist argues that *Shevardnadze's* objective included illegally electing a new speaker, probably to pre-empt the opposition's next move. Conversely, a lawyer reportedly claimed that although the CEC documents confirmed the authority of the new parliament, he believed

---

348   *Ibid.*, 10.
349   Gorgodze and Ekberg, "Shevardnadze resigns in war of the roses;" Temur Tatishvili. "A Chronology of coup d'etat." *The Georgian Times, International Edition.* (24 November 2003):2, 3.
350   Gorgodze and Ekberg, "Shevardnadze resigns in war of the roses."

that the 'storming' of the Parliament was unconstitutional. Nonetheless, he also described the Parliamentary meeting as illegal. While a variety of Government deputies continued to accuse the individuals who rushed into the Parliament of welding weapons, no weapons appeared in the television footage. As mentioned previously later reports reflected that no weapons were used, even if carried into the Parliament. In a slightly more romanticized version of the opposition's entry into the Parliament, one writer explains that when *Saakashvili* entered the session, he held a rose without a bud and dramatically announced that the Rose Revolution was successful.

One article reprinted from an earlier *Moscow report*, discussed the coup and added that troops and police blocked roads around the parliament armed mostly with truncheons (I observed guns). However, the soldiers made no effort to prevent the opposition from entering the buildings.[351] A Georgian government official, from the National Security Council, stated that if a civil war had resulted it would have been more disastrous than the one that erupted in 1991. Here the writer describes the coup as characterized by shoving and overturning chairs. Moreover, this writer claims that *Saakashvili* stated, "The velvet revolution has taken place in Georgia...We are against violence."

Shevardnadze's long career in Georgian and Soviet politics included being a member of the Soviet Politburo and holding the position of the Foreign Minister in 1985. *Shevardnadze* became the President of Georgia one year after the collapse of the USSR and generally was perceived as the man who brought order to Georgia. Across the West, *Shevardnadze* remains viewed nostalgically, particularly for his part in ending the cold war. However, one author describes his twelve years in office as characterized by increasing economic difficulties and systemic corruption. An emotional editorial in *the Messenger* explains that Georgians never loved *Shevardnadze* but rather only respected him as a consummate diplomat. *Shevardnadze's* inner circle encouraged him to continue the façade of democracy as he made his supporters rich off the backs of ordinary Georgians.[352] I heard him called the

---

351   Seth Mydans, "Foes of Georgian Leader Storm Parliament." *The Georgian Times International Edition* (24 November 2003): 6.

352   N.N., "Georgia's White Fox and "Revolution of roses." *The Messenger* (24 November 2003):2.

"white fox" and the "silver fox" by Georgians on several occasions. A caricature of him appeared as the joker in a deck of playing cards sold in a corner grocery store in my *Tbilisi* neighborhood. This mirrors Georgians negative attitudes about his presidency. While he seen as bright, in the end the Georgian people did not believe that he represented them. However, in another issue of *the Messenger* a different journalist provides a more positive review of his career during both the Soviet period and his tenure in post-Soviet Georgia.[353] The last name of this writer appears Slavic so his view remains juxtaposed to the previous perspective of a Georgian journalist. This Slavic author lauds *Shevardnadze*'s long career and describes him as committed to public service even before he became associated with *Mikhail Gorbachev* and *glasnost', perestroika* and the end of the cold war. *Shevardnadze's* credits are described as establishing relations with the United States and reunifying Germany. It was also under his tenure as Minister of Foreign Affairs that the Soviet Union left Afghanistan. When he became the Chairman of Georgia's State Council in 1992, he facilitated Georgia's entry into the Commonwealth of Independent States and in 1993 created the Citizen's Union of Georgia. He also managed to end the conflict with *Abkhazia* and orchestrated the receipt of a great deal of humanitarian and economic assistance for Georgia from the United States. Similarly, another article in the same paper elucidates a United States government public statement explaining, "Thanks to President *Shevardnadze*, Georgia emerged from a difficult period and civil war in the mid-1990's to become a valued member of the international community" and "Because of his contributions millions of people living in the former Soviet Union are free today to pursue their own dreams in states committed to political and economic reform."[354] The U.S. statement also indicated that they look forward to working with Interim President *Burjanadze* "in her effort to maintain the integrity of Georgia's democracy as she strives to ensure that this change in government follows the constitution."[355] The next day, President Bush called Interim President *Burjanadze* and offered his support,

---

353   Christina Tashkevich, "Georgia's White Fox, Transcends communism, democracy and decades." *The Messenger* (25 November 2003):1, 3.

354   N.N., "United States thanks Shevardnadze welcomes new government." *The Messenger* (25 November 2003):5.

355   *Ibid.*

expressing his hope that the forthcoming election will be held in a democratic transparent and fair way."[356] In a different vein, the Slavic newspaper writer also quotes *Shevardnadze's* last radio address on November seventeenth when he asked the people: "Do [you] not see that they are being used as weapons in the fight for authority." The President also argued that the opposition leaders were only fighting for the president's chair.[357]

On Monday the 24th, *Nino Burjanadze* officially became the Acting President of Georgia.[358] She met with the UN Under-Secretary General, Jean Marie Guehenno who reportedly told journalists that the international community appreciated the adherence to the constitution's requirements following *Shevardnadze's* resignation. She then met with the National Security Council and discussed the stability of the nation. The Chief of the Border Protection Department, *Valeri Chkeidze* reported that no current violence existed across the country. The Interim President discussed budgetary problems with the Chief of the Intelligence department who told her that the transfer of federal funds to his department had not occurred in over three months. The Interim President also met with Bruce George, President of the OSCE Parliamentary Assembly who explained that he supported holding new Parliamentary elections and hoped that they would free and fair. The acting speaker of the Parliament, *Gigi Tsereteli,* appointed by *Burjanadze,* announced that the Parliament would meet on Tuesday at 1600 to re-schedule parliamentary and presidential elections. Subsequently, the Parliament voted to adopt January 4th as the date for the Presidential election. While one newspaper claimed that six candidates announced their intention to run, this included only three political parties in addition to the Nationalists. Those candidates were *Saakashvili, Roin Liparteliani, David Agmashenebeli, Gieorgi Korganashvil, Igor Giorgadze* from the Initiative Party, *Zarab Kelekasvhili*, from the Political Union Party, and *Kartolos Garibashvhil* from the Georgian Advocate Party. Conversely, the next day another article in a different paper claims that fifteen

---

356   N.N., "U.S. President calls Nino Burjanadze." Rustavi-2 online news http://www. rustavi2.com.ge/print.php?id=5933 (as of 26 November 2003).

357   Tashkevich, "Georgia's White Fox, Transcends communism, democracy and decades."

358   Mary Makharashvili, "Interim President takes the helm." *The Messenger* (25 November 2003):1, 5.

people announced their candidacy for President.[359] One author argues that the most attractive candidate thus far seems to be *Saakashvili*.[360] Two additional candidates were virtual unknowns to citizens. Some other major party leaders such as *Patiashvili* as well as the Labor Party threatened to boycott the Presidential elections, apparently displeased about the recent coup. One journalist argues that this will create suspicions about the fairness of the process. *Saakashvili* has reportedly tried to encourage *Alsan Abashidze* to run for the Presidency hoping that this would engender *Abashidze's* support for the election process. However, *Abashidze* reports that neither he nor his constituents in *Adjara* will participate in the forthcoming elections and retorts that he expects the Nationalists to falsify the election. The writer doubts that *Abashidze*, if in the running, could defeat *Saakashvili*. This piece also reflects that in a recent interview on Russian television, *Shevardnadze* encouraged Russia to support *Abashidze*. He also suggested that *Abashidze* might become the man who could unite all of Georgia. This again suggests that as some have long argued *Shevardnadze* appears somewhat out of touch with reality. A new political opposition block has already emerged consisting of a splinter group from the Traditionalists' as well as a new party called the People's Movement. The people's movement previously broke away from the government bock. The Minister of Security expressed concerns that as the Presidential election draws nearer, these new oppositional parties may attempt some kind of "terrorist attack" on prominent politicians and businessmen including targeting *Saakashvili*. Even before the calm following the last storm settles, Georgian fears about new potential power holders and political violence appears. However, as usual Georgians have a variety of other social problems that require attention.

As the exciting and frightening events of the Rose Revolution ended, newspaper coverage returned to other more chronic problems common to many post-Soviet countries, human trafficking.[361] Specifically, from 1989 to 2002, 1,028,000 people emigrated from Georgia due to the poor economy,

---

359   N.N., "Saakashvili enters elections without serious rival." *The Messenger* (3 December 2003):2; Gia Bakradze, "Dismantling is Launched." *Georgia Today* (28 November 2003):1, 2.

360   N.N., "Saakashvili enters elections without serious rival."

although many of these were victims of trafficking. While the average age of Georgian out migrants ranges between twenty-five and forty years old, a representative from the International Migration Organization explained that those under twenty-five are usually more inclined to leave in order to pursue a University education abroad. Conversely, most traffickers recruit from the poorer rural regions of Georgia promising better jobs and higher incomes. These young women then become sexually exploited, and forced to turn over all or some of their earnings to the traffickers. Young male trafficking victims often end up working in low paying service sector jobs. The writer claims that Georgia has no established protocols to limit trafficking or curb illegal migration and further no form of rehabilitation for victims who return to the country. In spite of the absence of any government intervention, two Georgian NGOs assist Trafficking victims. These include the "Center for Rights and Safety of Migrants" in *Tbilisi* and a second called "Support." Whether the presence of civil organizations may in the long-run, prevent or disable the government from becoming more pro-active in alleviating social problems like this one remains debatable. Additionally, such developments may further disempower the already weak government.

Two days following *Shevardnadze's* resignation, election headlines begin to address the issue of the political parties who previously renounced the protests.[362] This piece reveals that the Labor Party, New Rights Party, and Industry Will Save Georgia Party will be re-organizing in order to win parliamentary seats in the re-scheduled election. One report reveals that these competing parties are already making a variety of inflammatory statements to debunk one another and denounce the old oppositional block. While another article in *Georgia Today* plays down the inter-political party animosity more visible in the latter piece, the evidence supports the previous view that new oppositional groups are emerging.[363] For example, the leader of the Labor Party, *Shalva Natelashvili* allegedly denounced the Nationalist's use of

---

361   Lali Javakhia, "Georgian population flees from the Country...Youth are lured into trafficking." *The Georgian Times International Edition* (24 November 2003):8.
362   Mary Makharashvili, "Parties on the Sidelines Having denounced protests, other opposition parties now struggle to find their place." *The Messenger* (25 November 2003):1, 7.
363   *Ibid;* Zaza Jgharkava, "Politicians in the Revolution Roses." *Georgia Today* (28 November 2003):2.

"force" to remove the President. He criticized the Nationalists and the *Bur-janadze* Democrats for protesting and exploiting the people since both parties had successfully crossed the seven percent threshold. An interesting statement to make in light of the fact that evidence of voting fraud already had been substantiated. Another Labor Party member, *Gela Danelia*, called the demonstrations, the "caprice of *Saakashvili.*" He expressed concerns that the opposition movement created a "dangerous precedent" that could lead to Georgia's destruction. He calls *Saakasvhili*, *Burjanadze*, and *Zhvania* criminals and argued that "according to Georgian law they should be arrested." He also exclaimed that *Shevardnadze* should not have resigned. He described his own party platform as socialist and explained that the leader of the party, *Shalva Natelashvili* will be their choice for the President. Interestingly, four days later, on November 29th, a hand grenade exploded in front of the central office of the Labor Party.[364] *Shalva Natelashvili* subsequently announced that his party would boycott the Presidential and parliamentary elections. He believed that the Nationalists-and *Burjanadze* Democrats orchestrated the attack in order to frighten him from participating in the presidential election. He also believed that the Rose Revolution's real focus was to destroy him. Although a separate piece covering the same incident reported that *Natelashvili* claimed the focus of the revolution was to destroy his party. Furthermore, he argued that *Shevardnadze* actually gave the government over to his own followers intentionally to keep the Labor Party from power.[365] The Press Secretary of the Labor Party, *Gela Danelia* joined in these accusations by stating that the new interim government came to power by violating the constitution and that these forces were not really oppositional party blocs, but rather forces within the government who wanted more power. She also claimed that: "Foreign experts conducted analytic research reflecting that the Labor party remains the most popular and thus *Natelashvili* has a fair chance to win the presidential elections."[366] Moreover, *Danelia* holds George Soros as well as a variety of foreign institutions responsible for orchestrating the Rose

364 Anna Arzanova, "Natelashvili pulls out of the race..Blames explosion on new leadership." *The Messenger* (1 December 2003):1, 5.
365 N.N., "Labor Party Boycotts New Elections." Rustavi-2 online news http://www.rustavi2.com.ge/print.php?id=5960 (as of 29 November 2003).
366 Arzanova, "Natelashvili pulls out."

Revolution. She said: "These foreign organizations allotted USD million [dollars] to carry out the events of November twenty-third." In a counterclaim, a National Movement party leader, *Petre Tsiskarishvili*, accused the Labor Party candidate of making such claims only because he has no chance of wining the election. Further, *Tsikarishvili* indicates that the Labor Party planned and carried out the grenade blast to increase their own power, and "to accuse the National Movement and the block of *Burjanadze*-Democrats." A member of the *Burjanadze* Democrats Party also reports that they had nothing to do with the explosion and that *Saakashvili* has already met with *Natelashvili* telling him that an investigation into the incident will follow. This is also an interesting claim to make considering *Saakashvili* authority to make such a statement is limited and he is not yet the elected President. As political parties continue to re-construct the Rose Revolution, the New Rights Party (supportive of business) also explains they have no regrets in refusing to join the Nationalist block. Yet David *Gamrelidze*, leader of the New Rights party also retorts that *Saakashvili* tried to discredit his party by declining an apparent offer to join the opposition. It seems somewhat unlikely that both statements are accurate representations of the truth. Next, the writer presents *Gamrelidze* as taking the position that protests or demonstrations by one party against another are inappropriate. Similar to other party claims, *Gamrelidze* then reportedly stated that the political block used the Georgian citizens simply to gain power. *Gamrelidze* also argued that nullifying the election results is more dangerous than falsifying the votes. [367] It remains unclear why he might make such a statement or believe it for that matter. One *Georgia Today* journalist calls him a "young gifted politician with considerable organization skills" but describes radicalism as alien to him.[368] This is an interesting characterization, considering that *Gamrelidze's* statements seem so contradictory, at least as they are presented. However, another member of the New Rights Party stands ready to break off from the party as he explains, that he has "sympathies with the *Burjanadze* Democrats and has relatives

---

367   Mary Makharashvili, "Parties on the Sidelines Having denounced protests, other opposition parties now struggle to find their place." *The Messenger* (25 November 2003):1, 7.

368   Zaza Jgharkava, "The New Rights to Face Split?" *Georgia Today* (28 November 2003): 2.

and friends who supported the revolution." No further description of his reasons for joining the Nationalist block were provided. *The Messenger* also relays that the Industrialists, who failed to reach the seven percent threshold, condemned the elections and refused to join the Nationalist block. Similar to other party's claims, the leader of the party, *Gogi Topadze,* told reporters he believed another country or international interests controlled the opposition. He later referred to this group as "financial monsters" who want to give us "orders." However, he approved of the President's decision to resign. As other parties re-analyze and re-interpret events surrounding the Rose Revolution, other changes continue to transform the former President's administration.

Political transformation continues to dot the landscape within the former President's administration. First, the Press Secretary, *Kakha Imnadze*, resigned explaining that he plans to continue to work with *Shevardnadze* for some time and then will pursue a diplomatic career.[369] As the old administration began leaving office, unfortunately the new administration began to threaten the freedom of the press.[370] Specifically, one writer stated that the new "de facto government" is using threats and violence to intimidate journalists." He further explained that over the last two days approximately ten instances transpired involving "pressure" exerted on journalists. Later the author stated that this pressure included physical attacks. The perpetrators were allegedly members of the student group *Kmara*, who were supporters of the Rose Revolution. A description of the violence included the following:

a. An attack on the home of a famous Georgian journalist *Luba Eliashvili* on November twenty-fifth.
b. On the same day, an armed group broke into the *Tbilisi* office of *Adjara* TV Company and demanded that the company shut down.
c. On November twenty-fourth members of the de-facto government broke into the state funded TV Corporation and demanded that the news programs shut down.

---

369   N.N., "Press Secretary of former President Shevardnadze resigns." Rustavi-2 On-Line News http://www.rustavi2.com.ge/print.php?id=5932 (as of 26 November 2003).
370   N.N., "SOS Special Appeal." *Daily Georgian Times* (27 November 2003):1, 5.

d. The same group has placed pressure on the newspaper *Sarketvelos Respublika* to cease their activities.

e. On November 26th after protests and demands by *Kmara* students for the Rector of the *Tbilisi* State University to resign, he complied. Under duress, a university Dean resigned.

f. This followed a protest by another group of students who were demanding that the behavior of *Kmara* and the de-facto government cease.

Moreover, five journalists applied for assistance as political refugees following these events. Additional accusations included actual assaults on journalists. However, the victims are reportedly not talking about the details because they are afraid of further repercussions. The independent Georgian Journalists' Association appealed for help from international NGOs, the UN, the EU, and the US as well as international journalists associations. The writer called for a united forum of Georgian journalists to discuss these encroachments on freedom of speech. Finally, the editorial asked all journalists to resist political pressure, while maintaining neutrality, clearly a difficult thing to achieve in this culture at this time.

Four days after *Shevardnadze's* resignation, *Saakashvili* announced his candidacy for President.[371] The headline reveals that other opposition parties are uniting behind him. Following the presidential election, assuming the new political block wins, they plan to change the constitution by creating a Prime Minister position. The Prime Minister's authority will revolve around managing domestic affairs while the President's role will remain primarily symbolic, with limited authority over foreign policy goals and defense issues. *Saakashvili* reportedly stated that he wants "regulated relations with Russia," "help from our Western friends," and "support from Russia." He also said that (speaking with the acting President and the most viable candidate for Prime Minister assuming *Saakashvili* wins the election), they want the elections to be free and fair and welcome other candidates to run for the office of President. The article also reports that recent opinion polls indicate that *Saakashvili* stands

---

371   Tamara Ninidze, "Mikhail Saakashvili to run for President, Opposition leaders unite behind a single candidate." *Daily Georgian Times* (27 November 2003):1, 2.

as the most popular candidate for the Presidency. Readers should recognize that another article provides a brief profile of *Saakashvili's* education and work history, noting that he received his law degree from Columbia in the U.S. and attended other universities abroad in both the Ukraine and Germany. President *Shevardnadze* relied on *Zhvania to* recruit *Saakashvili* to return to Georgia in 1995. Subsequently, *Saakashvili* won election to Parliament where he became a member of a powerful committee charged with creating a new electoral system, an independent judiciary system, and a nonpolitical police force. When *Zhvania* recruited *Saakashvili* to return to Georgia crime was so problematic that "few people walked the streets at night" in *Tbilisi.* Now *Tbilisi* residents frequently enjoy evening activities ranging from club life, to bowling, eating out, and plays and films without fear of street crime. In a recent interview, *Saakashvili* reported that his critics accuse him of being pro-Western. Conversely, he stated that being pro-Western is not a tactical consideration but reflects his party's values. He explained that he wants to make Georgia a model democracy for the entire region. While the previous article seemed supportive of the new party alliance, another piece claimed that a former National Democratic party member, Irina *Sairshvili-Chanturia* labeled the new leadership as a "force of dictatorship." Consequently, she is leaving the party. She also alleges she has received threatening phone calls from the Parliament and suspects the new block. Furthermore, she believes that the American Armenians sponsored the revolution in conjunction with the American intelligence service. She argues that this new leadership will "trample the national and religious values of Georgia." She also calls *Kmara* a terrorist group. She claims that the new developments in the country are a "looming threat" and that "a dictatorship has been established in Georgia and everyone will miss *Eduard Shevardnadze's* government quite soon." She contends that this new dictatorship uses "terror" again insinuating that they perpetrated the harassing phone calls as well as other vague threats that she has received. She perceives that the new government will result in "national and religious decay." She reports that she plans to I create a new party, called "New Force" to protect Georgia from this dictatorship.[372] In another ar-

---

372   *Idem.* "Irina Sarishvili to Form a 'new force' against dictatorship, ex-leader of NDP threatened." *The Daily Georgian Times* (27 November 2003):4.

ticle, her new party is referred to as "New Power." The difference probably relates more to accuracy of the English translation than anything else. However, this latter piece also reveals that she did not leave her party but that she was removed.[373] No further information was provided revealing the reasons for her removal. While she may have a valid reason for accusing the new status quo of sponsoring terror with from the Americans, she is not alone in making these accusations.

Mark MacKinnon's piece from the *London Globe and Mail accuses* Soros of planning the revolution and orchestrating *Shevardnadze's* resignation. This journalist offers evidence of the plan to catapult *Saakashvili* to the Presidency by mentioning that last year Soros personally nominated *Saakashvili* with an OSI Award. Moreover, *Kmara* also received a five hundred thousand start-up grant from OSI last April. MacKinnon suggests that these funds supported their activities throughout the Rose Revolution. In the same newspaper, another article discusses *Kmara's* receipt of training in protest organization and resistance from *Otpor,* the student resistance movement in the former Yugoslavia. The description of *Otpor* as a terrorist organization comes from an article in a Yugoslavian paper, *Politika,* written by a political party member from the Yugolsav Left.[374] In this article, *Uros Rkic* blamed *Otpor* for an attempted murder against two fellow party members, and claimed that the group was a "terrorist organization." Furthermore, he argued that members were not college students or high school students but rather were "criminals, psychopaths, lazy bums and destructive personalities directed by enemies of this country."[375] First he suggested that NATO supported the *Otpor* students then he accused the CIA of training *Otpor* (as they trained the Kurdish Liberation Army) to commit terrorist activities. While there is a degree of truth to his accusations, describing them as terrorists is a bit of a stretch. However, *Otpor* was responsible for *Milosevic's* resignation. Clearly, any group trying to topple or remove a despot from office may become labeled as

---

373   N.N., "Irina Sarishvili establishes a new movement." Rustavi-2 online news http://www.rustavi2.com.ge/rpint.php?id=5931 (as of 26 November 2003).

374   N.N. (translated from Politika, Belgrade), "OTPOR for Violence and Terrorism." *Daily Georgian Times* (27 November 2003):3.

375   *Ibid.*

terrorists, primarily as the result of the loose definition that United States constructed post-9/11.

New voices of opposition to the former opposition continue to surface in a variety of newspaper articles. In two different articles, writers again refer to the new government, under acting President *Burjanadze,* as a dictatorship.[376] Unfortunately, the critics were angry about recent *Kmara* activities aimed at removing *Tbilisi* State University's Rector. Specifically, three days after *Saakashvili's* supporters broke into the parliament, *Tbilisi* State University *Kmara* students began protesting in front of the University administration building demanding the Rector's resignation. They entered the Rectors' office threatening to nail up his office door if he refused to quit.[377] He capitulated and resigned on November 26th as *Kmara* activists also began to demand that chairs of all departments also resign. One article discusses reactions by non-*Kmara* students to the resignation of the *Tbilisi* State University, Rector, *Roin Metreveli.*[378] These students began shouting the slogan, "*Kmara, Kmara*" or "enough is enough". Students referred to *Kmara's* activism in pressuring the Rector and Chairs to resign as a reflective of a dictatorship. *Saakashvili* entered the fray by trying to quell the protests of both sides and by articulating that the proper authority to determine resignations was the University's Scientific Council. On the same day, the Council rejected the Rector's resignation, but Rector *Roin Metreveli* staid the course and indicated he felt this was the right decision. As the anti-*Kmara* protesters gained momentum, they blocked a portion of *Chavchavadze* Avenue in front of the university, demanding the Rector's return. Throughout several days of protests, demonstrators also blocked traffic from both directions of the main street on which the University administration building stands. The result was a terrific logjam down the main avenue of the city and throughout the remainder of the capital. Unfortunately, this resulted in canceling all university classes. At one point during the student demonstration, President *Burjanadze* met with the protestors and asked them to remain calm re-assuring them that there would

---

376   Kate Bojgua, "We are under threat of dictatorship! State University Students defending their Rector." *The Daily Georgian Times* (27 November 2003):3; Ninidze, "Irina Sarishvili to Form a 'new force' against dictatorship."

377   Gia Bakradze, "Rector's Back." *Georgia Today* (28 November 2003):1, 2.

be no dictatorship of the University or the country. However, the writer reports students failed to respond to her. Students from *Kmara* were also present at the protest arguing that other students were only protesting out of fear of punishment for their part in corruption with the University Rector. Later *Saakasvhili* met with the Rector and the students resulting in the Rector rescinding his resignation followed by the cessation of the student demonstration.[379] As the initial waves of change seemed to subside, accusations of wrongdoing perpetrated by the new power alliance continued and new political violence as well as new resignations, characterized the coming months.

III.5   December 2003 and January 2004

Ten days after *Irina Sarishvili-Chanturia's* initial report of the receipt of intimidating phone calls, several unknown individuals fired gunshots into her home.[380] One journalist explained that her "controversial" political positions occupied while the speaker for the political block called New Georgia may have provoked the attack. The writer seemed to justify political violence taken by blaming the victim. The journalist further describes the 1994 shooting that resulted in the murder of her husband, *Gia Chanturia* and her own injury. However, the writer provides these background events to provide further support to the tenet that she brought this trouble onto herself. Here the more recent threats she received included threats of revealing to her children the identity of their biological parents. Since that time, she moved her children to an undisclosed location. However, the Minister of Internal Affairs, *Gia Baramidze* tells the media that the police will do everything in their power to find the perpetrators. He also maintains that these criminals are trying to pit Georgians against one another and denies that the motive was political intimidation or murder. However, two MP's, *Irakli Gogava* and *Zviad Mukbaniani* believe that the shooting was an attempted murder. *Irina Sarishvili* told

---

378   N.N., "Students Protest in University Garden." Rustavi-2 On-Line News
     http://www.rustavi2.com.ge/print.php?id=5934 (as of 26 November 2003).
379   Bakradze, "Rector's Back."
380   Anna Arzanova, "Gunmen fire on Sarishvili's House Police Suspect Political Intimidation or assassination attempt." *The Messenger* (4 December 2003):1, 5.

reporters she would not speculate as to who was behind the crime. Nevertheless, the headline certainly attracts readers by claiming that the suspects were attempting to kill her or intimidate her. Although the Interior Minister denied political motives for the crime, considering her vocal opposition to the Rose Revolution and *Kmara,* it certainly may be possible that the shooting was an attempt to silence her, either temporarily or permanently. The newspaper devoted an entire page to an interview with *Sarishvili* following this shooting incident.[381] She discloses to the interviewer that she believes *Saakashvili* is a dictator but also argues that he is a puppet manipulated by *Zhvania* and *Burjanadze. Sarishvili* also explains that both the U.S. and Russia backed the opposition in the Rose Revolution. She claims *Burjanadze*'s father controls her, a rich oligarch sometimes referred to as the "Georgian Bread King". She called *Burjanadze's* father wheat mogul. She also believed that her husband's murder was part of a conspiracy to eliminate him as a potential Presidential candidate. She insinuates that the opposition movement currently holding power has been planning all these events for some time and she feels certain that they will destroy Georgia. A member of her new party "For New Georgia," *Irakli Gogava* also accuses the new interim government of political terror. He implied that the new government orchestrated both the phone calls to *Sarishvili* as well as the gunshots to silence the new opposition.[382]

Readers are probably wondering by now, why high levels of political violence continue to plague Georgia. The answer is three pronged; first Georgian young people still receive weapons training for civil defense purposes, a left over from the Soviet era. The Soviet curriculum required students to take military studies from ninth through eleventh grades. This includes a teaching students how to clean *Kalashnikovs* (the soviet issue military rifle), fire weapons, and identify different parts of tanks. Even still weapons are included in the classroom as a teaching tool. Sometimes they are real and sometimes mock. The second explanation for Georgia's political violence includes what Assistant Prosecutor *Giorgi Taladze* called availability.

381   A. Spurling, "Maybe now it will be Rosy Terror?" *Georgia Today* (5-11 December 2003):7.

382   N.N., "Irakli Gogava Speaks of Political Terror." Rustavi-2 online news http://www.rustavi2.com.ge/print.php?=6033 (as of 8 December 2003).

Taladze explained to Rustavi-2 that weapons and explosives remain fairly easy to obtain across Georgia. Illicit weapons' trafficking has become a burgeoning industry across the former Soviet Union as well as globally.[383] Finally, political cultural norms continue to maintain a sort of covert ideology that you should not argue with or contradict the extant power structure. Critiquing the existing order is simply not acceptable and parties are either all good or all bad, shades of grey simply cannot be perceived. The result of such compartmentalization inevitably leads to violence.

On December tenth this problem of the availability of weapons and explosives and the reality of political violence became visible again. This time an explosion occurred outside one of the branches of the mobile telecommunications company, *Magticom* Limited, located in downtown *Tbilisi*.[384] *Shevardnadze's* son-in-law, *Giorgi Jokhaberidze*, partly owns the company. While no injuries occurred, windows of nearby businesses were shattered in the blast. The extent of the damage on the *Magticom* business itself remained unreported. The writer proposed no supposition as to why *Shevardnadze's* son in law was targeted or even if this was the aim of the perpetrators. A few days later, another explosion rocked the same building, however, the State Security Minister failed to offer any new information, only indicating that the investigation was ongoing.[385]

In the context of this new political violence, western statements simply ignored the problem. Specifically, an OSCE report issued on November twenty-eighth regarding the post-election observations stated that the forthcoming presidential election will indicate whether or not the new administration will be able to hold truly free and fair presidential elections.[386] The report stipulated that the previous elections fell short of international standards for democratic elections and that "developments during the tabulation of results and the complaints and appeals process only served to further underline the extent to which the parliamentary elections failed to meet OSCE other international standards." The report also argued that the CEC "placed narrow

---

383   Kathi Austin, "Illicit Arms Brokers: Aiding and Abetting Atrocities." *The Brown Journal of World Affairs* 9:1(2002):203-227.

384   N.N., "Explosion at *Magticom* office." *The Messenger* (11 December 2003):1.

385   N.N., "Second attack on *Magticom* outlet." *The Messenger* (15 December 2003):5.

party interests above democratic principles."[387] The OSCE resolved that all those previous individuals on the Commission are unfit to serve, suggesting the necessity of a house cleaning. Furthermore, they informed the new administration that they must ensure that the courts can function independently and that judicial decisions are upheld and enforced. Finally, the OSCE report complemented the NGO Fair Elections and the Young Georgian Lawyers Association for conducting exit polls that helped illuminate the voting fraud. The OSCE mission to observe elections has been in Georgia since September and will begin new observations again this month.

It seems that when western organizations say jump, Georgian politicians comply, because following the above OSCE announcement, the prosecutor's office began filing criminal charges against local election commission officials. However, the Prosecutor declined to file charges against CEC members.[388] Moreover, no attempts to resolve the problem with the voters' lists were made. Clearly, Georgia's knee jerk reactions to Western criticism remain superficial. The U.S. and the OSCE are once again providing funding to facilitate fair and transparent elections with OSCE authorities indicating that they believe five million Euros will be needed. As mentioned above, after the OSCE recommended the replacement of all CEC members, they suggested that the head of the Fair Elections NGO, *Zurab Chiaberashvili*, become the new CEC Chairperson. Subsequently, his nomination and approval followed and *Chiaberashvili* became the new Chair of the Central Election Committee. Although an earlier offer was made to someone else, that person declined, leaving OSCE in the position of getting what they wanted.[389] *Chiaberashvili* was a huge critic of the manner in which the CEC previously managed elections and voting procedures and is reported to have said that [if he] fails to do the job properly he will admit that criticizing is easier than doing the job yourself. He exclaimed: "I am taking a big risk, I do not know if after January fourth I will walk the streets of *Tbilisi* with my head in the air as I do now."[390]

---

386   Allison Ekberg, "First Test: New Elections OSCE issues interim Report." *The Messenger* (1 December 2003):1, 9.

387   Ekberg, "First Test: New Elections."

388   Bakaradze, "Dismantling is Launched."

389   Sopho Gorgodze, "Fair Elections head to Chair CEC Says voter list problem is solvable." *The Messenger* (1 December 1 2003):5-8, 10.

now."[390] One of the primary problems yet to be resolved is the accuracy of the voter lists. However, he claims that he will eliminate this problem. He also believed that the absence of professionalism and the poor preparation of the local election commissions contributed to voter fraud. He communicated that his former NGO will continue with a new director and that they will again conduct a parallel voters' tabulation as completed previously. One parliamentarian, *Gurma Sharadze*, criticized *Chiaberashvili,* accusing him of having discredited the parliament. This writer also contradicts earlier reports that *Chiaberashvili* filed complaints with the Supreme Court. *Sharadze* described the court documents filed as efforts aimed at nullifying the proportional portion of the parliamentary elections, not the majoritarian portion. He also accused *Chiaberashvili* of working for the Freedom (Liberty) Institute, those who trained members of *Kmara.* Conversely, another MP, *Elene Tevdoradze* praised *Chiaberashvili* claiming that he founded Georgian civil society. Two other MPs also adduced that a quorum was not present in Parliament during the vote on *Chiaberashvili's* nomination. However, the writer argues that the record indicates a quorum was present. In a later interview with another Georgian English newspaper, *Chiaberashvili* disclosed that Lynn Pascoe, U.S. Deputy to the U.S. Secretary of State had been unrealistic with regard to what Georgia was capable of accomplishing before the November elections. However, *Chiaberashvili* suggested that Pascoe's idea to include a pre-registration process at each at local CEC location for all Georgians was a good one.[391] The interviewing journalist tried to inquire about *Chiaberashvili's* own political preferences, but he only intimated that there are three popular candidates and that Georgian people will decide who becomes the next President. *Chiaberashvili* also explained that the decision with regard to the proportional and majority portions of the election remains in the hands of the Constitutional Court. He also verbalized that he will comply with the court's decision. Finally, he acknowledged the importance of and welcomed election observers in both of the forthcoming elections. A few days, later Acting President *Burjanadze* appointed five new members to the CEC including *Zaza*

---

390   *Ibid.,* 10.
391   Misha Kobaladze, "Eternal Elections." *Georgia Today* (5 December 2003):1, 2.

Zaza Gorozia, Elza Guliashvili, Levan Samkharauli, Zurab Nonikashvili and *Karlo Kvitaishvili.*[392]

Other new appointees of the acting President's Administration include *Zurab Zhvania* and *Zurab Noghaideli,* both tasked with eliminating the current deficit.[393] They plan to mobilize resources from home and abroad to achieve that goal. No description of their methodology was provided. However, a later article from another media outlet reported that *Zhvania* presented a project for social employment in Georgia to the state chancellery that was designed to create jobs in spite of the patronage system currently in place.[394] The only details offered included the provision of some sort of job bank. The objective of this program as well as others not yet announced included the payment of arrears pensions and salaries. An article published two days later in the same paper provided the text of a press conference with *Noghaideli.*[395] This latter article referred to him as hopeful. He revealed that the current debt was two hundred and ninety three million U.S. dollars. Further, he disclosed that the government already spent seventy-four percent of what remained available.[396] He articulated the necessity of attracting continued international financial assistance and claimed that current negotiations with the German and the U.S. governments to receive additional financial support are underway. He also discussed the possibility of developing a trust fund managed by the World Bank who would distribute the funds as necessary. He purportedly planned to re-negotiate debts owed with the Paris club of the IMF and promised that IMF loans will resume in 2004. He assured the reporter that corrupt government employees within his department would be fired, prosecuted and among those found guilty, punished. Both this article and the formerly discussed piece agreed that the Georgian economy is in a shambles. One writer articulates that the new administration must make some structural

---

392   N.N., "New Presidential Envoys to CEC." *Georgia Today In What's New* (5 December 2003):12.
393   M. Alkhazashvili, "Zhvania and Noghaideli responsible for Georgian Economy." *The Messenger* (1 December 2003):3.
394   N.N., "Social Employment Program Presented." Rustavi-2 online news http//www.rustavi2.com.ge/print.ph;?id=6003 (as of 4 December 2003).
395   Christiana Tashkevich, "Noghaideli vows to make his least corrupt. New Finance Minister is hopeful." *The Messenger* (3 December 2003):1, 4.
396   M. Alkhazashvili, "Economy Uncertainty is Certain." *The Messenger* (4 December 2003):3.

changes to fight corruption within the upper echelons of government. However, the new administration argued that the constitutional changes should accomplish that goal by adding the post of Prime Minister and creating a Cabinet of Ministers. Although such changes do not necessarily portend that systemic corruption will be eliminated . Descriptive statistics provided in the article claim that sixty percent of public officials engage in corruption, unfortunately the writer failed to cite any reliable source. It is important to note that *Noghaideli* previously served as Finance Minister from 2000 to 2002 and his most recent job was as a consultant for United Energy Distribution Company. A third journalist the following day, also expressed concern about the state of the economy and mentioned that *Noghaideli* was probably re-appointed to the post because he maintained such good relationships with international financial institutions.[397] This kind of social capital is necessary in order to insure that the required one hundred million GEL needed to fulfill the 2003 budget will be provided. About one week later, the new finance minister stated: "Everything must be done in the few weeks remaining in the year to ensure maximally minimal losses" in the budget.[398] However, these figures reflect that only seventy-nine percent of the expected revenues have been collected for the 2003 budget and that almost two hundred million more GEL are needed to finance the state through the end of 2003. Reporting 100 million and then 200 million as required makes it more apparent that accurate reporting of facts remains illusive. Further, this writer reported that the debt probably lies between two hundred and forty and two hundred and fifty million GEL. The journalist makes it clear that foreign assistance is necessary. Subsequently, the Georgian government requested a five million U.S. dollar wheat grant, a five million EURO food safety grant from the CoE and another five million dollars for other urgent expenditures. Perhaps more realistically, one reporter states that "according to some calculations" reducing smuggling by ten percent would result in a 500 million GEL budget increase. The writer characterized *Shevardnadze's* administration as lacking the political will to fight the shadow or illegitimate economy. Then the journalist invited readers to wonder if the new opposition currently in power, the winners of the Rose

---

397   Alkhazashvili, "Economy Uncertainty is Certain."

Revolution, will really be able to eliminate corruption as they promise. A few days later, the same author reported that the new Finance Minister seemed to making some positive steps to prevent or eliminate smuggling by increasing the budget coiffeurs through legal taxation.[399] *Noghaideli* explained that the smuggling of cigarettes created a loss of 9.3 million GEL in the first eleven months of 2003. Other smuggled products creating financial losses for the state include petroleum, cars, and alcohol. He claimed: "Nearly every businessman involved in the cigarette industry trades illegally." He says: "If they don't play by our rules, we will take measures against them," including filing criminal charges. *Noghaideli* is also on a mission to find out which employees in the Finance Ministry have been accepting bribes and plans to remove them from their positions. He also expects to create one large taxpayers inspection office from twenty-nine separate legal entities in order to give him more control over major contributions to the budget.

Additional appointments to the Interim government continue, this time *Giori Baramidze* was appointed as the new Minister of the Interior. Other Ministers not yet replaced will remain in office until after the presidential election. As the new party in power established its authority, a variety of high-ranking officials began to resign from office. These included the Chairman of the Control Chamber, *Sulkhan Papashvili,* the *Imereti* Governor, Temur *Shashiashvili,* the President's representative to *Kakheti, Bidzina Songulashvili,* the head of the Presidential Press office *Kakha Imnadze,* the Chief Prosecutor from *Imereti, Tamaz Chumburidze,* and the *Kutaisi* Chief Prosecutor *Shalva Pkhakidze.*[400] However, the prosecutor's office denied any relationship between these resignations and the Rose Revolution. Shortly thereafter, the Chief of the state run Georgian Railway, *Akaki Chkaidze* was fired. The State Minister *Zurab Zhvania* reported that he was removed directly as the result of the Rose Revolution.[401] He was accused of representing the best example of

---

398   M. Alkhazashvili, "Government seeks "Maximally minimal losses." *The Messenger* (10 December 2003): 3.

399   M. Alkhazashvili, "Finance Minister launches fight against smuggling." *The Messenger* (11 December 2003):3.

400   John Horan, "Prosecutors Step Down." *The Messenger Press Scanner* (4 December 2003):8.

401   M. Alkhazashvili, "Finance Minister launches fight against Smuggling." *The Messenger* (11 December 2003):3.

official corruption. The government alleged that he used the train system to transport smuggled goods throughout Georgia. The new management of the Railway is comprised of a board of eleven persons. Subsequently, it was revealed that rather than this dismissal being a Georgian initiated decision, apparently both the IMF and the World Bank 'demanded' *Chkaidze's* resignation. Moreover, both international financial institutions also demanded that two other state enterprises be audited. Accusations that the Rose Revolution was orchestrated by foreign powers, seem accurate in light of these new revelations. However, the new opposition may just as easily being exploiting these partial truths to further their own agenda. Moreover, if the Georgian government so easily behaved according to the west's bidding, why not orchestrate the end of the political violence. Or perhaps such violence also serves the best interests of foreign powers as it ensures continued instability and the 'necessity' of on-going external control.

Political violence drove one member of Parliament from the New Rights Party to flee the country. This PM, *Levan Gachechiladze,* [402] After returning he expressed concerns about *Saakashvili's* ability to perform effectively as President if elected and stated that he does not plan to vote for him. He views the new leadership emerging from the revolution as retaining the same leadership style as *Shevardnadze.* Finally, he reports being concerned that elections were re-scheduled before making appropriate amendments to the constitution, although there is no indication of whether or not he suggested how that would have been accomplished i.e., with an illegitimate new Parliament or the old Parliament. Thus while some critiques of the new political power structure are offered by the media, the information provided often remains incomplete, shortsighted, and poorly timed. Moreover, the newspapers continue to maintain Georgian's fears that Russia remains a powerful threat. One journalist described a recent meeting of Russian administrative authorities with the leaders of *Adjara, Abkhazia*, and South *Ossetia* in Moscow minus Georgian government officials. While the subject of the meetings was omitted, the average Georgian reaction was mirrored in this statement from *Burjanadze* who said: "When such meetings are held without the agreement

---

402   Mary Makharashvili, "New Rights' Gachechiladze fled fearing bloodshed." *The Messenger Press Scanner* (4 December 2003):8.

of the central government of Georgia, it is natural that they arouse serious ir-
ritation in *Tbilisi.*"[403] This meeting may have transpired after Putin sent a note
to the head of the Russian Federal Council, *Sergey Mironov*, urging that the
mandate for the Russian peacekeeping forces in Georgia extend until one of
the parties decides that the situation is stable.[404] Putin's personal representative to *Abkhazia's* affairs, *Valerie Loschchinin* and the Russian Defense Ministry official, *Valerie Yevenvich* were announced as participants in what was
then referred to as a future discussion. This continuously conflict ridden relationship between Russia and Georgia is also exacerbated by discussions
with regard to additional changes to the Russian VISA requirements. It is currently easier for *Adjaran* and *Abkhazians* to obtain Visas than it is for Georgians. One piece alleged that Chairman of the Supreme Council of the *Adjaran*
Autonomous Republic of Georgia, *Aslan Abashidze* was attempting to negotiate this change himself. Conversely, *two* Westerner's reported that *Abashidze* was trying to make it more restrictive for *Adjarans* to enter Russia.
The later makes more sense than the former, although once again Georgians
received contradictory information. Nevertheless another writer reported that
on November twenty-eighth the Russian *Duma* met, voted on the issue and
the bill failed to pass. However, later a third article indicated that on December eighth the Russian government simplified the Visa process at least for
Russians going to *Adjara.*[405] This procedure, basically no visa requirements
for Russians, exists in both *Abkhazia* and *South Ossetia.*[406] During a press
conference the Russian Ambassador to Georgia, *Vladimir Chikvishvili,*
claimed that similar discussions were underway to relax Visa requirements in
Adjara first and then for all of Georgia.[407] This too will make Georgians frightened of Russian interference in Georgian affairs. Later an MP from the Revival Party, *Hamlet Chipashvili*, claimed that the *Adjara* has no information

403   N.N., "*Burjanadze* disappointed with Russia." *The Messenger News* (1 December 2003):4.
404   N.N., "Russia Urges Extension of Peacekeepers' Mandate in Abkhazia." Rustavi-2 On-Line News http://www.rustavi2.com.ge/print.php?id=5951 (as of 28 November 2003).
405   N.N., "Georgia Objects Russia's Decision." *Ibid.,* http://www.rustavi2.com.ge/print.php?id=6044 (as of 9 December 2003).
406   Anna Arzanova, "Relaxing the Russia-Adjara Visa Regime Reality Still Unclear." *The Messenger* (10 December 2003):1, 5.
407   *Ibid.*

about any relaxed Visa regime and that the reports of this are false although *Abashidze* recently discussed future plans for this in a meeting with Russian officials in Moscow. However, in another article, the Georgian undersecretary of the Security Council argued that such a simplified procedure should exist for all of Georgia not just *Adjara.* Conversely, Deputy Foreign Minister of Georgia *Kakha Sikharulidze* stated that such a decision would violate Georgian sovereignty. This last article written, by westerners, also claims that while *Abashidze* denies that he wants independence from Georgia, he expressed hope that he could rely on Russian military forces in *Batumi* to assist him in the case of any type of conflict.[408] In the articles written by Georgians, insinuations include allegations that the meeting was held to discuss *Ossetian, Adjaran* and *Abkhazian's* desires to be incorporated into the Russian Federation. *Abashidze* refuted this claim and argued that the discussion only focused on economic development. Unfortunately, sifting through the truth on this subject is clearly impossible given the variation in stories presented. Nonetheless, it remains clear that *Abashidze* continues to flaunt his opposition to the new Georgian central government.

Abashidze's opposition to the new Georgian government is symbolized in his declaration of a state of emergency in *Adjara* following the Rose Revolution. Interim President *Burjanadze* wanted to convince *Abashidze* to end the emergency as well as to persuade him to participate in the presidential election. *Abashidze* purported that the United States pushed S*hevardnadze* to resign, and that this justifies his refusal to participate in the presidential election. *Abashidze* also blamed *Shevardnadze* for the collision of interests between the U.S. and Russia regarding Georgia. *Abashidze admitted* that his perceptions of the Interim government remain negative but he hopes that Georgians will "wake up soon."[409] In response, Presidential candidate *Saakashvili* invited *Abashidze* to negotiate while concomitantly warning *Abashidze,* "Let no one try to intimidate us, we will not allow anyone to divide Georgia. Any step taken against the territorial integrity of our country will be

---

408   Tom Warner and Andrew Jack, "Russia and U.S. Drawn Deeper into Crisis." *Georgia Today In Web-Mix News Section* (28 November 2003): 8.

409   N.N., "Aslan Abashidze Predicts Quick End to Georgia's New Government." Rustavi-2 On-Line News http://www.rustavi2.com.ge/print.php?id=6030 (as of 8 December 2003).

punished severely."[410] This interesting remark comes from a man who currently holds no federal political office. The previously mentioned Moscow meeting returns to the headlines once again reminding readers that both the *Abkhaz* Prime Minister *Raul Khajinba* and South Ossetian President *Eduard Kokoti* attended.[411] Interim President *Burjanadze* was quite disturbed about the meeting especially since Georgia received no invitation to attend. A Georgian political scientist explains that he is concerned about the outcome of such an agreement given *Abashidze's* previous involvement with Russia.[412] This writer revealed that the *Abkhaz* and *Ossetian* leaders promised a negative reaction if Georgia demonstrated any aggressiveness towards them and they reiterated that they remain independent nations.[413] This writer seems incredulous that the Russian Foreign Minister met with Separatist leaders discussing their relations with Russia immediately following Russia's allegedly supportive visit to the new Interim Georgian government. The writer believes that Russia wants to absorb Georgia into its federation because they fear Georgia's growing relationship with the west. However, Moscow overtly contends that it remains supportive of Georgia's territorial integrity. Journalists continue to respond suspiciously to the slightest indication of Russian interference even when unsupported by the facts. This pattern is well established, when *Abkhazia* and Russia concurrently appear in any context, Georgian fears increase.

In attempt to resolve some of these issues, on December 10th, *Burjanadze* visited *Adjara* and met with *Aslan Abashidze* for approximately ten hours. *Abashidze* commented later: "I can only tell that the meeting showed that we could understand each other very well."[414] *Burjanadze* indicated that she was willing to continue the dialogue with *Abashidze*. Conversely, *Tsotne Bakuria*, head of the Revival Party told journalists that the only acceptable solution for *Abashidze* would be a postponement of the forthcoming election.

---

410   N.N., "Mikhail Saakashvili Ready to Compromise Aslan Abshidze." *Ibid.*, http://www.rustavi2.com.ge/print.php?id=6048. (as of 9 December 2003).

411   N.N., "Separatists gather in Moscow." *The Messenger* (1 December 2003): 2.

412   Anna Arzanova, "Visa Regime Discussed for Georgia or Adjara?" *The Messenger* (1 December 2003):4.

413   N.N., "Khajinba-"We are independent republic." *Rustavi2 On Line News* http://www.rustavi2.com.ge/print.php?=5963 (as of 29 November 2003).

414   Natia Mamistvalovi, "Political events on two fronts." *The Messenger* (11 December 2003):1, 4.

Another Revival Party member explained that he thought the meeting was a good idea but that his party still believes that the new government achieved power illegally. Meanwhile in *Tbilisi*, the Second Congressional meeting of the National Movement Party took place in the Sports Palace and *Saakashvili* formally announced his candidacy for President. He promised to create a new government where each Georgian citizen would have an opportunity to take part in state building. *Saakashvili* also pledged once again to restore the nation's territorial integrity. He claims that criminals orchestrated the spate of explosions occurring recently around the country. He further explained that these perpetrators want to stop the forthcoming election. Subsequently, another article claimed that *Saakashvili* launched his campaign for the Presidency much earlier on the 4th of December.[415] He announced that the Chair of his campaign headquarters would be cabinet member, *Zurab Zhvania*. He also referred to his competitors in the campaign as people who want to destroy Georgia. He also socially constructed his own candidacy powerfully, by referencing its similarity to the 1918 first independent Republic of Georgia. Of course, he held his speech in the same physical location presenting himself as the savior of the Georgian people. Finally, promised an end to the political violence claiming that his administration would find these people and punish them. *Zhvania* also spoke at the meeting and asserted that the new government was already making progress by arguing: "No force will succeed in shaking our unity."[416] However, *Zhvania's* references to progress remain unidentified. As the new Nationalist alliance began its campaigning, they received some assistance from the constitutionally recognized Georgian Orthodox Church.

More precisely, in a subsequent article the Georgian Orthodox Church Patriarch *Illia* II attempted to symbolically resolve the problems of territorial integrity *by* meeting with the Russian and Armenian Church Patriarchs. They discussed a variety of problems in their own internationally unrecognized geographical areas. The Georgian Eastern Orthodox Church Patriarch *Ilia* II also met with the Georgian Interim President telling her that it was necessary to mend fences between the former administration and the current admini-

---

415   N.N., "Saakashvili Launches Election Campaign." *Rustavi-2 On Line News In Brief.* http://www.rustavi2.com.get/print.phy?id=6004 (as of 4 December 2003).

stration for the welfare of Georgians.[417] Finally, the Georgian patriarch also met with Russian President Putin who continues to state that he supports Georgia's territorial integrity. Of course, Georgiains perceive this statement as incongruent with Russia's exclusive meetings with *Ossetian, Abkhazian,* and *Adjarian* leaders. Simultaneously, Putin's remarks occurred in the context of Georgia's growing relationship with the American government as illustrated by the on-going presence of American business people in *Tbilisi.*

This relationship between America and Georgia is illustrated in an entire center section of a newspaper (three pages total, labeled "Society") containing a color photo spread consisting of both Americans and Georgians. The headline touted: "The American Chamber of Commerce in Georgia celebrated its 5th Anniversary at the Sheraton *Metechi* Palace Hotel on Saturday."[418] Following dinner and an awards ceremony the description indicated that guests and members danced the night away to the music of the *Tbilisi* Concert Orchestra. The American Chamber of Commerce maintains a number of offices in foreign countries around the world as well as web sites for each office. The web page for this organization states that its aim is

> to promote the development of commercial relations between Georgia, the United States of America, and the international community in Georgia. At the suggestion of former American Ambassador to Georgia, Mr. Kenneth Yalowitz, a group of leading businesspeople representing American interests in Georgia convened to further examine and define the need for an international association of American, Georgian and international businesses. The Chamber was officially registered in Georgia as a non-profit non-commercial organization on September 29, 1998.The founding members of the American Chamber of Commerce: Fady Ashly, Managing Director of Agritechnics; Leigh Durland, President of Absolute Bank; Betsy Haskell, Owner of Betsy's Hotel; Dave Mayer, Vice Chairman of Sante-Walsh Products; and Dennis Stuart, Vice President of Georgia Pipeline Company, envisaged that the

---

416   Mamistvalovi, "Political events on two fronts."
417   Mary Makharashvili, "Georgian Patriarch Travels political circles." *The Messenger* (1 December 2003):4.
418   N.N., "Photographs." *The Messenger* (1 December 2003):6, 7.

Chamber would quickly emerge as the leading organization representing American and International business interests in Georgia. The Chamber protects and promotes the common economic interests of its members and represents their opinions on all types of business matters while striving to facilitate constructive solutions to economic issues concerning Georgia-US business relations. The Chamber promotes its goals by establishing relations with key policy makers and appropriate governmental bodies in both the US and Georgia on subjects of interest to its members. Additionally, the Chamber collects and disseminates timely information concerning areas of interest, organizes conferences and seminars, works on legislative initiatives of concern to the business community in Georgia, and most importantly, provides an ongoing forum for members of the American business community to gather to share knowledge, experiences, problems and solutions. Finally, the Chamber tries to encourage a strong sense of community among businesspeople in Georgia. The Chamber organizes regular social events such as parties, cookouts, receptions, dinners and cultural events. Roundtables and discussion groups are an integral part of the Chamber's commitment to further the sharing of knowledge and experience among its members. We at the Chamber encourage you to join this association either as a company member or as an individual who is interested in learning more about American-Georgian business opportunities. We are excited about the future of the American Chamber of Commerce in Georgia and would like very much for you, your company or your organization to be a part of it.[419]

This telling web statement illustrates the breadth of American postindustrial development and reflects the U.S. government's willingness to act in the interest of all new democracies and capitalist economies while more covertly serving its own best interests. While readers may think my view too jaded, support for this exploitative relationship appears again later, in another issue of *the Messenger*, in which a U.S. based non-profit organization called the Foundation for International Arts and Education (FIAE) reportedly hosted

---

419   The American Chamber of Commerce in Georgia, http://www.amcham.ge/about _us.htm (as of July 2005).

ten Georgians for a month in Washington D.C. While the initial purpose of the visit might have been unclear, Georgian representatives were from a variety of diverse institutions included the mass media, public relations, promotional companies, art and general exhibitions, insurance and banking organizations. The writer reports that the FIAE's stated purpose was to "protect and pre-serve the historical and cultural legacy of countries of the former Soviet Un-ion through supporting exhibitions, education programs, research and practi-cal training for entrepreneurs."[420] However, the FIAE's web page reports a more detailed mission:

> the Foundation for International Arts & Education (FIAE) is a non-profit, 501(c)(3) organization. Headquartered in Be-thesda, Maryland, the Foundation was created to help protect and preserve the historical and cultural legacy of the coun-tries of the former Soviet Union. The Foundation for Interna-tional Arts & Education was created with a set of very explicit goals and principles; Preservation and protection of artistic and cultural legacies; Presentation of first-rate art exhibitions; Adherence to the highest artistic standards in determining the contents and themes of these exhibitions; Protection of the dignity and reputation of the institutions whose artifacts are presented; Involvement of the local host community in all as-pects of planning exhibitions, cultural events and research projects; Assurance that quality educational programs are developed and presented throughout the exhibition's showing in each US community; Support of substantive research and analysis; and Development of practical training programs for entrepreneurs.

The final item listed clearly supports economic globalization with the U.S. at the helm. Thus it appears that support for history and culture probably comes with a price tag. The Georgian newspaper article reports that the FIAE founder was a former cultural attaché to the U.S. Embassy in Moscow during the years 1980-85. Subsequently the Coordinator of the U.S. Soviet Ex-change Initiative for the United States Information Agency (according to their

---

420   Zaza Gachechiladze, "Community Connection in Action." *The Messenger* (3 De-cember 2003):10.

web page USIA is: "An independent foreign affairs agency supporting U.S. foreign policy and national interests abroad) began conducting international education and cultural exchanges, broadcasting and information programs". This program has existed since 1986.[421] Under the subterfuge of cultural exchange, the United States gains more control and influence, and 'profit' than indigenous institutions. This disconcerting form of assistance could be dangerous for Georgians. An article reprinted from the United States newspaper *The Financial Times*, cogently illustrates my concerns about United States' aid.[422] Specifically, the author reports that while the U.S. state department's initial perspective of the November 2nd elections argued that reports of "significant irregularities were "overstatements", three weeks later the State Department stated that it was "deeply disappointed" with the election process. The author argues that the U.S. treated this election differently from the one which transpired equally fraudulently (and more violently) in *Azerbaijan* in October, primarily because the dynastic succession of *Heydar Aliyev's* son in *Azerbaijan* had been expected and he was viewed as more pro-U.S. Conversely, Georgia was viewed as having recently tilted towards Russia and therefore in need of some direction. Dinmore quotes Charles Fairbanks, an election monitor and expert on affairs in central Asia, "Washington Relapolitik school played the Georgian crisis badly. Still events had delivered the Bush administration its first great success in regime change."[423] Even an interview with *Shevardnadze* illustrates that he too believes that Western forces (although he says the United States was not involved) pre-selected *Burjanadze, Zhvania,* and *Saakashvili* as his successors months before the Rose Revolution.[424] *Shevardnadze* purports that a number of NGO's were responsible for creating this revolution by funding opposition movements. He recounts that his reasons for resigning were simply to avoid bloodshed. He also continued to insist that the November elections were fair. Some writers attribute *Shevardnadze's* allegations of interference to his declining state of mind

---

421 United States Information Agency, http://dosfan.lib.uic.edu/usia/ (as of August 2005).

422 Guy Dinmore, "Flaws exposed in strategy of Realpolitik." *Georgia Today* (28 November 2003):9.

423 *Ibid.*

424 Thomas de Wall and Margarita Akhvlediani, "Shevardnadze: A Bitter Resignation (IWPR Interview)." *The Messenger* (3 December, 3 2003):7.

while other journalists claim his inner circle of confidents lied to him about the state of his popularity. Nevertheless, plans for more U.S. assistance are forthcoming, as a U.S. delegation readies itself to come to *Tbilisi* to discuss how the U.S. can help in the forthcoming presidential election. Of course, the other issues scheduled for discussion include the U.S.'s on-going oil interests in the BTC pipeline.[425] In a later discussion of the BTC pipeline, the writer reviewed a UK Guardian article alleging that Russia plans to use Chechen terrorists to commit acts of ecological terrorism on the BTC pipeline.[426] While this writer argues that the BTC pipeline is a major economic security concern of Georgia's, I argue that the security of the pipeline is of more concern to Georgia's foreign investors than to Georgia. A recently re-published policy paper written by a research fellow at the Institute for Advanced Strategic and Political Studies in the United States similarly reflects this theme.[427] The paper argues that Georgia is of strategic interest to the United States for three primary reasons, first as an energy resource with regard to the BTC pipeline and secondly as a possible staging area in the ongoing war on terrorism in the Middle East. Finally, Georgia is an important asset in limiting Russia's ongoing attempt to influence and destabilize the country through their influence in *Abkhazia, South Ossetia,* and *Adjara.* This influence includes the formal Russian presence at three military bases that remain active in Georgia as well as Russia's on-going role as peacekeepers in *Abkhazia.* Of course it should also be noted that Russian clan based organized criminal groups maintain control over a large portion of the shadow economy throughout Georgia. Moreover, the writer argues that Russia's ongoing support of *Abashidze* appears mirrored in *Adjara's* high level of voting fraud observed during the November elections. Simiarly, the November Rose Revolution established more momentum, leading *Abashidze* to shut down all means of transportation to *Tbilisi* and the rest of Georgia to assert his condemnation of the demonstrations. His recent meetings with Moscow and the threat of his secession into the Russian federation, according the writer, warrants America's

---

425   N.N., "U.S. State Administration to Send Delegation to Tbilisi." *Georgia Today* (28 November 2003):2.

426   M. Alkhazashvili, "Anti-BTC terrorism threats." *The Messenger* (4 December 2003):3.

on-going provision of assistance to Georgia. The author also explains that this is necessary to ensure Georgia's future membership in NATO. The extant U.S. investment in Georgian 'national security' includes the sixty-four million dollar Georgian military training and equipment program. The U.S. military also provided assistance in 2002-2003 to help Georgia more effectively manage the *Pankasi-Gorge* located near the Chechen border. This area had become a logistical support route for Chechen rebels in their on-going conflict with Russia for independence. United States' funding and support becomes even more suspect in light of the two oil pipelines running through Georgia. One pipeline includes the three hundred and seventy-five kilometer pipeline from *Baku* to the Georgian Black Sea Port of *Supsa.* It has been operational since 1997. On at least two occasions in May 2002 and again in January 2003, illegal extractions of oil from the line occurred. This disclosure may be an attempt to allay Georgian fears of the possibility of theft from the oil transported in the future BTC line. However, the writer reports that the security system for the new pipeline will be "more advanced." A second front-page article virtually contradicts the previous article by discussing the absence of security with regard to natural gas and electric energy lines. In addition to concerns about poorly constructed and maintained lines as well as theft, the United States continues to be portrayed as rescuing Georgia. Specifically, the Georgia Energy Security Initiative (GESI) sponsored by USAID funds will provide assistance to ten rural Georgian communities to identify and develop alternative energy resources. Secondarily, the GESI also promises to improve economic development.[428] The writer reports that one community, *Dagva* (in *Adjara*) dropped out of the project after the conviction of the election observer in *Kobuleti Adjara* (see pages 126-127). Although not specifically stated, the project sponsors may have determined that *Adjara* was simply too unstable to meet one of the major qualifications of project, community willingness. While the writer asserts that this one incident led to the modification of the agreement, it may be more likely that this is an attempt to disempower *Abashidze* in light of his recent refusal to recognize the Georgian cen-

---

427   Vladimir Socor, "Georgia's Security Dilemma is a Georgian-American Opportunity." *The Messenger* (10 December 2003):7.
428   Christiana Tashkevich, "New Energy project to begin in rural areas Adjara eliminated due to detained election observer." *The Messenger* (4 December 2003):1, 5.

tral government. This kind of U.S. support for the new Georgian government continues to express itself in a variety of other domains.

In early December, the United States announced the allocation of five million dollars to Georgia for re-stabilization following the Rose Revolution. Furthermore, an additional two million will be provided for "The Winter Warmth Program". While this could involve maintenance or repair of natural gas lines, the writer fails to provide specific details with regard to the utilization of the funds.[429] Ideally, the utilization of money could provide safe gas heating across the country. Numerous families need reliable and safe heating both within and outside the capital city.[430] Some Georgians sometimes resort to chopping down trees illegitimately and burning the wood in their homes in order to remain warm. Others build their own natural gas heaters in their homes, resulting in a number of accidental asphyxiations each year. *Tbilisi* City Hall reports that *Tbiligazi* is responsible for keeping track of the prevalence of this problem, however they report that the only data collected comes from the gas heaters they install. *Tbiligazi* is also responsible for inspecting apartments in the city but their staffing shortages prevent them from consistently doing so. Furthermore, they only schedule inspections once every two years. My apartment contained two new and well-functioning gas-heaters therefore I remained warm throughout the winter (after GAZPROM lifted the gas restriction in late November). In contrast, I spent many cold days and evenings teaching classes at the State University as well as cold evenings in friends' apartments who could not afford gas heat. Unfortunately, some Georgian families not only lack heat, they also have no beds to sleep in and little food to eat. The NGO, Stages are sponsors of a project called: "Integration of Marginalized Groups into Society". They provided a series of articles to the newspapers about families or individuals living under critical conditions across Georgia.[431] One such story discussed a single mother living on the outskirts of *Tbilisi* with two children and her mother who earned a 45 GEL

---

429   N.N., "U.S. to Allocate $7 million dollars to Georgia." Rustavi-2 online news http://www.rustavi2.com.ge/rpint.php?id=6005 (as of 4 December 2003).

430   Christina Tashkevich, "Heating woes leave families with few choices Choosing between gas, wood, and electric there are no clear winners." *The Messenger* (12 December 2003):1, 5.

431   N.N., "Little Vika wants to study, but she is not allowed to go to school." *The Messenger* (12 December 2003):4, 5.

annual pension. She rented a two room flat in an old dormitory in *Mukhiani* with a tile floor in one room and a concrete floor in the other. They had no electricity because there is no wiring in the flat. They spent their evenings in candlelight. Her eight-year-old child cannot attend school as she has no birth certificate and it will cost 20 GEL to have a new birth certificate issued. As a result, the mother has home schooled the child for two years. The younger child has a birth defect, hydro-encephalitis, and requires a great deal of medication that the mother remains unable to afford. Thus, this mother placed the child in an orphanage to ensure that she would receive the required medical care. While her family also lacks sufficient food, her neighbors have been giving her food to sustain the family. Ironically, a country provided with so much U.S. and western assistance, growing oil transport lines, flounders when it comes to the welfare of its families. Of course, the same is clearly true of the poor in the United States who remain as poor as many people across the developing world.

In a later article, the Winter Warmth program is identified as a USAID program providing two million U.S. dollars to support regional electricity companies.[432] Yet electricity shortages across the country make it necessary to ration electricity to the regions, according to the Director of the United Georgian Energy Distribution Company (UDC), David Thorton. However, this rationing schedule is also necessary according to the UDC because of each region's poor record of payment for electricity utilized. Additionally, this rationing schedule is also the result of corruption within the regional branches of the UDC. However, then people suffering from this lack of electricity become constrained to bribe employees in order to receive electricity. UDC claimed that those offering bribes wanted to receive more electricity than others. However, the converse is certainly possible as well. That is UDC employees may refuse to provide services to people, unless they receive bribe money. Of course, both scenarios may also be true. All the financial assistance in the world may be unable to eliminate this kind of institutionalized bribery.

---

432   Christina Tashkevich, "Regional electric service to be rationed; not 24-hour." *The Messenger* (10 December 2003):1, 5.

Nonetheless, ignoring such norms regarding bribery, the World Bank and the EBRD developed a five month Power Sector Action Plan that systematically focuses on methods of handling payments, revenues, debts, and expenditures. The plan also involves teaching the Georgian government how to provide improved security to state owned electricity plants. It is dubious how an already financially strapped government, will be able to provide security for fifty-one electric substations. Problems like these previously led to the suspension of electricity imports from Armenia to the *Akhalkalaki* and *Ninostminda* branches of the *Samtskhe-Javakheti* region.

The European Union also pledged additional foreign aid to Georgia in early December.[433] H.E, Torben Holtze, head of the European Commission Delegation to Georgia, reported that the EU plans to furnish 5.26 million GEL to support a variety of other organizations that will provide educational, technical and logistical support for the forthcoming Presidential Election. These funds originated from the EU's "European Initiative for Democracy and Human Rights." The EC plans to accelerate receipt of an additional five million GEL under the Food Security program administered by the Ministries of Agriculture, Education, and Health and Social Services. Another program will also transfer funds to assist in improving Georgian Customs. All this assistance may never change these deleterious conditions but rather only facilitate more corruption and bribery. Illustrative of how little change this aid engenders, Georgia continues to be unable to close the cases involved with the criminal assassination attempts against former President Shevardnadze that occurred in the 1990's.

A suspected conspirator of one attempt is *Igor Giorgadze,* the former Minister of State Security. Recently, after living abroad for some time, *Giorgadze* decided to run for the Presidency. [434] *Giorgadze's* father, the leader of the United Communist Party, announced that his son would return to Georgia if *Shevardnadze* resigned. Since *Giorgadze* is a criminal suspect, he must first seek immunity from prosecution in order to return to Georgia and before running for the office of the President. One writer suggests *Giorgadze* has

---

433   *Idem.* "EU announces new aid package. Countries to fund election program and speed food assistance." *The Messenger* (11 December 2003):1, 5.

434   Anna Arzanova, "The Ultimate Dark Horse Georgian Fugitive provokes furry and possible candidacy." *The Messenger* (3 December 2003):1, 5.

been living in Moscow since his suspected involvement in the 1996 assassination attempt when a car bomb exploded near the President's motorcade.
This transpired shortly after the ratification of Georgia's new constitution.
Conversely, another writer claims that *Giorgadze* has been living in *Abkhazia*.
A member of the *Burjanadze* Democrats' block suggested that *Giorgadze*
should first seek to clear his name or prove his innocence before deciding to
run for office. Politician *Elene Tevdoradze* explained that *Giorgadze's* desire
to run for the Presidency substantiates his guilt, because if he does become
a candidate, he could avoid criminal prosecution. *Tevdoradze* purported that
no normal or sane person would support *Giorgadze* for the President's office.
Another spokesperson for the National Movement is quoted as saying that
Giorgadze has no right to participate in politics as "he has been a fugitive for
ten years and has been charged with terrorists acts-this is a very grave matter, I'm sure he that he won't gather any votes". All Presidential candidates
were required to register by early December and while *Giorgadze* was on the
Central Election Commission's list, the CEC makes the final decisions with
regard to which of the candidates actually meet the qualifications to compete.
Meanwhile, another journalist reveals that *Zurab Zhvania* and the Minister of
Internal Affairs plan to refuse to allow *Giorgadze* permission *to* return to
Georgia or to run for the election. Rather, the Minister of Internal Affairs will
arrest and detain him as soon as he returns. Related suspicions include information revealing that *Giorgadze's* previous appointment as the Minister of
State Security in the early 1990s transpired under pressure from Russia. Following the car explosion in 1995, *Giorgadze* arrested suspects whom he
claimed were previous supporters of *Zviad Gamsakhurdia*. When evidence
surfaced indicating that *Giorgadze* had been involved in the explosion, he
fled to Russia through a Russian military base in *Varian Abkhazia*. Whether
or not he was actually involved in the assassination attempt is now mute, as
his credibility as a potential Presidential candidate were eliminated as the result of these allegations of a relationship with the Russian government. *Saakasvhili* also warned Georgians that *Giorgadze* is preparing a counter-
revolution using "armed brotherhoods", suggesting *Giorgadze* is also involved
in organized crime. Subsequently, *Saakashvili* asked Georgians to support
the new government, explaining: "The situation in the country is really dan-

gerous and even one shot could trigger a thirty year war." [435] Shortly thereafter, the CEC refused to grant *Giorgadze* permission to run for the Presidency.[436] They explained the disqualification as related only to the fact that he had not lived in Georgia for the last two years. They also rejected *Giorgadze's* earlier request to register as a parliamentary candidate. *Giorgadze's* supporters claim that this reflects the absence of democratic principles of the new government, and that the new government simply resembles the old government. Interestingly, the writer argued that *Giorgadze* was a key contender of *Saakashvili's* and that the only other serious challenge to *Saakashvili's* candidacy remains *Temur Sashiashvili*, the former Governor of *Imereti*. Suspicious readers may begin to think that as *Saakashvili's* competitors begin to disappear from the landscape the likelihood of a landslide victory may be a foregone conclusion. However, six other registered candidates for the Presidency successfully accumulated the 50,000 voters' signatures necessary to place their names on the ballot. These six contenders submitted the lists as required to the CEC. After the new Nationalist block and government administration managed to debunk another one of *Saakashvili's* major competitors, they subsequently began to 'clean house' by initiating a series of dismissals and arrests, first within the police department.

Recently appointed Interior Minister reported in a news briefing that thirteen police officers were recently fired and six charged with "drug addiction."[437] The Minister also instructed regional police chiefs to begin similar proceedings against their corrupt staff. The interior minister also issued a decree that poppy seeds used in baking shops were actually drugs. Therefore, orders were to confiscate them from markets and stores and then destroy them. However, it later became apparent that this was also an error in translation and perhaps a mistake in judgment as another piece in a subsequent newspaper clarifies that the government destroyed opium poppy seeds. Journalistic mistakes like these make the Georgian news media virtually unpalatable at times. Nevertheless, opium abuse has become another social

---

435   *Ibid.*
436   Natia Mamistalovi, "CEC rejects Giorgadze's candidacy." *The Messenger* (15 December 2003): 5.
437   N.N., "Police clean house ban poppy seeds." *The Messenger News in Brief* (4 December 2003):4.

problem for Georgia. The Interior Minister stated that this drug is technically legal. However, he plans to ensure that this is changed. Congruent with this new American like war on drugs, the Interior Minister ordered the arrest and detention of the Director of the *Vake-Saburtalo*, who is the son of the Chief Prosecutor of *Tbilisi*, for abusing narcotics. Similar charges leveled against the Chief of Police of the *Saburtalo* district transpired before his arrest.[438] However, a variety of extant research reflects that the arrest, conviction, and incarceration of drug addicts and alcoholics, the supply reduction model, has no deterrent effect and that ultimately no criminal or prosecutorial war on drugs will ever eliminate or reduce drug or alcohol dependence. Rather effective reduction requires mandating drug treatment. Additionally the advent of the new drug courts that order drug treatment also successfully reduce drug related criminal behavior. However, Georgia seems to be following the American supply reduction model, the less effective and more costly method of intervening.

As the arrests of former officials continued, acting President *Burjanadze* met with the Regional President of British Petroleum, the company primarily responsible for building the *Baku-Tbilisi-Ceyhan* pipeline.[439] Both politely conversed and emphasized that the pipeline will benefit Georgia. The BTC pipeline will become operational by the first quarter of 2005. Similarly, *Burjanadze* states that she is also supportive of the *Shah-Deniz* gas pipeline. Conveniently, financial aid flows in, symbolic arrests transpire, and laudatory comments about new oil pipelines resound.

The new President also made her first official trip out of the country when she attended the OSCE Foreign Ministerial Council meeting in *Maastricht*.[440] [441] There the U.S. Secretary of State again announced U.S. support for Georgia's new leadership as well as for their continued territorial integrity. However, Russian Foreign Minister Igor Ivanov told journalists that he was

---

438   N.N., "Interior Ministry Cracks Down on Drug Abusers." *Rustavi-2 On Line New* http://www.rustavi2.com.ge/rpint.php?id=6006 (as of 4 December 2003).
439   N.N., "News In Brief. BP updates Burjanadze on BTC." *The Messenger* (1December 2003):4.
440   Allison Ekberg, "Interim President receives warm words in Maastricht. U.S. Opposes support to Separatists." *The Messenger* (3 December 2003):1, 5.
441   Gia Bakradze, "First International Acknowledgement." *Georgia Today* (5 December 2003):2.

against a U.S. Georgian relationship and believed that Russia and Georgia, because of their great alliance over the last two centuries, should be able to resolve any of their difficulties given enough political will.[442] *Burjanadze* also met with the OSCE President, Bruce George. George told the new President that it was important to ensure that the parliamentary elections were re-scheduled soon. While the CEC previously re-scheduled the election for late January, they recently asked the President for a postponement. Again, the OSCE President re-iterated that it is necessary that Georgia conduct fair and democratic elections by creating a "credible electoral administration and to eliminate the corrupt electoral culture of the past…if the forthcoming elections will not meet international standards, it will be detrimental to the international credibility of the democratization process in Georgia."[443] The OSCE President also promised financial aid, almost three million Euros for the Presidential election and three and a half million Euros for the Parliamentary Elections.[444] OSCE plans to send a delegation to Georgia to observe the next round of elections. The Office for Democratic Institutions and Human Rights (ODIHR) will also deploy thirty long-term observers and four hundred and fifty short-term observers.

Only weeks after the Rose Revolution apathy appears to have crystallized again as a recently scheduled parliamentary session met but failed to reach a quorum.[445] As a result, some MPs are questioning the lawfulness of confirming two new appointments to the government, one the new Chairman of the CEC, *Zurab Chiaberashvili*, and the other of the Foreign Minister, *Tedo Japaridze*. The Chairperson of the Parliament's procedural committee told reporters that a re-scheduled confirmation hearing would repeat the process with a quorum present. *Japaridze* was formerly the National Security Secretary, and prior to that served as Foreign Ambassador as well as in a variety of other capacities within the Foreign Ministry.[446] *Japaridze* claims that his priorities include strengthening relations with Russia and the United States as

---

442   *Ibid.*
443   Ekberg. "Interim President receives warm words in Maastricht."
444   Bakradze, "First International Acknowledgement."
445   N.N., "Quorum Remains to be a Feat in the Parliament." Rustavi-2 online news http://www.rustavi2.com.get/print.phy?id=6007 (as of 4 December 2003).
446   N.N., "National Security Council Chief is Taking over the Foreign Ministry." *Georgia Today* (5 December 2003):4.

well as resolution of the *Abkhazian* problem. He also promised to continue Georgia's partnership with the U.S. in the fight against terrorism. The U.S. military's Train and Equipment program goal is to develop four "anti-terrorist" battalions in Georgia. The parameters of this anti-terrorist battalion remain unspecified. The U.S. has spent sixty-four million dollars on the program scheduled to end in 2004. Once gain, money flows into Georgia and continues to have no effect on the poor. Even more disconcerting are the continuing arguments about whether or not to invalidate the proportional portion of the election or the proportional and the majoritarian portions.

Since late November, the number of MPs who voted to appeal the results of the majoritarian elections to the Constitutional court increased from seventy-three to eighty-eight.[447] However, some MPs subsequently withdrew their names from the petition even after the deadline leaving the current number appealing at forty-three. This invalidates the required one fifth of parliament necessary to take the case to the Constitutional court. The author speculates that the court will extend the deadline in order to allow some MPs to re-consider. In *Zugdidi,* a majoritarian independent candidate began a hunger strike protesting against the Supreme Court's decision to re-count the majoritarian portion of the *Zugdidi* votes.[448] Other political changes include a large number of Labor party members who continue to become members of the new government block.[449] However, one Labor Party leader, *Shalva Natelashvili,* held a press conference and proposed an alternative to the current crisis between *Adjara* and the new government. He suggested reconvening the November elected Parliament to resolve the conflict. Furthermore, he claims that the only opposition to this proposal is *Zurab Zhvania* whom he refers to as the "immortal gray cardinal." *Natelashvili* has also taken this proposal to the Supreme Court asking them to annul the November proportional election results. He argues that this is necessary in order to eliminate the possibility of *Adjara's* secession. He believes that *Adjara* will secede if the Presidential election occurs as currently scheduled for 4 January. In re-

---

447   Mary Makharashvili, "Mps withdraw support for invalidating majoritarian election results." *The Messenger* (4 December 2003):1, 5.

448   N.N., "Strike in Zugdidi." *Rustavi-2 news online* http://www.rustavi2.com.ge/print.php?=6029 (as of 8 December 2003).

sponse to his proposal, party members of the National Movement and the *Burjanadze* Democrats spoke on Rustavi-2's television program *"Kourieri"* and retorted that his proposal was unacceptable, without providing any additional information.

On December 9th an election observer previously convicted in *Kobuleti, Adjara* (see pages 126-127) for an alleged under a hooliganism charge was released after several rounds of meetings between the U.S. Deputy Assistant Secretary of State Lynn Pascoe and U.S. Ambassador Richard Miles.[450] *Giorgi Mshvenieradze*, a Fair Elections observer's detention followed an altercation at the polling station during the November election. MP *Hamlet Chipashvili* from the Revival Party and head of *Adjara's Tbilisi* headquarters blamed the media for inflaming the situation. The President of the Young Lawyers Association believes that the detention of the young man was retaliatory and followed the filing of a case against the *Adjaran* government asserting that they violated the media's right to free speech.[451] In a reporter's interview with *Mshvenieradzi,* questions focused on the incident in *Kobuleti.* The twenty-one year old husband and father to-be characterized the situation very differently than the description previously provided by *Adjaran* state TV. The young law student explained that as he continued to observe election violations and reported them to the Fair Election headquarters, local officials asked him to stop sending in his reports. However, he refused and subsequently the *Adjaran* authorities demanded his silence. Finally, the authorities threatened to assault him if he continued to report the fraudulent voting. Finally, after consistently refusing to submit to their demands, he explained that a police officer verbally provoked him and the verbal altercation quickly became a physical altercation. Although provoked, the young man confessed to throwing the first punch. While observers receive training requiring them to remain unresponsive if provoked, he was unable to confrom and in this way provided *Adjaran* officials an excuse to escort both he and his observation

---

449   Sopho Gorgodze, "Labour Party's new proposal." *The Messenger* (11 December 2003):4.

450   Mary Makharashvili, "U.S. insistence helped free observer Adjara credits U.S. Ambassador for raising attention to Abashidze's attention." *The Messenger* (10 December 2003):5

451   *Idem.* "Interpretations of Mshvenieradze's Release." *The Messenger* (12 December 2003):1, 7.

partner to the prosecutor's office. Subsequently, the *Adjaran* officials purported that after examining him they found him to be under the influence of drugs. The young man denied that he was under the influence of any mood altering chemicals. The *Adjaran* TV news reported that the observer thanked for police for intervening in his "drunken quarrel". *Mshvenieradze* purported that this was a distortion of his remarks and that he only thanked one police officer who safely escorted him away from the precinct following the incident. Although he explains that received no poor treatment during his six weeks in prison, he described the prison conditions negatively but provided no specific details. The GYLA President reports that they are filing a case with the Supreme Court for *Mshvenieradze's* complete exoneration. This provocation and arrest provides a salient example of how *Adjarian* television and government officials' manufacture and or manipulate public opinion with regard to the Georgian central government. While both constructed political violence and real political violence remain mainstays of the news, almost no media coverage of intimate partner violence appears in the Georgian press.

One of the most prevalent social problems in Georgia and globally that continues to be unreported and unresolved is domestic violence. This issue received no media attention from late July until mid December when one article briefly mentioned the existence of the problem. Moreover, the report provided no specific data on its frequency or prevalence.[452] Attending to women's issues is not high on the agenda of the Georgian government. I observed two incidents of violence against women on public streets during my ten months in Georgia. In one incident, a young man slapped a young woman during what appeared to be an intimate quarrel. In another incident, a middle-aged man pushed an elderly woman onto the ground after an exchange of angry words (passers by told me that he was her son and that they were IDPs). During each incident, witnesses simply ignored both the verbal altercation and the physical violence. In the second instance, I tried to get locals to call the police, but they were dismissive since those involved were just "IDPS."

---

452   N.N., "Families without violence International Day of Human Rights draws attention to domestic issue." *The Messenger* (11 December 2003):5.

I visited the first Domestic Violence Shelter opened to women and their children in *Tbilisi* in June of 2004. However, one article claims that Safari Union, a different NGO, was the first agency to open such a shelter. An NGO with private funds managed the facility that I visited in June. No public funds are available to support these endeavors. As mentioned previously, there has been no women's movement in Georgia to call attention to violence against women. Similarly, there has been no movement to increase public awareness of mental illness and dispel the stigma association with it. Therefore, mental health treatment also remains primarily managed and organized by private NGOs with grants from international organizations. While I know Georgian scholars, social activists and mental health practitioners who are working to ensure an end to violence against women, other educated Georgians seem to be either in denial or just as unaware of these problems as is the public and the traditional Georgian media. The absence a feminist movement explains this lack of awareness and social inaction. Moreover, it was the second wave of feminism in Western Democratic nation states that drew attention to the problem of violence against women by demanding government intervention. While women's issues are simply not on the Georgian's radar screen, relatedly, the countries economic issues are comparmentalized and viewed as separate problems unrelated to women. Gender is not seen as related to poverty, even though most elder street beggars are women, and my observation that women continue to be unrepresented within the government continues to be absent from public discourse as it might be related to Georgia's pervasive problem with bribery and corruption.

On December 12th, *Saakashvili* spoke to business leaders about his plans if elected President and used *Levan Mamaladze* as an example (see page 77) of "high level corrupt political authorities" that will be prosecuted.[453] He also accuses the *Tbilisi* City Hall of systemic corruption or "group debauchery and drunkenness." He promised to "take care" of corruption, stop tax collectors from accepting bribes, and eliminate administrative tariffs on businesses. He explained that politics should not interfere with business. He also asked businesses to contribute to improving Georgia in public projects

---

453   Christina Tashkevich, "Saakashvili shows support for businesses warns economic miracles are not a possibility." *The Messenger* (15 December 2003):1, 3.

like re-building roads. He espoused that the Georgian education system must be re-vamped and suggested that until then Georgians should go abroad for a higher education and then return to Georgia to help improve the institution. He refers to the conditions in *Adjara* as like those on a different planet and holds *Shevardnadze* accountable for this problem. In further political posturing, he promised to launch a campaign against smuggling. Another article discussed this speech and told readers that the participants at the meeting, while not surprised by *Saakashvili's* statements, reported feeling hopeful about the changes he promised to deliver.[454] However, this journalist also explained that the most powerful business leaders in Georgia were not invited to the event. These elite individuals include two thousand members of the Tax-Payers Union. Only twenty people from this group were invited. The writer interviewed the Chair of the Tax Payers' Union, *Batoni Lekishvili,* who stated that he was concerned about the state of the current parliament and feared that the new parliamentary elections will not transpire. He also complained about corruption and believed that bribe seeking custom officials were responsible for ruining business profits. Furthermore, he explained that while the new government has introduced Supervisory Councils to act as semi-regulatory agencies, they are primarily responsible for awarding government contracts. He also stated that the council maintains a separate committee for each type of business with only a few select business people maintaining seats. The problem with this is that these pre-selected businessmen abuse their power by shutting out their competitors from the bidding process. He further explained that the Council is supposed to ensure the transparency of economic policies not the preferential treatment of some businesses over others. The information provided in the article once again lacks clarity and readers are only provided with the opinion of one businessman with no opposing views presented nor further information detailing the exact mission or responsibilities of this new Supervisory council. Nonetheless, this is reminiscent of the no-bid contract offered to Vice President Dick Cheney's old company, Halliburton, to rebuild war torn Iraq, unfair, convenient, and unethical if not illegal. Defining corruption in such a manner as to

---

454   Nino Psaturia, "Call for More...." *Georgia Today* (19 December 2003):1, 5.

prevent clientelism is a necessity for the world's future, not just within Georgia.

As the government's fight against crime and corruption continued, the Prosecutor subpoenaed information from TBC bank with regard to the commercial transactions of two gold mining companies, *Kwartsis* and *Madneuli.*[455] *Madneuli* was co-managed by a Georgian and Australian company; however, Georgian Lawyers allege that their Australian partners attempted to swindle them out of their share of the profits. In the process of the investigation and subpoena, Georgian lawyers for a second bank, Investbank, that stored the gold (it is unclear if the journalist was referring to the actual gold or merely profits from the gold) claimed that law enforcement officials tried to forcibly remove the evidence (gold or profit from gold). If under a subpoena, the bank was obliged to release information listed in the legal paperwork. However, the bank in question, *Investbank*, refused to answer the inquiries of the investigative journalists. Interestingly, this gold came from the *Bolnis*i area, the same location where *Saakashvili's* entourage had been assaulted during the pre-November election campaigning. If the suspected theft perpetrated by the Australian business partners became substantiated the poor quality of models for ethical business conduct available in Georgia would be even more apparent.

Although not yet elected President, *Saakashvili's* campaign promises to arrest corrupt officials continues with the arrest of the President of Georgia's football association, *Merab Zhordania*. Supcisions were that he embezzled three hundred and fifty-two thousand dollars.[456] Law enforcement authorities discovered the missing funds after a scheduled transfer of money from the state budget to the state football association did not occur. Charges filed against *Zhordania* included the misappropriation of funds and tax evasion. While the new Minister of Internal Affairs denied any political motivations for the arrest, *Zhordania's* ex-wife believes that the new government's pursuit of alleged corrupt officials reflects efforts to eliminate the former associates of *Shevardnadze*.

---

455   Misha Kobaladze, "Georgian Gold Mines in Trouble." *Ibid.*
456   Anna Arzanova, "Zhordania charged with embezzlement." *The Messenger* (15 December 2003):1, 7.

Similar corruption charges against *Sulkhan Molashvili,* the out-going Chair of the Control Chamber, were filed and included the misappropriation of millions of GEL and murder. He is a suspect in the recent murder of *Nika Lominadze,* head of the Finance Department of the American Electric Service *Telasi* office. His suspeced involvement in the murder later led investigators to the evidence of corruption within the Control Chamber. Later *Molashvili* reported in a news conference that no such charges existed and no prosecutors had contacted his office. He also retorts that his office initially reported the corruption problem specifying the problem was within the Energy sphere. The control chamber acts as an auditing or inspection agency and reports suspicions of corruption to the Parliament and the Prosecutor's office for investigation. *Molashvili* told journalists that the allegations have more to do with his previous position in *Shevardnadze's* government, than any real wrongdoing. He also claims that authorities from the Security Council have been harassing him by making these false claims. Later in the month, *Molashvili* resigned, although he reportedly had intentions to do so regardless of the allegations made against him. Interestingly, he also explained that the harassment began after he collected documentation that revealed corruption among the relatives of some high-ranking officials. However, he refused to disclose if those involved were members of the current government or the former government. Finally, *Molashvili* accused *Burjanadze* of making false statements about his effectiveness as the head of the control chamber. Specifically he argued that his agency brought over five hundred criminal cases to the attention of Prosecutor over the last three years, compared to the minimal forty-eight that Russia's equivalent chamber submitted. He further reveals that his office successfully removed over three hundred people for bribery or corruption offenses using Control Chamber files.

While charges and counter-charges of corruption continue, another assault against a journalist occurred. Fortunately, the writer was not seriously injured.[457] The journalist, *Irakli Chikhladze,* was investigating problems among Georgia's minority population and had made recent inquires about corruption in the *Kvemo Kartli* region (where *Bolnisi* is located). Following the initial assault, he received additional verbal threats after pursuing additional

---

457   N.N., "Journalist Targeted." *Ibid.,* 5.

information about his assailants. The head of the American Chamber of commerce in Georgia, Fady Asly, contends that the government arrests and allegations against former and current government officials as well as the violence committed against journalists have become political tools used to eliminate the competition and silence critical media coverage.[458] Other victims, he claims are simply scapegoats, including the Georgian Football Federation President *Zhordania*. He stated that most Georgian officials are involved (99%) in corruption and therefore suggested that offering amnesty to everyone involved might be a better method of resolving the problem. He also explained that some of the new appointees of the new government are notoriously corrupt.

While the accusations continue to mount from both sides, the new administration against the old, another political block takes shape.[459] The National Democrats and the Traditionalists united behind a former member of the *Burjanadze*-Democrats, *Akaki Asatiani*. *Asatiani* criticized the new government arguing against their plans to nationalize previously privatized state property. Apparently, the new administration's intentions in planning this endeavor include an attempt to limit the corruption of business people. However, *Astiani* argues that such a solution is not viable. He refers to his new party block as the rightist opposition force and his co-leader, former Chair of the Traditionalists, *Bachuki Kardava,* reiterates *Asatiani's* claims. In an interview with a member of the *Burjanadze*-Democrats *Lado Papava,* he reports that he is pleased that *Asatiani* is uniting an opposition group. *Papava* argues that political opposition forces are good for Georgian politics.[460] Yet, *Papava* also has concerns about the administration especially with regard to future appointments that *Saakashvili* might make if elected as President. *Papava* suspects that *Saakashvili's* administration will have western educations and unless they are experts in their fields, he questions the appropriateness of such decisions. He also expresses concerns about the indebtedness of the country and the need to convince the Paris club that Georgia can re-pay its debts on a regular schedule. He insinuates that the new minister of finance, *Noghaideli*, is not a real economist and thus may be unable to manage the

---

458   Nino Patsuria, "Progress will be very slow." *Georgia Today* (19 December 2003):4.
459   Zaza Jgharkava, "Opposition Unites." *Georgia Today* (19 December 2003):2.

ministry, although he voices no complaints about what the new Minister has done thus far.

During the holiday season, I was out of the country. Therefore, throughout the remainder of December and the entire month of January the only reviewed articles analyzed were from *Rustavi-2*'s online Internet service provider. The main objective during this time was to keep track of the presidential election and any major political, social, or economic changes made immediately following the election period.

Over seven hundred election observers from a variety of international organizations were located in two hundred and twenty-six election districts across Georgia during the election conducting exit polls. GSG's poll revealed that although 12.8% of voters refused reveal for whom they voted, 85.6% of voters' reported voting for *Mikhail Saakashvili*. Only three other candidates individually each received less than one percent of the vote. [461] [462] Organizations sponsors of the election observers included the Organization and Security Council of Europe's (OSCE) Office for Democratic Institutions and Human Rights, the OSCE and the EU Parliaments. Other organizations observing the election process included the Georgian "Young Lawyers Association" and the Georgian NGO "Fair Elections." Additional election observers present in Georgia included a group from the Commonwealth of Independent States. The supervisor of these one-hundred and twenty observers called the Presidential election "fair and legal."[463] The chief of the party was quoted as indicating that this Presidential election "was the best among all previous Georgian elections"…with a "high voter turnout." By the end of the voting day, both the preliminary government's Central Election Commission as well as the international and national election observers revealed that *Mikhail Saakashvili* won the Presidential election by collecting ninety-six percent of the vote.[464] Unfortunately, this writer did not differentiate between government results

460   *Idem.* "IMF program must Resume." *Ibid.,* 3.
461   N.N., "Results of Exit Polls." Rustavi-2 Online News http://www.rustavi2.com.ge/ view.php?id=6273 (as of 5 January 2004).
462   N.N., "Election Observers Make Preliminary Conclusions." *Ibid.,* http://www.rustavi2.com.ge/view.php?id=6275.
463   N.N., "CIS Observers Asses Presidential Elections Positively." *Ibid.,* http://www.rustavi2.com.ge/view.php?id=6276.
464   N.N., "Preliminary Data Say Saakashvili Wins Elections by 95% of Votes." *Ibid.,* http://www.rustavi2.com.ge/view.php?id=6277.

and monitoring reports. The journalist provided a brief education and employment history of *Mikhail Saakashvili* including his foreign education credentials from a variety of universities abroad including U.S., Ukrainian, and French institutions. The author mentioned *Saakashvili's* graduation from Columbia University law school graduate, a very prestigious U.S. school. The author reviewed his role as a two time elected Parliamentarian in Georgia and his membership in *Shevardnadze's* party, the Citizen's Union of Georgia. The author also discussed his later appointment as *Shevardnadze's* Minister of Justice in 2000. Following his departure from that that position he formed the National United Nationalist Movement-Democratic Front Party. Finally, the article briefly summarizes *Saakashvili's* role in the Rose Revolution and his ouster of *Shevardnadze*, referred to as *"Shevardnadze's* twelve year regime." Another brief article reports that the former President, *Eduard Shevardnadze,* also reported casting his vote for *Saakashvili*. The former President said he believes that *Saakasvhili* is a "skillful and initiative person" although he lacks "experience."[465]

Following the post-election celebratory comments and the Eastern Orthodox Christmas festivities, the new government's pursuit of official corruption continued. In mid January, the head of the Post-Bank of *Saburtalo* was detained for corruption related offenses. Specific charges included embezzling 500,000 GEL (approximately 250,000 dollars) and misappropriating 1.2 GEL (600,000 dollars) allocated for IDP support.[466] The on-going investigation is seeking other suspects that may have been involved in the offense, what the article calls "his accomplices." However, this man has been in pre-trial custody for three months. Therefore, this should not necessarily be attributed to the new political order, but rather to *Shevardnadze's* administration. Another journalist reported that sixty IDPS forcefully entered the Post Bank *Samegrelo-Zemo Zvaneti* region Presidential office demanding their late support payments.[467] The IDPs were from *Zugdidi* in *Abkhazia* and explained that they had not received any social security payments for several

---

465   N.N., "Georgia's Ex-President Pledges to Assist Saakashvili." *Ibid.,* http://www.rustavi2.com.ge/view.php?id=6279.
466   N.N., "Head of Post Bank Saburtalo Branch Detained." *Ibid.,* http://www.rustavi2.com.ge/view.php?id=6276 (as of 13 January 2004).

months. Outside the building, another three hundred IDPS from *Abkhazia* also gathered in protest. As the elite steal from the poor making the rich richer, Georgia's poor suffer enormous losses as the possibility of gaining class privilege escapes them. As a result, IDPS and others who do not have the necessities that are required seek these resources from the cheapest available place. Often this means buying through illegal markets or from illegal sellers because the goods are less expensive. Inevitably, this means such markets or sellers become associated with the poor and earn bad reputations even if undeserved. The same was true in *Tbilisi*. When the privileged class members discussed these problems, they becomce framed in the context of public health.

Similarly, a Tbilisi City Assembly meeting discussed a variety of sanitary problems across the city capital but exclusively focused on the open market.[468] Three men recently died after eating contaminated food sold at the market. Ten additional men were recently hospitalized after suffering from botulism from similarly contaminated foods. The City Assembly gave "market authorities" 24 hours to clean up the area. This particular area is a section of the city near the railroad station that is also located next to the local market where authorized/licensed retailers sell food, meat, flour, seasoning, vegetables, and fruit. The illicit open market sets just in front the legal market. It is here where unlicensed Georgian retailers sell similar goods more cheaply and on a smaller scale. These sellers are poor and sell their few products in order to survive. I received warnings from some locals to beware of pickpockets in the area. Others also suggested to me that the food sold there might not always be fresh or safe. Although I purchased food from the unlicensed traders on many occasions, including fruit, vegetables and cooking oil and never suffered any consequences. By the time I left *Tbilisi* in June 2004, this open-air illicit market near the legal market was gone. I do not know what happened to these former sellers, but I felt sad that they had no other options for earning wages. Meanwhile, some middle class Georgians seemed to believe that these street vendors were thieves or robbers who charged too

---

467   N.N., "Leri Chitanava Demands Institution of Criminal Charges Against Post Bank." *Ibid.,* http://www.rustavi2.com.ge/view.php?id=6343.
468   N.N., "Anti-sanitary Situation in Tbilisi Discussed in the City Assembly." *Ibid.,* http://www.rustavi2.com.ge/view.php?id=6345.

much for spoiled goods and "dirtied up the place." Other complaints included the allegations that the vendor's booths blocked automobile traffic. This was accurate; they occupied a two to four block area in both the middle of the streets and sidewalks. These illegal market sellers could have easily been too poor to afford a license to sell their product or pay taxes on items sold.

The traders told reporters that they would comply with the new law if the government made other jobs available. While mortality from botulism is a serious problem, the exploration of some other less punitive and harmful public policy is necessary. Another article reveals that this new law passed by *Tbilisi* City Assembly banned all street trading for anyone selling goods without a proper license (thereby avoid paying taxes). The city promised tax paying street vendors covered stalls' regardless of their location, while there was talk that use of force might be necessitated to remove the" illegal" street vendors. However, in my neighborhood, every day from dawn until dusk near my apartment, several local women sold fruit on the corner as they sat on uncomfortable looking boxes. After the new law passed, they just moved to the underground walkway beneath the main street and continued to sell their small baskets of fruit. These women survivors found a way to subvert and resist the government's attempt at social control. This effort to rid the city of the poor and create a front-stage appearance of respectability mirrored the continuing wave of arrests of allegedly corrupt government officials. Specifically, on January ninteenth, the Minister of Finance announced that he fired the heads of three regional Tax offices for suspected involvement in violating trade asset laws. These infractions cost the state budget an estimated eight million GEL, probably a substantially greater amount than is lost from illegal street sales.[469] In addition to these efforts to make Georgia look better, *Saakashvili's* previous suggestions with regard to constitutional changes also begin to take shape.

The first symbolic change to the constitution included a new national flag. The Parliament met in mid January without a quorum, as the writer argues that they frequently do, to discuss a variety of draft amendments, in-

---

469   N.N., "Several Heads of Tax Offices have been fired." *Ibid.,* http://www.rustavi2. com.ge/view.php?id=6388 (as of 19 January 2004).

cluding the new flag.[470] The proposed flag is an ancient Orthodox Christian Church Flag called the Five Crosses. The flag also was a replication of President *Mikhail Saakashvili's* Nationalist Party flag. As parliament discussed the bill, National Movement supporters carried the flag into the Parliamentary session and subsequently stationed flags on the balconies of the building. Other significant issues discussed by the parliament included the President's nomination for the post of the Prosecutor General. *Saakashvili* recently nominated the current Prosecutor, *Nugzar Gabrichidze,* for a position as a Supreme Court Judge. As these transformations continue across the Georgian political arena, what remains consistently irritating to Georgians is the Russian military presence. However, Georgian Foreign Minister, *Tedo Japaridze*, expressed as his belief that negotiations with regard to the closure of the remaining Russian military bases in Georgia will eventually end successfully.[471] However, the Foreign Minister also told the media that Russia has demanded eleven more years to complete the process of withdrawing from Georgia. Nevertheless, The Georgian government responded that they considered three years a sufficient period to withdraw troops and equipment. The Foreign Minister disclosed that the Russian government concession to less time is contingent on the provision of five hundred million dollars in compensation. The continuing Russian presence, in concert with the elimination of *Abashidze's* rule in *Adjara,* and the problem of re-integrating *Abkhazia* continues to create dissention and debate among Georgians.Recently the Chairperson of the Supreme Council of the *Abkhazian Autonomous* Republic of Georgia in exile resigned from his post.[472] While the extent of the powers of this council are absent from the report, the post represents at least some symbolic value in light of Russia's presence, the IDPs, and the secession of *Abkhazia*. One member of the council, describes this resignation of the Chairperson (*Tamaz Nadareishvili*) as an "ouster." Conversely, *Nadareishvili* reports that he will meet with the President of Georgia to discuss a potential future assignment. The journalist argues that this is

---

470   N.N., "Parliament to Accept Prosecutor General's Candidacy and Approve National Flag." *Ibid.,* http://www.rustavi2.com.ge/view.php?id=6351 (as of 14 January 2004).
471   N.N., "Georgian Foreign Minister Believes Russia will Sooner or Later Withdraw its Bases from Georgia." *Ibid.,* http://www.rustavi2.com.ge/view.php?id=6354.

this is only the beginning, that additional changes in the make-up of the Supreme Council in exile are forthcoming.

Meanwhile the founder of the non-governmental organization, "Our *Adjara*" filed a law suit against *Aslan Abashidze. The* suit *charges that Abashidze* illegally instituted a state of emergency in *Adjara*[473] It also argues that *Abashidze* has no right to declare an emergency, that only the Georgian President and the Parliament have that authority under the constitution. The constitutional court will review the case soon.

In mid January, the Central Elections Commission released the final tally of the votes for the President reflecting *Mikhail Saakasvhili's* victory with 96.27 percent of the vote. The commission reported that almost two million citizens voted, with thirteen thousand ballots invalidated. However, two other political parties, the New Rights and the Labor Party, renounced the voting as improper due to what they called errors in the preliminary registration procedures.[474]   Complaints by rival parties at this point might have been more successful had they argued that the new constitutional changes proposed by *Saakashvili* were occurring too rapidly or even before the new parliamentary election.

While no political complaints appeared about the constitutional changes, Journalists provided their own weak criticisms of the proposed changes. One journalist writes that *Saakashvili's* appointment of a Prime Minister and a new cabinet were all so young, they resembled kindergartners who should be hidden in any case of a visit from Michael Jackson. This followed the worldwide announcement of charges against Jackson for child molestation, although the jury later found Jackson innocent. Shortly thereafter, *Saakashvili* appointed *Zurab Zhvania* as the new Prime Minister. *Zurab Zhvania was* a front stage co-leader in the Rose Revolution. *Zhvania* promptly met with the High Representative of the European Commission for

---

472   N.N., "Nadareishvili Decided to Resign." *Ibid.,* http://www.rustavi2.com.ge/view.php?id=6347.

473   N.N., "Diasamidze Sues Aslan Abashidze." *Ibid.,* http://www.rustavi2.com.ge/view.php?id=6346.

474   N.N., "CEC Released Final Results of Presidential Elections." *Ibid.,* http://www.rustavi2.com.ge/view.php?id=6360 (as of 15 January 2004).

Foreign Affairs and Security in mid January in *Tbilisi*.[475] Discussions centered on Georgia's future relationship with the European Commission. The Prime Minister interpreted the visit as reflective of the EU's support of Georgia. Later the European Commission's head of Foreign Affairs and Security met with President *Saakasvhili*. *Saakashvili* reportedly quipped that Georgia had proven its European origins to the whole world, it is not clear if he was referring to himself, to the revolution or to his new administration.

As is mentioned above, other changes include *Saakashvili's* appointment of a new Prosecutor General to launch his on-going "fight against corruption."[476] The Parliament approved *Irakli Oqrusavhili* as the Prosecutor General on January forteenth. One article describes the Prime Minister's introduction of the Prosecutor to his staff. The Prime Minister proudly explained that *Irakli Oqruashvili* would restore the rule of law throughout the country. In his speech to his staff, the Prosecutor promised that his office would launch a "real" fight against crime and corruption and incompetent prosecutors' dissmisal would follow. The administration continues to construct the appearance of a genuine attempt to eliminate or at least reduce corruption.

More constitutional changes came from by the Parliament in a bill reccommending that the eletion of Parliamentarians from *Abkhazia*. However, the bill would require the election of these PMs using the majoritarian system rather than the proportional system currently used. The bill also framed that the PMs elected should be members of the New Rights and Fund of Social Programs Party. The introduction and passage of the bill would result in these PM positions being chosen in the forthcoming elections scheduled in late. This would represent a challenge to the existing political block, a good thing in a democracy, probably perceived as a bad thing to the new administration.[477] These parliamentarians would represent Georgian IDPs who originally lived in *Abkhazia*.

Current negotiators on the *Abkhazian*–Georgian issue include the Special Representative of the United Nations Secretary General, the Georgian

475   N.N., "Zhvania and Saakashvili Met Javier Solana." *Ibid.,* http://www.rustavi2.com.ge/view.php?id=6358.
476   N.N., "New Prosecutor General Pledges to Really Fight Corruption." *Ibid.,* http://www.rustavi2.com.ge/view.php?id=6361.

Minister for Extraordinary Matters, *Malkhaz Kakabadze* and the head of Georgia's Intelligence Department as well as members of the *Abkhazian* separatist government. New proposals in this process include the continuing work by the coordinating council to manage the peace talks as well as make recommendations to resolve the crime problem in the *Gali* border region. Unfortunately, the Georgian delegation "demanded" that the armed custom checkpoints in the area be dismantled and that *Abkhazian* authorities arrest any suspected criminals. They also demanded the arrest of nine prison inmates who recently escaped from the *Rustavi* prison. These escapees are reportedly hiding in *Abkhazian* territory. The negotiations lasted six hours, however, the reporter declined to offer any detailed information about the outcome of the meetings. The writer insinuated that the *Abkhazians* were unresponsive. Readers are left feeling either angry, hopeless, or at a minimum frustrated as they perceiving this as an irresolvable problem.

The ambiguous characterization of the Georgian *Abkhazian* peace talks are exacerbated by *Rustavi-2*'s headlines describing additional problems in *Adjara*. *Adjaran* Special Forces (masked soldiers) were described as forcibly dispersing a group of "Our *Adjara*" protesters in the *Gonio* area who were planning to raise the new Georgian flag in front of a local government building.[478] The protesters marched from a local school to the government building while holding placards as well as the new Georgian flag. They again demanded *Abashidze's* resignation and the re-institution of freedom of speech. The newspaper journalist wrote that *Adjaran* Special Forces officers attacked the protesters and tried to prevent *Rustavi-2* journalists from reporting the details of these events.

Another journalist reported that representatives from "Our *Adjara*" s described a recent politically motivated assassination.[479] The victim was the Director of the Emergency Department of the Interior Ministry of the *Adjaran* Autonomous Republic. Movement members believe that his victimization resulted from his support of the new Georgian government. "Our *Adjara*" also

---

477   N.N., "MP Khmaladze Urges MPs from Abkhazia to Be Elected." *Ibid.*, http://www.rustavi2.com.ge/view.php?id=6362.
478   N.N., "Adjaran Special Forces Dispersed Peaceful Protesters in Gonio." *Ibid.*, http://www.rustavi2.com.ge/view.php?id=6392 (as of 19 January 2004).

told reporters that they believed that *Abashidze* and his administration planned and perpetrated the assassination. The victim, Minister, *Temur Inasishvili* had previously publicly criticized *Abashidze's* regime and verbalized support for the new Georgian President. One of the founders of "*Our Adjara*" explained:

> The President Elect of Georgia will not hold any kind of negotiation with the *Adjaran* leader which could work to the detriment of the interests of the *Adjaran* and on the whole, Georgian citizens as it was the endless negotiations between *Shevardnadze* and *Abashidze* that contributed to the reestablishment of the *Abashidze* regime and his already twelve year rampage in the region.

The violence and protests continued as tension between *Adjara* and Georgia mounted throughout the remainder of the month.

Armed with a machine gun and wearing a face-mask a Russian soldier was photographed in *Batumi*, a sea port in *Adjara*, near the end of the month.[480] This sighting of an armed and masked Russian soldier created even more anxiety with regard Abashidze's previous threats to secede from Georgia. In an interview, a member of *Abashidze's* Revival Party discussed a recent telephone conversation with the *Adjaran* Minister of Internal Affairs about the presence of armed Russian soldiers. While the journalist explained that *Abashidze's* supporters carried arms beginning back in 1992 in order to maintain *Abashidze's* power, the fact that this armed masked individual was a Russian soldier was ignored as relevant by by the writer. Conversations with a revival party leader as well as an alleged expert in Southern Caucasian issues, *Mamuka Areshidze*, and the writer of this article reflected that a variety of armed groups are prepared to fight for *Abashidze* to remain in power. However, others are similarly poised to fight for his removal. Concerns continue to be that Russia will take advantage of this growing split by supporting *Abashidze* and thus endangering Georgia's security and territorial integrity as

---

479   N.N., "Our Adjara" assesses Assassination of Temur Inaishvili as Politically Motivated." *Ibid.*

480   Iamze Khositashvili, "Armed Groups Appear in Batumi, Russian Force to seize the opportunity for their purposes." *Daily Georgian Times* (30 January 2004):1, 2.

well as limiting any possibility of winning such a conflict. Another revival party member revealed that recently the *Adjaran* police arrested "several persons", allegedly planning to depose *Abashidze*. Subsequently, President *Saakashvili* telephone *Abashidze* asking him to attend to the letter of the Georgian law. The revival party member insinuated that the central Georgian government is stirring up discontent in *Adjara* and that *Adjaran* police will uphold order. In an interview with a legal expert from IREX, revelations are that "some forces" in Georgia want a destabilized *Adjara*, suggesting that this is not the view of Georgian leaders, but rather Russian politicians. He further indicated that if relations between the *Tbilisi* government and *Adjara* deteriorated, "a foreign force" would exploit the situation for its own benefit. The IREX expert also explained that if fair and democratic elections transpire in *Adjara* in March, *Abashidze* and his clique would not win. Conversely, a different Caucasus area expert claimed that Russia supports both *Abashidze* and his opponents, but that this two sided support is clearly only aimed at buttressing their own agenda. The Caucasus expert refuted a suggestion by one journalist that *Adjara* will actually secede from the Union just like *Ossetia* and *Abkhazia*. This ambiguity surrounding the geographical integrity of Georgia's national borders may even be more salient now following *Saakashvili's* campaign promise to restore Georgia's territorial integrity. In a related vein, President *Saakashvili* told journalists after a recent meeting with UN Secretary General, Kofi Annan: "Until the Georgian Army becomes stronger no UN will help us in *Abkhazia*. Whatever steps the Georgian government will make in its relations with *Abkhazia*, the international community should support Georgia".[481] In response, the President of the autonomous republic of *Abkhazia* explained that "such statements run counter to all the agreements reached under the UN aegis, especially as the statements are made after the meeting with the UN Secretary General. The Former President of Georgia made similar statements during the war claiming that Georgians would win the war as they were right and were supported by the UN and international community." The author then stated that the *Abkhazian* president recently complained about the U.S. Georgian training and equipment program. The

---

481   Ketevan Lomaia, "Scared breakaway republic addresses Kofi Annan for help, Avtandil Ioseliani: Ardzinba realized he is going short." *Daily Georgian Times* (30

Abkhazian President argued that Georgia signed the 1992 *Tashkent* agreement mandating no military assistance moneys in support of any aggression against South *Ossetia* or *Abkhazia*. He further complained that Georgia previously broke that agreement when they attacked *Abkhazia*. This alleged attack remains unidentified in any other media sources, so it appears the *Abkhazian* President's rhetoric was intentionally inflammatory or that he was simply referring to the previous conflict. This writer reports that the *Abkhazian* government claimed that other countries are somehow involved in providing battleships to Georgia and that Georgia has used these ships to commit piracy in the Black Sea. Conversely, later the *Abkhazian* President claims to be open to a dialogue with the Georgian government. The Chief of the Georgian Intelligence Department explains that the *Abkhazian* President *Vladislav Arbzinba* makes these wild claims followed by offers of his willingness to negotiate because he is worried that he new government will "restore Georgia's territorial integrity." The intelligence chief (*Avto Ioseliani*) then predicts that soon *Abkhazians* will be recruited into the Georgian armed forces to further strengthen Georgia's military. He denied the *Abkhazian* reports that Georgia committed acts of piracy explaining that in one instance the detention of a Turkish ship occurred as the ship was suspected of illegally removing some type of Black Sea resource. Finally, the writer explained that each time *Saakashvili* makes a statement about re-uniting Georgia, the autonomous republics "get serious headaches" and then make a variety of accusations to posture against President *Saakashvili.*

This rhetoric of ethnic nationalism continues to reverberate throughout Georgia. For example, the southern portion of Georgia near the Armenian and Turkish border is called the *Javakheti* region and remains primarily occupied by ethnic minority group members who are either Turkish or Armenian. As *Abashidze's* separatist regime continues to increase Georgian anxiety, newspaper headlines and politicians raise additional fears about the ethnic Armenians' desires for autonomy in this area. A letter written by the Council of Armenian NGOS condemned the Georgian Parliamentarian representing this region (also an Armenian) after he allegedly reported that most *Javakheti* Armenians do not want autonomy from the Central Georgian gov-

January 2004):6.

ernment when the NGOS argue that in fact they do.[482] The article stated that eight percent of the Georgian population are Armenians and live either in the capital city in *Tbilisi* or within the *Javakheti* region. Here over eighty percent of the residents are Armenian. NGOs throughout the region claim to express the Armenian desire for autonomy from Georgia. Conversely, a Parliamentarian from the region told reporters that only the NGOS have these motives, not the Armenian people who simply want the central government to meet their wishes and needs. Further, this Parliamentarian revealed that the Russian government pushed these Armenian NGOs into this position because of their own geo-political interests in Georgia. However, the journalist suggested that the Armenian Diaspora movement has also argued for autonomy from Georgia. The Parliamentarian dismissed that idea and stated that the U.S. would never support such a move, only Russia would. Another later article also referred to this predominantly Armenian area in Georgia. Here the article referred to the Armenian NGO Council's frustration with a Parliamentarian of Armenian *Van Baiburtian* who represents the *Javkkheti* region.[483] The parliamentarian reported previously that the Armenians did not want autonomy from Georgia but the council refutes that claim, indicating that *Baiburtian* is out of touch with his constituents' wishes and desires. Conversely, *Baiburtian* argues that the NGO's fail to speak for the people but merely reflect the views of the leaders of the NGOs. In this instance, the readers' ability to discern the truth seems highly improbable.

In a replication of President *Saakashvili's speech to* the PACE Council of Europe in late January of 2004, *Saakashvili* reported that he plans to cut police forces and then improve salaries of the remaining officers in at attempt to reduce the problem of police corruption.[484] *Saakashvili* disclosed that as his administration continues to remove and arrest corrupt officials, and that the forfeiture of their financial assets will eliminate their power and influence.

---

482   Rusudan Kbilashvili, "Armenian NGOs invite the Georgian Times to inquire. Discrepancies among the Armenians over the autonomy in Javakheti Region." *Daily Georgian Times* (30 January 2004):4.

483   N.N., "Armenian NGOs Regret over Armenian MP's Statements in GT." *The Georgian Times International Edition* (2 February 2004):11.

484   N.N., "Address by Mikheil Saakashvili, President of Georgia PACE Session on 26-30 January, 2004. Excerpt From the Verbatim Report of the debate." *Daily Georgian Times* (30 January 2004):5-6.

While acknowledging his view that Russian people are his neighbors not his enemies, *Saakashvili* reminds listeners that the Russian government continues to refuse to remove military bases from Georgia even though they promised to do so several years ago. *Saakashvili* reiterates his campaign promise to restore the territorial integrity of Georgia through peaceful resolution means with both South Ossetia and *Abkhazia*. He denies that the war with *Abkhazia* was a "separatist war" but reframes it as "a Russian Georgian war" characterized by interference from Russian as a way punish Georgia for seeking independence. Resentfully, he further explains that what we got afterwards was Russian 'piecekeeping', because the rest of the world did not want to intervene. He refused to call it genuine peacekeeping; but "piece keeping"—maintaining control of the former pieces of the Russian empire, rather than a desire to re-establish genuine peace in the region. When asked about his constitutional reforms, *Saakashvili* responded by describing his new cabinet that will allow him to delegate more of his duties as he brings Georgia toward the European model of liberal democratic reform. *Saakashvili* revealed that he plans to provide additional training to the army to ensure that they uphold democratic principles and eliminate corruption (he mentions nothing about doing away with the masks law enforcement officials wear when making arrests as they appear on television news reports). *Saakashvili* verbalized that the Rose Revolution was neither a U.S. sponsored coup nor a European sponsored Coup and argues that the absence of violence during the Rose Revolution is a testament to the strength, will, and desire of the Georgian people to improve their country. Additionally, *Saakasvhili* promised to eliminate poverty in Georgia and improve the Georgian economy. These lofty goals are dubious probable achievements for one administration in either one or two five-year terms in office.

III.6   February 2004

Saakashvili gave his inaugural speech in late January at the *Gelati* Monastery. The *Tbilisi* Monastery was the home of King David IV who united most of what has become modern Day Georgia.[485] The writer argued that this location metaphorically reflected the theme of *Saakashvili's* speech, the reunification of all Georgia, including *Adjara, Abkhazia,* and *South Ossetia.* Additionally, *Saakashvili's* presentation on the front stage of the former home of one of Georgia's most respected monarchs is not lost on readers. The fact that his administration chose this location and the journalist's comments together framed *Saakashvili* as a monarch and as savior of the people. Moreover, the journalist referred to *Georgia's most* pressing issue as *Adjara,* while *Abkhazia* was referred to as the "most daunting." *Saakashvili* explained: "The *Abkhaz* conundrum cannot be resolved in a week", and that these areas will not be reintegrated until:

a. Georgia revives its economy.
b. Georgia builds up its military.
c. Georgia enforces order (omitting the law) .

Saakashvili also promised not to use force in *Abkhazia* because he said he would resolve these problems peacefully. The statement makes sense in the context of the resignation of the Chairperson of the Legitimate Soviet of *Abkhazia* in exile (Mr. *Tamaz Nadareishvili*) labeled as a Georgian Hawk. He resigned after receiving a no confidence vote from the *Abkhazian* council. This should make a peaceful resolution to the conflict more likely. Apparently, there were also suspicions that *Nadareishvili* was involved in corruption. Following his resignation, some of his administrative assistants were arrested for embezzling public funds. Perhaps these new developments will assist in eliminating the current stalemated peace dialogue between *Abkhazia* and Georgia. Georgia's recent political quagmire also may have facilitated the stalled talks. Recently, high-level negotiations were postponed and only border and security negotiations took place. The writer claims that *Abkhazians* remain wary of *Saakashvili* because they see him as a populist and nationalist and therefore as a threat. The deputy chief of the National Intelligence Agency, *Zurab Erkvania* a former member of the *Abkhaz* government who worked for *Nadareishvili* until March of 1998 when tens of thousands of Georgians fled the *Gali* area. Recently *Erkvania* stated:

> I would recommend that the new leaders of Georgia hurry to declare their commitment to political dialogue with the *Abkhaz*, their intention to promote economic relations between *Tbilisi* and *Sukhumi*, reopen mutual railway, marine, road and air traffic, denounce Georgia's economic sanctions previously imposed in *Abkhazia*, and start talking about restoring Georgian-*Abkhaz* relations rather than Georgia's national integrity.[486]

Erkvania argues it is time to disband the government in exile and replace it with a more flexible coordinating body. *Erkvania* explains: "This body, whose original mission was to deal with the social economic and cultural problems of refugees, gradually lost its function and was reduced to the state of mere bureaucratic accessory serving one man" Referencing *Naradieshvili*.[487] While this sentiment might be accurate, it is unlikely to receive acceptance until the IDPs regain what they lost and their struggle to achieve economic and educational equality ends. As a result, Georgian IDPs staged of several protests and hunger strikes over the last few months in an attempt to express their discontent with the current political stalemate. IDPs recently detained the Georgian Minister of IDPs, *Eteri Astamirova,* in the Western Georgian town of *Zugdidi demanding* their late benefits. As a Civic Education Project Fellow at *Tbilisi* State University, I met a group of IDPS from *Abkhazia* who were originally from all economic strata, while they all now struggled to provide for their families and fellow IDPs. IDPs include husbands, wives, and children as well as college students. The college students have spent their entire childhood in

---

485 Gocha Khundadze, "Georgian Leader's Abkhaz Choices: New Georgian President Mikheil Saakashvili begins a rethink of his country's policy on Abkhazia." *The Georgian Times International Edition* (2 February 2004):10.

486 Khundadze, "Georgian Leader's Abkhaz Choices."

previously designated temporary housing that has become their permanent home for the last ten years. For example, grammar school aged children know of no other kind of life. A small group of women IDPS volunteered to visit my ethnic sociology class at *Tbilisi* State University during the spring semester of 2004. These women explained their initial grief, anger, and sadness at loosing their homes, livelihoods, family members, and friends during their forced exodus from *Abkhazia*. Jobs here in central Georgia were difficult to find and they were unable to send their children to local public schools because they were unable to afford to purchase the required books. Families must buy textbooks because the public schools have such poor funding they remain unable to purchase books and then issue them to the students. *Tbilisi* also maintains the *Abkhazia* University in exile where traditional college aged students can earn their university diploma. Their professors are former University professors who lost their jobs at Universities in *Abkhazia* during the war. The monthly allowance for an IDP includes 14.00 GEL for those who do not live in collective centers, or 11.00 GEL+ bread free of charge for those who do live in collective centers. Ms. *Astamirova*, the Minister for Refugees, is also an IDP and a member of the Supreme Soviet of *Abkhazia in* exile. This institutionalization of the government in exile defies over ten years of the social fact of the "exile" and as subtlety argued previously by *Erkvania,* may persist in fueling Georgian nationalism and resentment especially in the context of the presence of so many IDPs who continue to struggle to regain their former socio-economic status. For them returning home remains a powerful dream fueled by the ideology of a government in exile. The *Abkhazian* government in exile is a thirty-eight person council with members who have held their positions for twelve to thirteen years. Another voice of reason, *Armaz Akhvlediani*, the director of the School of Political Studies in *Tbilisi* commented on the stalwart resentful position of many Georgians: "Georgians must stop thinking that Russia is the cause of all evil....we must get rid of this complex and make a clean start in our relationship with Russia while the option is still there."[488] Another factor involved in keeping this contentious issue alive is the presence of armed Georgian guerrilla groups operating in

---

487   *Ibid.*
488   *Ibid.*

Abkhazia.[489] One writer alleges that *Shevardnadze*'s government in *Tbilisi* financed these guerilla groups and that the guerillas continue to perpetrate acts of sabotage against the separatist government of *Abkhazia*. The writer argued that these groups were controlled by former Chairperson of the *Abkhazian* government in exile, Mr. *Tamaz Nadareishvili,* recently forced to resign because of his hawkish ideology. However, *Nadareishvili* argued: "My removal was encouraged by the separatist government of *Abkhazia.*" Further, he claimed that he received warnings about that many times. "As I resigned, that core of the legitimate government was in fact removed. Now the structures of the legitimate government are being dismantled and if that keeps going this way the processes will yield grave consequences." *Nadareshvili* denied that the *Shevardnadze* government administration financially supported his illegal soldiers however he also stated that the when the new government is ready to re-take *Abkhazia*, his militiamen are ready to perform. A government source reports that the new Nationalist-Democratic coalition government will disband these guerillas partly because of a recent violent confrontation that occurred on January 26th in the region of *Tsalenjikha* within the Georgian-*Abkhazian* conflict zone. The writer explained that these Georgian guerillas continue to fight against armed Abkhazians despite the peace accords. In this latest incident, an armed group of *Abkhazians* attacked a police station in the village of *Lia* killing four police and wounding seven more and two of the "criminals" (*Abkhazians*) died. However, the *Abkhazian* government claims that the Georgian guerilla forces perpetrated the crime. The *Abkhazian* Minister of Security, *Givi Agrba* explained:

> Over the ten years since the end of the Georgian *Abkhazian* conflict, *Tbilisi* has been conducting peace talks with *Sukhumi* and at the same time supported the guerrilla movement that on its turn perpetrated terrorist acts on the *Abkhaz* territory. The Georgian rebels are responsible for the death of ninety-six Russian peacekeeping soldiers, *Abkhaz* militias and thousands of civilians on *Abkhaz* territory.[490]

---

489   Temur Tatishvili, "Georgian leadership poised to cooperate with separatist republics. Georgian guerrilla bands to be dismantled on Abkhaz territory." *The Georgian Times International Edition* (2 February 2004):3.

490   *Ibid.*

Finally, *Agrba* retorts that Georgian claims that *Abkhazians* led the January shootout were false. He argues that Georgians promoted the claim to discredit the *Abkhazian* government. The journalist indicated that following the 1991-92 ceasefire, both sides formed partisan groups and continued to fight in a variety of skirmishes. Two of these Georgian groups include the "Forest Brothers" and the "White Legion." References to the *Abkhazian* groups included the label 'punitive police'. All of these groups are guilty of shedding blood well after the signing of the peace agreement. The *Abkhazian* militia are described as more extremist and as exacting brutal revenge on the ethnic Georgians living in *Abkhazia*." The writer contends that Georgian civilians have been tortured to death or shot by the *Abkhazian* militia.

As previous journalists' reported, Russia's portrayal as culpable with regard to the refugees and internally displaced peoples across the Caucasus continues. These refugees include Ingush and Chechens as well as IDPs living in the Russian Republic of North *Ossetia* and *Inguesh*.[491] However, in this case the writers are not Georgian but rather citizens of the former Republic of *Chechneo-Ingusheitia* in the Northern *Caucasus*.[492] One *Inguesh* IDP family is described as living in North *Ossetia* because they are unable to return to their home village, currently in rubbles. The director of the *Inguesh's* IDPs Committee explains: "The *Ossetians* living in these villages don't want their [former] *Ingush* neighbors to return. "The *Ingush Osesstian* conflict occurred in 1992 and lasted five days resulting in hundreds killed and thousands taken hostage. The writers claim that this area (one writer writes in N. *Ossetia* and the other from *Ingheshetia*), called the *Prigorodny* region, previously consisted of *Ingushetia* until Stalin gave the land to North *Ossetia* in 1944 after deporting the *Chechens* and *Ingush* to Central Asia. While many *Ingush* returned in the 1950's, they never received official documents substantiating their official residence in the area. An Ossetian political analyst further explained that the old *Ingushetia* constitution calls for the return of disputed ter-

---

491   Albina Olisayeva and Madina Khadzieva, "Ingush Refugees Find Way Home Blocked. A dispute is still raging over how many Ingush refugees deserve the right to return to North Ossetia." *The Georgian Times International Edition* (2 February 2004):4 Written originally for *Vladikavkaz and Nazran. IWPR*.

ritories to the *Ingushetia*. However, *Ossetians* worry that more conflict will follow such a return. Interestingly, one North *Ossetian* official reported that three thousand and five hundred North *Ossetians* also currently live in *Ingushetia*. Another report indicates that twenty-one thousand of the twenty-seven thousand *Ingush* who led the fighting in 1992 have returned to North *Ossetia* (Other reports reflect that thirty-two thousand five hundred originally lived in North *Ossetia*.) However, the government states that only nineteen thousand *Inguesh* actually returned. The others are unable to do so because of the absence of official documentation about their original status. Conversely, the Russians maintain different figures claiming that approximately eleven thousand *Ingush* currently reside in *Ingushetia* who have registered as forced migrants from North *Ossetia* while only five hundred *Ingush* live in North *Ossetia*. This is the first instance in the newspapers in which attributions cast much of the conflict in the Caucasus region to Stalin's forced ethnic re-locations in the 1930's and 1940's. Yet these writers are not Georgians, because from the Georgian perspective only Russia itself was responsible for these atrocities, not their own Joseph Stalin. Georgians' denial and inability to accept responsibility for their part in the creation of the Soviet Union also persists with regard to other subjects when they often blame their bigger northern neighbors for a variety of Georgian social problems. For example, it seems that even with regard to Georgia's population of HIV infected individuals, Russia and Ukraine are held responsible for "bringing on the infection."[493]

Blaming others for their social problems is also something they share with other countries, particularly those nations who embrace ideologies of civic or ethnic nationalism. National ideologies grounded in ethnic nationalistic identities rapidly develop into the scapegoating of those who fail to fit inside the rigid normative definition of the 'group'. For example, one HIV positive drug addict told a journalist that police beat him when they suspected his HIV positive status. Such behavior reflects the social stigma associated with any kind of non-traditional behavior. Only four hundred and forty-six were

---

492   G.U. Soldatova, "The Former Checheno-Ingushetia." *Russia Social Science Review* 34:6 (1993):52-73.

493   Tamuna Nachkebla, "AIDS-the Plague of our Century, "We don't care about the HIV infected, why should they care about us?." *The Georgian Times International Edition* (2 February 2004):4.

registered as HIV positive in 2004, most of them having developed the disease as the result of sharing needles while abusing drugs. The author argued the real estimate might be closer to two thousand. Although there is some minimal recognition of this problem, Georgian HIV positive mothers are frequently rejected for beds in local "maternity houses". This indicates the level of stigma still attached to the disease as well as the gendered expectations of Georgian women. Then in another infusion of nationalism and ethnocentricity, the writer argues that Russian HIV mothers abandon their babies while Georgian HIV mothers continue to care for their babies who remain at risk for HIV. This thinking exists in concert with the fact that only five of the four hundred and forty six registered HIV Georgians are receiving state funded medical treatment and the preventative drug cocktail. While some Georgians are getting generic drugs from non-western drug markets, most are not taking any medication and will not do so until the Global Fund begins providing financial assistance. As Robert Merton argued, addiction may provide the best method to avoid the pain of failing when the traditional means of achieving normative goals are unavailable. If this addiction and its sequela continue to wreck havoc, it may contend with another leading cause of death in Georgia, traffic accidents.

As a passenger having ridden in automobiles or mini-buses in the city of *Tbilisi* regularly, I can verify one writer's claim that "the capital is overcrowded with vehicles". The author also reports that this results in "increases air pollution and of course traffic jams".[494] The Head of the City economic Committee and Commission for Reforms, David *Ioseliani*, provided documentation showing that over six thousand mini-buses, the *martshrutkas*, provide mass transportation to many people without automobiles. Forty to fifty *tetra* (twenty to twenty-five cents) will get you almost anywhere in the city on a *martshrutka* (a mini-van). The writer argued that the mini-buses are more efficient than the publicly financed subway or the trolleys, trams or larger buses. Currently the owners of the mini-buses do not pay taxes and if they were required to do so, that would bring almost eight million GEL into the state's budget that *Ioseliani* claims would pay many pensioners' salaries. While traffic in downtown *Tbilisi* may be as bad or worse as any other

---

494   Lali Javakhia, "Traffic jams-another challenge for Tbilisi." *Ibid.*

densely populated major Western or Eastern metropolitan area, I have never before seen this degree of congestion in concert with the willful disregard for traffic laws and dividing lanes. The Chief of *Tbilisi* Police Traffic Management Department, *Avtandil Jashiashvili* indicates that six hundred to seven hundred people die annually in car accidents across the country and one hundred and twenty to one hundred and thirty of those in *Tbilisi*. Cars hit many pedestrians as they crossing the street illegally (not a bona fide crosswalk). There are no mandatory seat belt laws in Georgia and certainly none available in public transportation vehicles. While I thoroughly enjoyed my rides in *martshrutkas,* I sometimes felt as if I was on a roller coaster even though the ride was just as disconcerting as it was exciting. A later piece written in late February by an American reflects some of my own experiences as a frequent customer of the *martshrutka.*[495] He wrote about the norms or rules that riders should keep in mind while on the *martshrutka*. These included keeping a large amount of cash out of sight and tucked neatly into zipped containers, after all crime is about economic survival. However, he also reminded riders not to take Georgian's poverty and need to survive as evidence that they are inhospitable people, because they are kind, loving and hospitable, only they have no money and it is easy to steal in a *martshrutka*. As all Criminologists know, typically thieves and pickpockets are not seriously violent criminals, at least not against strangers. He also tells Westerners', particularly Americans to leave their fanny packs home because stealing a fanny pack in a *martshrutka would* be easy. I once observed a young man on a *martshrutka* who was watching a middle-aged woman carrying a purse with her cell phone hanging out of the purse pocket. As he reached up once or twice to quickly take it, he noticed me watching him, at least I think he did, and changed his mind and quickly got off the van, without paying. The author also advises riders to look as if you know where you are going even if you do not. Thieves know that lost passengers are also easy targets. I got on the wrong *martshrutka* on a number of occasions and often just pretended to know exactly where I was going, until I could get off at a place with which I was more familiar. However, once I was so unfamiliar with my location, I ended up at the

---

495   Andy Hastings, "Marshrutka diaries: Rules of the Road." *The Messenger* (20 February 2004):17.

drivers' rest stop, where the driver tried unsuccessfully to get a date with me. He also happily placed his hand on my knee, until I explained that I had a husband (I do not, I made that up). He was very polite and courteous following my rejection of his advances and helped me find the right *martshrutka* to get back to my neighborhood. Another rule included avoiding riding in a *martshrutka* where the driver lets passengers stand in the isles, he called it a "Pick-pocket's smorgasbord." Sometimes, he explains, the drivers have a collegial relationship with the pickpocket and share the proceeds. He also wrote that one should ignore the drunks, well I would argue not necessarily. Case in point, I was on a *martshrutka* one day when a very drunk man sat near me, he was relatively quiet until he noticed a young toddler with her parents and began to try to engage her in a jovial conversation. While I didn't understand all of it, at some point, the man asked if he could give the little girl a kiss on the cheek, the young girl said out loud "*ara ara,*" which means "no no." The passengers in the *martshrutka* laughed loudly at the little girl's assertiveness and obvious dislike for the overly friendly drunken man. Clearly the writer's term for this as is reflected in my previous story is a "communal experience" as all the passengers experienced the same "sudden stops, starts, and swerves and social events. "You all envy the Mercedes with VIP tags that just veered into on-coming traffic to make it to [some special Western event in a Western style restaurant]." "But can all rejoice when he lands in jail charged with expropriating the Mercedes from a state enterprise." Finally, after opening his editorial with a constructive criticism of the recent changes in the constitution, especially with regard to the current administration's skipping of the "one month of public debate clause" he stated: "Cheers to the new Constitution. Enjoy your ride." He offered a humorous metaphorical prediction of the future of Georgia's journey on the road with the new administration.

The author of the *Martshrutka Dairies* also mentioned the absence of seatbelts on public transportation as does a previous article describing government officials' plan to reduce the number of mini-vans on the streets and mandate seat belts in order to reduce traffic injuries and fatalities. A few days after the article that described *Tbilisi's* problems with traffic accidents, the Chief of the Traffic Police resigned, under the usual allegations of corruption. This followed his "interrogation by the prosecutors' office for illegally importing cars". Are arrests such as these reflective of the Georgian media's influence on the government or just coincidentally related to the newspaper story headlining the problem with Georgian automobile traffic? Of course another possibility is that this just another in a long series of resignations in *Saakashvili's* battle against corruption. The former seems more accurate as three additional members of city or state government also simultaneously resigned.[496] One of these resignations was the state Minister of the Passport and Registration Bureau. Moreover, both the Chief of Traffic police and the Minister subsequently had charges filled against them for engaging in corruption. A number of other staff at the customs bureau also lost their jobs, some for "exceeding authority." This translates into inappropriate use of their office or corruption.[497] Another arrest of a local public official in the *Khashuri* District occurred allegedly for misuse of office. This official is the father of a party official in *Zurab Zhvania's* party block, the National Democrats.[498] Additionally, a court case is ongoing with regard to the former President's son-in-law, *Giorgi Jokhtaberidze* and his cellular company, *Magticom.*[499] The lexicon chosen to relay this story reflects that *Jokhtaberidze* was "interrogated" by the prosecutor's office, and further that *Shevardnadze's* former Minister of Communications, *Fridon Injia*, provided a letter of confirmation to the Prosecutor General of Georgia promising that *Jokhtaberidze* would testify in the investigation. This letter's design was to prevent authorities from detaining *Jokhtaberidze* for the usual lengthy period. This substantiates that economically elite Georgians have the class privileges that are similarly available to the same elite from richer nation-states.

Amidst the new administration's house cleaning, via arrests for charges of corruption, and or voluntary resignations, the Parliamentary Assembly of the Council of Europe (PACE) complains to the Georgian government: "deploring" the Georgian administration's failure to act on a voters' referendum

---

496   Lali Javakhia, "Why has Traffic Police Chief Resigned." *Daily Georgian Times* (3 February 2004):1, 3.
497   N.N., "Staff Changes at the State Customs Department." *The Georgian Times, International Edition* (2 February 2004):11.
498   N.N., "Deputy head of the Khashuri District Arrested." *Ibid.,* 14.
499   N.N., "Ex-Minister of Communications Left General Prosecutor Office without Giving Testimony." *Ibid.*

passed during the November election".[500] The referendum asked Georgians whether or not they wanted to change the current proportional representation policy of parliamentarians holding office from seven percent to four or five percent. Georgians voted to do so, but the current administration refuses to abide by the people's vote. Further, PACE also stated that the current/new election commission remains "undemocratic" and "biased" due to overrepresentation of persons who were selected by the new administration. A number of International NGO's also have urged the administration to make the referendum law. They note that an emergency session of Parliament, if scheduled before the March parliamentary elections could easily enact the people's referendum into law.[501] Another journalist argues that any referendum by the people automatically becomes law following the publication of the results, available since November 2003. The writer also reports that recent amendments to constitution failed to include this particular change. Politicians offered three reasons for not making the required changes:

a. Absence of a respective legislative framework.
b. Absence of a plan for territorial arrangement of the country.
c. Political will of the government.

Finally, the writer claims that the inherent legal contradiction in the constitution consists of references to one time-period with regard to enforcement of referendums, while another statute describes a different timeframe. Specifically, the constitution requires that referendum decisions be legislated two months following the vote, while the Law of Referendums explicates that immediate implementation. Two politicians interviewed about the referendum provided disparate rationales for the failure to implement the change. One argued that more time is required to implement such changes, cautioning that "we cannot replace figures (numbers so easily) because we don't know how many actual parliamentary seats that will translate into." While relatively simple to multiply four percent by the number of people in the region, utilization

---

500   N.N., "PACE appeals to Georgia to Amend Election Legislation." *Daily Georgian Times* (3 February 2004):2.
501   Maka Chambashidze, "Where has November 2nd referendum disappeared?" *Ibid.*, 3.

of math appears irrelevant. Readers should note that this referendum would reduce the number of representatives in parliament resulting in some politicians possibly losing their positions of power. This politician also retorts that no legislation exists to make this change. He then maintained that since the majority PMs previously elected in November remains viable, they are unable to make any further changes. However, this seems incongruent with the Constitutional court's previous declaration of a fraudulent proportional portion of the November election, although the logic of only invalidating the proportional results seems incredulous. Finally, he stated that PMs must obey the constitution of Georgia. The writer reports that no stipulation of an effective date exists in the referendum. Later another politician argued that 2007 was the effective data on the referendum. Another minority party parliament member disclosed that her party submitted the change in proportional representation following the referendum although the bill failed to pass (she claimed it was blocked). Another opposition party member explained that the majoritarian party members do not want to implement the law because it would decrease their representation in the parliament. One MP argued that the motivation to refuse to declare the majoritarian portion of the election fraudulent centered around maintenance of the current political block's power thus preventing the implementation of the referendum. More realistically characterizing Georgia's non-violent Rose Revolution as simple 'regime change could be in order. Western newspapers are beginning to explore this possibility as they call attention to *Saakashvili's* new alleged campaign against corruption.

One section in the *Daily Georgian Times* reviews articles about Georgia published in Western newspapers. An article originally published in the Christian Science Monitor explained that, "observers are worried that a much needed campaign against corruption in Georgia led by President *Mikhail Saakashvili* has taken a sinister turn---which a new zeal for law and order has led to police abuses." [502] The pattern reveals that public officials suspected of engaging in bribery are first losing their government jobs and then prosecuted (note that first officials' experience removal then prosecution…not ex-

---

502   Khatya Chhor, "Elections in Iraq, Georgian Corruption and Putin's Russia." *Daily Georgian Times* (3 February 2004):6.

actly innocent until proven guilty). Another piece reveals the arrest of five high-ranking government officials on charges ranging from tax evasion to embezzlement, and misappropriation of state property. One of those arrested was the former President's son-in-law, previously interrogated about illegal behavior with regard to the company *Magticom*. Approximately ten days after this new wave of arrests, the administration created a new law enforcement agency designed to pursue financial crime and corruption. The journalist called them the Financial Police described as having a mission to investigate, analyze, and collect intelligence with regard to tax evasion, the shadow economy, and other economic crimes.[503] Unfortunately, they also collect taxes, a task previously accomplished by the Tax Office that also had a history of official corruption. The government transferred twenty-eight cases to this new agency. The agency will consist of fifteen to twenty personnel assigned to "defend the nation's financial and economic interests with force, if necessary." Previously these functions belonged to an Investigative Department of the Finance Ministry. However, it remained undecided whether or not this new law enforcement body will become a part of the finance ministry or the Interior Ministry. The new department chief, *Davit Kezerashvili*, was formerly an assistant to *Saakashvili*. While the organization might improve investigative procedures and conviction rates of white-collar criminals, it is unknown if agency will function as intended or if it is simply a part of *Saakashvili's* front stage performance. Specifically, critics postulate that the new presidents' campaign against corruption has thus far focused on his political enemies. Even Human Rights Watch, the international NGO, accused the Georgian government of using methods that while popular with the public continue to violate human rights. The focus of human rights complaints are on Georgian law enforcement behavior when making arrests as well as lengthy pre-trial detentions. As mentioned previously, police frequently make arrests while wearing military fatigues with their faces covered by masks, hardly the hallmark of free and democratic society, but rather more like the representatives of a police state. The journalist clarifies that it will take more than a few arrests to transform Georgian institutions built on "cronyism and

---

503   M. Alkhazashvili, "Financial Police join fight on Corruption." *The Messenger* (5 February 2004):1.

preferential treatment." This cronyism remains influenced by the huge amount of Western aid flowing into the region. Unfortunately, this influence also extends to media companies.

Media mogul, *David Alaverdyan,* Editor in Chief of an independent Armenia news agency called *Mediamax* founded in 1998, describes his company's objective as covering political issues in the Caucasus region including those in Iraq and Turkey.[504] *Alaverdyan* denied that western moneys supported Caucasus journalist outlets in TV or in newspapers. However, he agreed that Georgian journalists' coverage of the *Rose Revolution* facilitated the effectiveness of the social movement that ousted President *Shevardnadze.* While the interviewee argued that Soviet journalism is a relic of the past, he also stated that the Caucasus mentality (although he does not say what that mentality is) limits the ability of journalists to achieve more success. It is not clear what the writer means when referring to the Caucasus mentality, but I have heard the expression used both in Georgia and other parts of the FSU with respect to the attitude that the state should 'take care' of its citizens in all respects, like a mother cares for a dependent child. However, it also seems to reference the denial of some young adults that the Soviet period had no effect on them because they were children when the USSR disintegrated. Yet Georgians and other former Soviet citizens seem to accept what the media or the government tells them at face value without criticism. Unfortunately, this is a pervasive problem not unique to the FSU. Moreover, the writer contends that Georgian newspapers have become a powerful influence on the Georgia public. According to *Medimax's* web page, *David Alaverdyan* continued to hold the Editor in Chief position as recently as 2005. While I suspected Western funding, I could find no evidence of that other than a recent U.S. state department grant that allowed them to install an electronic news-line on the front of one of their building in downtown Yerevan.[505] Mediamax's web page publishes an EU newsletter called: "The European Union in Armenia" claiming to be a newspaper covering events in Armenia and the South Caucasus. They also purport to interview politicians around the world. Interestingly, their website states:

---

504   N.N., "Rose Revolution' went right due the Georgian journalism"-David Alaverdyan, the editor-in-chief of the news Agency Medimax." *Ibid.*

> *Mediamax* is ready to become your partner in this region, the interest towards which is growing day by day. The South Caucasus will be one of the priorities of the Euro-Atlantic community in the course of next years, and our company is ready to become your ally in this part of the world which links Europe and Asia and serves as a gate to the Greater Middle East. Trust us, and we will give you the most valuable that we have - quality, efficiency and reliability.

Who is the advertisement appealing to, and why? Their presentation of self is grandiose yet, they need advertisers and readers. The appeal seemed aimed at big business seemingly supporting economic globalization and the G-8. The privatization of previously owned communist assets, as the FSU embraced capitalism, for Soviet republics became a more sophisticated term for theft. Simultaneously while the previous state owned media prevented any critique of government, Georgian newspapers now offer critiques on everything and everyone simply because they can. However, often the critique becomes a story based upon poorly constructed evidence or partisan opinion. Sometimes all the news becomes simplistically conceived editorials.[506]

Georgian journalists' interpret the free press, as a press free to criticize the government. Similarly, politicians seem to misunderstand wining a democratic election as a justification to weld absolute power and do whatever one wants' regardless of the constitution. In Georgia, this behavior results in the disintegration of old alliances and the formation of new ones. For example, one headline described a split in the newly constituted nationalist block.[507] The recently elected majoritarian parliamentary leader (*Davitashivili*) resigned in protest to *Zurab Zhvania's* appointment as the Prime Minister. He explained:

> I find it unacceptable to change the country's constitution for one person, just so *Zurab Zhvania* can be prime minister. It is

---

505   http://mediamax.am/special.htm (as of 23 June 2005).
506   Anna Araznova, "Crack in the National Movement-Political Secretary Koba Davitashvili resigns in opposition to Zurab Zhvania." *The Messenger* (5 February 2004):4.
507   *Ibid.*

also unacceptable for me to be a member of the same party as *Zhvania*. I want to call once again on the members of the National Movement to oppose *Mikhail Saakashvili's* plans with this action to save *Saaksashvili*, our country and those who support constitutional changes.[508]

Davitashvili also reported misgivings about another constitutional change permitting the President to dismiss the Parliament. *Davitashvili* also opposed the unification of the National Party and the United Democrats and threatened to resign as the Chairperson of the National Party if members supported the union. The unification of the two parties should not surprise anyone who watched the Rose Revolution unfold in November as *Zhvania* stood beside *Saakashvili* each time he spoke at rallies in front of the parliament. On *Saakashvili's* right, stood *Zhvania* and on his left, stood *Burjanadze*. *Zhvania* announced the unification of both parties on January 28th when President *Saakashvili* was abroad. *Saakashvili* responded by saying:

> there were more important problems facing the nation such as the life and death battle against the mafia....everybody has the right to leave [the party] if they want. If somebody wants to deviate from this plan it is his or her own business. I am not interested in individuals. Georgian people support me and I will make every effort to see this matter to the end.

Moreover, the President explained that the unification of the parties was necessary to eliminate the problems created by *Shevardnadze's* presidency. In the midst of these protestations, *Saakashvili* promises: "I want to tell everybody that the members of the mafia will never come back." *Zhvania* responded to this situation by stating: "I am very disappointed about what happened today. We are all obliged to work together and fulfill the promises that we made to the population. This is not the time to be offended by each other to make the problems in the country." Another National Movement party member also reassured the public that *Saakashvili's* decision to unify the three parties is and should be acceptable. However, a member of the *Burjanadze* Democrats reported that he expected *Davitashvili's* decision, indicat-

---

508   *Ibid.*, 1, 4.

ing that political rivalries and jealously may have precipitated *Davitashvili's* resignation. As illustrated above in *Saakashvili's* statement about the recent resignation, his administration's on-going fight against crime continues to dominate the headlines.

A second front page article described a police raid orchestrated by the Interior Minister, *Baramidze* in *Zugdidi in early* February. This resulted in the arrest of tobacco, petroleum, and drug smugglers.[509] Thirty arrests were made and while observers reported concerns about "aggressive legal tactics" no specific details were provided. Illegal arms confiscated during the arrest included forty-five automatic rifles, machine guns, hand grenades, grenade launchers, and mortars.[510] Additionally, law enforcement officers shot several suspects, however it is not clear if these suspects were injured or killed. A photograph illustrated the police in military uniforms wearing facemasks and carrying what appeared to be automatic weapons. The Chief of the Interior forces indicated that these "criminals" were linked with "*Abkhaz* criminals" and that "everyone knows how these criminals infuriated the residents...robbing, killing, and raping people". Contrary to this report, the Regional Head of Police explained that the suspects were "an ordinary criminal group pretending to be partisans." Later President *Saakashvili* arrived on the scene welcomed by crowds shouting his nickname "*Misha! Misha!*". In a later speech, he promised to continue to fight crime: "All families should be protected from surrounding criminals. Starting from this day, none of these families will be persecuted by criminals." In subsequent meetings, *Saakashvili* reportedly encouraged police to meet any resistance by force: "Anyone who resists the orders of the police will be wiped-out." Seemingly, he provides permission for the use of deadly force without any constraints. The same day he issued a Presidential order to the Minister of Internal affairs permitting law enforcement officers to shoot, on the spot, any criminal who refuses to obey their orders. The author subsequently interviewed a lawyer from the NGO "Article 42 of the Constitution," who argued that such orders/decrees are unconstitutional. It is a forgone conclusion that since Georgia has no death penalty, ordering to shoot to kill a suspect before a trial is a human rights vio-

---

509   Mary Makharashvili, "Fighting Fire with Fire Aggressive tactics alarm legal observers." *Ibid.*

lation. *Manana Kobakhidze* also explained that guidelines in place specify rules of deadly force similar to those in the U.S. i.e., shoot to disable a fleeing felon suspect, the minimum amount of force necessary to apprehend a suspect. Another lawyer for the for this NGO revealed that violations of the Procedural Code of Georgia also occurred when police arrested and detained the Deputy Director of the Georgian Electricity Company without a warrant. This also characterized the recent arrest of the Transportation Minister. The *Tbilisi* Prosecutor claimed that such methods were appropriate for political officials or high-ranking authorities "we have no other way."[511] While this statement justifies illegal state violence, it remains congruent with Georgia's one party authoritarian history and perhaps illustrates another example of the previously referred to 'Caucasus mentality'. However, the United States federal law enforcement post-9/11 policy similarly results in unauthorized and illegal arrests and detentions of numerous foreign nationals utilizing similar justifications. Georgian authorities continue to emulate their newest and biggest benefactor, the United States government.

In spite of a increasingly repressive police state, the government's claims of sweeping reforms continue. Specifically, the head of the Committee to reform Internal Affairs, *Gia Kiknadze*, recently re-structured the entire department. Of course, this included financial requests from donor agencies and other countries in order to implement the reforms.[512] The improvements included increases in police salaries and new benefit packages (they reportedly need three hundred thousand GEL or one hundred and fifty thousand U.S. dollars). This aid will facilitate the re-structuring of the federal police department into separate patrol and criminal divisions. Interestingly, three districts in *Tbilisi* will receive twenty-four new patrol vehicles and each of these areas are predominantly middle class neighborhoods (*Vake/Saburtalo, Mtatsminda/Krtsanisi and Didube/Chuguerti*). The government hopes to begin funding for some of these projects in the next two to six months. This will make the federal government responsible for all internal policing across the

---

510   N.N.,"Police Raid in Zugdidi." *24 Hours Rustavi-2* (6 February 2004):6.
511   Makharashvili, "Fighting Fire with Fire Aggressive tactics alarm legal observers."
       Ibid., 5.
512   Sopho Gorgadze, "Georgian Interior Ministry plans Sweeping reforms: Appeals to
       donors for funding." *Ibid.,* 1, 5.

country. Government representatives tout that this will improve effectiveness in fighting crime. My daily observations in *Tbilisi* rarely included seeing police officers. When police were visible, their cars remained parked on the side-walks with officers' asleep inside. Sometimes the officers were just standing around smoking cigarettes. On rare occasions, I observed motorists stopped by police at rudimentary police blockades. There officers sometimes pulled *martshrutkas* over and checked all the identity cards or passports of the passengers. Unlike other major cities in the Western world, that I have visited or lived in, I only occasionally heard police or emergency sirens after the hours of darkness in *Tbilisi*. However, making a police department more effective does not necessarily require the federalization of the police. Once again, the America government's recent creation of Homeland Security and allegedly improving federal law enforcement coordination, under the auspices of protecting American's from terrorism, provides an easy justification for *Saakashvili* to begin federalizing Georgian law enforcement. Fortunately, although *Saakashvhili's* new party block appears to be consolidating its power, some competition has been lining up for the new parliamentary elections.

A number of political parties aim to break the seven percent proportional threshold required for election to parliament in the forthcoming March elections.[513] Fifty new parties registered before the January 31st deadline after collecting the fifty thousand signatures required before permission to register was authorized. Following the CEC's development of the computerized voters' lists planned for after the March parliamentary elections, the Ministry of Justice will be responsible for maintaining and updating voters' lists. Assigning the Ministry of Justice to a function that could easily result in criminally charging potential voters with crimes in order to prevent their electoral participation is clearly incongruent with democratic values. However, it also resembles many American states' policies that prohibit convicted felons from electoral participation. This U.S. policy has been highly criticized by a number of human rights organizations. Nevertheless, at least the new Georgian government block has some competition for the forthcoming parliamentary election. The following parties are currently registered:

---

513   N.N., "Election Picture takes shape, sort of." *Ibid.*, 2.

a. National Movement + United Democrats=One party Block
b. Revival Party-*Adjaran* Leader *Aslan Abashidze's* party
c. Our Adjara-opposition part to Revival Party and Abashidze
d. Labor Party-radical critic of current government
e. Socialists-invited Labor Party to join them in a party Block
f. Freedom Party + Centrist Party-one party consists of one party block. Konstantine *Gamskhurdia*, son of Georgia's first President *Zviad Gamskhurdia* joined the party after living in Switzerland since his father's fall from power in 1992.

The above parties reportedly represent the left, while parties on the right include:

a. *Akaki Asatiani's* Traditionalists + National Democrats-one party block
b. New Rights-pro business party
c. Industrialists-pro business party

One journalist wrote that he believed that the election turn out across *Adjara* would improve compared to the presidential election turn out. This writer viewed this as possible because of the rapidly growing opposition to *Abashidze's* party. The writer also predicted that the block of the Nationalists and the United Democrats would win the parliamentary election. Undoubtedly in an effort to compete with the Nationalist block, another electoral block recently united from two opposition parties in *Adjara.* However, Our *Adjara* and Democratic *Adjara,* joined forces in effort to drive out *Aslan Abashidze.*[514] Discussions about *Adjara* often occur in conjunction with references to the *Abkhazian* republic, this time the connection between the two seems related to reports of recent violence perpetrated by the *Abkhaz* militia.

The *Abkhaz* militia perpetrated an attack in the *Gali* region of *Abkhazia* and kidnapped the head of a NGO called "The Union of *Abkhaz* and Georgian Artists."[515] Apparently, the *Abkhaz* militia planned to trade him for the

---

514   N.N., "Adjara has united opposition." *The Messenger Press Scanner* (*Tuesday on Mzera*) (5 February 2004):3.
515   N.N., "Georgian NGO Representative Kidnapped to Abkhazia." *24 Hours Rustavi-2* (6 February 2004):2.

bodies of two alleged "criminals" killed during an attack on a police station in *Tsalenjikha, Samegrelo*. One witness reported that the kidnappers were indeed *Abkhazian* (although it is not clear how such differential recognition is possible). While *Adjara* and *Abkhazia* continue to receive support from Russia, such assistance is unsurprising given the on-going support from the west to Georgia. On the one hand, while it sometimes seems that neither side seems aware of how such competitive support exacerbates the on-going conflict, on the other hand perhaps they do know. While the former cold war was about control of land and political power, the new cold war, seems like old water in new bottles, or perhaps 'new oil' in old barrels.

This new Western funding, once again appears financed by George Soros. He supported the development of a new resource called the Fund for Reform and Development.[516] These moneys and a second pot of financial resources called the Presidential Fund provide, will provide discretionary funds to the President. The Soros financed funds will support and implement institutional and public reforms, retrain public servants, ensure adequate compensation, and develop an environment conducive to reform. However, later the writer indicated that at least one of the funds actually comes from a variety of sources. These included anonymous donors, international organizations, and legal entities, all unidentified. While parliament approved the funding, the constitution indicates that salaries of government officials must be provided by the government and thus the Soros sponsored fund violates the constitution. The writer gathered this information from another Georgian language newspaper called the *Mtavari Gazeta*. The author further explained that opposition political party members are concerned that salaries paid by anonymous donors imply a clear patronage system. However, the Presidential Fund is not new, in 2002 the government used twenty million GEL from the Fund. Although the writer indicated that the moneys were only "spent in special or unforeseen circumstances." Yet even these specific "circumstances" also remain unidentified. Such western financial support especially from sources that remain obscured, illustrate the degree to which the West attempts to manage or manipulate Georgian geo-politics. Further evidence of

---

516   M. Alkhazashvili, "Two funds for the President." *The Messenger Economic Analysis* (5 February 2004):3.

Western influence or neo-imperialism are reflected in *Saakashvili's* new appointments to public office, primarily Georgians educated in the West. While Georgians may get a better education in the West, the degree of influence that this gives the West in administrative decisions that could harm Georgian government and society. This may be especially true if that influence leads to the uncritical acceptance of all forms of Western aid and assistance.

Saakashvili continued to make new ministerial and staff appointments and touted the value of young people educated in the West and their high level of professionalism.[517] Interestingly, the writer suggested that the new President must change the appointments to the National Security Council since the old post members did nothing to defend *Shevardnadze* following his resignation. Loyalty seems more important than professionalism, perhaps even loyalty to the west as symbolized by *Saakashvili*. However, as the author mentioned later, many of *Saakashvili's* appointments to high posts are going to those who were actively involved players in the *Rose Revolution*, and of course his political loyalists. The writer argued that these new appointees are either more loyal to *Zhvania* or to *Saakashvili* because both men need loyal followers throughout the cabinet. One new candidate for Defense Mininster is a member of the *Zviadist* wing of the Nationalist Movement and former supporter of Georgian's first president *Zviad Gamskhurdia*. This reflects the growing strength of nationalist sentiments within the new administration. While *Saakashvili* appointed these new western educated cabinet members or *Zviadists*, he also continued to eliminate a number of government agencies, allegedly to save money. While staff position cuts range from thirty to forty percent, the cuts may not save government money but rather help pay for the raises promised new cabinet members as well as the new police program. Cutting extant spending to expand new spending does not exactly reflect sound fiscal policies. In the context of these contradictory moves, more arrests of allegedly corrupt officials continue to occupy newspaper headlines.

Two criminal cases discussed in the news in brief section involve more allegedly corrupt public officials. One such case involved the arrest of the former Minister of Transport and Communication, *Merab Adeishvili*, by a

---

517   *Idem.* "On new Staff Appointments." *Ibid.*

dozen masked law enforcement officers. Accusations include misappropriat-ing between ½ million and thirteen million GEL.[518] Similarly, in another article *Adeishvili* is accused by the Prosecutor General *Irakli Okruashvili* of embez-zling anywhere from ½ million GEL to up to thirteen million GEL. *Okruashvili* suspected that *Adeishvili* also misappropriated Air Force funds.[519] Addition-ally, the Prosecutor arrested *Adeishvili's* brother, the former Deputy Minister of Fuel and Energy, although later he was released. The Prosecutor insinu-ated that corruption always existed throughout the fuel sector. Further, he explained that every sector of *Shevardnadze's* government was character-ized by crime and corruption. However, he reported that those who return stolen funds might avoid later prosecution. In another criminal investigation, accusations against a member of the National Movement included extortion and bribery. The former Governor of *Kvemo Kartli, Levan Mamaladze faced the same accusations.*[520] Other arrests for corruption charges included the former Minister of Transportation and the Chief of the state owned Georgian Railway, *Akaki Chkaidze.*[521] He and three other incarcerated officials, *Merab Zhordania*, President of the Football Federation and *David Mirtskhulava*, for-mer Fuel Minister were reportedly transported to the jail hospital, although there's no indication why the jail hospital was necessary.[522] *Chkaidze* is ac-cused of modifying established tariffs for some individuals or organizations resulting in a loss of approximately thirteen million GEL. The author reported that the Prosecutor General told another newspaper that such arrests should not threaten people who are engaging in honest business-practices but only those current and formal officials who engage in corruption and bribery. He is quoted as stating: "If they return everything they stole, we will be lenient and some can be freed from responsibility". The journalist made inquires about recent allegations of human rights abuses with regard to the arrest without a

---

518   N.N., "Adeishvili accusations to be known Thursday." *The Messenger* News *in Brief* (5 February 2004):4.

519   Christina Tashkevich, "I will not say who will be next." *The Messenger Press Scan-ner* (*Tuesday on Mzera*) (5 February 2004):6.

520   N.N., "Investigating Mamaladze." *The Messenger News in Brief* (5 February 2004):4.

521   Sopho Gorgadze, "Law enforcers work in emergency regime." *The Messenger Press Scanner* (5 February 2004):6.

522   N.N., "High Authorities Sent to Jail Hospital." Rustavi-2 online news http://www.rustavi2.com.ge/view.php?=6384 (as of 19 January 2004).

warrant of the Deputy Chair of the Electricity Wholesale Market. The Prosecutor denied the allegations and explained: "I do not think we have done anything illegal here. I think that the state is an emergency situation and we have to carry out emergency operations." The Prosecutor told reporters that an informant, the Minister of Transportation, *Akaki Chkaidze,* helped build the case. The former Minister of Energy also provided evidence with regard to the case. Finally, the reporter indicated that the suspect's family will also be queried about the source of their wealth. Here it is important for readers to understand something my Georgian students often told me, that in Georgia money earned via corruption is often buried or hidden in the accounts or properties of family members of the corrupt politician so that he or she can avoid implications of any impropriety. As arrests continue, the new changes in the constitution also remain a central focus of the newspapers.

The 24 Hours, a formerly Georgian language news publication published in English for the second week in a row, dated February 6th 2004, provided information about the potential changes to the Georgian constitution. Almost the entire paper was devoted to a discussion of the proposed changes and related critiques. The most significant change included the addition of the position of a Prime Minister with the authority to dismiss the entire Parliament. The President would appoint the Prime Minister and the Prime Minister could then dismiss parliament "in case of disagreement over issues of extraordinary importance" or a no confidence vote. A variety of NGOs including a famous Georgian scholar and analyst for the NGO, Caucasian Institute for Peace and Democracy, *Ghia Nodia*, argued that this change is inappropriate. As previous critiques of the proposed modifications in the constitution have maintained, such changes ignore the current requirement that Parliament discuss constitutional amendments for one month prior to making final decisions. Therefore, the proposed changes increase the power of the executive branch over the Parliament. Moreover, this is a unique development globally, as normally a Prime Minister post usually precedes the constitutional addition of the office of the President. Nevertheless, one hundred and sixty-five MPs voted to introduce the post of Prime Minister. Critics argued that this occurred simply because *Zurab Zhvania* wanted to become prime minister. The Prime Minister will manage and direct the cabinet although his power comes directly from the President who holds the power to dismiss the whole cabinet as well as the parliament.[523] According to one front-page article, the President can perform these dismissals without any explanation. However, the next sentence lists three specific justifications available to the President. He can dismiss the parliament if (1) the parliament fails to approve a budget or (2) fails to approve a cabinet appointee three consecution times, or (3) their vote disagrees with the President on three consecutive occasions.[524] This is clearly a usurpation of executive power and an undemocratic move. While Parliament can also dismiss the Cabinet, they can only do so with 3/5 of the votes. Moreover, if the parliament fails to deliver such a vote to dismiss the cabinet, the President may dismiss the cabinet or the parliament. The head of the constitutional court expressed concerns about this development. However, *Saakashvili* believed that the parliament will make the changes. Further *Davitashvili* also argued that the post of Prime Minister decreases the role of parliament and increases the power of the executive branch of government. *Davitashvili* stated that this will harm Georgia's new democracy and will reduce support from the West, although he's probably wrong about the latter. Congruent with his opposition to the new government, *Davitashvili' also* refused to accept three different posts offered to him within the new government. Other NGO's including representatives from the Young Lawyers' Association as well as the U.S. National Democratic Institute argue that these changes are not democratic. Apparently, in responding to these criticisms, *Saakashvili* dismissed the issue and simply stated that Georgia struggles with organized crime and "those who want to join the fight with us are welcome." Leaders of both the National Party and the United Democrats reported that *Davitashvili's* withdrawal from the party would not change the forthcoming union of both political parties. In a related article, *Davitashvili* also criticized *Zhvania's* support for Georgia's entry into the Commonwealth of Independent States. Fortunately, here this Georgian newspaper article provided a cogent criticism of *Saakashvili's* sweeping changes and included the concerns of a political opponent.

---

523   Giorgi Asanishvili, "Commission Gives Consent on Constitutional Amendments." *24 Hours Rustavi-2* (6 February 2004):1.

524   Giorgi Kandelaki, "Constitutional Changes Spark Controversy." *Ibid.*

Unfortunately, the above criticism of *Saakashvili's* administration fails to have any effect on his determination to continue to transform the government. This time the modifications were made to the Central Election Commission.[525] Interestingly, five of *Nino Burjanadze's* appointees to the Central Election Commission resigned following the inauguration of President *Saaksashvili*. Subsequently, *Saakashvili* appointed two new members although three earlier resignations later resulted in reinstatements. However, interestingly this new CEC recently denied registration to two political parties. While the CEC reports that these two groups failed to meet some of the requirements necessary to register, the specific requirements the groups' failed to meet were not provided. These two groups included the Unification of Georgian Professional Unions and the State Independent Lawyers Board. This may reflect the on-going consolidation of executive power in the new political block. In a related article, the Council of Europe asked the Georgian government to consider reducing the proportional barrier for party blocks from seven to five percent, to protect democratic pluralism.[526] Unfortunately, the writer claimed little time remained to accomplish this before the March 28th parliamentary election. Additionally, the Council of Europe asked the Georgian Central Election Committee to complete the computerized list of Georgia's voters in time for the forthcoming election. Apparently, the CEC previously allowed new voters to add their names to the list on Election Day and the Council of Europe suggested that this practice cease. However, the recently appointed Chair of the Central Election Committee, *Zurab Chiaberashvili* indicates that insufficient time remains to complete the computerized list in time for the March election.

Another writer reviewed the constitutional changes and reported that the President's authority extends to appointment of the local Mayors and regional *Gamgebelis* (regional administrators) previously elected.[527] This new procedure was described as a temporary measure with officials explaining that elections will occur later. However, the new procedure was assigned no expiration date. Russian President Vladimir Putin also maintains similar

---

525   N.N., "Central Election Commission Fully Staffed." *Ibid.*
526   N.N., "Council of Europe Seeks Improved Election Code in Georgia." *Ibid.,* 2.
527   Eka Kvesitadze, "Secret of Development Lies in the System, Not in the Individual." *Ibid.*

power as he now appoints all the regional Governors, who were previously elected by their constituents. The writer argued that history illustrates that the concentration of power within the executive branch of any government never bodes well for the survival of a nation and used Putin's new executive power as an example. In its usual historical demonstration of wartime power, the United States of America also exemplifies a similar concentration of power within the executive branch, especially since 9/11.

Another article written by *Niko Melikadze* of the Center for Strategic Research, the history of different types of constitutional democracies, including France, the United Kingdom, and the United States of America were reviewed.[528] The essay occupied an entire page of the newspaper and pointed out that Georgia's new constitutional changes fail to reflect democracy. While the author agreed that arresting corrupt officials stands as good policy and should facilitate systemic changes, in the context of the President's increasing power, arresting corrupt officials offers little meaning and may have no long-term positive effects.

In an interview with the new Minister of Justice, *Zurab Adeishvili* the constitutional changes are discussed further.[529] *Adeishvili* reported that the President would only overrule or reject decisions made by the cabinet if they were illegal. Furthermore, he described the Parliament as also maintaining the authority to issue a vote of no confidence in the cabinet. If a three fifth majority makes such a decision, the entire cabinet will be required to resign. However if the parliament takes such a vote with only a simple majority once, and again within three months by simple majority vote, the President must either fire the cabinet or dissolve parliament. The Minister also indicated that President's similar authority remains limited to two circumstances, when the parliament fails to approve a cabinet member, or when parliament fails to approve a budget. While *Adeishvili* seems to think his characterization paints a different picture of the new expansiveness of *Saakshvili's* executive power, he is mistaken. As mentioned above this new bill in the parliament will authorize the President to appoint the previously elected regional governors called *Gamgebelis*. The administration rationalized that this change is necessary

---

528   Niko Melikadze, "Opinion: Why not to Introduce the Post of Prime Minister." *Ibid.,* 3.

only because there is no time or money to pay a for a third set of elections following parliamentary election. During the previous president's administration, the locally elected city or town councils, or *Sakrebuloes* appointed the *Gamgebelis*. When the Minister was asked why not continue this, his answer revealed the poverty of information among Georgian institutions managing democracy as well as the legacy of the soviet period. He explained, "We cannot afford having pro-*Shevardnadze* officers in the transition period." However, he promised that elected *Gamgebelis* will take office in the fall of 2005. A recent talk show aired on the *Iberia* television channel when a New Rights politician stated that during the pre-election campaign *Saakashvili* previously promised the election of city or town Mayors, not appointments.[530] This New Rights politician, *David Saganelidze* argued, "Self governance as well as freeing small and medium businesses from taxes was promised in their campaign but as soon as they came into power they pushed these things back until 2005 and in some cases until 2009." *Saganelidze* also explained that his biggest disappointment with regard to new cabinet members is the absence of representation from other political parties. Other complaints by a local caller were that the ministers were too young and inexperienced. *Saganelidze* also insinuated that the government has all their friends working around them and that while this is okay, these young new Ministers needed to learn to work with the more experienced politicians. Another caller expressed concerns that all the new cabinet members were educated abroad, leaving few opportunities for those people who cannot afford an overseas education. These arguments reflect the growing public perception of the new ministers as economically privileged, and thus out of touch with majority of Georgian citizens' lives. Furthermore, *Saganelidze believed that* Saakashvili remains too exclusively focused on solving immediate social problems, rather than doing more unpopular things that might better help the country in the long-run. Another caller argued that new cabinet members were chosen only because they spoke English and knew how to use computers.

---

529   Tamara Khorbaladze, "Three Initiatives of the Ministry of Justice, Interview with Zurab Adeishvili." *Ibid.,* 4.

530   Sopho Gorgodze, "Tuesday on Dialogue, news analysis on the Iberia Channel." *The Messenger* (19 February 2004):6

Perhaps in reaction to the above television program and the cumulative effect of the venom building over the disappointing behavior of the new Administration, one journalist revealed renewed administrative efforts to repress the Georgia television media.[531] The background of the article discussed *Saakashvili's* contentious arrests of high-level businessmen and politicians since taking office, and told readers that in one police "raid" officers were wearing face masks and carrying military assault weapons. Georgian newspaper writers typically fail to comment on this style of paramilitary dress of local law enforcement authorities. This followed a police raid on a company that owns a local television channel. In this case, the writer quoted the Prosecutor General, *Irakli Okrusavhili* who responded to concerns in this instance that the government is interfering with the rights of a free press by saying: "We will take appropriate measures against everyone who has committed crime. We don't differentiate if this person stole a camera or a needle." The police raided several subsidiaries of a company called *Omega* that in addition to owning the TV channel *Iberia* remains one of the largest tobacco exporters in the nation. On local television, law enforcement agents were shown surrounding the building and denying permission to anyone to exit or enter for an hour. Subsequently, an outraged public appeared on the scene leading law enforcement officers to depart without conducting a search of the station. The owner of *Omega, Zaza Okrushvili,* is also a parliamentarian. He was reportedly angry about the raid and claimed he was not afraid of these "raiders" and would "defend himself if necessary." Another employee of *Iberia* revealed *to* a reporter that officers beat up at least one journalist during the incident. *Akaki Asatiani*, party leader of the Traditionalists, referred to such behavior as resembling the tactics of Trotsky and Stalin. A different daily paper also reported these events on the front page with a headline describing the event as a real effort to shut down the media, not just its parent company.[532] The headline read "Police Raid *Omega* Group's Iberia TV." The phrase police search also was used to describe the incident. This journalist revealed that *Omega* group owns the newspaper *Akhali Epocha* as well an-

---

531   Misha Kobaladze, "Attack on Media or Criminals?" *Georgia Today* (20 February 2004):1, 2.

532   Sopho Gorgodze, "Police Raid Omega Group's Iberia TV." *The Messenger* (20 February 2004):1, 14.

other media outlet called Media News. The journalist wrote that suspicions of the company included tax evasion and involvement in cigarette smuggling. *Zaza Okruashvili's* spouse, MP *Nato Chkeidze,* also works for the *Omega* group. The Prosecutor General, *Irakli Okruashvili,* reportedly continues working on lifting their immunity from prosecution. The day following the raid (the article mentions nothing about a legal warrant) Georgian protesters carrying a coffin with the words, "Free Press" marched down the main avenue in the capital city. The writer reported that the group consisted of Parliamentarians, NGO representatives, journalists and others who were angry about the previous day's search. Meanwhile, the prosecutor general told the press that *Omega* group's illegal activities cost the government twelve million GEL. The police search discovered seven printing machines used to make fake excise stamps and illegal firearms. He explained that arrests of four company Presidents would be forthcoming along with others involved in the scandal. The prosecutor also reported that lawbreakers hiding behind the safety of the free press are not immune from prosecution nor are parliamentarians. As these activities transpired, the Council of Europe Secretary General Walter Schwimmer held talks with politicians from opposing non-government parties. In a conversation with President, *Saakashvili* allegedly assured him that the recent search was not an attack on the free press only an investigation of the Omega group. Additionally, the new Prime Minister *Zurab Zhvania* exclaimed "It is funny how our opposition tries to compare the action taken against illegal excise facilities to the raid on Rustavi-2 during the previous government." *Zhvania* made no comment about the assault that occurred during the raid. *Zhvania's* reluctance to compare the two incidents was probably related to the fact that the incident under *Shevardnadze's* administration resulted in a two people being killed. Nonetheless, what remained unstated is the fact that two Georgian PMs own and control a local newspaper. None of the journalists or any politicians commented on how such ownership might be a conflict of interest. Such biased ownership could clearly result in intentional deceit or the misrepresentation of facts. *Saakashvili's* administration could have used this incident to make some systemic changes with regard to promoting political ethics and journalistic ethics that are more reflective of democratic values, but the opportunity was lost. Instead, the moment was utilized to make critiques of the extant power structure and while this also remains important, it is already normative in Georgian politics and therefore not representative of progress. Nonetheless, as his predecessors accomplished, this behavior similarly reveals *Saakashvili's* effort to centralize power and authority within the executive branch. In later news reports, S*aakashvili's* own advisors unabashedly stated that increasing executive power was a primary objective.

Specifically even the Minister of Justice *Adieshvili* reported that a priority for the new administration includes the development of a strong central government. Other objectives included the elimination of seventy-five territorial units as well as the reduction of administrative units. He claims that these measures will eliminate loss of funds from corruption as well as assist in restoring the territorial integrity of Georgia. Arguments might also maintain that eliminating additional levels of democratic representation to achieve lower corruption and a reduction in the number of government administrators will result in little or no effect on decreasing corruption.

Another journalist questioned *Adieshvili* about a second proposed anti-corruption bill labeled by *the opposition as* an anti-free market free bill. The bill's central focus reportedly is the investigation and punishment of government bribe takers. The new law would require state officials proven guilty of stealing from the state budget to return the stolen funds. Otherwise funds or property not relinquished will be confiscated unless in the name of a relative for over one year. However, if a relative fails to claim the said property, it will be confiscated. Interestingly, there is also a portion of the new bill indicating that some corrupt officials may have sentences suspended, particularly if the offender provides additional information about other instances of bribery or corruption. In this instance, the new law seems to represent *Saakashvili's* attempt to institutionalize honesty, something that grew to be non-normative throughout the Soviet period because telling the truth was dangerous.

Following the reports of new anti-corruption laws, tax evasion charges were filed against the marketing Director of an energy sector company, *Soso Natroshvili*.[533] However, his supervisors, all foreign nationals, reported that he was innocent. Subsequently, additional arrests included the former Transpor-

---

533   Sopiko Chkhaidze, "Dominoes Principle Second Ex-Director-in-Chief of Wholesale Market Arrested." *24 hours Rustavi-2* (6 February 2004):6.

tation and Communications Minister, *Merab Adeishvili* and the head of the Aviation Ministry, *Chankotadze*. Again, the charges were corruption. Their offenses allegedly resulted in the bankruptcy of the Aviation administration.[534] While one aviation official accused the above officials of gross levels of misappropriation of Georgian government funds, another government official claimed that these were all legal distributions of funds based upon the law as well as World Bank agreements. This spate of recent arrests remains either unrelated to any involvement of officials in organized crime or simply uninvestigated or unspoken.

In an interview with the Interior Minister, *Giorgi Baramidze,* the new amendments to the criminal code will reportedly make it easier to prosecute what he calls the Georgia Mafiosi or thieves in law.[535] This will permit prosecution if evidence substantiates the person's membership in the organization. The Minister explained that law enforcement officials have been unable to apprehend these suspects previously because they never commit crimes in person and instead use their army of soldiers to perpetrate crimes. Subsequently, the deputy director of the Georgian Energy Wholesale Market, was arrested for the murder or "assassination" of the Director of the American Elective Service in Telasi, *Nika Lominadze.*[536] This murder revolved around the misappropriation of two and a half to almost four million GEL by the suspect, *Natroshivili.* Other suspects included the previous director, *Jibashvili.* Apparently, they both gave unauthorized credits to private companies in addition to expropriating funds. The writer also reported that Russian armed forces were involved in some of these activities. The current Director of the Energy Market told journalists that there was no warrant authorizing the arrests. While the initial implication here is that these suspects are members of an organized criminal group, arresting them without a warrant is clearly a violation of their civil and human rights.

In another report of corruption, the Mayor of a village where the British Petroleum pipeline is scheduled for construction was arrested for stealing

---

534   Tamara Dvali, "Will the Aviation Case End Up in the Prosecutor's Briefcase?" *Ibid.,* 5.

535   Khatue Jangirashvili, "New Anti-Mafia Legislation." *Ibid.,* 6.

536   Sopiko Chkaidze, "Dominoes Principle Second Ex-Director-chief-of Wholesale Market Arrested." *Ibid.*

one hundred thousand GEL from a six hundred and twenty-nine thousand GEL compensation fund scheduled for allocation to forty-two residents of the city.[537] The mayor, *Roden Pilpan*, and a village resident, *Gilvi Tchkadua*, will face ten years in prison for corruption, if convicted. The prosecutor General's office has indicated that dozens of such cases exist. He promised to identify and prosecute the perpetrators. Similarly, a separate article reports that Interpol wants the former Governor of *Kvemo Kartli*, *Levan Mamaladze*, for extortion and bribe taking.[538] His mother was recently subpoenaed to appear for questioning with the Prosecutor General. She argued that the case against her son is political and that she will refuse to answer any of the Prosecutor's questions. Journalists reveal another problem with regard the BTC pipeline construction. Some Georgian citizens living near the new oil pipeline, demanded compensation for exposure to environmental hazards.[539] The group, residents of the city of *Rustavi*, plan to sue even though the *Rustavi* Mayor maintains that he will not allow anyone to prevent the construction of the pipeline. Obviously, the Mayor's concerns are economic rather than local residents' victimization. The continued exploitation of Georgian land and Georgian citizens seems to have little impact on Georgian sentiments with regard to ethnic minority group members, as they become likely scapegoats for other problems plaguing Georgia.

Specifically, in rare coverage of a local murder, an ethnic minority group member, an *Azeri,* was described as murdered by a Georgian. The incident occurred in *Dmanisi and began as a* conflict between Georgians and *Azeris* in the nearby town of *Useinkenti.*[540] Unfortunately, the conflict erupted as the result of the dissemination of inaccurate information passed to the Georgian *Svan* population that the *Azeris* were attempting to take over their land. Shortly thereafter, one *Svan* attacked and killed an *Azeri* and subsequently the *Azeri* population threatened mass protests if the suspects remained free. The police were unable to locate the suspect. Considering the series of events leading to the death, it is unlikely the police will ever locate the suspect. Furthermore, it is also unlikely that *Saakashvili's* nationalistic policies

---

537   N.N., "Village Head Arrested Fraud in BTC Controversy." *Ibid.*
538   N.N., "Levan Mamaladze's Mother Summoned For Questioning." *Ibid.*
539   N.N., "Oil Pipeline Construction Delayed in Rustavi." *Ibid.*
540   N.N., "Ethnic Azeri Murdered in Dmanisi." *Ibid.*

even while aimed at re-integration and the elimination of corruption will resolve these kinds of problems, as they are never raised as social-political issues. Nonetheless, *Saakashvili* does appear to want to bury the hatchet with Georgian's powerful neighbor to the north, Russia.

In mid February President *Saakashvili* visited President Vladimir Putin in Moscow telling him "I came here to befriend you".[541] The writer continued quoting the remainder of *Saakashvili's* statement to Putin: "...Russia is a great power and we are a small country but we have our interests, our pride, our history and this history is connected to Russia." Putin reportedly acknowledged *Saakashvili's* by explaining that he pays attention to what President *Saakashvili* states both in Georgia and abroad and that he perceives *Saakashvili's* expressions as "positive signals driven toward restoring Georgia-Russian relations." The author referred to a statement from Putin's administrative assistant who described the talks as "deep and frank", and that "they...lend themselves to a change in the character and nature of Georgian-Russian relations." During this visit, *Saakashvili* also reportedly claimed that Georgia is neither pro-Russian nor pro-American but rather pro-Georgian. Georgia's President spoke to a group of students and Professors at the Moscow State Institute of International Relations quoting a statement made by Fidel Castro about *Saakashvili*, "*Saakashvili* overthrew a regime, which only stole from the people....*Saakashvili* is exactly the same as myself." *Saakashvili* then explained: "I tried to be like him, but a beard does not suit me." It seems both fascinating and foreboding that Castro compares himself willingly to *Saakashvili* and similarly that *Saakashvili* embraced his comparison to dictator even if benevolent one.

This writer further criticizes *Saakashvili* by accusing him of ignoring Chinese journalists while granting interviews to many other foreign journalists at the recent World Economic Summit in Davos. The journalist points out a comment by a rather angry Chinese journalist at the apparent elitism of *Saakashvili* after he bragged about ignoring Chinese journalists. It remains unclear where this anti-Chinese sentiment comes from, other than the usual ethnocentric or jingoistic fear of any neighbor (especially a large one) who

---

541   Sopho Gorgodze, "Hand of Friendship now in Moscow, I came to Russia to befriend you." *The Messenger* (12 February 2004):1, 5.

appears to look less like the self-identified nationalist group. In a recent visit to Far Eastern Russia, I also observed a rather pervasive fear of the Chinese, although this seemed to be based on both jingoism and the proximity of Russians on the Chinese border.

A number of Ministers, businessmen, and other politicians accompanied *Saakashvili* to Moscow including the Head of the Border Guards. They were invited to Moscow to discuss the Georgian-Chechen border with their Russian counterparts. This meeting may have transpired in part as the result of an earlier report indicating that the exiled President of *Chechnya, Aslan Zakaev,* in a separate interview, thanked the Georgian people for their support of *Chechnians* in their struggle to avoid Russia's clutches.[542] In this interview, the President of *Chechnya* also insinuated that Russia's strategy of dividing and ruling in the Caucasus is not over. He further explained that he holds Russia responsible for the separatist conflict in *Abkhazia, Ossetia*, and the *Karabakh. Saakashvili* met with Russian businessmen re-assuring them that their investments in Georgia would be protected unlike his predecessor whom *Saakashvili* later accused of 'saying one thing, thinking another and doing yet another.' Apparently, there a number of Georgian Diaspora live in Moscow and *Saakashvili* spoke to them at the St. George church. *Saakashvili* told them that he would do everything he could to get them back into Georgia and or *Abkhazia.* The author focused on the Russian media's emphasis on *Saakashvili's* visit to Russia as transpiring before his visit to the United States. Apparently, the intent is to make it seem that Saakashvili's priority is Georgia's relationship with its closest geographic neighbor, not the distant U.S. The writer also focused on *Saakashvili's* choice to travel on a commercial economy class flight, rather than first class. By extension, *Saakashvili* told the media that he sold the old Presidential residence and lives in a small apartment (but it is a new building) because "as long as the people live they way the do, the government officials should not live better." *Saakashvili* also informed the Russian press that Georgia would never loose *Abkhazia* but that it would not wage a war to ensure its return. In response to questions about Russia's military bases remaining in Georgia he explained,

---

542   N.N., "Zakaev: "Divide and Rule" Politics should be over in the Caucasus." *24 Hours Rustavi-2* (6 February 2004):4.

'the soldiers deployed in Georgia have no combat importance for Russia but rather emotional meaning and "the bases that have no warfare importance should be withdrawn." When asked for a proposed date by a Russian radio host, he replied: "the sooner the better" and also promised that Russian bases would not be replaced with American bases. However, shortly after the closing of one Russian base in early 2000, a small American detachment was posted to Georgia as a part of the U.S.-Georgian military training and equipment program. Russia had previously agreed to close all their bases at the 1999 Istanbul summit but continues to postpone closing a number of these posts that remain operational. Another contentious issue between Georgia and Russia is the Pankasi Gorge near the Chechen border. Chechen rebels or 'terrorists' depending on whose perspective one takes on the issue, continue to take refuge in Georgia and the Russian government wants Georgia to prevent this as well as to turn over any Chechens found in the area. *Saakashvili* recommended a joint Russian-Georgian patrol in the area, although this would not be well received among Georgians. Another salient issue is that Georgia owes Russia one hundred and sixty million U.S. dollars. *Saakashvili* indicated that he intends to re-pay the debt. However, he insisted that the debt was the result of corrupt Georgian officials, who have been arrested. He seems to be suggesting that Russia forgive the obligation to pay the debt. *Saakashvili* also concurred with a former Georgian Security minister who acknowledged that one person arrested in the Moscow subway bombing was from *Abkhazia*. This comment seemed aimed at reminding the Russians that they may have created this problem with the Chechens themselves. *Saakashvili* promised to continue assisting Russia in their on-going investigation of the Moscow subway bombing. *Echo Moscow*, a Russian radio station recently polled Russians on the air and found that seventy percent of callers believed that *Saakashvili* viewed Russia favorably. However, in January sixty-one percent of *Echo Moscow* listeners polled believed that Russian-Georgian relations were cold and forty-three percent thought that the *Chechen* problem prevented normalized relations between the two nations. In another article discussing *Saakashvili's* visit to Russia, a journalist articulated Georgia's on-going stressful relationship with Russia, explaining that Russians view *Shevardnadze* as a traitor to the Soviet Union and blame him for participating in *Gorbachev's perestroika,* the results of which have not been particularly successful. The author argues that one goal of *Saakashvili's* was to eliminate Russian negative attitudes about Georgians and suggested that the objective may have been achieved. However, *Saakashvili* also told Russians that Georgia wants to acknowledge and respect the interests of Russia in the Caucasus as long as is does not conflict with the interests of the Georgian state. *Saakashvili* also suggested the possibility of connecting an oil pipeline from *Novorossiik* with the *Baku-Supsa* pipeline currently under construction. *Saakashvili* reminded the Russian authorities that Georgia's territorial integrity is very important. *Saakashvili* asked the Russians to stop supporting the separatist regimes *Ossetia* and in *Abkhazia.* In addition to the Georgian debt owed Russia, *Saakashvili* reportedly stated that he hoped that the Paris Club would re-structure their debt programs with Russia. Finally, when asked what bound Russia to Georgia, *Saakashvili* stated "History, language and a common faith." Finally, *Saakashvili* spoke optimistically about dropping Visa requirements between the two nations while encouraging Russia to preserve and deepen cultural ties to Georgia. Unfortunately, one cultural and historical tie connecting Georgia and Russia that Saakashvili failed to mention includes the second-class status of women and the related development of the post-soviet victimization of women through human trafficking.

In a recent seminar addressing the issue of human trafficking in *Tbilisi,* one group called the "advocates expressed hopes that the new government would fight trafficking."[543] The Georgian Young Lawyer's Association (GYLA), the American Bar Association, and the NGO Women for the Future sponsored the development of this new organization whose goal is to eliminate trafficking. A GYLA member explained that human trafficking remains a serious problem and is a form of slavery. In one interview with a representative of the NGO Women for the Future, she explained that one of their surveys' illustrated that eighty percent of Georgians want to leave the country to find jobs. Unfortunately, this makes them vulnerable to traffickers who frequently make false promises of economic success and a better life. Richard Emmons, the ABA Country Director of the Eurasian Criminal Law Program reports that this

---

543   Mary Makharashvili, "Advocates hopeful new government will fight Trafficking." *The Messenger* (12 February 2004):1, 7.

is a problem far beyond *Tbilisi* stretching throughout the Caucasus region. He also indicated that two major goals are to increase public awareness of the problem and to draft legislation in Georgia to prevent and or punish trafficking. The GYLA representative told the reporter that in a recent meeting of the Georgian Security Council, other state agencies, and NGOs, are developing an action plan to implement *Shevardnadze's* anti-trafficking laws adopted in 2003. A working group created within the Public Defender's office, will coordinate the resolution of this problem. This is one of the few instances when the identification of women's issues appeared in the Georgian press. Additionally, the article made no further mention of information that might begin this future public prevention program or offer suggestions or advice to women who might be susceptible to being trafficked. No gendered analysis of any of Georgia's salient socio-economic or political issues ever seems to appear in the press. Georgia needs a women's movement. Georgian women need the first wave of feminism to protect them from violence, poverty and other forms of exploitation. While there are significant numbers of women in civil society and some college Professors who include an analysis of gender in their classes, it is not on the public's radar screen and is invisible to the government. Crime is a gendered phenomenon and while there is no published scientific research to support any tentative hypothesis that corruption is gendered, I suspect, like its sister white-collar crime, that it is also a gendered phenomenon and is closely related to the ideology associated with capitalism.[544] [545] While *Saakashvili* appointed a number of women to his cabinet, these are largely symbolic gestures as the preponderance of his staff are men.

Saakashvili appointed *Irakli Chubinishvili* to hold a new post as Chief of the Presidential Staff while *Zurab Adeishvili* received the an appointment as the new Minister of Security, replacing *Valery Khaburdzania*, who will remain in the administration in a different post.[546] This new position of Chief of Staff

---

544   James Messerschmidt, *Crime as Structured Action: Gender, Race, Class and Crime in the Making* (Thousand Oaks, CA: Sage, 1997).

545   Louise Shelley, "Organized Crime Groups: 'Uncivil Society.'" In: Alfred B. Evans, Jr., Laura A. Henry, and Lisa McIntosh Sundstrom, eds., *Russian Civil Society: A Critical Assessment* (Armon, NY: M.E. Sharpe, 2006), 95-109.

546   Anna Arzanova, "Picking the new Team Three Key Appointments in Georgian Government." *Ibid.*, 1, 4.

(or Chief of the Presidential Administration) reported that his position entails observing and guarding the new Presidential powers. Such a definition of his responsibilities seems more focused on security than administrative management. He indicated that his orders will come directly from the President. Furthermore, he will ensure that Presidential decrees result in full implementation. He reported that these decrees will supersede any measure passed by the cabinet of ministers. Interestingly, *Chubinishvili* reports that he requires a large staff of 150-200 people, somewhat incongruent with other administrative plans to reduce federal agencies and staffing levels. Nevertheless, the constitutional changes and *Zhvania's* nomination as Prime Minister remain the most controversial aspects of *Saakashvili's* sweeping changes. Some view *Zhvania's* appointment as a sort of political debt owed for his participation in the Rose Revolution. Again, the President claims that the office was not created just for *Zhvania* but rather to ensure that the "government can work better."

Concerns about *Saakashvili's* sweeping changes specifically regarding the large number of recent arrests of allegedly corrupt officials seemed to have affected the President's resolve as in a recent press conference, *Saakashvili* promised an end to the arrests. He explained: "We took such steps because it was necessary to respond to illegality that has existed in Georgia over recent years." He also referred to the necessity of "law and order" a phrase employed frequently in the United State by politicians to garner public support. "The arrests will come to end soon—though the members of the new government should know that if they take illegal steps they will also be held responsible for everything they do."

Saakashvili continued to replace cabinet members and create a number of new governmental positions for his political allies. *Saakashvili* also explained "the government should not look like a Kindergarten."[547] Apparently, *Saakashvili* was speaking about replacing the old political guard (from the Soviet period) with young people who have fresh ideas, but not so young as to make the government look like a kindergarten. It is unknown if he was the first to adopt the use of the term or if he employed it as a response to the on-

---

547   N.N., "The government should not look like a kindergarten." *The Messenger Press Scanner* (12 February 2004):6.

going criticisms that his cabinet members were too young and inexperienced. Another writer revealed statements made by *Koba Davitashvili*, National Movement MP, who denied rumors of the development of another political block that included the son of former President *Gamsakhurdia, Koko Gamsakhurdia.* [548] He also commented about the new constitutional changes, "...reducing the powers of the parliament is an expression of mistrust towards the government". He warned that the unification of the National Party with the *Burjanadze-Democrats* will "bring no good to the National Movement". He further implied that this political block will lead to the reduction of he parliamentary seats available for other parties. As other critics previously warned, the loss of political plurality will silence the voices of dissent that are necessary and sufficient for the maintenance of democracy. However, on-going problems with *Abkhazia* also threaten Georgia's weak democracy.

The former Chair of the pro-Georgian Supreme Council of *Abkhazia, Tamaz Nadareishvili* negatively evaluated the recent visit of the *Abkhaz* delegation to *Tbilisi.*[549] She believes the *Abkhaz* delegation's insistence that Georgia sign a non-aggression statement is unacceptable. She praises *Saakashvili* for indicating that force might be necessary, although in other public statements *Saakashvili* reported that force is not an option, although he intends for all of Georgia to re-unite. Of course, his other ambiguous objectives include a rather large budget with little systematic ability to garner the resources necessary to support such expenditures.

Specifically, the details of 2004 budget offered by one journalist, are described as "lofty".[550] The revenue anticipated for 2004 as well as the outlays for the year as delineated by the Finance Minister, *Zurab Nobhaideli* are illustrated in Table four.

---

548   N.N., "Zhvania will not bring any good to Saakashvili." *Ibid.*
549   N.N., "Nadareishvili likes Saakashvili's brave steps." *Ibid.*
550   M. Alkhazashvili, "2004 budget sets lofty goals." *The Messenger* (12 February 2004):3.

Table 4: Georgia's Budgetary Problems

Anticipated Grants 2004	Anticipated Tax Revenues 2004	Expenditures 2004	Budget Deficit 2003	Pensions and Unpaid Salaries 1997-2000	Pensions and Salaries Owed 2004
200 million GEL	1.522 billion GEL	930 million GEL	600 million GEL	280 million GEL	100 million GEL

Clearly if tax collection falls short of expectations, the government could be in serious trouble…again. By February 18th, the parliament was poised to approve the new President's cabinet.[551] In an attempt to silence any parliamentary opposition, the nominees met with parliamentary committees on the eve of the scheduled confirmations. Georgians continued to refer to his new cabinet by making jokes about their youth and inexperience, calling them the kindergartners. Only *Zurab Zhvania* has significant political experience. Each minister met with the press and explained their five-year plans for Georgia. *Zhvania* told reporters that the new President's plan included re-organizing the government to create smaller administrative offices, reforming law enforcement, increasing wages and pensions, increasing social services, improving foreign relationships, and supporting private business. Of course, one business desperately in need of promotion has been Georgia's need for its own oil resources that the BTC oil pipeline will provide.

Russia expressed concerns about the *Baku-Tbilisi-Ceyhan* oil pipeline, believing that threatens Russia's economic and political interests in the region.[552] This journalist argues that Russian authorities view the BTC pipeline as an effort to get Caspian Energy resources to the world market while "circumventing Russia." Specifically, the Russians argue that this project will result in a five billion dollar loss to the Russian economy. Certainly, while local Georgians' whose lands were purchased by the company at minimal costs to the oil giants may fail to benefit from this gargantuan project, some hope that other Georgians will reap rewards. However, the company involved in this operation is referred to by one American watchdog organization, as repre-

---

551   Sopho Gorgodze, "Zhvania lays out plans Parliament expected to approve appointments in late night session." *The Messenger* (18 February 2004):1, 10.

sentative of colonialism, just as *NAFTA* and the World Trade Organization are representative of rich countries' best interests not developing countries' best interests. For example, critiques of NAFTA argue that the constitutions of the three countries become virtually nullified as companies' profits drop. This economic treaty usurps the power of elected officials and operates in non-public meetings with appointed not elected officials. Russian authorities view Georgia's participation in the oil project as a great "misdeed". Apparently, the Russian government is also displeased with recent restrictions placed on its oil tankers that are passing through the Istanbul Bosporus and Dardanelles ports, making it unprofitable to transport oil from the Russian port of Novorossiisk.

The above budget also seems extravagant in light of the IMF's suspension of loans to Georgia though the loans were recently re-instated. However, the new payment plan has not yet begun.[553] Implementing the new restructuring of the debt will only begin after Georgia meets the following objectives. Georgia must initiate reforms in the financial sectors, achieve parliamentary approval of the 2004 budget and pass a group of laws designed to combat money laundering. Georgia must also provide evidence of their continued effort to combat smuggling. The government must carry out reforms in the energy sectors and complete audits of the three largest state enterprises, *Madneuli*, a copper ore mining company, *Poti Port* in *Adjara*, and the Georgian Railway. The IMF Georgian agreement also necessitates that Georgia collect 350 GEL more in tax revenues than last year. Once all these tasks are completed, Georgia will receive an additional thirty-six million dollars from the IMF. However, the anticipated 2004 budget revenues may total 1.294 billion while forecasted expenditures stand at 1.438 billion (clearly more than the earlier forecast, see page 257). This necessitates that Georgia seek additional financial assistance from other international financial organizations as well as donor countries. The Georgian government anticipates receiving 400 million GEL in total. In 2003, the government expected 95.4 million GEL but received only a 1/3 of that amount. Coincidentally the promise of new financial support followed *Saakashvili's* election as President. Relatedly, keeping

---

552   M. Alkhazashvili, "Russia searches for BTC alternatives." *Ibid.*, 3.
553   *Idem.* "IMF gives government a chance." *Ibid.*

his critics at bay seems to occupy a great deal of the new President's time as efforts to control the media continue.

Government pressure on the media continued when a political talk show host working for one of the privately owned television stations, Rustavi-2, resigned under duress.[554] This controversial show criticized governmental positions on a variety of issues. Some MPs argued that pressure from the new government ended her career. More specifically, *Saakashvili's* administration was accused of encouraging her to resign. The former talk show host refused to confirm or deny any coercion with regard to her decision. However, some MPs pushed for an investigation into the allegations. Interestingly, reports leaked that in the near future, she will begin working for one of the state owned television stations, Channel *1*. However, the article does not explain what her new job will entail. The parent company, of *Rustavi-2* is *Magticom* (a cell phone company), partially found and currently owned by the son-in-law of the former President *Shevardnadze* who has been previously questioned about arrears taxes and allegations of falsely reporting mobile phone fees. Following the journalist's resignation, law enforcement officers interviewed *Shevardnadze's* son-in-law. Earlier in the year, a raid on *Magticom* transpired due to suspicions of company involvement in illegal sales of products and the possession of weapons. While no other information about this second interview was revealed, another public official was arrested under suspicion of tax evasion. This time the suspect was the director of the Marneuli Technical Bureau District.[555] Additional accusations included the misappropriation of 35,000 GEL as well as violation of other duties and responsibilities. He could serve five years in prison if convicted. While the arrests continued, politicians historicized national sentiment by referring back to the *Abkhazian* conflict. Keeping the citizens angry and resentful seems to be the on-going objective here, especially when continuously referring to the *Abkhazian* injuries.

This time politicians reminded one journalist about an incident that occurred ten years ago in the *Gali* region. On February 17-18, 1994, during the war with *Abkhazia*, *Abkhazian's* allegedly massacred nine-hundred and fifty

---

554   N.N., "Inga Grigolia moves to Channel One." *Ibid.*, 4.
555   N.N., "Prosecutor's Office arrests Levan Mamaladze's relative." *Ibid.*

Georgians (including 17 children).[556] However, one Parliamentarian also claimed that fifty Georgians also were kidnapped and later forced to serve in *Abkhazian* separatist army. The speaker of the Parliament gave her condolences to the relatives of the dead and stated: "This is our common tragedy, and I hope we will manage to change the situation with regard to *Abkhazia*." Unfortunately, no further discussion of the allegations of the massacre or the kidnapping followed. In the same article, the writer mentioned that Russian and Georgian authorities were trying to re-institute a former train route that previously ran between *Sochi*, Russia to *Tbilisi* Georgia through the disputed *Abkhazian* region. However, this is unlikely to occur as recently *Abkhazia* refused to meet in the United Nations talks originally scheduled for February in Geneva.[557] Once again, in the same issue of this newspaper a story about *Adjara* and *Abashidze's* party, the Revival Party appears.

The Chair of the Revival Party in *Tbilisi* recently returned from a trip to the United States. He was attempting to garner support from leading Western nations although it remains unclear if this support was financial or ideological. However, opponents of the Revival party argued that his visit focused on the forthcoming Parliamentary elections.[558] The writer implied that this was an attempt to keep international observers away from the forthcoming rescheduled parliamentary elections, even though it remains unlikely that international observers would ever agree. Later, the author's supposition was corrected following a report by a Revival Party member revealed that *Adjara* would welcome the presence of international observers, "as many as possible." The writer then asked him about his opinion with regard to the new cabinet ministers and he responded that the future will tell how professionally and patriotically these people will behave. Questioning the patriotism of one's competitor represents an effective method of creating doubt about the opponent's value. Finally, the Revival Party member endorsed *Abashidze's* ongoing leadership by refusing to criticize it, and stated "it is up to the leader of the *Adjara* Autonomic Republic to decide whether or not "I will stay as the chair of the Revival *Tbilisi* Branch." As the *Adjaran and Abkhazian* issues step off the front stage, corruption returns to the headlines.

---

556   N.N., "Ten Years since the Tragedy in Gali." *Ibid.*
557   N.N., "Conflicting reports out of Sokhumi." *Ibid.*

This time accusations of corruption were made against the former Minister of Defense. A parliamentary committee on defense and security released a sixty-three page report documenting corruption throughout the Defense Ministry.[559] The journalist wrote that the former Minister of Defense, *David Tevzadze*, had papers waved at him threateningly by MPs while he shouted "there is some misunderstanding, but "if anyone is at fault that he should be punished." Subsequently, the President *Mikhail Saakasvhili* appointed him as Georgia's ambassador to NATO. Readers are left wondering if *Saakashvili* is really committed to routing out corruption or just eliminating opposition.

Subsequently, President *Saakasvhili* called upon the political opposition parties to "unite" for the forthcoming parliamentary elections. However the writer indicated that this unification seems only to characterize the current government block of Nationalists and Democrats.[560] The writer anticipated that only the government bloc would dominate the election and that no other parties will be able to the new seven percent threshold required. While there has been some discussion of the Labor Party unification with the Revival Party, the current leader of the Labor Party, *Shalva Natelashvili*, denied the possibility that this will occur unless his appointment as the leader of both parties transpires. Institutional and individual power holders are reluctant to relinquish their positions except under duress.

The story of the American Electric Services Corporation in Georgia illustrates this dynamic. Although no longer managing the electricity, the AES logo remains visible on many of the Capital electric meters. A recently released documentary film reviewed the American Electric Services Corporation's take over of Georgia's state electricity company in the early 1990's.[561] The film ran in local *Tbilisi* theaters during the spring of 2004. When the American company purchased the state run company, Georgians hoped that their electricity problems would end. However, AES failed to deliver regular electricity as promised and claimed that its major problem consisted of col-

---

558   N.N., "Bakuria recounts his U.S. visit." *Ibid.*, 6.
559   N.N., "Why has compromising information against Tevzadze vanished?" *Ibid.*
560   N.N., "Opposition might be saved by unification only." *Ibid.*
561   Christina Tashkevich, "Georgia on the Big Screen, "Power Trip" in Tbilisi." *The Messenger* (19 February 2004):1, 5.

lecting payments from local residents and businesses. AES eventually sold the company to a Russian electricity company. This documentary film, entitled: "Power Trip" directed and produced by Paul Devlin, told this tumultuous story at the premiere screening in *Tbilisi* on February nineteenth. Co-producers included two Georgian women, *Claire Missanelli* and *Valery Odikadze*. The first line of the film, according to the article was "Corruption, assassination, and street rioting surround the story of chaotic post-Soviet transition told through culture class, electricity disconnections, and blackouts."[562] While I have not seen the film, the previous quote with the exception of the street rioting reflects *Tbilisi's* on-going problems, although the capital city's electricity problems remain considerably better those that existed ten years ago. Although it should be noted many rural parts of Georgia continue to have problems with electricity or have no electricity at all. Moreover, in the capital, new social problems have become more pressing since those days, and this includes the growing problem of illicit drug abuse and drug smuggling.

In mid February representatives from Georgia, Armenia, *Azerbaijan*, the European Commission, and the United Nations Development Program met to review and extend the goals and objectives of the Southern Caucasus Anti-Drug Program designed to fight drug smuggling.[563] The objective of this three year old program is prevent drug smuggling by training border guards to implement a variety of intelligence activities. The head of the Georgian National Bureau against Drug Trafficking reported that the UNDP has been the only agency to provide assistance to eliminate this problem. The journalist cited the UNDP report that indicated, "drug-trafficking from Asia to Europe is being fulfilled through the South Caucasus corridor" that includes Georgia as a transit point. The head of the European Commission in Georgia explained that drug trafficking remains problematic across Georgia because of "the slow pace of economic reforms." Jacques Vantomme told newspaper reporters that, "suppression is not the only method of fighting against this evil." Vantomme also added that a more comprehensive strategy would focus reforms at eliminating poverty, reforming the education system, and improving

---

562   *Ibid.*

health protection. Finally, Vantomme added the "absence of a wide approach brings down the effectiveness of assistance." Similar honest appraisals rarely become verbalized in the United States, even when extant research shows that a truly comprehensive approach cannot simply be based on criminalizing the drug problem or supply reduction efforts. As clearly articulated here, illegitimate drug markets often develop as the consequence of a poor legitimate economy and concomitant demand for illicit substances. This program in the Caucasus is called SCAD, Southern Caucasus Anti-Drug Program. Unfortunately, later, Vantomme reverts to a simplistic social control policy to manage the drug problem by indicating that border control is a key factor as well as strengthening the cooperation between the three Caucasus republics. The United Nations development representative Lance Clark encouraged other legal reforms and mentioned the need to fight against corruption. He explained that program effectiveness develops from efforts to combat corruption in concert with the political will to eliminate the problem. Interestingly, another article in the same newspaper announced accusations of corruption by authorities against the Chief of the Border Guard.[564] Charges of corruption against the former Director of the Border Guard, *Valeri Chkeidze* also emanated from other high-ranking officials of the Georgian Border Guard. The writer indicated that the accusations were made only to force the current director to resign, implying that the allegations were false. However, the journalist explained: "It is a secret to no-one that smuggling in Georgia is an extremely widespread problem." This writer stated that the entire border-guard service was responsible for the problem and that previously only the apprenehensvion of lower level officials occurred while the eleven-year Director of the Border Guard was responsible for most of the systemic corruption. Former employees of the Border Guard claimed: "The Border Guard is the most corrupt defense structure in the government." Three former border guards disclosed that corruption has characterized the entire system for many years and that the Director knew the problem existed. Former employees also indicated: "For ten years, we have been waiting for *Shevardnadze* to leave. He made the Border Guard off limits and put *Chkeidze*, a member of his clan, at

---

563   Anna Arzanova, "Crossroads bring benefits-and trafficking Caucasus Countries link up to combat drug smuggling." *Ibid.,* 1, 4.

the top of the structure." Finally, the former employees' disclosed, "petroleum, children, and Mujahadeen fighters have left the country for some time
through this system." Later in the article, one of the former employees revealed that he was also receiving money, from 1000 to 1500 dollar a month,
to allow the passing of illegal cargo across Georgian borders. He reported
that funds were set aside as large as 35,000 dollars for the Director and other
high ranking officials, although it is unknown if this was a regular monthly
payment or a one time payment occurring each time an illegal substance
crossed the border. Finally, the writer claimed that such confessions are
smoke screens hiding other motives. Specifically, recent legislation allows
the perpetrators of lesser corruption offenses to receive a pardon if they admit their guilt and provide information that can lead to the arrest and prosecution of higher-level offenders. The writer seems somewhat dismissive of this
tactic, although similar arrangements are often negotiated by U.S. law enforcement, i.e., let the little fish off to catch the big one. On the other hand,
the writer also indicated that such tactics often focus on removing the old
cadre to replace them with the new power elites. This is patronage and was
illustrated shortly thereafter by President *Saakashvili's* appointment of a National Movement party member, *Tamaz Lursmanashvili to* run the Border Patrol.

The autonomous republics in Georgia are again on the front page of
one newspaper this time with regard to diplomatic talks in Geneva and Moscow.[565] Also discussed in the meeting were Russian military bases in Georgia. In Moscow, the OSCE Chairman Solomon Passy met with Russian Foreign Minister *Igor Ivanov*. The talks centered on the future of the OSCE and
regional issues affecting Georgia and Moldova. This is an interesting political
gesture to offer to Russia, the OSCE talking to Russian authorities about two
independent nations no longer a part of the Soviet Union or the Russian
Federation. However, both Moldova and Georgia suffered civil wars with notable parts of their countries seceding following the disintegration of the FSU.
The OSCE reported that Minister Passy explained to his Russian counterparts that OSCE"s plan to do "it's utmost to help the new Georgian govern-

---

564   M. Alkhazashvili, "Border Guard chief accused of corruption." *Ibid.,* 3.

ment implement political, legislative, and economic reforms". This includes OSCE on-going support of the dialogue with regard to the Georgia-Abkhaz and Georgian-Ossetian conflicts. Representatives of "the Friends of Georgia" met in Geneva at the UN office for two days to dialogue about the *Abkhaz* conflict. The head of the UN peacekeeping mission chaired the meeting (Jean-Marie Guehenno) that included delegations from France, Germany, Russia, the United Kingdom, and the United States. The outgoing Georgian Minister for Emergency Affairs, *Malkhaz Kakabadze* and his new replace-ment, *Goga Khaindrava*, participated in the talks as well. Unfortunately, the *Abkhaz* representative refused to attend the meeting. The *Abkhaz* Foreign Minister, *Shergei Shamba*, explained that he believed the Group of Friends should not be involved in the meetings. *Shamba* argued that the coordinating council should be the central arbiter of the dispute reminded others that the Group of Georgian Friends are merely observers. The UN admitted that the ten-year peace process and the monitoring of the ceasefire, has stalled, nev-ertheless diplomats hoped that the recent change in power in Georgia might re-invigorate the process. The UN head of peacekeeping, Jean Marie Gue-henno, argued that the nations on the Security Council must push for a solu-tion to this on-going problem.

An editorial (never labeled as such in Georgian newspapers), referred to the leaders of the *Rose Revolution* all of whom have gained or maintained political power in the wake of the revolution and the presidential election, as the "Rose Triumvirate." This label seems to symbolize the probability that these players will continue to work to maintain and nourish their power.[566] Of course, the players include *Mikhail Saakashvili*, the new President, his new Prime Minister, *Zurab Zhvania*, and the Speaker of the Parliament, *Nino Bur-janadze*. The author insinuated that while the three have argued over ap-pointees to the executive and judicial branch of government, their relationship is strong, and all three of their parties continue remain united. The author ar-gued that most decisions about the appointments transpired during the pre-revolutionary and revolutionary time-period, including adding the new Prime Minister position. Again, the author mentioned that only the friends of both

---

565   Warren Hedges, "Georgia at the negotiating table. Abkhaz party declines to take a seat." *Ibid.*, 1, 5.

Zhvania and *Saakashvili* gained appointments to various posts. Moreover, this writer argued as others before him have, that *Saakashvili* created the post of Prime Minister specifically for *Zhvania* through the constitutional change. It was not chosen by the people or debated in the parliament. However only *Zhvania's* party, the United Democrats and *Saakashvili's* party, the Nationalists will be unified into a single part block for the forthcoming election scheduled for next month. This election will determine the proportional candidates who will subsequently serve in the parliament. Walter Schwimmer, the General Secretary for the European Council, arrived in Georgia on Wednesday and met with *Saakashvili, Zhvania, and Burjanadze*.[567] Schwimmer will go to *Batumi* to meet with *Aslan Abashidze* and subsequently wants to bring *Abashidze* to *Tbilisi*. The President reportedly said that *Abashidze* should come to *Tbilisi* on his own rather than brought here by a foreign dignitary as if he were the Russian Foreign Minister. This reflects *Saakashvili's* frustration at having his authority usurped by *Abashidze*. Meanwhile, the opposition to *Abashidze's* position as de facto President called for *Abashidze* to leave *Adjara* as seen in posters reading "Aslan Go Away." The leaders of the "Our *Adjara*" movement continued to demand his resignation. Interestingly the posters hung by the group in *Adjara* quickly disappeared from public view, apparently removed by Revival Party supporters. Another front-page article reviewed the details of Schwimmer's visit to *Tbilisi*.[568] This writer reported that Schwimmer visited with a number of other government officials including the new Chairperson of the Central Election Commission, *Zurab Chiaberashvili*. Schwimmer stated that he was satisfied with the administration of the CEC and hoped that the re-scheduled parliamentary elections would significantly improve compared to the previous one. Contrary to the former writer, another journalist reported that *Saakasvhili* invited *Abashidze* to meet Schwimmer at the capital. *Saakasvhili* revealed that he will not go to *Batumi* but rather expects *Abashidze* to join he and Schwimmer in *Tbilisi*. In response to *Saakashvili's* statement, *Abashidze* stated that he would not go to *Tbilisi* until the "terrorist acts against him" were investigated. A third writer reviewed the February visit by Walter Schwimmer in which he spoke with the Chairman of

---

566   N.N., "Rose Triumvirate sticks together." *Ibid.*, 2.
567   N.N., "Schwimmer may bring Abashidze to Tbilisi." *Ibid.*, 4.

the Chairman of the Central Election Committee, *Zurab Chiaberashvili.* During that conversation, he *reportedly* underlined the importance of improving the voters' list while avoiding election fraud.[569] He also suggested that Georgian officials consider lowering the percentage of votes required for election to the parliament. While the current proportional system requires seven percent, Swimmer suggested a 4.5 percent threshold, thus reducing barriers to opposition parties to enter the parliament. At least Georgian journalists are providing a cogent criticism of the new administration with regard to the proportional threshold continued in another review of *Saakashvili's* earlier trip to Strasburg Germany.

In President *Saakashvili's* initial trip to Strasburg Germany, he met for his first time with the Council of Europe's Secretary General Walter Schwimmer. The journalist asked Schwimmer what he thought about Georgia's constitutional changes.[570] Schwimmer responded by indicating that the constitutional changes were made too quickly and further should not have been made before the re-scheduled parliamentary elections. He also exclaimed that these constitutional amendments require review immediately after the new parliament takes office. Additionally the journalist made inquiries about criticisms from the Venice Commission. Their concerns mainly centered on the President's new constitutional authority to dissolve the parliament. Unfortunately, Schwimmer's comments on this subject were not included in the article. Subsequently, questions posed the Secretary General included the recent cancellation of three political television talk shows. The journalist implied that the media had been under pressure by the government to refrain from criticisms. Later the Speaker of the European Parliament agreed to appoint a commission to investigate this allegation. Schwimmer disclosed that it would be "deplorable" if the government prevented the media from engaging in public debate on candidates, parties, or programs before the election. The reporter revealed that each of the three broadcast channels stated that the canceld television talk shows resulted from government pressure. Although

---

568   Galina Gotua, "Schwimmer For Peace." *Georgia Today* (20 February 2004):1, 2.
569   N.N., "CEC Chairman meets CoE's Schwimmer." *The Messenger* (20 February 2004):6.
570   Mary Makharashvili, "CoE's Schwimmer talks to the Messenger, sees amendments as provisional." *Ibid.,* 1, 13.

the networks also disclosed these shows would return later in the spring after re-structuring occurred. Schwimmer refused to call these acts "a breach of freedom of expression" but did indicate that open and transparent methods of keeping the public informed are required before the elections in order that voters can make up their own minds. While Georgia joined the Council of Europe in 1999, the reporter mentions that many of Georgia's commitments to Europe remain unfulfilled. Schwimmer agrees that Georgia is behind the original timetable set by the EU Parliament however, the EU Parliament has given the Georgian government permission to submit a modified timetable. Furthermore, he suggested that the Georgia must immediately ratify the European Charter on local self-government, the social charter, and the Convention on the Protection of National Minorities. The interviewer explained that while the Georgian government has signed the Convention on the Confiscation of Property targeting money laundering and corruption, it remains ungratified by the parliament. She asked Schwimmer what the council might do to encourage ratification. Schwimmer reported that he plans to speak to authorities and encourage them to ratify it. Finally, the journalist told Schwimmer that President *Saakashvili* recently gave orders to law enforcement personnel to shoot anyone who attempted to resist their authority and asked him how the Council of Europe views such orders. He replied: "I do not know the exact text of this order, I hope it is not an order for extra-judicial execution, but shooting without need or as a case of an extra-judicial execution would be against the Council of Europe Standards and against human standards."

Despite OSCE's concerns, they released one million additional Euros to assist Georgia in covering the costs of the scheduled March parliamentary elections.[571] This included operational costs for the Central Election commission in managing the elections. This brings the total funds authorized from the EU to Georgia to 5 million Euros, 2 million Euros for the previous presidential elections and the remainder for the March parliamentary elections. During Secretary Schwimmer's visit to *Tbilisi,* supporters of the *Omega* group protested in front of the Marriot on *Rustaveli* Avenue (probably where Schwimmer was staying) to reflect their disapproval of government repres-

---

571   N.N., "OSCE Check for Elections." *The Messenger* (19 February 2004):4.

sion of the media. They carried a coffin down the street symbolizing the death of Freedom of the Press. *Zaka Okuashvili,* the Prosecutor General, met with Schwimmer and reported that he felt 'satisfied' with the meeting. However, in an attempt to dissuade journalists from viewing the recent raid on the parent company of the television station as an attack on the free press, *Okuashvili* met with and presented journalists with evidence removed from *Omega's* offices. This included machines used to print fraudulent excise stamps, counterfeit stamps, as well as weapons. The Prosecutor General indicated that the fraudulent excise stamps represented a loss to the state budget of millions of lari. While no arrests or detentions of high-ranking *Omega* officials followed, the Prosecutor claimed that this would be forthcoming.

Journalists continued to criticize the new administration's behavior ranging from the constitutional changes to the appointment of young and less experienced Ministers.[572] One reporter however, argued that most of the changes particularly *Zhvania's* appointment as Prime Minister was what *Zurab Zhvania* wanted all along, power; and that this was his only motivation for getting involved in the revolution. Moreover, he argued that *Saakashvili* manipulated the Parliament to approve the constitutional changes and the new cabinet. While the Parliamentary vote reflected an overwhelming victory, with one-hundred and sixty-five votes to five, parliamentary members of three other parties, the Socialists, the New Rightists, and the Traditionalists refused to vote signaling their resistance to this new one block government. Although more women received appointments to this cabinet than previously, four out of sixteen women are unlikely to tip the balance of the extant patriarchal nature of the Georgian government. The presence of these women is largely symbolic, and probably reflects more of an effort to dissuade critics from focusing on Zhvania's powerful new role in the government.

Most of *Zhvania's* support is partisan as other oppositional party members' reportedly have no trust or confidence in him or other members of the new cabinet. All the new cabinet members are either Nationalists or *Burjanadze*-Democrats and earned higher educations in the west. The author reflected that as a result they engendered the nickname "Soros-Bred." The re-

---

572   Nino Patsuria, "New Cabinet's Mission." *Georgia Today* (20 February):1, 3.

porter also criticized *Zhvania's* late submission of his reform package to the Parliament, received just prior to the scheduled deadline. Conversely, a member of the *Burjanadze* democrats and a PM told the reporter, this cabinet, "...is excellent, its members are professionals, purposeful, honest, uncorrupted, and each of them acknowledge the great responsibility to pull the country from its deplorable conditions." The new Prime Minister's program goals included stability and economic growth. Other objectives included:

a.   Democratic government

b.   Improve government by reducing red tape

c.   Establish real local government

d.   Improve government efficiency

e.   Improve health care

f.   Protect cultural heritage

g.   Protect territorial integrity

h.   Raise pensions by April 2004

i.   Raise salaries by June 2004

The new Prime Minister promised to increase wages and pensions by April.[573] The average Georgian earns a pension of fourteen GEL a month while minimum wage stands at twenty GEL a month. *Zhvania* also reportedly promised a new sixteen-month energy program aimed at ending the chronic power crisis across the country. Specific implementation details were unavailable. While the rhetoric of these goals may sustain Georgian faith in the new administration, the President concurrently made gestures aimed at generating nationalistic sentiments as he focused on the necessity of military service.

President *Saakashvili* explained that any person (he means male persons) failing to comply with the mandatory military obligation will be unable to hold a government post.[574] He also called the sons of politicians and state officials who have refused to serve in the military 'shameful and 'intolerable'. After publicly exposing this, *Saakashvili* failed to threaten any consequences

---

573   N.N., "Wages and Pensions to be raised in April." *Ibid.*, 3.

to deter the elite from exploiting their status and avoiding military service. In another article, the Minister of Defense disclosed plans to begin implementing a variety of structural changes in order to facilitate Georgia's acceptance into NATO within five years.[575] In this context, again Georgia hopes to encourage Russia to remove their military bases. Becoming a member of NATO will require that Georgian military funding increase from a little over one-half of one percent of the budget to two percent. This may be extremely difficult in a country that remains characterized as one of the poorest nations in the world.

According to recently released World Bank information, Georgia's ranks as the twenty-fourth poorest nation across the globe with fifty-four percent of the population living below the poverty level.[576] Russia stands at fifty-second on the list with only forty percent of their population living in poverty. The World Bank indicated that both post-Soviet nations and African nations remain the poorest in the world. One reporter wrote that Georgia's external debt was almost two billion U.S. dollars. This necessitates that Georgia raise eighty-eight million GEL just to pay the extant debt. Furthermore, if future meetings with the Paris Club are unsuccessful, Georgia's debt will only increase. Additionally, Georgia's owes money to a number of individual nations, those are illustrated in table five.

---

574   N.N., "Army for Everyone." In What's New Section." *The Messenger* (19 February 2004): 2.
575   N.N., "NATO Candidate in five years." *Ibid.*
576   Zaza Jgharkava, "24th Among the Poor." *Georgia Today* (20 February 2004):3.

Table 5: Georgia's Foreign Debt

Country	Debt Owed in U.S. Dollar
Austria	96.7 million
Azerbaijan	16.2 million
Russia	159.9 million
Germany	25.9 million
USA	36.9 million
Japan	37.7 million
Kuwait	13.2 million
Uzbekistan	802,000.0 million
China	3.3 million

A viable alternative in the midst of such debt and poverty might be the development of improved working relationships among competing political parties to meet the needs of better Georgian citizens. Unfortunately, self-serving party interests, and the maintenance of exclusive hold on power appears more important. Previously some journalists reported that the alliance between the Nationalists and Democrats weakening. Similarly, one other journalist stated that the Nationalists remain dubious about their political block with the Democrats.[577] This contentious point has nothing to do with the resolution of Georgia's myriad problems, but rather remains focused on the number of 'star politicians' from both the Democratic Party and the Nationalist Party with current cabinet positions that leaves few worthy candidates available for parliament. Subsequently, both parties began considering the possibility of entering the Parliamentary race singularly, rather than as the extant block. Some nationalist party members also began threatening to leave the party block because of their dislike of *Zhvania*. Gaining, holding, and maintaining power ranks as more important than solving Georgia's numerous social problems.

Other front-stage issues among Georgia's power holders, businessmen and oligarchs are concerns about the possibility of being arrested. A reporter described the oligarchs as becoming excessively concerned about the administrations' pursuit of their illegal activities. Specifically, the writer argued the possibility of arrest can only be escaped by becoming an elected PM, making the immunity provision very attractive. The writer also weaved a new twist on the tale of the political plot engineered the Rose Revolution. The writer claimed that *Zhvania* will only be a temporary member of the cabinet after *Saakashvili* pays him back for favors provided during the protests in November, *Saakashvili* will "get rid of *Zurab Zhvania*". First *Zhvania* will be held responsible for the government's initial failures. In retrospect, this article is particularly foreboding because while still in office, in early 2005, *Zurab Zhvania* died, allegedly accidentally. Initial suspicions of fowl play were later discounted following an investigation revealing that he was a victim of Georgia's poor infrastructure. His death was accidental, the result of a natural gas leak in a friend's apartment (see epilogue for more details).

Information revealed in the newspapers continues to reflect Georgia's emulation of American or Western models of exploitative capitalism. One journalist discussed a new NGO called the Economic Policy Research Center who described themselves as consultants to the state and to business. They purport to develop a market economy as exemplified by the United States, the World Trade Organization (WTO) and the North American Free Trade Association (NAFTA).[578] It is important here to revisit much of the extant research on both the WTO and NAFTA illustrating that both organizations often make wealthy countries richer while increasing poverty and economic inequality among poor countries.[579] Additionally, such funding may lead also to the development of ethnic nationalism and civil wars. Similarly, the second writer reviewed a recent training seminar organized by the International Finance Corporation aimed at teaching Georgian businessmen the corporate model of business leadership.[580] This Corporation provides training seminars for over three thousand different companies. *Irina Gordeladze*, the project manager, reportedly stated that such training would eliminate the problem of violating shareholders rights as frequently occurs in Georgia. Moreover the

---

577   *Idem.* "Nationalists Resist Teaming up with Democrats." *Ibid.*, 3.
578   Nino Patsuria, "Panacea for Georgian Economy?" *Ibid.*, 4.
579   Rebecca S. Katz, "Genocide: The Ultimate Racial Profiling." *The Journal of Law and Social Challenges* 5:1 (Summer 2003):65-92.

training would help to develop a Georgian stock market that is currently described as "nonfunctioning". This reflects a Western model, with one exception. The Project Team-leaders argued that the state should own no more than twenty-five percent of the shares in these new companies. The third piece appeared in the economic section and revealed that the Georgian Wine Industry has continued to report increasing profits particularly within the Russian market.[581] For example beginning in 1993, the Georgian Wine and Spirit Company earned a number of international wine competitions. Located in *Telavi,* the factory maintains cooperative relationships with local grape farmers and '[assists] ing them in producing higher quality grapes'. The company employs over two hundred and fifty permanent personnel and they earn "relatively high wages." The writer also stated that the company exports wines to a number of different countries in the EU. While this kind of growth is important to note, many Georgians realize that this kind of post-soviet growth is rare. They also remember that as the Soviet Union disintegrated, factories closed, and many people lost their jobs, never to regaining permanent or positions again.

One of Georgia's most salient social problems is the absence of stable industrial work. For example, my students once replied when I asked them: "Where are the factories?, they exclaimed together "what factories? "We have no factories in Georgia anymore." Many of the cold war military industrial complexes closed their doors. While a few continued to operate, they maintained a reduced and underpaid workforce. The FSU industrial plants were primarily engaged in building parts and equipment for the Soviet military and were simply no longer necessary. Some new factories have developed since then, like the *Tbilisi* bottled water company as well as several beer companies, most of which sell only internally, they are not yet part of the global economy. While it might be intuitively evident that Georgia's struggling economy would negatively affect political participation, one reporter's interview with Till Bruckner, Project Director of the International Foundation for Elections systems, revealed that all three elected Presidents received an

---

580   Nino Patsuria, "More Comprehensive-More Prosperity." *Georgia Today* (20 February 2004):4.
581   N.N., "Georgian Wine Wins." *Ibid.*

overwhelming consensus of the voters' voting.[582] However, Bruckner's organization, a private nonprofit organization established in 1987 to monitor and provide support for elections by promoting the rule of law and by strengthening civil society, argues that participating in only one or two elections a year does not reflect the existence of a competitive electoral processes nor the active engagement of citizens with their political representatives. Bruckner argues that it is latter not the former that makes a nation democratic. When the reporter asked Bruckner why previous Presidential elections indicated such overwhelming popularity of specific Presidential candidates, she guessed that there was a high level of consensus building prior to these elections. Moreover, people want to elect politicians perceived as strong leaders or strong personalities. While Bruckner does not indicate that the legacy of post-Soviet society and forced hero worship might contribute, I would argue that it does. This remains the remnant of the Stalinisque 'cult of personality'. The final question posed included whether or not Georgia might become substantively more democratic twenty years from now. Bruckner replied that while she did not know for sure, she estimated that if people continue to struggle economically, it will more difficult to become politically or civically engaged. Her organization received a grant from the United States of America's International Development Agency to support its ongoing work on democracy and civil society. Most of its funding supports building democracy and community involvement in public schools through student government and parental involvement in children's education. One element that facilitated the development of the cult of personality around *Saakashvili* was his inaugural promise to restore Georgia's territorial integrity.

The President's inaugural promise to unit Georgia's autonomous religions of *Abkhazia* and *Ossetia*." in the context of *Aslan Abashidze's* posturing prior to the presidential elections probably led to growth of *Saakashvili's* popularity.[583] *Abashidze* was characterized as a threat to the democratic election process as well as potential future separatist conflicts. The writer explained that *Abashidze's* visit to Moscow during the *Rose Revolution* and prior to the presidential election mirrors his dangerousness to Georgians.

---

582   N.N., "Democracy Beyond Election Day." *Ibid.*, 7.

However, the presidential election proceeded unimpeded although *Aba-shidze's* regime and his party "Revival" are the last bastion of support for *Shevardnadze*. The author speculated that *Abashidze* will not be able to garner seven percent of the parliamentary votes necessary to ensure the Revival Party maintenance of power in the Parliament. Moreover, *Saakashvili* continues to demand that *Abashidze* come to *Tbilisi* to meet with him, while *Abashidze* refuses. *Saakashvili* referred to his refusal as "disobedience" and stated that such behavior will result in a "relevant reaction" insinuating military action. Of course related to the threat of conflict or secession surrounding *Adjara* are the separate republics of *Ossetia* and *Abkhazia*.

Saakashvili's visits to Moscow are described as focused on asking Russia to stop supporting *Abkhazian* and *Ossetian* separatists in order to resolve the current stalemated conflict. *Saakashvili* created a new State Minster post, and appointed *Goga Khaindrava* to the position to devote complete attention to the re-unification of the autonomous regions with Georgia. Following *Saakashvili's* visit with the President of *Ossetia* just prior to the presidential elections, the *Ossetian* President claimed that he will "arrest him...if he comes here again." The reporter explained that local experts (not cited by name or by position) argue that only when Russians close their military bases in the regions and withdraw as peacekeepers, will restoration of Georgia's territorial integrity ensue. It seems more relevant to address the impoverishment of Georgian citizens before trying to re-integrate the country, after all senior citizens, disabled adults, and children are continuing to beg on the streets for money or food.

As mentioned previously among poor struggling Georgians bread is a staple and affordable product, and unfortunately, at various times throughout this year, journalists reported concerns that the price of bread would increase to the extent that the poor would be unable to afford it. In late February, the government announced a plan to begin regulating the price of bread.[584] Once again, Georgia's new big brother, the United States, donated fifty thousand tons of wheat to Georgia's Ministry of Food and Agriculture to maintain current bread prices. The writer explained that bread consumption has in-

---

583   N.N., "Population excepts promised united Georgia." *The Messenger* (20 February 2004):2.

creased over the last decade particularly as the result of the drop in incomes. Thus, the writer assumed any increase will hit Georgian families particularly hard and probably affect the outcome of the March 28 parliamentary elections. Reportedly, prices had already increased by ten tetre (about five U.S. cents) over recent months. The current Minister of Agriculture reported that no further price increases will take place as U.S. assistance will provide enough wheat to last an additional month and a half and Russian and *Kzak* wheat will supplement the Georgian reserves. Georgia is a part of a U.S. program called "Food for Progress", this program may make available up to fifty-thousand additional tons of wheat. While details were not available, it seems to resemble the U.S.-Iraqi "Food for Oil" program, currently under investigation in the United States for fraud. The head of the *Tbilisi* Oil and Grain Exchange, reports that seven thousand tons of U.S. wheat was sold on the market last week, for about four-hundred and twenty to four hundred and forty GEL, just under average market prices. The writer explained that while this was good for Georgia, the world wheat market could worsen and if that occurs, Georgian bread prices will rise. Recently Russian bread prices reportedly increased by forty percent, however four hundred grams of white bread sells for eighty Georgina *tetre*, thus easily purchased by Russians who receive state subsidies. The journalist reported that some "experts" maintain that government subsidies could soften the blow of such an increase while other "experts" indicated bread price increases would lead to an increase in price of other foodstuffs and that any state sponsored effort at social welfare for food would result in increased corruption.

Another international loan discussed on a subsequent page, reveals a United States Agency for International Development loan to Georgia for ten million dollars through the Microfinance Stabilization and Enhancement program. The loan will assist rural and female owned enterprises as well as non-bank microfinance institutions.[585] USAID director for the Caucasus reports that they have been providing such aid through similar programming for many years. Interestingly, a subcontract for program management belongs to a U.S. consulting firm called Chemonics International Incorporated. Additional

---

584   M. Alkhazashvili, "Government to regulate Price of bread." *Ibid.*, 3.
585   Christina Tashkevich, "USAID renews support for microfinance in Georgia." *Ibid.*, 4.

U.S. corporate subcontractors also included Shorebank, and Bankwood. USAID also finances another project called the Georgian Enterprise Growth Initiative, also contracted to another U.S. company, Bearing Point, that aims to establish a corrupt free credit bureau system. Who is this assistance really benefiting, Georgia or U.S. economic interests? It seems that USAID facilitates U.S. control of the global market under the auspices of repairing Georgia's institutional infrastructure and public services.

One of these public services disparately in need of improvement is the *Tbilisi* water supply company. This is *Tbliskalkanali* and one journalist wrote that "massive repairs" are required.[586] Apparently, maintenance of the plant suffered neglect for many years, not unlike other public across the FSU, and the writer reported this might lead to serious water problems in the capital city in the near future. The current cost of water lies between ninety-tetra and 1.2 GEL per person per month, much lower than its actual value. Additionally, as with the electricity in Georgia, only forty percent of customers actually pay their water bills and including individual households, businesses, and other organizations. Analysts indicated that the company needs five hundred million GEL to repair the facility and that this amount consists of half of the Georgian annual budget. Recently, the World Bank provided Georgia a low interest loan of twenty-five million US dollars to repair the water company. However, the World Bank will not release the funds until Georgia is able to substantiate that the companies' requesting the bids are actually capable of doing the repairs. This may indicate the likelihood that no locally owned companies would be able to meet the criteria so the contract would be globally outsourced. As anticipated, a French company, Generale des Eaux, won the contract to work on the *Tbilisi* water system. The writer reported that the outsourcing of the work angered the Nationalist Party President *Mikhail Saakasvhili*. Rumors followed that *Paata Shevardnadze*, the son of the former President, owned a part of the French company. However, the French Company explained that it will turn the ownership back to the city government following the completion of repairs and thereafter will only operate the company, meaning high-level management will remain in the hands of foreigners, while low-level positions will belong to Georgians. As greater power among the G-7 na-

---

586   M. Alkhazashvili, "Tbilisi Water Supply Company in Limbo." *Ibid.*

tions accumulates, nationalistic parties like *Saakashvili's* will rally against this oppression by the rich of the poor. Undoubtedly, they will do so by mimicking such global unifications and creating large political blocks of power at the national level.

Across Georgia, other political parties followed suit as two of the nation's best-financed parties, New Rights, and Industrialists, registered as a new political block with the Georgian Central Election Commission.[587] One leader of New Rights Party includes *David Gamkrelidze,* owner of *Aldagi* Insurance Company, a company with advertisements located all over the capital. The Chief of the Industrialists' party is *Gogi Topadze,* the founder of *Kazbegi* beer-corporation. The new block party is the Rightists Opposition. Other parties were given additional time to accomplish similar objectives as the Central Election Commission postponed the deadline for parties to register as electoral blocks for several more days.[588] Six political parties have already indicated that they will be registering as blocks, this includes one block of The Union of Georgian Traditionalists and the National Democratic Party, and another that includes the Union of Georgian Countrymen and the Helsinki Union of Georgia.

While *Saakashvili* and his predecessor before him were both criticized for media censorship, legal statutes remain partly to blame for the presence of an inadequate independent media. Specifically, one report revealed that the creator of the Georgian investigative news program called "60 minutes," modeled after the U.S. CBS program "60 minutes" is taking parliament to court over an article in the civil code requiring journalists to apologize when covering information that may offend specific groups. Previously, the producer of the program appeared in court after accusing the head of the Georgian railway of corruption. Subsequently the head of Georgian railway was arrested and currently remains in jail on corruption charges. This astounding absence of any historical precedent institutionalizing the value of investigative journalism in a democracy continues to shock the conscience, but seems clearly related to the FSU's totalitarian regime and before that the rule of the Czars' and Georgia's own history of monarchies. Perhaps it is this notion of

---

587   N.N., "Big Money Unites." *Ibid.,* 6.
588   N.N., "CEC gives parties two more days." *Ibid.*

Monarchy, of the divine right to a piece of geography that is also an active force in Georgia's nationalism; reflected in their inability to let go of *Abkhazia* and *Ossetia*.

Of course, once gain global powers continue to support the issue of territorial integrity by providing vast amounts of funding for security, money that might be better spent improving the Georgian infrastructure. Specifically, in a later discussion of OSCE's defense of Georgia's territorial integrity, the details of an interview with the Chairman of the Organization for Security and Cooperation in Europe who recently visited both Moscow and *Tbilisi* are revealed.[589] A reporter from *Vremia Novostei* newspaper interviewed the Chairman of OSCE in *Tbilisi*. The Chairman indicated that OSCE expects Russia to fulfill its obligations IAW the OSCE (Conventional Armed Forced in Europe-CFE) treaty signed in 1999 requiring them to close military bases in Georgia as well as in Moldova. Moldova's recent history reveals a number of secessionist movements and an internationally unrecognized separatist state. For the first time, a journalist revealed that the OSCE maintained a Border Monitoring Organization in Georgia to ensure that the Chechen conflict will not spill over into Georgia. OSCE claimed it remains committed to the territorial integrity of Georgia with regard to *South Ossetia* and *Abkhazia*. OSCE reportedly expects that Georgian IDPs will return home and political re-integration with the central Georgian government will transpire. The European Union also provided 2.5 million Euros to economically rehabilitate the zones of conflict and return the IDPs. The United Nations Development Program and United Nations Human Rights Commission also are involved in this project. The OSCE Strategic Police Matters Unit also proposes funding to improve policing in the *Georgian-Ossetian* conflict zone and to combat crime. As global support for 'territorial integrity' seems to remain a priority, its not surprising that Georgia seems unable to move forward. As old wounds are transformed into abscesses due to Georgia's own nationalistic ideology and the global powers' deep coiffeurs, leaving Georgia in a beholding position with the G-8. In this report, the Georgian media demonstrates its ability to

---

589   Mikhail Vignanskii (Correspondent of "Vremia Novosti"), "OSCE Defends Territorial Integrity of Georgia." *Ibid.,* 7.

maintain an independent free press by providing this critical information to Georgian citizens.

While journalists sometimes make substantial efforts to offer information, particularly with regard to public officials, the truth is often rejected by the privileged. One journalist revealed that the spouse of the former Governor of *Kvemo Kartli*, *Levan Mamaladze* (described as a fugitive from justice), is suing Rustavi-2 television for allegedly slandering her family.[590] She filed the case after the television station reported that she owned several *dachas,* or summer homes. The spouse referred to these allegations as "moral terror and blackmail" against her family. She also reported receiving threatening mail stating, "if you managed to hide money and assets, you will not be able to hide your children." In similar news, a television political talk show conducted an interview with the new Minister of Health and the Minister of Culture.[591] The Minister of Health, *Gigi Tsereteli*, reported that he wants to provide affordable health care to all Georgians. One viewer who called in asked why the salaries of all the Ministers increased while Doctors salaries remain low. He replied that international funds were providing some of the funding to improve government officials salaries and that such improvements would prohibit corruption of public officials who previously earned low salaries and thus stole from the federal budget. He also explained that his administration stopped taxing medical institutions and now these funds could be utilized to improve the quality of health care. During the interview with the Minister of Culture *Goka Gabshvili*, a former employee of the Open Society Institute, revealed that new funds were needed to support the perseveration of cultural heritage sites including folklore, sports, and archives. He indicated that attracting grants to meet this need would remain a priority. He also mentioned new legislation that encourages contributions from businesses to the arts and culture as well as sports.

Revelations of more global financial assistance to Georgia continue, this time sponsored by the European Bank for Re-construction and Develop-

---

590   N.N., "Mamaladze's wife sues Rustavi-2." *Ibid.*, 8.
591   Sopho Gorgodze, "Wednesday on Dialogue of Iberia Channel. New Minister Promises affordable health care, and Minister of Culture saves monuments, urges donations." *Ibid.*

ment (EBRD).[592] The Director for the region reported their support of the Georgian infrastructure as well as the development and assistance to small and medium businesses. ERBD will specifically provide support to banks, the energy sector, and the *Enguri* Dam. Additionally, he indicated that assisting the Georgian Railway to restructure was also a priority as well as the expansion of the port at *Poti*. Finally, the EBRD provided 125 million US dollars to the *Baku-Tbilisi-Ceyhan* oil pipeline (BTC) even though criticisms continue to emanate from environmentalists about the safety of the line. However, the EBRD claims they are observing the process to ensure that the environment will be protected. He reports that the *Shah-Deniz* gas pipeline is also a priority. Economic development always seems the priority for international organizations while local NGOS and other national groups struggle to re-build civil society.

One group struggling to improve the rule of law is The Georgian Young Lawyers Association (GYLA). They recently demanded that the Parliament amend the election code and urged them to make the changes immediately.[593] A government official explained that changing the law so near a major election would not permit the CEC time to become familiar with and implement all the necessary changes. The GYLA is also reportedly angry about violations of the election code by employees of the CEC who remain uninvestigated or punished. They expect the CEC to complete the investigation and mete out the punishment. However, the CEC cannot effectively or legally investigate and punish itself for illegal behavior, and a CEC spokesperson explained that they only administer disciplinary action for employees who fail to perform their jobs correctly. Furthermore, they explained that only the parliament is capable of making behavior illegal and subsequently the courts are responsible for administering punishment following a trial. A lawyer should have some knowledge about this process, although attorneys in the GYLA apparently do not. It should be noted that some members of GYLA may be graduates of Georgian style law schools, sometimes requiring only a Masters degree in Legal Studies. This mirrors the problems that exist within higher education in Georgia (and some other post-soviet nation-states) and demon-

---

592   Christina Tashkevich, "EBRD keeps a full plate in Georgia." *Ibid.*, 13.

strates how these "trained" young lawyers do not always appear to understand how a democratic legal system function. Of course as with other institutions across the country, corruption remains problematic partly as the result of low pay. Therefore, certainly some of these law students could have bribed their teachers for good grades rather than earning them. Of course, the Georgian journalist could have erred in the details of the report. Finally, the spokesperson for the NGO Fair Elections agreed that the passage of prohibitive laws with appropriate consequences for those found guilty of fraudulent voting are necessary. Related to political domination by fraud is the issue of domination of the polity by exploiting the seven percent proportional requirement for election to parliament. Both organizations insisted that the barrier requires adjustment to facilitate democratic development, diverse ideologies, and thus fruitful debate.

In another rare case of coverage of a homicide, one front-page article discusses an unsolved murder committed in July of 2003.[594] A Regional Prosecutors' office charged two individuals with the murder of the adult son of a MP. However, neither suspect was subsequently located. Prior to the murder, a gunfight transpired between one of the suspects and the deceased although no further details were available. Later, a lawyer for the family of the defendants argued that two of the four photographs placed on display by law enforcement officials erroneously labeled photos of the brothers as the two suspects. The family's lawyer argued that it is illegal to display photographs of non-suspects (i.e., no warrant) and that the display made the brothers so frightened that they were reluctant to leave their homes. The lawyer also argued that the utilization of the photos occurred intentionally to manipulate the brothers into the prosecutor's office for questioning. The reporter reiterated that the caption under the photos reflected that all four were wanted for "illegal possession of firearms and murder" Another lawyer for the Judicial Rights Advocate's office also told the reporter that placing the two brothers in the photo violates the constitution stating that warrants for arrest are required before posting public notices. One of the attorneys also checked with the local

---

593   Mary Makharashvili, "Young Lawyers calls for accountability, supports rapid improvement of election code." *The Messenger* (24 February 2004):1, 10.
594   *Idem.* "Wanted for being related Brothers o suspects wrongly wanted, says lawyer." *Ibid.*

court and found no charges filed against any suspects. Additionally, the advocates' office reported that it is illegal to declare a public search for a witness. The Judicial Rights Advocate's office filed a court case against the police for making false accusations. What initially appeared to be an honest mistake to be intentional misinformation promoted by the prosecutor's office. Unfortunately, the promotion of misinformation is not limited to the prosecution of typical street crimes.

Even though government and business players involved in BTC oil pipeline have repeatedly claimed that its structure will prevent accidental leaks as well as theft, this is inaccurate because journalists reported that an oil leak was recently discovered coming from the pipeline.[595] International financial institutions including the European Bank for Reconstruction and Development (EBRD) subsequently requested an investigation into environmental safety of the pipeline. The bank's investments in the British Petroleum pipeline project total over 2 million dollars. Several representatives from BP continue to report that they have built the pipeline using the "highest international standards" designed to protect the environment. While unreported here, there are no enforceable international standards, no environmental protection agency for developing countries. Resolving these oversights might eliminate future risks for the developing world and emerging democracies who are now under the serious threat of environmental devastation from global oil companies and other industries from the West. A recent Public Broadcasting television station in the U.S. aired a documentary called Extreme Oil detailing information about the BTC pipeline. Photographs of the pipeline reveal what appears to be a plastic pipeline, laying one to two feet above the ground as it traveled through portions of *Azerbaijan* and Georgia. Several NGOs investigating the pipeline report that the banks providing the loans violated the "Equator Principles" requiring banks to assess and manage environmental and social risk" before financing a project. Unfortunately, a principle is not an enforceable human rights law. However, such cases have been won in U.S. court. These cases were civil suits for damages to indigenous tribal peoples and their environments caused by U.S. companies.

---

595   Christina Tashkevich, "NGOs warn of oil leakage Environmental Concerns follow BTC." *Ibid.*

Foreign nationals won these human rights suits using the U.S. Alien Tort Claims Act. Thus the precedent has been established. One NGO, Cornerhouse, claims to have documentation showing that BP has built sections of the pipeline using substandard materials. Another NGO, "Green Alternative" is currently involved in a court case attempting to nullify the original agreement with BP and the Ministry of Environmental and Natural Resource Protection (signed in November of 2002) to construct the pipeline. The director of the South Eastern Europe and Caucasus branch of EBRD claims that they are constantly supervising the building of the BTC pipeline to ensure that the environment remains protected. Protecting the environment of developing countries and their citizens is clearly not a priority for international oil and gas companies. The appearance of environmental safety seems much like the appearance of cleaning up corruption; looks are deceiving.

As *Saakashvili's* administration continues to look like they are working to 'clean up' crime and corruption across Georgia, the amnesty plan for tax evasion gains media attention.[596] *Saakashvili* purportedly promised that businessmen who pay back taxes before one April will not be prosecuted for tax evasion. The writer reported that this may not be possible as the previous administration's tax system was unfair and that most businessmen [and women] cannot afford to pay their taxes without considering bankruptcy. However, *Saakashvili's* administration promises to overhaul the tax system in the future but insists that businesses pay back-taxes. Threatened with bankruptcy, the owners of businesses could face joining the ranks of Georgia's poor. Although in a separate article, the same author reports on a fifteen-year World Bank poverty reduction program planed for implementation in five-year increments.[597] Georgia has received money for poverty reduction in the past, and still Georgia's rural poor and urban poor remain poor, we must ask ourselves where are these funds going? If recent history as exemplified by other poor countries stories might reflect, the money may be flowing into the pockets of corrupt officials.

While large amounts of funding continues go to Georgia to develop the free market economy with some of it allegedly earmarked to assist the poor,

---

610   M. Alkhazashvili, "Paradox of Tax Amnesty." *Ibid.,* 3.
597   *Idem.* "Economy Ministry's New Plan." *Ibid.*

the status of women and children continues to decline. A recent review of UNICEF's mid term report reveals the low status of women and children in Georgia. The implementation of a 1999 joint UNICEF-Georgia cooperative agreement aimed to improve maternal-child well-being, child development, child protection, and social policy development. However, Georgia's 2002 state budget only allocated about four percent to health and education.[598] The most recent report reveals that half of Georgia's children continue to live under the poverty level and twenty-five hundred children beg for their livelihood on the streets or engage in prostitution. Interestingly, there is no evidence that these children belong to any particular ethnic group even though rumors persist that street children are Roma's or Kurds, not Georgians. This denial is the result of poor public awareness and the extremist ideology of ethnic nationalism. Also unaccepted is the fact that almost five thousand children remain institutionalized in places also characterized by extremely poor conditions. Over ninety-five percent of these children ended up in these institutions because of family economic hardship. Almost ten thousand children are disabled and not receiving proper care and forty-two thousand children are IDPs and continue to lack access to basic health care. However, only one hundred and thirty-one juveniles remain institutionalized for delinquent behavior. Georgia's infant mortality rate stands at 23.8 per 1000 live births. Thirty eight percent of Georgian children suffer from iodine deficiency, which could later lead to mental retardation. This state of affairs grows from the fact as of 2000, fifty percent of the Georgian population lived under two GEL a day. While the feminization of poverty and childhood remains problematic across Georgia, it becomes easier to deny as a small middle class grows in *Tbilisi*, particularly among those employed by international NGOS or international aid agencies. Georgian middle class women remain highly visible within civil society, and while I only rarely observed middle-class men involved in similar activities. Additionally, most senior citizens begging for money on the streets of *Tbilisi* also were women. There are virtually no social services for the aged, for the disabled, for the children and no child welfare programming or community mental health services, and further no govern-

---

598   Mariam Kobaladze, "Mid-Term Review of UNICEF." *Georgia Today* (27 February 2004):12.

ment grants for treatment programs. Local counseling centers exist only through private foundation or foreign grants. With so few of Georgia's real social problems on the table it seems impossible that a one party Parliament would be able to dialogue about this issue much less resolve it.

Journalists continue to analyze and critique the "prospect of a one party parliament".[599] One unidentified author discussed the seven percent minimum required for political party members' election to parliament and also argued that with the new coalition of the Nationalists and the United/*Burjanadze* Democrats, the parliament may contain only one party block. The writer described the Revival Party as weakened considerably and while this is positive in terms of decreasing *Abashidze's* ability to control the results of the vote, it results in the concentratation of more power in the hands of the current administration. The left wing Labor Party was left devastated by the Rose Revolution. While they could increase their strength if they united with the Socialists, they refuse to do so. This also plays into the hands of the new three party block government. Similarly, expectations are sanguine that the Communist Party will be able to garner much support among voters. Moreover, a former Minister of Defense, a Communist party member, continues to remain in hiding after accusations that he attempted to assassinate former President *Shevardnadze* in 1995. The political parties on the right consist of the Traditionalist Party and the National Democratic Party as well as two other parties, the Industry Will Save Georgia, also called the Industrialists, and the New Rights. Apparently, they are no threat to the new government block. Interestingly, the writer also reported that *Konstantine Gamsakhurdia*, the son of Georgia's first President *Zviad Gamsakhurdia*, plans to run for Parliament in another new party, the Freedom Party. Another article discusses this development further described *Konstantine Gamsakhurdia* as living in self-imposed exile in Switzerland.[600] *Gamsakhurdia* explained his pleasure with the new administration and the coup that removed *Shevardnadze* from power. The author reminded readers that the day after *Saakashvili's* inauguration; the new President pardoned over thirty members of *Gamsakhurdia's* administration previously incarcerated by signing a national decree of recon-

---

599   N.N., "Prospect of one party parliament." *The Messenger* (24 February 2004):2.

ciliation. The author referred to these individuals as "political prisoners." *Konstantine Gamsakhurdia* explained to the reporter that the followers of his father remain active in his new political party. However, the writer argued that it is too late to register the party for the parliamentary election. *Gamsakhurdia* indicates that he will join forces with other parties while building the Freedom party, as long as "their hands are not dirty with blood". Readers should remember that according to a variety of reports, his father died at the hands of opposition political parties. This writer further indicated that *Gamsakhurdia* plans to return to Georgia at some point in the future. In other political news, the Republican Party leader, *David Berdzenishvili,* predicted that *Aslan Abashidze* will soon lose all of his power. *Berdzenishvili* accused *Abashidze* of lining his pockets with millions of dollars. He believes that *Abashidze's* prosecution by the *Tbilisi* Prosecutor General is forthcoming. As expectation and tension with regard to the next election grows, the new government continues their assault on the media.

According to one newspaper editor, the government's recent closure of the newspaper, *Akhali Epoch* resembles the actions of an "emperor" not a President.[601] The editor stated: "We should answer only to the law and not to *Saakashvili* for what we are doing. ...The President cannot dictate to journalists what to do and what not." A newspaper person from a another Georgian paper contends that the government should be investigating and combating corruption and tax evasion without destroying freedom of speech. Marina *Salukavadze*, the editor of a third newspaper, the *Mtavari Gazeti*, discussed the raid by masked law enforcement officers. She argued: "We are few (Georgians) and maybe those people were worried to be recognized, maybe they were somebody's neighbors, etc." A member of the New Rights Party, *Pikria Chikhradze,* complained that that the new government seems unconcerned about the previous achievements of freedom and independence. She also expressed hopes that the population will not stand by and watch *Saakashvili* eliminate those previously hard won rights. Finally, a Traditionalist political party member explained that while he has not been surprised by the new government's behavior, he believes that the attack on the media and the re-

---

600   Anna Arzanova, "Picking up Zviad's torch Gamsakhurdia's son plans to return to politics." *Ibid.*, 5.

cent arrests of the "Georgian bourgeoisie who finances, printing houses, and brings investments into the country" may have even more detrimental affects on the Georgian economy. As Georgians face these numerous changes which bode poorly for democracy, President *Saakashvili* visited the U.S. and touted his administration's achievements over the last thirty days.

Two front-page articles described President *Saakashvili's* visit to the U.S.[602] *Saakashvili* spoke to students and professors at the John Hopkins School for International Studies at Washington D.C. in a speech titled "Georgia after the Rose Revolution -- Rebuilding Democracy." He reviewed the administration's post-election achievements and future goals including, improving salaries, ending corruption, providing electricity, finishing the BTC oil pipeline, and improving the investment climate. *Saakashvili* joked that he garnered more attention than Britney Spears as he walked up and down the U.S. Congress' hallways. *Saakashvili* told his audience that Georgians shared many common values with the U.S., while insisting that the Rose Revolution was not a U.S. or CIA sponsored coup. Finally, he argued that he had no plans to intervene militarily in any part of Georgia including *Adjara*.

President *Saakashvili* described his mood following the meeting with President Bush as euphoric because the U.S. promised continuing financial assistance. Specifically, the United States will continue to support the "Train and Equip" program for the Georgian army. This includes fully equipping a brigade of five thousand Georgian soldiers and the provision of American style military training. *Saakashvili* also asked for increase of 200 million dollars in assistance. However, the U.S. Secretary of State reported that increases would probably include up to 166 million dollars. *Saakashvili* said that this money will go towards security and defense. This seems to be an unfortunate use of the funding, considering the numerous social and economic problems facing Georgian citizens. However, *Saakashvili* also stated that the IMF and the World Bank intend to continue to support Georgia with additional aid. Specifically the IMF will transfer 30 million dollars to the Geor-

---

601   Christina Tashkevich, "Friday on Dialogue, opinions on the Iberia Channel." *Ibid.*, 6.

602   Allison Ekberg, "A swagger that makes Britney jealous, Saakashvili describes revolution, reform at John Hopkins." *The Messenger* (26 February 2004):1, 10; Anna Arzanova, "Saakashvili's Washington homecoming touts euphoria-and success-of U.S. visit." *Ibid.*, 1, 5.

gian National Bank. Other funds transferred will include some slated for *Airzena,* the Georgian airline company. This money will come from the American Export-Import Bank. *Airzena* is the only Georgian Airline company currently in existence. These funds will allow it to purchase another Boeing aircraft. However, the journalist reported that she could not confirm the validity of these reports of financial aid. She wrote that *Saakashvili* was interviewed on CNN during his stay in the United States primarily consisted professed Georgia's desire to be a part of the European Union and the need for the removal of Russian military bases.

In this context of the reported need for financial aid to build up the military and national security for Georgia, another front-page article discussed the poverty-stricken "crumbling communities" across Georgia.[603] The author described one such village called *Zkmeri* located in the region of *Racha* setting 1741 meters above sea level. Before the 1989 earthquake, four hundred families lived in the village. Subsequently as the result of the failure to seek funding to repair the damage, only about thirty families remain. Few children attend school beyond the primary years' as parents are unable to afford books. While *Iza Gagnidze,* the chairperson of the village city council or *Sakrebulo,* reported that she asked for funds from the district office, the district also has no money. Ms. *Gagnidze* reports that she would like to apply for a grant to facilitate improving the village's main source of income, raising livestock.

These issues of rural poverty were addressed in a recent conference in *Tbilisi* called "Needs Assessment for Future Local Governance Activities".
Research conducted in 2003 on the functioning of district and local government and the attitudes towards village and district government illustrated that only fifteen percent of local civic agencies exercised their power or implemented changes because of the absence of financial resources, "imperfect legislation," and "poorly qualified local staff," and "the Soviet Style of governance." This translates into highly centralized control from the capital, *Tbilisi* preventing the rebuilding of communities like *Zkamri.* Interestingly, the study also found that the general population remained cynical about non-government organizations that were viewed primarily as profit oriented busi-

603   Sopho Gorgodze, "Providing Hope to Crumbing Communities." *Ibid.,* 1, 10.

nesses. People also believed NGOs became dependent on specific donor organizations while failing to target the populations that most needs the assistance.

With regard to the problem of government centralization, one representative from an NGO reported protesting against the recent changes to the constitution that increased the authority and control of the central government. He argued that the government must provide a deadline when these extensive federal powers will end, a detailed explanation for their implementation, and a long-term plan for a de-centralized government. Another economic problem, according to the executive Director of the Councils Association of *Lanchkhuti,* includes the federal government's recent decision to terminate the land tax, a decision that will further reduce local government funding.

While the economy appears to be at risk from new federal government policies, the debate continues with regard to the government's pressure on a variety of independent television programs airing political talk shows.[604] These shows include "*Mzera*" which television-producers claim is being re-formatted, and *Rustavi* 2's series called "Night Kourieri" that was canceled. While some representatives from independent television stations deny that the government has pressured them, *Nato Oniani* who hosted such series called "Time-Out" reported that the government did coerce him. A member of *Saakashvili's* own political party, *Koba Davitashvili* who opposed the new Prime Minister position, argued that all these TV magazines disappeared shortly after criticisms surfaced about the new constitutional changes. Fortunately, the Parliament has created a special commission to investigate these allegations. This writer explained that Rose Revolution would not have transpired if not for the free press. Furthermore, these television shows were optimal venues for Georgians to hear about the issues since most people cannot afford newspapers.

After the fall of the FSU many of the former republics privatized the government owned lands and businesses, resulting in a free for all as many individuals fought to buy up former state properties. Recently, *Saakashvili* began discussing the possibility of de-privatization. One journalist bemoans

---

604   N.N., "Political Talk Shows a Symbol of Democracy." *Ibid.,* 2.

the "threat of de-privatization", especially in the context of *Saakashvili's* other rapid transition policies.[605] However, this de-privatization, as the author calls it, seems related to *Saakashvili's* efforts to combat corruption. Specifically, the Minister of Justice sent a proposal to the Parliament aimed at fighting corruption by changing the current three-year statute of limitations for pursuing bribery charges against state officials engaging in illegal privatization transactions. The newspaper writer argued that the law would less stringent in pursuing corruption while a representative of the Minister of Justice reports that the new law stipulates that the three-year statute of limitations only covers disputes about privatization and that it will not apply in criminal cases. Conversely, the Chair of the Economic Committee of Parliament explains, "this draft gives the government the opportunity to secretly review any privatization deal." The writer cautioned readers that re-thinking private property rights could harm the free market economy, politicize the Prosecutor's office (it's already politicized), and might result in a re-distribution of property. The writer interviewed another opponent of the law from the Taxpayers' Union who stated that "Instead of attacking property titles (this is not mentioned anywhere in this article), the government must not hold businessmen [and women] accountable-if a government official illegally bought or sold something, we must punish only him and make him pay a fine." Interesting spin, punish the corrupt official but not the budding capitalist, when both may have intentionally broken the law. What remains ignored here is that sometimes the capitalist also holds a government position. Again, the precise details about this new bill are missing or simply incorrectly communicated by the press or politicians.

Another journalist joined the parade of cynics criticizing George Soros, making accusations that Soros funded the Georgian revolution. Moreover, the journalist argued that the new administration and his financial backers only want power and that social, political, or economic change was never really on the agenda.[606] Conversely, a Georgian language newspaper *Akhali Taoba*, reported that some Parliamentarians are demanding that President *Saakashvili* stop provoking *Adjaran* authorities and instead de-escalate the

---

605   M. Alkhazashvili, "Turning back the clock, the threat of de-privatization." *Ibid.*, 3.

political situation. Other demands for change included insistence that the Prosecutor General resign due to his "non-professionalism and irresponsibility". *Chkeidze* called the situation in Georgia one of "terror." Another MP, a former *Shevardnadze* follower, also accused the government of "shameful activities" (violence) not a fight against corruption. Regardless of the criticisms of the new administration, the effects of the Rose Revolution reverberate even in neighboring Abkhazia.

A number of recent public protests have occurred in *Abkhazia* aimed at the *Abkhazian* President, *Valdislave Arbzinba*. The protests are related to a recent executive decree by *Arbzinba* forbidding commercial use of all forests by any private companies except the one owned by one of his relatives, *Pavel Arbzinba*. The protests and public discussion centered on the necessity of the President stepping down. Even some discussion of impeachment followed, but the *Abkhazian* parliament had no codified statute by which to implement an impeachment process. Following the public protests, the government modified the decree on commercial forestry. One of the opposition political party leaders in *Abkhazia* reported that he plans to run in the next presidential election (scheduled for October 2004). The writer then begs the question: "Where is he, the *Abkhaz* '*Misha*'?" the leader organizing all the protests in *Abkhazia*, "show him to us" he pleads.[607] The *Abkhazians* apparently want to clone *Saakashvili* hoping for their own version of the Rose Revolution.

The on-going *Magticom* corruption scandal continues with more focus on *Shevardnadze's* son-in law, who continues to be accused of tax evasion.[608] *Shevardnadze's* daughter reportedly called the investigation a witch-hunt. The writer stated that the new President's "crusade' to deal with the "entrenched corruption of *Shevardnadze's* regime is in full swing." The writer explained that both receiving bribe payments as well as evading taxes co-occur among corrupt officials. He also claimed that this amounts to millions of lari. Other suspicions with regard to *Magticom* include involvement in pres-

---

606   Natia Mamistvalovi, "Javelidze vs. new government" and "Chkheidze demands resignation of Prosecutor General." *Ibid.,* 6.
607   Inal Khashig, "Abkhazia: Ardzinba under pressure-The opposition in Abkhazia is broadening its campaigning against the republic's leader." *Ibid.,* 6.
608   Nino Pasturia, "Political Witch-Hunt?" *Georgia Today* (27 February 2004):3.

suring another telecommunications company, Georgian Telecom, to merge with it. The writer also alleged that recently *Shevardnadze's* son-in-law allegedly attempted to flee the country by applying for a U.S. Visa. Although the Visa was denied, he was subsequently arrested on a plane scheduled to leave for the U.S. The author suggested that he planned to sell all of his shares in *Magticom* after arriving in the U.S. While *Shevardnadze's* son-in-law is pursued by law enforcement, the current administration granted immunity from any future corruption charges to former President *Shevardnadze*. *Jokhtaberidze, Shevardnadze's* son-in-law, later spoke to journalists and told them: "The press should think twice before reporting on the news." He indicated that the media has publicized false information about his company's financial behavior. He also told journalists that reporting this information will scare investors and damage the country. He informed reporters that the questions that the prosecutor's offices were asking were only technical and regarded the founding of the company. He explained that while he found the company with his American partner, he takes no part in the management of the company. However, then he acknowledged that he developed the business plan every year. He also denied other accusations that his company had driven Georgian Telecom out of business, and claimed that this was not likely as there are numerous competitors of Georgian Telecom currently in existence. Specifically, he claimed twenty-seven other international calling businesses are operating in Georgia. Mark Hauf, Chairman of the company, reports that *Magticom's* dealings are legal and that the company has invested one-hundred and twenty million USD into the Georgian company and an additional one hundred and forty-three million GEL into the Georgian economy. After all *Jokhtakberidze's* defensive posturing, the writer then claimed that *Jokhtakberidze* offered to pay the court to stop the investigation, the court refused and sentenced him to three months of pre-trail detention. *Shevardnadze's* daughter and other recent arrestees of *Saakashvili's* new government continued to argue that these on-going series of arrests were motivated by politics not probable cause. The journalist agreed by explaining that a number of individuals continue to be involved in corrupt activities are free and have not been investigated. The writer quoted a political scientist who asked: "Why hasn't *Geocell* also been subjected to a similar financial audit?"

Another writer reviewed the recent police raid on the Omega-Group, owners of a cigarette a company, a publishing business and a newspaper.[609] Contrary to previous reports, this journalist explained that police fired shots during the raid and subsequently closed the publishing office. Subsequently the President of the company and a Parliamentarian were arrested. He called for the resignation of the Prosecutor General, referring to him as incompetent. The author argued that some MPS continued to call the incident a violation of democratic values and the rights of the free press. However, other MPs claimed that the police were within the rule of the law by shutting down the press while the investigation of suspected tax evasion continued. The Prosecutor's office also accused the Omega group of maintaining a monopoly on the sale of cigarettes. The Omega group publishes "Omega Magazine" as well as the newspaper *Akhali Epoka* or *The New Epoch*. The Omega group also owns the *Iberia* TV station. A famous Georgian journalist, the editor of the Omega Magazine, went on a hunger strike in protest against these arrests. One employee of the Omega group claimed that law enforcement officers also entered the Omega premises illegally and attacked several employees. While the prosecutors' office initially claimed that no illegal activity occurred during the arrest, later he admitted that police officers committed some assaults and that they would be punished. The prosecutor also revealed that four leaders of Omega group's subsidiaries are missing and need to report for questioning (there was no statement in the paper as to whether or charges were filed on these four individuals, whether or not an arrest warrant was issued or if they have just been asked to come in for questioning). Conversely, an employee of Omega stated that these individuals are available for questioning. Another politician explained that the law does not support halting an industrial process in the process of an investigation, while a second person working for the Prosecutor's office reports that his office does have the authority to suspend any work process in the interests of the investigation including the media. This slippery slope is one of many that Georgian authorities seem to walk as one crisis after another envelops the new administration.

---

609   *Idem*. "A Storm in a Teapot." *Ibid.,* 2.

Asian *Abashidze* continued to resist changes suggested by President *Saakashvili*.[610] Recent events in *Adjara* include protests organized by the student movement *Kmara*, formerly active in the November Rose Revolution. *Kmara* is currently calling for a change in the government in *Adjara*. Other activists groups include "Our *Adjara*", also demanding an end to *Abashidze's* regime. However, the pro-*Abashidze* group "The Revival Union "continues to support Abashidze. In one recent protest, the *Adjaran* authorities allegedly assaulted some *Kmara* activists in an effort to repress this movement. The writer alleged that speculation is growing that *Abashidze* plans to use Russian military bases to demonstrate its military strength in resisting the movement to avoid changes in the autonomy of *Adjara* relative to *Tbilisi*. Subsequently, the Russian military began training maneuvers in *Adjara* reinforcing Georgian's fears of another confrontation. One Georgian politician denied that Russia would support any such efforts even as the opposition groups in *Adjara* continue to call for *Abashidze's* resignation. In turn, *Abashidze's* supporters assaulted a member of an oppositional political party, the Christian Democratic. Nevertheless, opposition forces continue to predict that their campaign will soon result in *Abashidze's* resignation.

While *Abashidze* tries to shut down this opposition, Prime Minister *Zhvania* continued to promise that the new administration and cabinet will fight against corruption and restore the country's territorial integrity.[611] *Zhvania* also urged citizens to understand that they must pay for the energy that they use to provide support for the new government. *Zhvania* reminded the public that government institutions and ministries changes included reductions from forty departments or agencies to fifteen. Chancellery transformations will result in a two third reduction of staff. *Zhvania* is showing citizens that the government is doing its part to reduce expenditures and thus citizens must do their part by paying the bills to provide tax income to the government. Conversely, *Zhvania* then announced his promise to strengthen the armed forces by increasing military spending to two percent of the GDP. Additionally, *Zhvania* promised to raise pensions by April and change the minimum wage to a living wage. An oppositional party member from the Social-

---

610   Zaza Jgharkava, "Abashidze throws down Gauntlet." *Ibid.,* 1, 2.
611   Gorgodze, "Zhvania lays out plans Parliament."

ists' ranks argued that *Zhvania* was dishonest because *Zhvania* had previously promised that wages would increase by January. *Zhvania* also promised that health care would be available by the end of the year for the entire population. Moreover, he alleged assured those who were unable to afford health care would receive it from the government. He also promised to have every school connected to the internet and that every school student would learn a foreign language. The writer offered no indication of a timeframe for the accomplishment of these lavish promises. Most interestingly, the article reports that *Zhvania* explained that Georgia will "remain a member of the European family and a partner with the United States, while relations with Russia will be changed." *Zhvania* may be offering far more than Georgia can afford even with notable administrative cuts in staff and agencies.

As the promises continue, the political opposition to the new cabinet appointees remains unfaltering. Specifically, the New Rights Party, the Liberty Party, and the Socialist Party opposed all the new cabinet appointees. Their complaints focused on the absence of detailed goals and objectives as well as the relative unknown status of many of the new appointees. The writer quoted one Liberty Party member who retorted: "Maybe they are planning to destroy everything". This same politician also explained that the lack of information about these appointees is "insulting for sensible politicians and political circles....these are some 'pig headed' people, 'slaves' in the Parliament who supported *Shevardnadze* yesterday and now they support *Saakasvhili*....they will destroy this President just as they have destroyed *Shevardnadze*." The writer than quoted Imedi TV's disclosure that a socialist party member explained that his party would not support the new ministers, particularly if no work plan is presented first. This party member also reported that the only thing they knew about some of the candidates was that they worked for the Soros Foundation. Finally, a member of the Industrialist party reported that his party would not support the new members until after they evidence revealed they worked diligently. It is unclear how the new ministers could work diligently until after the confirmation of their appointments by the parliament. Opposition parties also demanded a meeting with the nominees. As political opposition and criticism builds around *Saakashvili's* new administration, newspaper headlines create more angst by reporting on the presence of *Chechen* terrorists hiding in Georgia.

Chechnya borders Georgia's Caucasus mountain range and as mentioned in Chapter 1 *Chechen's* were one of the many ethnic groups forcibly transported from place to place during Stalin's tenure as Communist party leader. While this may partially explain their motives as terrorists, their much longer history of previous repression at the hands of Russia is also salient factor. Apparently, Georgia remains unaware of this fact as they continue to assist Russia in pursuit of alleged *Chechen* terrorists. A front-page article revealed that two *Chechens* recently escaped after being detained by Georgian authorities for eighteen months while awaiting extradition to Russia.[612] While the author explained the presence of a *Chechen* Diaspora in Georgia, the Russian President claimed one hundred *Chechens* are currently living in Georgia and asked President *Saakasvhili* to turn them all over to Russian law enforcement authorities. Apparently, Putin does not differentiate between Diaspora and terrorists. The writer argued that the *Chechen* lawyers' blamed the Georgian authorities who they claimed planned this "escape" who never intended to release the *Chechens* to Russia. *Chechen's* lawyers may be trying shift accountability for the escape to Georgia in attempt to get their clients off the list as runaway detainees. This incident began in August of 2002, when eight *Chechens* and five other non-*Chechens* illegally crossing the Georgian border. Subsequently detained, all thirteen requested political asylum. The request for asylum was denied and in November 2002, the Georgian prosecutor ordered the extradition of five of the Chechens to Russia. Five *Chechens* were extradited while three others remained held by the Georgian authorities until this recent escape. A delegation from the European Court will travel to Georgia to investigate the condition of the two men who allegedly escaped, although interestingly later the author refers to them as "released". The European Court representative also plans to travel to Russia to talk with the five individuals previously extradited to the Russian authorities. There is growing evidence that the Russian government has resorted to inhumane practices with *Chechen* arrestees and civilians alike. This makes

---

612   Mary Makharashvili, "Released Prisoners go missing Layers hold authorities responsible." *The Messenger* (18 February 2004):1, 5.

articles like this one re-invite Georgian fears of Russian interference in their small country. With this unconscious collective effort to increase Georgian anxiety about social problems, another front-page article reminded readers of the on-going electricity problems that they face.

In a rather foreboding manner this journalist reported that the leading electricity distributor to Georgia's rural regions, UDC, needs to restructure itself to take "advantage of recent changes in government."[613] The company announced these transformations as primarily changes in leadership positions. Interestingly, the former director of the company is now the head of the newly created Energy Crisis Advisory Board. Clearly, Georgian government authorities seem to imitate the American legacy of movement from the private sector into the public sector. While information of this sort appears to flow more freely to the Georgian public it may also be perceived as more normative given the legacy of the Soviet era corruption. Other changes that the company promised to make included improving the electricity supply, customer services, and financial performance. Recently the company received funding from USAID under a security initiative to up-date its entire system including meter equipment across four-hundred and forty sites. It is interesting that USAID provides funding for this improvement under the auspices of a security initiative. In order to receive the assistance Georgian is probably required to fight terrorism. Interestingly, the journalist interviewed a company member, an American named Dean White who is managing the company through a consulting firm, who reported that UDC would "work very closely" with the Georgian government to remove small power companies in the region allegedly because they overcharge Georgian citizens. However, then accusations are made that UDC has stolen payments from citizens and fraudulently billed the state for claims of unpaid electricity bills. UDC management argued that they plan to fight this sort of corruption as exemplified by the recent firing of two regional branch directors and the detention of others on suspicion of corruption. UDC also asked the government to protect electricity substations from sabotage. UDC promises that they will begin working with the government to improve their collection of payments from

---

613   Christina Tashkevich, "Dire straits require UDC staff changes UDC commits to reorganizing its management-and the system." *Ibid.,* 1, 4.

customers. Nevertheless after making this commitment both company representatives and government officials that it is "hard to assure a reliable 24 hour electricity for the country, that the previous twelve years of underinvestment, corruption and thievery cannot be addressed overnight." Then the company argues that both government assistance and donor involvement is necessary to improve electricity supply to rural Georgians. As usual, elites often seem to talk out of both sides of their mouths leaving readers feeling frustrated and probably more hopeless about their future.

III.7 March 2004

Tension continues to mount in *Adjara* as *Kmara* student activists disclosed another assault on one of their members by four men. The attack occurred in *Batumi* several days ago and *Kmara* claims that *Abashidze* is responsible.[614] The day following the assault *Adjaran* Special Forces mobilized and "greeted" *Kmara* activists as they crossed the *Choloki* border checkpoint from *Tbilisi*.[615] The students had previously testified about two supporters' of *Abashidze's* Revival Party charged with the illegal possession of firearms. *Adjaran* police detained *Kamara* students and searched their belongings. Additional details were unavailable. While it remained possible that this report might have been an exaggeration aimed at inflaming nationalist sentiments, a later report verified that the an assault occurred but that the victim was a *Rustavi*-2 TV journalist, *Vakho Komakhidze*. The assault occurred as the journalist was investigating *Abashidze's* family background.[616] The reporter alleged that the *Adjaran* government ordered his attack to suppress his investigation. *Adjaran* government representatives denied the allegation arguing that Georgian politicians created the incident to disparage the reputation of the *Adjaran* government. Recently, the President of *Adjara* filed a legal suit against a Georgian language newspaper, the Tribunal, the sister newspaper of the Georgian

---

614 N.N, "Enough activists express outrage at wounding of their co-member in Batumi." *Rustavi-2 news online* http://www.rustavi-2.com.ge/print.php?id=6841 (as of 3 March 2004).

615 N.N., "Adjaran Law enforcers Detained and searched Enough Activists." *Ibid.*, http://www.rustavi-2.com.ge/print.php?id=6852 (as of 4 March 2004).

Times for similar reporting. Later the Interior Minister of *Adjara* explained that a criminal investigation would ensue regarding the alleged physical assault. However, he asked Georgian journalists to ensure that their reporting remained unbiased and uninfluenced by political forces. Moreover, the *Adjaran* Interior Minister reportedly indicated believing the *Tbilisi* government unduly influenced TV stations. Therefore, it is the government's responsibility if journalists' lives become at risk. The *Adjaran* Minister also blamed *Tbilisi* for the politicization of media arguing that this raises a number of serious concerns about *Saakashvhili's* administration. There is no doubt that the *Adjaran* government perceives the new Georgian government as a threat to *Abashidze's* dictatorship. A third article reporting on the assault indicated that the attack against *Komakhidze* occurred after he passed a police checkpoint leaving *Adjara*. The *Adjaran* special task force units appeared there and physically attacked *Komakhidze*, who was subsequently hospitalized with "serious injuries". *Adjaran* police also allegedly confiscated *Komakhidze's* film and video camera.[617] A fourth report revealed that the assault occurred near a police station while officers stood by unresponsively. Shortly thereafter, President *Saakashvili* ordered *Aslan Abashidze* to have the assault investigated within ten days and punishment meted for those found guilty. If *Abashidze* fails to act, *Saakashvili* will request that the Georgian prosecutor's office begin a criminal investigation against *Adjaran* state officials. However, the Georgian Prosecutor's office and ordered law enforcement agencies in *Adjara* to investigate the incident. The Georgian Prime Minister and the Minister of Health and Social Welfare visited the injured journalist and condemned the attack calling it 'inhuman'. This is the second attack on a journalist this month in *Adjara*. Such events could be precursors of a violent *Adjaran*-Georgian confrontation and readers are undoubtedly thinking this even before any reports of the possibility surfaced.

Subsequently, on March fifteenth a large front page headline alarmingly reads: "War in *Adjara*!!! Georgia Army on Alert after President Barred" and

---

616   N.N., "Journalists Beaten in Adjara." *Georgia Today* (12-18 March, 2004):2.
617   N.N., "Rustavi-2 Reporter Beaten in Adjara." *Rustavi-2 news online* http://www.rustavi-2.com.ge/print.php?id=6858 (as of 5 March 2004).

"Russia warns Georgia not to invade *Adjara*."[618] While this sensationalistic piece may overstate the seriousness of the situation, it does logically follow a series of instances of *Adjaran* abuse of authority. The remainder of the article, located five pages from the front page, provides a more innocuous description of events than justified by the front-page headline. Yet a great deal of information remains left to the imagination as readers are forced to look for other sources of information to gain a clearer picture of events. Moreover, a clear description of Russia's ultimatum only appears in a second article located underneath the first one. This incident follows on the heels of *Abashidze's* continued refusal to participate in the forthcoming March elections and the allegations of the two assaults on journalists and the illegal detention of the Georgian Finance Minister. The writer described the most recent incident as a physical blockade of Georgia's primary Black Seat port at *Batumi* by *Adjaran* authorities. Subsequently, an airport blockade followed the scheduled arrival of President *Saakashvili's* plane. However, weather conditions also prohibited the flight so the President's motor vehicle convoy and his entourage of political advisors including Prosecutor General *Irakly Okruashvili* and Interior Minister *Georgy Baramidze* drove to the *Adjaran* border. At the *Adjaran*-Georgian checkpoint, *Saakashvili* and his aids were unable to cross the border. Of course President *Saakashvili* only choice was to posture, saying: "If *Abashidze* intends to blackmail the Georgian President like a feudal lord from the Middle Ages, he is making a big mistake."[619] The word "invasion" appeared in the context of a speech by *Joseph Tsintskaladze*, the *Adjaran* Parliamentary Leader, who exclaimed, "What does it mean when the President wants to invade? Who does he want to invade with his retinue? When he wants to travel in the country he can go everywhere, but not like this." Conversely, *Abashidze's* son, the Mayor of *Batumi*, *George Abashidze*, explained that *Adjaran* authorities were unaware of the President's intended visit. Interestingly, nothing in the text of this article reflects any type of alert status for the Georgian Army as indicated in the headline. A Russian Ministry official reportedly told *Interfax* that his government suspected that *Tbilisi* planned to use force and explained: "If there is a crisis, all responsibility will

---

618   Niko Mcedlishvili, "War in Adjara!!! Georgia Army on Alert after President Barred." *The Georgian Times* (15 March 2004):1, 6.

lie with the Georgian Leadership." Also recently, *Abashidze,* while visiting Moscow, explained that he possessed information revealing that one hundred thousand soldiers were planning to move into *Adjara.* In both articles, *Abashidze's* administration insinuated that Georgia and *Adjara* were on the horizon of a looming crisis comparable to the secession of *Ossetia* and *Abkhazia,* especially if the situation remained unchanged. Unfortunately, newspaper editors, writers, and *Adjaran* politicians each socially constructed this crisis almost to the brink of war. However, near the end of March, the growing fear of confrontation between *Tbilisi* and *Adjara* began to diminish when *Saakashvili* and *Abashidze* came to an agreement.[620] It seemed that some journalists appeared disappointed in the negotiated agreement as a later headline also located on the front page, reads: "Swift Revolution number two failed." The text casts aspersions that *Saakasvhili* weakened at a pivotal moment by giving in to *Abashidze* who continues to cater to the Russian media and government.[621] The author compares *Saakashvili's* rhetoric about restoring democracy in *Adjara* to the U.S. justification for the war in Iraq. Noting his disappointment, the author writes that after receiving concessions from *Abashidze* to turn control of the *Batumi* Port and the *Sarpi* Customs Office (located on the Turkish border) back to *Tbilisi, Saakashvili's* motives to restore democracy waned. The author, as denoted by the title, insinuated that the President's motives were economic all along. Specifically, over ten million tons of oil will enter the *Batumi* port in 2004. If the blockade of the port were to continue, it could have irreparably damaged a number of trade relationships for Georgia. Ships entering the *Batumi* port include those from a number of countries, including Russian, China, Iran, Ukraine, Armenia, and *Azerbaijan.* Attribution of blame for the crisis fell on Soros as the result of his vocal and financial support for the Rose Revolution. Some politicians alleged that Soros' motivation remains his own desire own property in strategic parts of Georgia. *Akaki Asthiany,* leader of the Traditionalists party, argued that the new government promised Soros a number of state industries in return for his

---

619   *Ibid.*
620   Jaba Tatiashvili, "Tbilisi-Batumi, political aggression and economic interests, Why did Abashidze and Saakashvili reconcile?" *The Georgian Times* (22 March 2004):1, 4.
621   Rusudan Kbilashvili, "Swift revolution number two failed." *Ibid.,* 1, 3.

financial support during the revolution. The writer reviewed the history of fraudulent voting in *Adjara,* and anticipated that similar results may occur in the new Parliamentary election. Revival Party members continued to charge that the *Tbilisi* government came to power by force and that they are threatening *Abashidze* and *Adjara.* Writers' construed Russia's motives in mediating the crisis as suspicious. Apparently, Russia sent the Mayor of Moscow, *Yury Luzhkov,* to *Batumi* as a negotiator. Moreover, a Russian company owns a part of the *Batumi* coastal area, making their interest in *Adjara* seem more self-centered rather than altruistic. Specifically, the author wrote that *Luzhkov* and *Abashidze* plan to develop tourism in the coastal area. Another article referring to the failure of the second revolution, a statement actually attributed to a member of the international NGO Helenski Human Rights group, suggested that *Saakashvili's* motivation was to provoke a war, although reports thus far indicated that *Adjaran* troops initiated the conflict by blocking the *Batumi* seaport. The spokesperson reiterated *Abashidze's* long history of human rights violations including, the repression of the press, fraudulent elections, and the implementation of a curfew enforced by armed soldiers. A third article located in the back of this particular newspaper co-written by two authors, one in *Batumi* and another in *Tbilisi* illustrates a slightly different perspective on these events. First, these journalists told readers that *Abashidze* and *Saakashvili* met together for four hours and that the blockade began on March 14th when *Saakashvili's* convoy tried to enter *Adjara.* Moreover the blockade was described as an economic blockade orchestrated by the Georgian President *Saakashvili* not a physical one implemented by *Abashidze* as suggested by previous articles. Another detail not mentioned previously, includes *Abashidze's* concession to participate in the forthcoming parliamentary elections. *Abashidze* also agreed to cooperate with the *Tbilisi* prosecutor's initiation of an investigation into all illegal detentions in A*djara*. Additionally, *Abashidze* agreed to collect weapons from all armed groups in *Adjara.* Writers' viewed these concessions optimistically making *Saakashvili* the perceived winner. *Saakashvili* spoke with Putin and the U.S. Secretary of State throughout the crisis and both offered their continuing support of Georgia's territorial integrity. However, Putin denied orchestrating the Moscow Mayor's visit to *Adjara.* Another presentation of these events also described *Saakashvili* as winning concessions from *Abashidze* including the release of all political prisoners.[622] While Russia and the United States officially proclaimed their neutrality, they expressed a desire for a peaceful non-military solution to the problem. Another journalist described *Abashidze* as "mean with words" after the conference with *Saakashvili* vaguely referring to his angry or sardonic verbalizations. The inaccurate information illustrated in the initial reports of this incident reveals that little investigative journalism exists across Georgia. However, building animosity, sensationalizing, and distorting the truth are firmly institutionalized. Even though this crisis was manufactured rather than real, the newspapers continue to foment fear of conflict with *Adjara*.

One journalist reported that the Georgian Prosecutor General began investigating the murder of *Temur Inaishvili* in *Adjara* allegedly perpetrated by the Deputy Security Minister of *Adjara, Davit Bakuradze*. Another article in the same paper better elucidates *Davit Bakuradze's* role in *Adjaran* affairs by quoting a Nationalist party leader, *Givi Targamadze,* who refers to him as the operational manager.[623] *Targamadze* believes that *Soso Gogitidze*, the *Adjaran* Security Minister, also *Abashidze's* brother-in-law, controls *Abashidze's* government while *Bakuradze* carries out the dirty work including illegal arrests, detentions, and organized violence. *Targamadze* also insinuated that *Bakuradze* was the paramilitary leader responsible for perpetrating the violence against journalists, *Kmara,* and election observers. Unfortunately, these allegations disclosed by *Targamadze* remain unsubstantiated. Finally, as the title of the article states, *Targamadze* predicted that *Abashidze's* departure from office would resemble *Shevardnadze's* political demise. Conversely, a political scientist, *Soso Tsintadze* adamantly insists that *Abashidze* will never resign and *Saakashvili* may have to resort to force to re-unite *Adjara* and *Georgia*.[624] *Tsintadze's* retorted to the interviewer when faced with these rumors: "Do you really believe this stuff?" *Tsintadze* argued that *Abashidze* gained his foothold in the region because of *Shevardnadze's* need for electoral support for his Revival party and while not supportive of *Saakashvili*, he believed that *Saakashvili's* decision to implement the economic blockade

---

622   Zaza Jgharkava, "Deadlock Broken." *Georgia Today* (19 March 2004):1-2.
623   *Idem*. "Abashidze will have to follow the same way as Shevardnadze." *Ibid.*, 2.

was appropriate. As the possibility or at the least the on-going social construction of war with *Adjara* looms on the horizon, newspapers unremittingly focus on bad news, this time smuggling.

Georgian border guards at the *Tsiteli Khidi* checkpoint recently fired shots at the tires of vehicles suspected of carrying smuggled goods from *Azerbaijan*. The vehicles drove through the border barricade without clearance from customs. The article indicated that the drivers were complaining about the incident and wanted to protest at the checkpoint. This new willingness to protest even if illegitimate seems to be the result of the social climate that the Rose Revolution created.[625] While the writer painted a picture of dutiful border guards maintaining law and order, another article revealed that the former Chief of Traffic Police, *Davit Kobakhidze*, remained under suspicion of corruption involving illegal custom clearance activities. Similarly, suspicions of misappropriating 300,000 Gel focused on Former Deputy Interior Minister, *David Todua.* He is also a witness against the first suspect. A third witness, Director of *Telasi* Electric Company, *Ilya Kutidzealso* also faces accusations of embezzling 40,000 GEL. A few days later, an elected MP from *Tkibuli*, *Bondo Shailikiani*, was arrested following a police search of his home during which two machine-guns and an anti-tank shell were confiscated. Interestingly *Shailikiani* also belongs to the *Kutaisi* city council and owns a television company, "*Kutaisi.*"[626]Another arrest of a suspected corrupt politician followed. This time the Prosecutor's office and the Interior Minister jailed the Majority Party PM from his home in *Kutaisi.* This arrest was the result of an investigation into organized crime and car hijacking. Additional arrests that resulted in the detention of twelve suspects also involved a shoot-out and the deaths of three police officers and an innocent pedestrian (note the writer calls the suspects, criminals). The political party block of the Industrialists and the New Rights criticized the police following the death of the bystander. The National Independence Party also lamented the arrest of the Minister *Bondo Shailikiani,* only because the arrest transpired during the early morn-

---

624   Nino Pasturia, "On the Brink." *Ibid.,* 3.
625   N.N., "Border guards shot at Smugglers." *Rustavi-2 news online* http://www.rustavi-2.com.ge/print.php?id=6860 (as of 5 March 2004).
626   N.N., "Law Enforcement Agents Arrested Bondo Shalikiani." *Ibid.,* http://www.rustavi-2.com.ge/print.php?id=6854.

ing hours and television news broadcasted his arrest while he was only dressed in his underwear. Under criticism for this new wave of arrests, *Saakashvili* retorted that his administration did not fear apprehending corrupt officials like his predecessor. However, *Saakashvili* also criticized the journalist for filming the suspect half-naked and broadcasting it on television. The suspect, *Bondo Shalikiani,* received a three-month pre-trial detention sentence. As discussed throughout this book MP's are immune from prosecution according the constitution, however, following this last arrest, the writer reported that the CEC, not the courts, abolished his immunity. Either the reporter is mistaken or the CEC continues to exert more authority than it should.

Another journalist discussed the alleged Financial Amnesty offered by S*aakashvili's* administration to Georgian businessmen with regard to unpaid taxes. The government established a 1 April deadline for businesses to pay arrears taxes in order to avoid prosecution. Interestingly, this excludes *Shevardnadze's* son-in-law and the Omega Group. *Shevardnadze's* son-in-law previously received a sentence of three months pre-trial detention following the discovery of 740,000 GEL in his Magi Com coiffeurs. While release on bail for two million lari was possible, the court refused to grant the bail. While it remains undisclosed why this one exception to the amnesty prevailed, it seems possible that the administration's motivation is unrelated to justice but rather to politics. One Georgian Economic expert argued for the universal application of the amnesty to all businessmen [and women], after all the current program forgives back taxes up to one million GEL and should include *Shevardnadze's* son-in-law. One individual retorted that the government's behavior remains tantamount to bullying individuals, particularly when threatening arrests. This person argued that during the Rose Revolution, *Saakashvili* encouraged businessmen [and women] to refuse to pay taxes to the corrupt government while now arguing that such a position remains untenable. The final complaint was that big businessmen [and women] have not been dodging payment of taxes and that the modification of the bankruptcy laws would better facilitate business survival, not threats of criminal punishment. However, the President of the Georgian Times favored *Saakashvili's* policy as well as the financial amnesty. In another negative view of *Saakashvili's* new approach to government, one reporter revealed that the *New*

York Times called *Saakashvili's* administration of the country a Stalinesque approach. In a second perspective of *Saakashvili's* new approach to back taxes, revelations include the fact that the law has not passed the parliament. Moreover, the detailed bill includes a provision giving permission to businessmen [and women] to submit a declaration on arrears taxes covering the previous year. The bill would then require the delinquent taxpayer to provide ten percent of his or her debt to the state within four months of filing the declaration. This financial amnesty will not apply to anyone previously indicted on criminal charges. However, the bill remains in draft form only and may fail to pass in the parliament until after the March parliamentary elections. [627] The Vice-President of the Georgian Chamber of Commerce suggested that the government just simplify the tax system and improve the management and administration of the system rather than pass this new law.

Although it looks as though *Saakashvili* is attempting to facilitate institutional change, another journalist also believed that the government resembles a one party government.[628] Similar to previous reports, the writer explicates that the new government mirrors the November political triad of the Rose Revolution. This writer also criticized *Saakashvili's* five-year economic and political plan without providing specific details. The author predicted that the Nationalist party block could become as politically ineffective as the former *Shevardnadze's-Zhvania-Saakashvili* Citizens Union of Georgia became during *Shevardnadze's* first term in office. Moreover, most candidates running in the forthcoming parliamentary elections are all members of the large party block of the Nationalists, *Zhvania's* Democrats, or *Burjanadze* Democrats, again reflecting a one party government stifling the possibility of fruitful parliamentary debate. Considering the rather unlimited financial support that Georgia continues to garner from the United States, the absence of criticism of Georgia's one party government should not be surprising. This continued unremitting influence of the United States in Georgian affairs seems self-perpetuating.

---

627   N.N., "Bill on Hidden Tax Declaration Considered by the Cabinet." *Ibid.*, http://www.rustavi-2.com.ge/print.php?id=6859.
628   Jaba Tatishvili, "Will the government bloc break up?" *The Georgian Times International Edition* (8 March 2004):3.

However, the U.S. recently chastised the Georgian government and called upon Georgia to eliminate 'Hate Crimes' as revealed in a reprinted letter from the United States Helsinki Commission. The letter strongly suggested that Georgia's new President ensure that violence against religious minority members' end. This development is interesting considering that Georgia has not yet had a civil rights movement for minorities therefore, fighting hate crimes when minority rights and issues remain unrecognized is a rather large leap. The Helsinki Commission mentioned an on-going investigation with regard to crimes against 'Jehovah Witnesses'.[629] The letter included a strongly worded statement that "[we].look to you for justice against criminals whom Georgia's law enforcement has refused to prosecute seriously." The letter also congratulated the new President and complemented the Georgian nation for its first post-soviet non-violent "rose revolution." The U.S. Helsinki Commission is a watchdog organization also known as the U.S. Commission on Security and Cooperation in Europe established to monitor the activities of the European Commission on Security and Cooperation. Georgia's new Big Brother continues to watch them and weld undue influence.

Another questionable U.S. influence on Georgia includes the International Republican Institute, operating with funding from USAID. They recently conducted a Gallup style survey of Georgian's attitudes about politics and the economy.[630] Some of the findings of the survey revealed that while last year eighty-three percent of respondents believed that the political environment or the government in Georgia was poor; the most recent survey conducted during February 11-17, reflected that seventy-eight percent of respondents believed that "Georgia is going in the right direction." Last year only twenty percent of respondents reported feeling satisfied with the development of democracy, whereas this year, seventy-seven percent indicated that they felt satisfied with the level of democratic development. In questioning Georgians about how rapidly they thought Georgian situation might change last year,

---

629   Multiple Authors CSCE, "CSCE Eager to Work with Georgian President to uphold rights," "U.S. Helsinki commission releases 12 February letter to Saakashvili." *The Georgian Times* (8 March 2004):5.

only twelve percent believed changes would occur soon. Whereas this year, forty-one percent reported that changes would occur more rapidly. Another primary concern currently reported by Georgians included jobs, the economy, and political and civil instability. Also Georgian's interest in politics improved since the previous survey. Last year only twelve percent of Georgians reported any interest in politics, whereas currently forty-six percent reported interest. Moreover, ninety-three percent reported approving of *Shevardnadze's* decision to resign. Georgians also disclosed that the characteristics of parliamentarians that they would vote for included, "speaking the truth and respect for human rights". Additionally, when asked what the government needed to do to improve public support, the list included resolving problems like, unemployment, low pensions and salaries, economic recession, corruption, as well as restoring Georgia's territorial integrity. Of course, Georgian's reported that they would loose faith in the government if promises were "broken or unfilled" Finally, eight-four percent of respondents believed that the new administration would regain all of Georgia's lost territories but eighty-four percent reported that they trusted the media more than other social institutions. The International Republican Institute, founded in Georgia in 1998, aims to "to work directly with Georgian political parties. This includes working to "strengthen grassroots political organizations and further develop campaign skills for democratic activists."[631] The IRI also launched the Election Media Center to monitor the forthcoming elections, although the article fails to explain this clearly. The center also maintains a web page with posted election results.[632] Interestingly, once again, the members of the International Republican Institute's board of directors, reads like a whose who of U.S. politics and businessmen [and women] including names like Senator John McCain, Former Secretary of State Lawrence Eagleburger, former UN Ambassador Jeanne J. Kirkpatrick and former National Security Advisor, Brent Snowcraft.

---

630   Lali Jvakhia, "Pre-election sociological research has rounded up, What population expects from the new government?" *The Georgian Times, International Edition* (8 March 2004):14.

631   International Republican Institute, World Web Page http://www.iri.org/region.asp?region=2005361763 (as of June 7 2005).

632   *Idem.* World Web Page http://www.civil.ge/eng/elections.php?id=32 *Ibid.*

A similar review of another opinion survey appears in the same pa-per.[633] These survey sponsors included the Institute for Policy Studies and the Open Society Institute. Neither of these articles provides information about how respondents were gathered and since it remains difficult if not im-possible to maintain or develop a population list in order to collect a random or representative sample in Georgia, the validity and reliability of the findings are questionable. The data is more likely to reflect a convenience sample of capital city residents, rather than a genuinely scientific methodology. Data collection occurred from June to November of 2003. This survey found that from a list of fifteen problems, the major concerns of Georgians following the November elections were in order of importance, unemployment, corruption, low salaries, pensions, and entitlements and territorial disintegration with percentages ranging from seventy-two to forty-one. Respondents also listed the same four issues as priorities requiring government's attention. Unem-ployment remained listed as the most important problem to be resolved, then salaries followed by territorial integrity and the fight against corruption. More-over, most respondents (ninety-nine percent) characterized the United States as friendly towards Georgia compared to forty percent who perceived that the European Union was friendly to Georgia. Interestingly, the nation considered most hostile to Georgia was Russia, with seventy-two percent of respondents choosing their northern neighbor. Almost forty-four percent of respondents believed that punishing corrupt individuals would resolve this Georgian prob-lem in addition to improving the legislature (forty four percent). Another inter-esting finding revealed that ninety one percent of respondents supported state ownership of a variety of sectors of the economy. Moreover, a notable increase of persons reported their willingness to engage in protest. In June 2003, sixty five percent of respondents reported believing that increased civil participation would improve the Georgian situation and by November, sev-enty-two percent believed it. Also in June, only fifteen percent believed that that one person could influence the government, whereas by November forty-seven percent believed that one person could influence the government. Ad-ditionally, forty percent of respondents indicated that they participated in the

---

633   Nana Sumbadze and Georgie Tarkhan-Mouravi Institute for Policy, Tbilisi, "Public
       Opinion in Tbilisi: In the Aftermath of the Parliamentary Elections of November 2,

protest rallies following the November 2nd parliamentary elections. Most tragic included the finding that only forty-six percent of respondents indicated that they would appeal to the courts following a violation of their civil rights. Most people would rather appeal to their network of friends or family members for help (seventy-seven and seventy-one percent respectively). Approximately eighty percent of respondents reporting preferring a democratic government while almost nine percent indicated they preferred authoritarian rule while twelve percent were unsure. While democracy clearly remains highly desirable to Georgians (at least those living in the capital city), capitalism remains more dubiously regarded. Fifty percent believed that economic inequality was normative or expected while the other fifty percent indicated that they preferred an egalitarian society where economic equality existed. Most, seventy-seven percent, argued that success remained an individual endeavor, undoubtedly a belief affected by the influence of western capitalism.

In other economic news, *Gazprom*, *Tbilisi's* Russian gas supplier recently signed a twenty-five year agreement with the *TiblisiGaz* to re-schedule its debts.[634] While the previous Minister of Fuel and Energy actually signed the agreement, the new Minister, *Nika Gilauri* plans to visit Moscow on March 15th to meet with the Director of the daughter company of *Gazprom, GazExport,* for a discussion of debt repayment. *GazExport* began supplying *Tbilisi's* gas beginning last October. *Tbilisigaz* has already accumulated 7.5 million USD in debt to *GazExport* just over the last five months. Part of the problem was that the Georgian government failed to turn in their allocation of welfare vouchers to the company.

In the midst of Georgia's continuing accumulation of debts, the national currency rate reportedly strengthened against the dollar with one writer citing an increase of 1.98 GEL to the dollar.[635] [636] However, another author argued that the increase remains meaningless as the GEL lost its value against the EURO. A third journalist reported that the increase resulted from recent offers

---

2003." *The Georgian Times International Edition* (8 March 2004):16.
634   Maia Misheladze, "Weekly Economic Review, Energy." *Ibid.,* 7.
635   Nino Shubitdze, "GEL yesterday and today." *Daily Georgian Times* (11 March 2004):4.

of financial amnesties to corrupt politicians and corporate executives. Another description of this change included labeling it as a brief fluctuation that will not positively affect the economy over the long run. Furthermore, a representative from the Young Georgian Lawyers association explained that when the exchange rate rises, it hurts the "entrepreneurs who will receive twenty-five percent lower earnings then envisaged by the business plan."[637] The government's recent impetus to collect back taxes by arresting suspected corrupt businessmen also may explain this increase in the value of the LARI. Another factor may include a government proposal to increase taxes paid by casinos.[638] Taxes on slot machine gains by customers as well as state lottery winners remain poorly reported to both the city and the federal government. Allegations presented here argue that tax collectors remain corrupt and often pocket the money collected rather than turning it in to the state and city. Numerous casinos exist in downtown *Tbilisi with* at least three setting on the main avenue where the Parliament also stands. Located near these casinos sit the street beggars previously described, again primarily senior citizens trying to survive in desperate times. Other beggars include children, sometimes coerced by parents, reportedly manipulated by organized criminal groups. Sometimes the presence of poor beggars and children became so sad it felt psychologically unbearable. Also impossible to eliminate is the extensive breadth and depth of the Shadow economy, of which organized crime is a large part.

In revisiting the issue of the shadow economy, a journalist wonders to what extent underground money may be financing the forthcoming election campaign.[639] Unfortunately, no NGOS or International organizations monitor party or campaign financing, and neither does the government. Secondly, as is true elsewhere, the party that spends the most remains most likely to earn more seats in the parliament. In an interview with a political expert, *Soso*

636   Maia Misheladze, "Weekly Economic Review, National Currency Rate Surges on Dollar." *The Georgian Times, International Edition* (8 March 2004):7.

637   Shubitdze, "GEL yesterday and today."

638   Maia Arabidze, "Taxes rise for casino owners." *Daily Georgian Times* (11 March 2004):4; Nino Patsuria, "Georgian Lari vs. Dollar." *Georgia Today* (12 March 2004):1, 4.

639   Khatuna Kviralashvili, "Will Black Money be laundered during the March 28 elections? Political Parties cannot specify how much they will spend on the elections." *Daily Georgian Times* (11 March 2004):3, 4.

Tsintsadze, a journalist revealed that a great deal of "black money" supports election campaigns and although the amount spent remains publicly available, no legal requirement exists to disclose amounts provided by specific contributors. Although the Anti-Corruption Bureau published a report on finances spent by political parties in the November election, apparently no one reads the report or utilizes it to make policy changes. The author also asserted that the Anti-Corruption office recently declared bankruptcy and that this seemed of little interest to the new government. The government block discloses that it will finance its campaign through donations and according to *Saakashvili* with "tiny contributions from the owners of shops and drug stores." The journalist writes that the "sources of incomes for the Industrialists - New Rights alliance is legal and crystal clear...the members of these two parties run their own business and people know where they get their money." This seems a rather naive or ignorant assumption to make, considering the number of allegations against businessmen [and women] suggesting involvement in corruption. Finally, the article notes that while the campaign remains open, no political parties have begun campaigning. It seems that the perception of a victory by the political block of the former Rose Triumph is undeniable.

In another discussion of the shadow economy, a writer argued that it was the drop in the circulating cash that led to the strengthening of the GEL against the dollar.[640] A decrease of activity in the shadow economy, the author explained, results an in increase in demand for the Lari. Moreover, the drop in interest rates from forty percent to twenty percent also increased the demand for the lari, which accordingly increased the currency's value in exchange for the dollar. Although the MP, *Nodar Javakhisvili,* and the former head of the National Bank denied any decrease in moneys circulating in the shadow economy would cause such an affect. In an interview with the National Bank of Georgia, responsible for implementation of the national monetary policy, their representatives assured the journalist that the fluctuation in the rate of exchange is not problematic. However, another journalist suggested that this phenomenon could reflect mistakes or involvement in corrup-

---

640   Shubitdze, "GEL yesterday and today."

tion or other covert activities designed to deceive the Georgian people.[641] Similarly, this author also viewed the Finance Ministry, responsible for implementing the monetary policy, as culpable for what he refers to as an economic meltdown. The author revealed that the Finance Ministry might spend only 1/12 of the old budget monthly, but that fifty million GEL surplus remains from moneys collected in January and February. This might also explain the strengthening of the Lari. Conversely, the writer later reported that spokespersons for the National Bank and the Finance Ministry explained that the Ministry of Finance maintains no deposits in the National Bank. This writer also quoted the MP mentioned above, *Nodar Javakhisvili,* who argued that all this reflects deceit orchestrated by the government. In a related article, the Finance Minister, *Zurab Noghaideli,* confirmed a surplus for February and reported that plans are to utilize the funds to pay arrears pension checks. He explained that the money remains available due to improvements in tax collections from the *Adjaran* Autonomous Republic.[642] Purportedly the Finance Ministry investigated forty-nine cases of tax evasion with four cases subsequently transferred to the prosecutor's office for further investigation while others were transferred to court for trial. The writer hinted that some of these proceedings may result from a number of recent dismissals of tax officers, including department heads from *Marneuli, Dedoplistskaro, Akhmeta, Telavi, Lagodekhi, and Kobulieti,* in addition *to* some tax inspectors. Finally, the Finance Minister explained that to continue the strengthening of the GEL, it is necessary to attract transnational corporate investments. The most salient issue in this increase of the value of the Lari, remains whether or not the change is temporary or permanent; especially in terms of its effects on Georgian voters' choices come election day.

Director of the OSCE Office for Democratic Institutions and Human Rights, Ambassador Christian Strohal visited *Tbilisi* for two days on March 9th and 10th as a precursor to the OSCE election observer mission consisting of four hundred and fifty personnel.[643] The Director focused on the need for

---

641   Shubitdze, "GEL yesterday and today."
642   Galina Gotua, "Budget not on Paper." *Georgia Today* (12 March 2004):4.
643   Rusudan Kbilashvili, "OSCE urges Georgian authorities to promote human rights in the country." *Daily Georgian Times* (11 March 2004):3; Galina Gotua, "OSCE calls for Dialogue." *Georgia Today* (12 March 2004):3.

Georgian society to promote human rights, democracy, and the rule of law especially in the context of the recent Rose Revolution. He encouraged the on-going dialogue between NGO's and the government in order to continue to develop civil society and improve the social and economic welfare of Georgian citizens. In December at the OSCE Ministerial Council, four million Euros were devoted to the Georgian Election Assistance Program that will both manage the money and the country's election process this month. The Ambassador held meetings with the Prime Minister and *Nino Burjanadze* as well as civil society representatives during which discussions focused on prison reform, the anti-corruption program, and land legislative reform. Opposition party members were included in the meeting.[644] Strohal emphasized the necessity to implement administrative reforms with public involvement. The ambassador noted Georgia's on-going problems in implementing human rights reforms with regard to the criminal justice system as well as maintaining an independent media. Recently, the CEC began implementing OSCE's earlier suggestions by reducing the number of CEC members from fifteen to five. In the future, the parliament will appoint CEC members to office. Other changes included limitations on local precinct commissions and fewer members on the board. Additionally, the CEC will implement the new OSCE proposal protocols for voting and vote tallying beginning in April 2004. However, the Leader of the Labor Party insinuated that OSCE is wasting its time monitoring the elections if CEC members primarily belong to the Nationalist-Democratic Block Party. CEC chair *Chiaberashvili*, continued to visit a variety of election districts throughout Georgia as he verified the accuracy of recently computerized voters' lists. One exception is in *Adjara* where he fired the chair of the election subcommittee due to various irregularities in the voters' lists.[645] The journalist reported that the political parties competing against the Nationalist block have remained relatively quiet which she interpreted as an indicator of a Nationalist block victory. Meanwhile *Saakashvili* continued to make new appointments in his administration.

After *Saakashvili* returned from a visit to France, he announced the appointment of the Georgian Ambassador to France, Mrs. *Salome Zurabashvili,*

---

644   Gotua, "OSCE calls for Dialogue."
645   Nino Patsuria, "CEC pledges to be Nonpartisan." *Ibid.*

as the new Georgian Minister of Foreign Affairs.[646] However, she is not a Georgian Citizen and reporters' questioned how a non-Georgian could hold the post. The President responded by saying that the constitution allows the appointment if the individual is granted citizenship "in the country's best interests." *Zurabashvili's* Georgian grandparents fled Georgia in 1921 after the *Bolshevik* revolution (note the writer said after the Communists seized Georgia). Born in France, she is the granddaughter of the famous Georgian Statesman *Illia Chavachavadze*. After granting her Georgian citizenship, she will hold dual citizenship status. Perhaps this provides even more evidence of S*aakashvili's* nationalistic sentiments. Moreover, as other events continue to unfold, revelations of his unlimited Western support as well as his endorsement of traditional Eastern Orthodox values and reliance on the police to enforce his policies became more apparent.

In mid-March, a front-page news article revealed that the Georgian police arrested a church Patriarch, *Basil Mkalavishvili,* for a series of "aggressive attacks" occurring in the late 1990's. The author referred to the group as an "aggressive sect of Jehovah's Witnesses." The offense involved "setting fire to Jehovah Witness' property."[647] A stalemated court case existed against the Patriarch since January 2003. This incident in question included his resistance to arrest including barricading himself in a church with a number of his supporters. As mentioned previously, just a few days before his arrest, the Helenski Commission wrote a letter to President *Saakashvili* urging him to raise the issue "of the longstanding campaign of organized violence against members of minority faiths, especially the Jehovah Witnesses."[648] The letter also suggested Georgia would fail in its commitment to the OSCE if it refuses to take legal action against such "uncivilized behavior" or "international norms." However, the arrest of the Patriarch poorly reflected the letter of the law. According to the writer, the conditions surrounding the arrest were that "...one hundred police destroyed [the church] door with trucks, before using

---

646 Misha Kobaladze, "Tbilisi-Paris-Tbilisi French Ambassador Made Foreign Minister." *Ibid.,* 1-2.

647 Jaba Tatishvili, "Religious themes from political angle, Basil Mkalavishvili's arrest following the recommendations of American congressmen." *The Georgian Times* (15 March 2004):3, 4.

648 *Ibid.,* 3; Commission on Security and Cooperation in Europe, http://www.csce.gov/ (as of 25 August 2005).

tear gas and batons in a violent clash with [*Basil Mkalavishvili's*] supporters in the building. Some twenty people, including children were injured." Although *Mkalavishvili* barricaded himself inside the church, it was unclear if the pursuit of other options were considered before selected the more aggressive law enforcement option. NGO's and opposition parties registered their disillusionment with the operation. Previous proselytizations of the Helenski Commission seem fascinating given the context of the U.S. government's behavior with regard to such laws as the Patriot Act in defiance of international norms, due process, and human rights laws. Similarly ironic, is the U.S. maintenance of its lease on Cuban territory of Guantanamo Bay and the continued illegal detention of hundreds of foreign nationals without due process, abuse of prisoners at Abu Gabi and the recent disclosures of secret CIA bases in Europe holding alleged terrorist suspects. Moreover, on November 29[th,] five days following the Rose Revolution, the Justice Minister registered two NGO's, one a subsidiary organization of the Jehovah's witnesses. This registration preceded receipt of a letter from George Soros to the Georgian government recommending the registration of the Jehovah's Witnesses. Subsequently, a conference was held at the *Metechi* Palace on March 16th during which Georgian Orthodox church patriarchs and NGO representatives discussed the Georgian church's role in supporting the law in an attempt to distance itself from *Basil Mkalavishvili's* deviant behavior. [649] Conversely, another article in the weekly newspaper denies that *Mkalavishvili* was a Georgian Orthodox Priest, instead referring to him as the leader of his own religious sect at the *Gldani* Church.[650] Of course Labor Party members, New Rights Party members, and National Independence party members all criticized the government's behavior calling it "barbaric" and "shameful" and in one instance requested the resignation of the Interior Minister and other administrative officials.

As the election approached, journalists continued to focus on the new government's refusal to comply with due process and human rights laws. A number of NGOs complained that since *Saakashvili's* election, an increase in the use of torture and the decline of democratic values has characterized the

---

649 Nino Patsuria, "Orthodoxy and Human Rights." *Georgia Today* (19 March 2004):1, 3.

new administration.[651] *Nana Kakabadze* the leader of the NGO, Former Political Prisoners for Human Rights explained that Georgia incarcerates more political prisoners than its neighbors and that reports of increased instances of police torture have continued. *Kakabadze* also mentioned the increased degree of repression of the free press and limits on freedom of association as other examples of a return to the communist past. She also claimed that seven people are languishing in jail for participating in organized protests, meetings, or demonstrations. Congruent with other criticisms of the party in power, this article also discussed the previously described extradition of five *Chechens*. The author referred to this as problematic because Georgian officials know that these people were likely to be tortured and or illegally executed. Another on-going criticism of the new government included the inexperience of many of the new government cabinet members. These unfavorable views all seem to center around another primary concern, the development of a one party state.[652]

These admonishments seem to be taking place in a vacuum as candidates of the National-Movement Democratic Block continue to expect a parliamentary victory and thus campaign minimally. Expecting a victory with so many non-democratic and unpopular practices seems either horribly naive or extremely savy. Specifically, there may be safety in assuming that no Georgians are reading the print media and this coupled with the fact that the television news has already been suppressed by *Saakashvili*'s new administration leaves his party in the best position for victory. The forthcoming vote will elect one hundred and fifty PMs through proportional representation. Eighty-five previously elected PMS' from the November elections will continue to hold their seats. The Council of Europe continued to argue that the seven percent proportional representation requirement remains too high for a pluralist democracy and that Georgia should set the proportionally requirement at four or five percent. Although their victory seems assured, arguments con-

---

650   Misha Kobaladze, "Basil Mkalavishvili in Jail." *Ibid.*, 2, 5.
651   Jaba Tatishvili, "New Government and old problems in Georgia Today human rights violation is much graver-human rights defenders say." *The Georgian Times* (15 March 2004):4.
652   Revaz Sakerarishvili, "Is Georgia Set to Become One-Party State? Georgia may find itself being governed by one all powerful political party, after forthcoming ballot." *Ibid.*, 17.

tinue inside the government political block over a variety of issues, most recently with regard to the list of candidates. Meanwhile, other critics hope for the break-up of the political block arguing that the result would be a positive outcome for Georgia. Additionally, *Abashidze* continues to threaten nonparticipation in the forthcoming election and if that occurs, it may result in a conflict similar to Georgia's wars with *Ossetia* and *Abkhazia*.

The *Ossetian* conflict and the events preceding it, as well as the election of President *Gamsakhurdia*, a fervent ethnic nationalist is re-visited in a article written by the "Public Movement for a Multinational Georgia and the Georgian Association of *Ossetians* Against the Supreme Court of Georgia."[653] This public statement revealed previously undisclosed information about the events preceding the ethnic conflict. Specifically information included revelations that *Gamsakhurdia* and his followers forced *Ossetians* to leave their homes and appropriated the homes for themselves at gunpoint. In one *Ossetian's* story, the writer disclosed a 2003 Georgian Supreme Court decision stating that these actions were human rights violations. However, the Georgian courts failed to prosecute one perpetrator who stole the home of an *Ossetian* and threatened the family of the rightful owner. Moreover, the public statement also alleged that threats against the *Ossetian* owner continued until in 2001 when the *Ossetian* was murdered. However, no charges were subsequently filed. This is the first mention of any Georgian culpability in the ethnic conflict in a Georgian newspaper article. Unfortunately, the source of this information, an *Ossetian* NGO, may result in Georgian's discounting of the information.

Attributing blame for the separatist wars to the *Ossetians* and the *Abkhazians* is facilitated by the continued references to the first post-Soviet President and this case his son, *Konstantin Gamsakhurdia*, the leader of the New Freedom Party. He recently arrived in *Tbilisi* in late March and spoke to a group of about five hundred supporters.[654] He promised that his party would succeed in the forthcoming election. He retorted that he lived out of Georgia for the last twelve years because *Shevardnadze's* administration would not

---

653   The Public Movement Multinational Georgia and Georgian Association of Ossetians, "We Call for Justice Against the Supreme Court of Georgia." *Ibid.,* 6.

654   Misha Kobaladze, "Gamsakhurdia arrives for victory." *Georgia Today* (19 March 2004):1.

permit the presence of political competitors. However, the writer also reported that *Gamsakhurdia* also had "political refugee" status in Switzerland where he lived since 1992. Even with pressure from the West and the presence of *Gamsakhurdia*, the outcome of the election seems certain. Even as the election approached, journalists continued writing about Georgia as if it were a commodity owned or bought and sold for the benefit of the Western world.

Specifically, on March 18[th,] the third Georgian International Oil (GIOGIE) conference took place in *Tbilisi*. The participants included a variety of oil companies; BP, Chevron Texaco, Georgian Oil, SOCAR (State Oil Company of *Azerbaijan*), *Botas, Kazmunalgaz*, Botax, *Ukrtransnafta*, Marsh, Ernst and Young, AON, McConnell Dowell and interestingly USAID representatives, with delegates from fifteen countries. Announcements include the initiation of the construction of the *Shah-Deniz-Erzerum* pipeline following completion of the BTC pipeline. The presence of these international oil transportation lines reflects that Georgia is becoming an exploited nation, referred to only as a transit corridor between Asia and Europe.[655] Georgia expects to get something from this deal. Apparently, they anticipate collecting about sixty two million dollars in revenue from the BTC pipeline annually.[656] Moreover, the Georgia Today piece reported that a European or an American stated that the *Batumi* Oil Terminal and the *Baku-Batumi* rail transit corridor "are keys to Georgia's economic stability".[657] A more accurate translation might be that they are keys to the continued wealth of western industrialized nation states. BTC representatives also claimed that a number of forthcoming projects will help residents along the pipeline route become fully employed thus improving their social conditions. One of the shareholders in the BTC project is Statoil, a Norwegian company based in Turkey that reportedly produces one million barrels of oil annually. The writer claimed it is the third largest oil company in the world. They are also shareholders in the *Shahdeniz-Tbilisi-Erzerum* pipeline, scheduled to become operational in 2006. The writer tried to frame Georgia as a powerful ally in the world of oil needs and oil companies as opposed to an exploited victim. However, the writer juxtaposed this

---

655   Galina Gotua, "Oil, Gas, Energy and Infrastructure." *Ibid.*, 4.
656   *Ibid.*

by reminding readers that Russia still controls most of Georgia's electricity.[658]Russia's Ministry of Fuel and Energy also participated in the conference and disclosed that Russia's Energy Council wants to help Georgia develop its energy potential by creating a common energy sector for all of the CIS through Georgia. The author argued that Russia feels threatened by Georgia's forthcoming energy independence especially since the Russians are not involved in the BTC or *Shahdeniz-Tbilisi-Erzerum* pipelines. It seems more likely that Russia feels threatened because the West is becoming Georgia's new imperial wizard, rather than Russia.

Other external powers also continued to exert control over Georgia. Specifically, the World Bank provided a sixty million dollar loan to the Georgian Ministry of Education for reform of the Educational system.[659] As mentioned previously, such assistance may ultimately prevent Georgia from finding an internal solution to their financial problems and may facilitate more corruption. While the Georgian government has difficulty in collecting the VAT sales tax, collecting taxes from regional public education institutions may be somewhat less difficult but more harmful. Apparently, when such taxes are collected they reduce the amount of funds delivered to regional public education institutions leading to loses of up to twenty percent of their awarded funds from international loans. As a result, school Principles attempting to utilize their minimal one thousand dollars of grant money end up owing two hundred in government taxes. *Saakashvili's* new arrest campaign against corrupt officials targets these unpaid taxes from the limited grant moneys. The author argued that this is not the battle to fight, as Georgian schools already suffer from serious economic problems. For example, one principle in the *Pankasi* area traveled into *Chechnya* to purchase necessary school materials from the black market in order to avoid the twenty percent VAT. Finally, as mentioned by many other writers throughout this year, tax collectors themselves are a part of the problem as they receive pay-offs for turning the other cheek when businesses fail to pay their twenty-percent. Yet schools are not the only institutions that fail to pay the VAT. The author alleges that even "Big Ben," a European style grocery store where foreign na-

657   *Ibid.*
658   *Ibid.*

tionals and elite Georgians with high incomes buy groceries, also fails to collect the twenty percent VAT sales tax from consumers. However, not collecting the VAT is also problematic because of the number of items bought and sold in the shadow economy where clearly nobody pays taxes.

Many of the items traded in the shadow economy include a variety of counterfeit goods. Perhaps the real issue has less to do with VAT and more to do with economic competition, especially for smaller businesses. Specifically, one writer described the Caucasian Brand Protection Group (BPG) as more concerned about the counterfeit competitors who are avoiding paying the VAT than they are concerned about their large corporate competitors like British American Tobacco, JT International, Nestle, Philip Morris, Procter and Gamble and the *Borjomi* Water Company.[660] Minimal awareness appears to exist here with regard to how difficult it remains for the poor to afford major name brand products or to pay the twenty percent VAT. The author even quoted the General Manager of Nestle and the President of BPG Mr. Esben Emborg, who explained counterfeit products will "Kill Georgian Business." I argue that Georgian business already may be dead, murdered by economic globalization and transnational corporations.

The central issues revolving around Georgia's economic collapse since the disintegration of the Soviet Union may not be as complex as they are difficult to measure. Moreover, it remains difficult to collect accurate empirical data with regard to these issues for a variety of reasons. One difficulty remains the absence of a reliable census and although the most recently collected census was administered in 2002, the data remain viewed as unreliable. However, census data collected prior to 2002 only occurred twice previously, in 1989 and in 1897, both also considered somewhat unreliable.[661] Additionally, with so few measurement periods as well as unreliable methodologies, it is difficult to understand comprehensive migration or economic patterns. While census taking in western democratic nation states remains imperfect, their methodologies have improved over time and certainly remain more reliable that that collected in FSU. Specifically, the west's ability to scientifically understand and explain poverty, economic crime, street crime, and

---

659   Anthony Schierman, "Educational Reform, Taxes, and Corruption." *Ibid.*, 5.
660   Nino Patsuria, "BPG Steps Up." *Ibid.*, 4.

general demographic trends including migration patterns has improved significantly over the last twenty years. However, also Georgia's 2002 census was a significant improvement over previous data collection efforts. The State Department of Georgian Statistics conducted the census and employed twenty-four thousand people in its administration. In order to complete the census, Georgia received approximately thirty percent of its funding from the United Nations, Germany, the Netherlands, and the United Kingdom. In light of Georgia's on-going economic problems, the population has decreased by sixteen percent since 1989. Moreover, fifty-two percent of residents live in urban areas, compared to fifty-five percent in 1989. Fifty three percent of Georgians are women. Surprisingly, the data reveal that there are over one-hundred and twenty ethnic groups living in Georgia, even though nationalistic rhetoric would have Georgian residents believing otherwise. Nevertheless, in 2002, almost eighty-four percent of the population identified themselves as Georgians compared to only seventy percent in 1989. Almost six percent are Armenians, six and half percent Azeris, one and half percent Russian, with Ossetians, Abkhazians, Greeks, Jews, Ukrainians, and others making up 1% to .9%. However, rumors circulate that even these statistics are unreliable due to excessive sampling error. Readers can access census data from Georgian government web page in English or Georgian at www.statistics.ge.[662] Doing effective and efficientl science, should improve when higher education improves. This is an institution in desperate need of reform and money.

Education thus far does not seem to be high on President *Saakashvili's* agenda as he continues his crackdown on crime. The most recent arrest was of an alleged organized criminal group (not suspected group) in the village of *Eceri* within the *Metia* Region. [663] The press referred to the gang as the "*Aprasidze* Clan," all blood-related individuals. The Ministry of Internal Affairs and the Anti-Terrorist Center of the Ministry of Security made the arrests. The President referred to the group as "a private army" and explained that with the group gone, the area could become a tourism destination. Of course, this

---

661   Mariam Kobaladze, "General Population Census of 2002." *Ibid.*
662   http://www.statistics.ge /index_eng.htm (as of 1 September 2005).
663   N.N., "Law Enforcement Agents Raid on Aprasidze's Clan." Rustavi 2 on line news http://www.rustavi2.com.ge/view.php?id=7045 (as of 30 March 2004).

remains unlikely with a minimal tourism budget. Another one of this group of criminal arrestees included, *Vkhtang Kipiani*, accused of "murder, drug addiction, and carrying unlicensed guns". *Saakashvili* claimed the previous administration supported this particular 'criminal'.[664] *Kipiani* later received a sentence of three months pre-trial detention.[665]

The substantive test of *Saakashvili's* commitment to rid of Georgia of fraud and corruption began on the day of the election. However, media attention remained singularly focused on election processes in *Adjara,* not in Georgia proper. By the early evening hours, the CEC Chair claimed observers reported serious voting irregularities in *Adjara.* Moreover, an attack on the headquarters of an *Adjaran* precinct occurred, allegedly perpetrated by *Abashidze's* forces. In another location, disorder prevented the election process from continuing unabated and in a forth location voters were intimidated and prevented from casting their ballots.[666] Additionally, busloads of people were transported to unauthorized precincts, where they voted illegally. Observers also witnessed ballot box stuffing at another precinct location. While the headline of this piece suggested that elsewhere in Georgia the voting process remained problem free, reports of other violations came from all over the country. However, the writer claimed that those in *Adjara* were the most serious. These violations included voting without presenting identification, attempted ballot box stuffing, and multiple voting, as well as failing to remove campaign posters from precinct poles. Furthermore, one assault on an observer also transpired in the *Khelvachauri* district in *Adjara.* Yet on the same page, despite these voting irregularities, another Messenger journalist prematurely stated that *Mikhail Saakashvili's* party won the Sunday elections.[667] As the administration attended to the possibility of fraud in *Adjara,* the President sent the Prime Minister and other administration officials to *Adjara* to observe the election in hopes of deterring further instances of fraud. The

---

664   N.N., "President Referred to Anticrime Operation in Mestia Region." *Ibid.,* http://www.rustavi2.com.ge/view.php?id=7051.

665   N.N., "Kipiani Sentenced to Pre-Trial Detention." *Ibid.,* http://www.rustavi2.com.ge/view.php?id=7052.

666   Sopho Gorgodze, "CEC casts heavy doubt on Adjara. Voting goes smoothly across the country." *The Messenger* (29 March 2004):1, 9.

667   Anna Arzanova, "Adjara under the magnifying glass." *The Messenger* (29 March 2004):1, 12.

writer reported that the President threatened consequences for fraudulent election procedures after receiving information that *Adjaran* forces planned to disrupt mobile phone service in order to prevent the reporting of violations by election observers'. Unfortunately, some of these efforts to block mobile signals were partially successful. The U.S. Ambassador, Richard Miles met with *Abashidze* on Friday before the Sunday vote and commented that the U.S. only wants *Tbilisi* and *Adjara* to settle their conflicts. However, Miles reported that he would use his "influence to regulate the situation in Georgia".[668] *Abashidze* accused *Zhvania* of involvement in previous fraudulent elections, as he tried to dismiss the presence of government observers in *Adjara*. *Abashidze* also disclosed his concerns that the central government will try to depose him following the election and retorted that this would provide evidence of Georgia's receipt of support from the United States. *Abashidze* also accused international organizations of plotting his demise. The framing of the elections as only problematic in *Adjara* leaves readers feeling more optimistic about the remainder of Georgia. However, the social constructions omitted information disclosed in other articles that voter turnout in *Tbilisi* remained low, especially when compared with the high turn out in the January presidential election. The constitution necessitates that unless thirty-three percent of voters vote the election results are invalid. The writers reported that interviewes with voters about their decisions after exiting the polls revealed that most people reported voting for the Nationalist Block, a small majority also indicated that they marked out their ballots in protest.

Interestingly, the *Georgian Times* fails to mention the parliamentary election on the front page but rather reserves front-page headlines for a lengthy diatribe about the life of the late first freely elected President of Georgia, *Zviad Gamsakhurdia* and the possibility of building a tomb in his memory. This reflects an interesting celebration of nationalism coinciding with the apparent parliamentary victory of the Nationalist Block.[669] Only as a sideline, this newspaper writer reported that unofficial results of the election reflected that *Saakashvili's* party won over seventy-five percent of the vote and that if

668   *Ibid.*
669   Radio Free Europe, "Georgian Times President Appears to Win Parliamentary Election." *The Georgian Times* (29 March 2004):3; N.N., "Zviad Gamsakhurdia. Georgia Seeks to Honor Deceased Former President." *Ibid.,* 1.

this continued the entire one-hundred and fifty parliamentary seats up for grab would be occupied by the Nationalist party block. The other eighty-five seats remained valid from the previously uncontested part of the parliamentary election in November. The writer also reiterated the previous review of voter fraud as well as destruction of property in *Adjara*. The journalist further reported that *Abashidze* continued to control local armed militias and that he is refusing to disarm them. Although *Abashidze* finally agreed to allow oppositional parties to campaign in the area, only fourteen parties campaigned for seats in *Adjara*.

The victory of the Nationalist Party remains cautionary for at least two reasons. First, while fifty-eight percent of Georgians of voting age were women, only six percent of those running for the parliament were women. This social fact remains ominous considering my observations of the large proportion of Georgian women active in civil society that far outnumbers men.[670] A recent seminar, sponsored by the Gender and Media Component Project (Gender Media Caucasus) funded by the United Nation's Development Program, addressed this absence of gender representation They sponsored talk shows and newspaper articles to discuss the issue and raise awareness about gender related issues. The director made it clear that the neglect of women's rights in Georgia is problematic. However, even this piece utilized nationalist rhetoric by referring to the strength of Georgian women as reflected in Queen *Tamara*, usually referred to as such a great leader that she should be called 'King *Tamara*'. Moreover, the person who brought Christianity to Georgia, the former slave and later Saint Nino, was utilized an example of women's strength and contributions to Georgian society. The project director addressed women's reluctance to speak their voices as the result of their domination through physical violence perpetrated by their male partners in conjunction with other forms of subordination such as institutional discrimination. bell hooks and Patrician Hill Collins, both black feminist writers and theorists in America, refer to this discriminatory and re-

---

670   Rusudan Klilashvili, "58 percent of voters are women in Georgia but only 6 percent appears on the ballot lists Perfect democracy is hard to observe in a similarly un-balanced gender environment." *Ibid.*, 4.

pressive process as the triple matrix of oppression.[671] The term refers to the third class citizenship of poor, ethnic minority women in America who remain triply discriminated against as they occupy three devalued and powerless positions, class, gender, and race or ethnic membership. Georgians need a feminist social movement that can address the multiplicity of forms of domination and subordination of Georgian women, the poor and ethnic minorities.

In another interesting analysis of the election especially when compared to the November elections in central Georgia, one journalist called them "bizarre." [672] The writer observed that *Saakashvili's* administration silenced the voices of competing political parties by preventing the airing of political talk show television broadcasts over the last two months. Moreover, other political parties made no efforts to replace November's political posters that littered telephone posts and walls prior to the first parliamentary election. Additionally, the head of the Council of Europe's Parliamentary Assembly (PACE) reported disappointment with the Georgian administration's refusal to adjust the proportional election threshold from seven percent to five percent. Finally, the Center for Sociological Research and Marketing surveyed one thousand and four hundred and sixteen Georgians across the country from 18-23 March, querying their voting intentions. Ninety percent surveyed reported that they would vote and seventy-three percent reported supporting the Nationalists. Two percent intended to vote for *Konstantine Gamsakhurdia's* party, Freedom, while only three and half percent support *Abashidze's* party. Three percent supported the Labor Party, three percent the Rightists, and ten percent would not answer the question. Approximately three percent intended to nullify their vote. The survey also asked people to indicate who they believed was responsible for the recent stand off between *Abashidze* and the central government. Fifty-six percent believed that the *Abashidze* was responsible, 4 percent thought *Saakashvili* was at fault, and seventeen percent blamed Russia. Only six percent believed that both sides were party responsible for the crisis. Forty-nine percent surveyed also be-

---

671   bell hooks, *Feminist Theory: From Margin to Center*, 2nd edn (Cambridge, MA: South End Press, 2000); Patricia Hill Collins, *Black Feminist Thought: Knowledge, Consciousness and the Politics of Empowerment Perspectives on Gender.* (New York: Routledge, 2000).

lieved that *Abashidze* should follow the lead of the central government while twenty-six percent wanted him to resign. Finally, when Georgians were queried about the consequences of potentially falsified votes in *Adjara*, over half believed that the central government should protest such behavior or file a lawsuit. However, about one quarter of the respondents refused to answer the question.

While election processes remain the center of media attention, one journalist reviewed the status of *Saakashvili's* first arrestee, the son in law of former President *Shevardnadze, Gia Jokhtaberidze*, who remains in prison.[673] At a press conference, *Jokhtaberidze's* new American Lawyer revealed that threats against Jokhtaberidze occurred before he sold his shares in *Magticom*. According to his lawyer, the threat came from someone known to him who also claimed a plan existed to murder *Jokhtaberidze* during his incarceration. *Jokhtaberidze* recently initiated a hunger strike in protest of what he calls his illegal detention. He and his wife as well as his lawyer argued that the charges against him are false and that the threats against his life are coming from a specific group that they will later reveal. He explained everyone "knows" who they are". The implication is that the threat comes from the new government, the Nationalist Party.

---

672   Jaba Tatishvili, "Bizarre general elections in Georgia." *The Georgian Times* (29 March 2004):4.
673   Lali Javakhia, "Ex-President's son-in-law faces threat of murder. Who wants to seize *Magticom* shares?" *Ibid.*, 6.

IV   Conclusion

Two days before Georgia's historic parliamentary election, the first instance of any reference to Joseph Stalin's genocidal campaign appeared in print, although the author was not a Georgian.[674] The first sentence stated that 1.3 million died in Stalin's purges. The evidence evolved from ten years of research sponsored by the Russian Presidential Commission and the *Andrei Sakharov* Museum. Their goal was to rehabilitate the victims of political repression. A CD Rom publication developed from this work, listing the names of Stalin's victims. The foundation, Open Russia, also sponsored the project with funding from the jailed Russian businessman, *Mikhail Khodorkovsky*. This project led to the inception of two others resulting in the release of over 600,000 victims' names. The Memorial director of the *Sakharov* Museum, *Arseny Roginsky* revealed that the number of names published so far only "scratches the surface of political repression in the Soviet Union."[675] He also believed that ten times that many people probably died during Stalin's purges. Alexander *Yakovlev*, head of the Presidential commission indicated that Russian federal authorities are not "devoting enough attention to the rehabilitation of repression victims" while the head of the Russian Federal Service Bureau, the new version of the former KGB, claimed that they have cooperated with the project, "for the most part." The CD Rom contains photos and personal stories of life in the gulags as well as other repression related government literature. The Presidential Commission representative argued that they have not granted anyone permission to search through the archives. However, a number of other researchers explain that they have done just that. *Yakovlev* disclosed that scholars estimate twenty million people perished during Stalin's era. As mentioned previously, this information appears absent from institutionalized Georgian memory. Interested readers should make note of Anne Applebaum's Pulitzer Prize winning historiography "Gu-

---

674   Carl Schreck, "List of Stalin's Victims on CD-Rom." *Georgia Today* (26 March 2004):8.
675   *Ibid.*

lag-A History."[676] She mentioned the Memorial Society in Moscow and the *Sakharov* Institute as well as other societies and museums across the former Soviet Union dedicated to revealing historical abuses. Georgia needs a similar museum. She accessed their collected repositories as well as recent memoirs and soviet archives including Stalin's special archive and records of Party meetings in writing her book. Her account is harrowing and reminds me of how little Georgian politics seems to have changed since the disintegration of the Soviet Union. For example, the March election resulted in only two political parties earning the required seven percent of the votes for parliamentary seats, the National Democratic Movement with sixty seven percent of the votes and the Industrialists and New Rights block with almost eight percent of the votes.[677] However, at least one other political party exists in the Parliament in addition to the Nationalist block.

This narrative analysis illustrates the difficulties Georgia continues to have in making the transition from a state run economy to capitalism as well as from a totalitarian government to a democracy. However, the results of this research also reveal how difficult it remains for Georgians who can afford newspapers to find any objective truth about daily, political, social, and economic events. While this work would not have been possible except for the willingness of Georgian journalists to write about some objective truths as well as subjective truths, it remains difficult to disentangle one from the other. It also remains apparent that the marketing of Georgian newspapers, both the presentation and content is highly nationalistic and only occasionally objective, while often giving voice to the anger, angst, and the sometimes naïve hopes and dreams of the Georgian people. In the midst of this chaos, I never ceased to be amazed at the Georgian propensity for kindness and for humor as they lived daily lives fraught with political corruption, economic deprivation, and a tattered infrastructure. As I close this project over two and half years in the making I feel much less optimistic than I did when Georgians first went to the streets in protest in November of 2003. While many things remain unchanged, some movement toward change has transpired. First in May of 2004, *Saakashvili* managed to orchestrate *Aslan Abashidze's* resignation

---

676   Anne Applebaum, *Gulag A History* (Penguin Press 2003 and Anchor Books Published in the United States of America, 2004).

even though fears of military confrontation loomed on the horizon before he surprisingly stepped down. In November 2004, the IDPs living in the *Tbilisi Iveria* hotel were re-located. However, it remains unclear if they were re-located to better housing or not. Moreover, the building's status remained disputed as some wanted to preserve it as a historic site while others preferred demolishing it. Unfortunately, several spates of military fighting between the autonomous region of Ossetia and Georgia occurred in 2004 and continued off and on through 2006 as I wrote this last chapter.

Interestingly, in the winter and spring of 2004-2005 the Ukrainian Orange Revolution, almost a mirror reflection of Georgia's Rose Revolution, occurred. Similar, to Georgia's revolution, it originated out of Russia's political support, this time for a candidate they openly endorsed. However, the difference here was that the oppositional candidate, *Victor Ushchenko* was poisoned. While the motive was murder, *Ushchneko* survived to build the revolution. The Ukrainians mounted the Orange Revolution protesting against a fraudulent election backed by Russia. This revolution too had support from a variety of Western financial institutions and a student movement given the same training as *Kmara* by former students of Otpor from Serbia. While their revolution was successful, *Ushchenko* has already fired two cabinets in his fight to end corruption and cronyism.

Sadly, in March of 2005, Prime Minister *Zurab Zhvania* died in what was eventually determined to be an accidental natural gas leak in the *Tbilisi* apartment of a friend. I was surprised and initially suspicious of foul play, but apparently, such things occur periodically as the result of the mismanaged maintenance and poor condition of gas lines across the country.

President George W. Bush visited *Tbilisi* in the spring of 2005. Prior to his arrival President *Saakashvili* suddenly initiated a brief spate of road repair projects, at least in the sections of the city that Bush was likely to see. Subsequently, the discovery of a live explosive device planted near the podium where Bush stood in what was supposed to be a secure area were revealed (enclosed by bulletproof glass). The dismantling of the bomb occurred without incident. It is unclear what motivated the act but it could have been an at-

---

677   Zaza Jgharkava, "Only Two in Parliament." *Georgia Today* (2 April 2004):12.

tempt to make a statement about Georgia's new symbiotic relationship with America.

The TBC pipeline officially opened in May of 2005. It remains questionable as to how or when this may actually benefit ordinary Georgians. Moreover, my colleagues tell me that *Tbilisi* State University is in transition as departmental faculty are re-assigned released and re-shuffled in an attempt to end corruption and improve the efficiency and credibility of higher education across Georgia.

Most tragically is that since March of 2004, the new government continues to be criticized for a variety of usurpations of the free press, human rights violations of jail detainees and prison inmates and a one party government. However, in August of 2005, *American National Public Radio* aired a number of positive reports about the improvement in professionalism and decreasing amount of corruption among police and border guards as the result of improvements in training and salaries.

In even more good news, Russia has promised to close all of its remaining bases in Georgia by 2008. As some based have already closed, many have become American-Georgian ant-terrorism posts. As I have argued throughout the book such a move simply exchanges one powerful neo-colonial force for another, neither of whom have ever really been very interested in Georgians' welfare. Even more recently, as I understand it, Americans no longer need Visas when entering the country. It is beginning to look more like an American colony.

While these newspapers in Georgia represent the free press, they are certainly not detailed, nor always truthful nor completely accurate or unbiased. However, I certainly cannot argue that American newspapers or television are unbiased or objective either as I have mentioned previously, American newspapers and television stations are owned by large transnational corporations that clearly have an interest in maintaining the status quo. Even more frightening, some of these same companies own some Georgian media outlets. It remains impossible for citizens to function effectively in any democracy without accurate, reliable freedom of information. Some Georgian writers seem to be better at reporting facts while others seem to obfuscate the truth with maximum editorializing characterized by little investigative work. Georgian newspaper journalists like their counterparts in the United States also seem to feed on sensationalistic non-professional appeals to emotions and sentiment. Moreover, Georgians without the financial ability to purchase and read a variety of different accounts as I did here may never really know what is going on in their society. Georgian citizens need an objective truth, not nationalistic emotional based rhetoric. Rather these citizens, like Americans who only watch television news, may both begin to believe the nationalistic distortions and social constructions offered by the writers and their corporate moguls (in the U.S.) or their politicians and oligarchs (in Georgia).

This phenomenon transpiring across Georgia and other post-soviet nations, as well as across the developing world are reflections of the movement of industrialized democracies toward transnational corporate ownership. This includes outside ownership of media outlets, an elitist government, rising economic inequality and free trade run and managed by a small elite group of European and Americans ideologues whose own power and bank-accounts grow faster than the rest of us can begin to imagine. Other narrative analyses of newspapers and media outlets across post-soviet space have identified similar dynamics.[678]

While U.S. television media provide similar distortions of politics and crime, they completely omit the problem of public corruption. Specifically, across the U.S. in 2004, over one thousand convictions of government officials occurred for bribery. The media only occasionally calls attention to these events in the U.S. however, then it only perceived as a scandal rather than as an event structured by the nature of the post-capitalist political economy. Similarly, the same kind of nationalistic rhetoric promoted in Georgian papers also occurs across the United States, particularly within the U.S. television news coverage. Certainly, in both nations' television media coverage of news, discerning truth from fiction or myth is sometimes difficult. If Georgians become more skilled at differentiating truth from fiction, it could be the country's most important asset as it grows and develops over the course of the next several decades. For Americans the solution revolves more around becoming less interesting in making money and more interested in protecting

---

678   Stephen Kotkin and Andras Sajo, *Political Corruption in Transition: A Skeptic's Handbook* (Budapest: Central European University Press, 2002).

the first amendment. Of course, in Georgia eliminating attempts by whatever party holds political power to obfuscate or suppress the truth must also end before any independent media will be able to fully mature.

In addition to attempts to control the media, the use of corruption as a political tool in post-soviet societies must end. Corruption has become a tool welded within Georgian politics to disparage the competition as often as U.S. politicians use street crime rhetoric to beat the competition. Both become fodder to de-legitimize a politician or a political party in power or remove them as potential threats to power. In fact, the use of the idea of corruption in political and media discourse across the former Soviet Union remains more pronounced in some instances than the actual prevalence of corruption. While Americans deny the pervasiveness of the problem of corruption and corporate collusion in it, American, politicians and the media similarly exploit our own version of ethnic nationalism through the promotion of the idea that street crime is a minority problem, and more recently with the use of similar rhetoric about the 'war on terrors'. These alleged American social problems take up as much social space as does the battle between the corrupt and the non-corrupt across Georgia. The discourse about crime and corruption in the Georgian media is easily comparable to the discourse on crime and politics in the United States media. In both places the media have allowed themselves to become exploited as political weapons rather than reflecting our human and civil right to be informed of relevant social, economic, and political issues in order to further support democratic and civic development.

A variety of other scholarly work reveals that corruption and organized crime are not unique to post-communist states or post-colonial nation states although its etiology varies considerably cross-nationally.[679] Sometimes it remains true, as Kotkin and Sajo argue, that political corruption has become a stereotype in Eastern Europe often used against political opponents to gain a public advantage.[680] They also argue that the West uses corruption as method of criticizing post-Soviet nation states in order to bid them to do their will. This truth resonates throughout this narrative analysis particularly with regard to the international financial assistance provided to Georgia that could

---

679   Mark Galeotti, "Inside the Russian Mafiya." In: *Idem*, ed., *Russian and Post-Soviet Organized Crime* (Burlington, VT: Ashgate, 2002), 23.

eventually result in cutting off the struggling nation at its own knees and encouraging corruption rather than prohibiting it.

Money flows into Georgia for the purposes of assistance while numerous transnational corporations take business away from local Georgians and enrich their already deep international corporate pockets. Cross-national research also shows that economic inequality explains corruption and that these effects are greater in non-democratic countries, particularly among nation-states with socialist or communist origins.[681] Therefore, as transnational corporations and the wealthy nation-states that control global trade continue to usurp indigenous economic growth they create or maintain the inequality that continuously reproduces the corruption they criticize. Moreover, media coverage of corruption and criticisms of the government, whatever political party remains in power, will only increase Georgian's anger and angst.[682] The media must address Georgia's other salient problems, ethnic-nationalism, the accurate history of the nation, the poverty of their people, women's issues, child abuse, educational reform, the elimination of corruption and the reduction of violence in the home. Of course, they must also cover Georgian successes to provide hope to the masses. Only then, will Georgians become empowered rather than overwhelmed with powerful feelings of anger, pain, and hopelessness.

In the midst of all these social, economic, and political problems, Georgians' retain an amazing ability to laugh and experience joy. Their resilience in the face of so many problems continues to amaze me. These qualities have motivated me to tell their story. Their voices resonate throughout this book, through the words of the Georgian journalists. The Georgian people transformed my thinking about poverty, crime, the developing world, and my own western privilege. I close this feeling frightened for all our futures, for all the citizens of world, as transnational corporate growth exceeds nations' wealth, and profit and control of other nations and peoples seems to become more important than the quality of human life. Even more disturbing remains

680   Kotkin and Sajo, *Political Corruption in Transition.*
681   You Jong-sung, Sanjeev Khagram, "A Comparative Study of Inequality and Corruption." *American Sociological Review* 70 (February 2005):136-157.

the reality that the media is not telling this story but rather is creating our social reality.

As Weitzer and Kubrin argue, the creation of public perceptions develop as the result of the distortions provided in the media, both in entertainment television and in alleged news programming. Georgia's media representations also similarly create or skew Georgian perceptions. For example, I watched my Georgian friends and colleagues fears grow more pronounced throughout the protests in November. These times were extremely frightening to those who previously experienced protests that resulted in violent government repression. Local television coverage was ongoing every minute of every day. Clearly, media reform is necessary both in Georgia and across the globe to better empower and inform all of us. Only a critical and pluralistic media will facilitate change socially, politically, and economically and in a more institutionalized and profound ways than just changing Presidents or political parties. It is clearly apparent that party and personnel changes are often superficial rather than transformative. Decreasing corruption will require increasing Georgians' standard of living and improving the quality of the information they receive through public education and media reform.[683] While some authors also claim that greater trade openness and less economic regulation of economic activity will reduce corruption, I would contend the opposite is true. Some scholars argue that elected and career officials are all corruptible, making it a core assumption of their theoretical model. Thus, they argue that when any party or organization monopolizes political power, corruption will occur as the power holders begin to fear the loss of their own control. In other words, when *Saakashvili's* party gained most of the parliamentary seats, he sealed his party's own fate of continuing to make the same mistakes as his predecessors.

Ultimately, neo-colonial political interference in Georgia's economy and political infrastructure must end. This will reduce some corruption in politics. Moreover, creating jobs will improve income and reduce economic inequality.

---

682   Ronald Weitzer and Charis E. Kubrin, "Breaking News: How Local TV News and Real-World Conditions Affect Fear of Crime." *Justice Quarterly* 21:3 (September 2004):497-520.

Lifting parliamentarians' immunity from prosecution is also a necessity. The pursuit of education reform is underway however, whether or not the product will be an improvement remains unknown. Additionally, the IDP's and ethnic minorities must have adequate housing and jobs. In the end, Georgians also may have to let go of territorial re-integration or at least grieve their losses for now and only hope for a long-term resolution in the distant future. Moreover, politicians and elite bourgeoisie capitalists must cease exchanging roles. This must become a reality in my home country and others if we are to prevent a global political and economic collapse.

All these socio-political and economic dynamics at the national and international level must become a part of criminological theorizing in order to assist in eliminating our most serious problems. Georgia's recent experience provides a more comprehensive approach to understanding the context of crime given a nation's history and the development of a national consciousness or national identity. More specifically, the manner in which the history of a nation becomes framed and generally accepted affects the criminal landscape. For example, while many Georgian journalists attribute the organized crime problem to the Russians and their exploitation by Russian throughout the Soviet Period; contrary evidence disputes that argument. Louise Shelley argues that the most powerful of the organized criminal underworld throughout the Soviet period grew out of Georgia in the mid-1970s.[684] They controlled the shadow economy throughout the Soviet Union. At that time, their perception of themselves resembled the notion of a Soviet version of Robin Hood, resisting the oppressive state and giving the people the things they needed.

Shelley also suggests that these criminal organizations mediated conflicts and provided safety and security otherwise unavailable to many Soviet citizens. In Russia, organized criminal groups often still provide these services. However, even more fascinating is Shelley's claim that half of all the identified thieves in law 'vory v zakone' were Georgians. Moreover, he reports that a Georgian, *Dzaba Ioselani,* a former inmate who spent many years in

---

683   Alok K. Bohara, Neil J. Mitchell, and Carl F. Mittendorff, "Compound Democracy and the Control of Corruption: A Cross Country Investigation." *The Policy Studies Journal* 32:4 (2004):481-499.

684   Shelley, "Organized Crime Groups: 'Uncivil Society.'"

the Gulag, began to preside over the criminal world in 1982 following the death of Brezhnev. It was at this time that the Georgian thieves-in law became more involved in politics and the legitimate economy. *Ioselani* held a position in the parliament after Georgia's independence from 1992-1995. Later Shelley claimed *Ioselani* became the 'right hand man of President *Shevardnadze*'. *Saakashvili's* allegations associating *Shevardnadze* with organized criminal groups during the Rose Revolution were apparently valid. However, it was *Ioselani* who proposed and helped institutionalize the relationship between the polity and organized criminals. Of course, *Ioselani* died in 2003, the year of the Rose Revolution.

If Shelley's claims are correct and Georgia as a criminal state has existed for over thirty years, one new administration is unlikely to change this. While it seems the real Georgian national identity is a criminal identity, the nations' perceived identity provides the primary impetus of all behaviour at the institutional level and individual level. Perceived identities might include the nation as a hero, a victim, an island, a proud warrior, or the chosen people. I argue that such identities motivate all behaviour, normative or deviant. This perceived core of national identity is central to the nature of the unique crimes that characterize each nation's government and economy. In Georgia, the perceived identity seems to be that of victim, and it is this perception that continues to motivate corruption, bribery and organized crime as well as the types of crimes individual citizens commit.

In comparison, the genocide of the Native Americans by Western European settlers in the United States helped to form the core of American identity. Perhaps, this factor constitutes the reason for the high murder rate that plagues the United States. This American identity remains characterized by an attitude of superiority, a sort of global elitism. Moreover, the United States' official ideology, the notion of democracy and freedom for all, was obviously a smokescreen in the context of the exploitation of African Slaves, disenfranchisement of all people of colour and women as well as the injustices that continue against these groups today. That false ideology, moreover, continues to inform military-industrial expansion and justifies the United States' infringement of the rights of other nations and peoples.

In contrast, Georgia's history remains characterized by victimization at the hands of many of its larger neighbours to the North, South and East. As it sees itself only as a victim, it becomes easy to avoid seeing itself as the perpetrator of any type of injustice. More recently, the core of Georgia's national identity revolves around its victimization by Russia. Georgia's identity also seems to be focused on fear and suspicion of bigger, powerful others, so much so that it often misses the forest for the trees: Georgians believe that only Russia can hurt them, nobody else will do so. Similarly, they certainly deny their own history of involvement in Soviet and Post-Soviet organized crime. A Soviet ministry of Internal Affairs report in the early 1990s revealed that three hundred and thirty nine thieves in law functioned at the top of the organized crime hierarchy across the Soviet republics. Thirty one percent of these crime bosses were Georgian while thirty-three percent were Russian. Perhaps this on-going criminal competition fuels the antagonism between Russians and Georgians increasing their mutual hatred and distrust. Georgian denial of their own role in perpetrating crime and in the heinous results of the Communist revolution and Stalin's purges leads to their projection of the role of perpetrator onto other nations or groups, particularly those groups or nations perceived as most unlike Georgians, i.e. Russians. Georgians' inability to perceive themselves honestly may lead to the disintegration of their nation-state. Perhaps more importantly as Shelley reveals, Georgian and Russian organized groups continue to cooperate and profit within the conflict zones in Georgia, hampering the political will to resolve any disputes.

National denial of historical facts as well as socio-political and economic motives will result in the disintegration of the modern world and the devastation of nation-states. Only recognizing and embracing historical and concurrent truths will end this acting out behavior and facilitate change in national identity and subsequent behavior across the globe. This kind of transformation will facilitate a decrease in crime and corruption and perhaps the birth of social altruism. The impetus for such social change is a free, critical, independent, and unbiased media. Without such a force for change all nations will remain plagued by crime, murder, corruption, bribery, war, and probably, crisis after crisis. I hope my country and Georgia can both achieve such transformations in the future.

Illustrations

1   The Iveria Hotel is located in downtown Tbilisi and is one of many
     homes of Internally Displaced Georgians.

2   Reflecting Georgia's lack of control over their own economy as well as the effects of economic globalization, the billboard advertisement stands at the airport just as passengers board their flights to leave *Tbilisi*.

3   Dilapidated exterior of an apartment building in the outskirts of Tbilisi
where Internally Displaced families' live.

4   This political advertisement was located on the main street in downtown
     Tbilisi before the November elections. It tells potential voters that
     choosing Burjanadze and or her party as Parliamentarians will result in
     a better economy and more jobs.

5   A crowd gathers listening to a political speech in downtown Tbilisi before the November elections. The sign read "Burjanadze Democrats
Tbilisi's Electoral Headquarters." *Burjanadze* and *Zurabshivili* are
standing near the podium.

6   This resembles the conditions of many Tbilisi buildings remaining from
     the Soviet era or earlier with poor foundations receiving little or no
     maintenance.

7   An old woman waits for change on the street in Tbilisi by the entrance
of a Russian Orthodox Church.

8   This illustrates the poor condition of the floor in one of the buildings where IDP children attend school in *Tbilisi*.

9   The demonstrators in front of the Parliament building in mid-November with the Nationalist party flag seen in the foreground.

10   The new Georgian national flag standing in front of the monument to Soldiers killed during Georgia's nationalist conflict in the 1990's.

Dr. Andreas Umland (Ed.)

SOVIET AND POST-SOVIET POLITICS AND SOCIETY

ISSN 1614-3515

This book series makes available, to the academic community and general public, affordable English-, German- and Russian-language scholarly studies of various *empirical* aspects of the recent history and current affairs of the former Soviet bloc. The series features narrowly focused research on a variety of phenomena in Central and Eastern Europe as well as Central Asia and the Caucasus. It highlights, in particular, so far understudied aspects of late Tsarist, Soviet, and post-Soviet political, social, economic and cultural history from 1905 until today. Topics covered within this focus are, among others, political extremism, the history of ideas, religious affairs, higher education, and human rights protection. In addition, the series covers selected aspects of post-Soviet transitions such as economic crisis, civil society formation, and constitutional reform.

SOVIET AND POST-SOVIET POLITICS AND SOCIETY

Edited by Dr. Andreas Umland

ISSN 1614-3515

9   *Алексей Юрьевич Безугольный*
     Народы Кавказа в Вооруженных силах СССР в годы Великой Отечественной войны
     1941-1945 гг.
     С предисловием Николая Бугая
     ISBN 3-89821-475-3

10   *Вячеслав Лихачев и Владимир Прибыловский (ред.)*
     Русское Национальное Единство, 1990-2000. В 2-х томах
     ISBN 3-89821-523-7

11   *Николай Бугай (ред.)*
     Народы стран Балтии в условиях сталинизма (1940-е – 1950-е годы)
     Документированная история
     ISBN 3-89821-525-3

12   *Ingmar Bredies (Hrsg.)*
     Zur Anatomie der Orange Revolution in der Ukraine
     Wechsel des Elitenregimes oder Triumph des Parlamentarismus?
     ISBN 3-89821-524-5

13   *Anastasia V. Mitrofanova*
     The Politicization of Russian Orthodoxy
     Actors and Ideas
     With a foreword by William C. Gay
     ISBN 3-89821-481-8

14   *Nathan D. Larson*
     Alexander Solzhenitsyn and the Russo-Jewish Question
     ISBN 3-89821-483-4

15   *Guido Houben*
     Kulturpolitik und Ethnizität
     Staatliche Kunstförderung im Russland der neunziger Jahre
     Mit einem Vorwort von Gert Weisskirchen
     ISBN 3-89821-542-3

16   *Leonid Luks*
     Der russische „Sonderweg"?
     Aufsätze zur neuesten Geschichte Russlands im europäischen Kontext
     ISBN 3-89821-496-6

17   *Евгений Мороз*
     История «Мёртвой воды» – от страшной сказки к большой политике
     Политическое неоязычество в постсоветской России
     ISBN 3-89821-551-2

18   *Александр Верховский и Галина Кожевникова (ред.)*
     Этническая и религиозная интолерантность в российских СМИ
     Результаты мониторинга 2001-2004 гг.
     ISBN 3-89821-569-5

19   *Christian Ganzer*
     Sowjetisches Erbe und ukrainische Nation
     Das Museum der Geschichte des Zaporoger Kosakentums auf der Insel Chortycja
     Mit einem Vorwort von Frank Golczewski
     ISBN 3-89821-504-0

29   *Florian Strasser*
      Zivilgesellschaftliche Einflüsse auf die Orange Revolution
      Die gewaltlose Massenbewegung und die ukrainische Wahlkrise 2004
      Mit einem Vorwort von Egbert Jahn
      ISBN 3-89821-648-9

30   *Rebecca S. Katz*
      The Georgian Regime Crisis of 2003-2004
      A Case Study in Post-Soviet Media Representation of Politics, Crime and Corruption
      ISBN 3-89821-413-3

31   *Vladimir Kantor*
      Willkür oder Freiheit
      Beiträge zur russischen Geschichtsphilosophie
      Ediert von Dagmar Herrmann sowie mit einem Vorwort versehen von Leonid Luks
      ISBN 3-89821-589-X

32   *Laura A. Victoir*
      The Russian Land Estate Today
      A Case Study of Cultural Politics in Post-Soviet Russia
      With a foreword by Priscilla Roosevelt
      ISBN 3-89821-426-5

FORTHCOMING (MANUSCRIPT WORKING TITLES)

Nicola Melloni
The Russian 1998 Financial Crisis and Its Aftermath
An Etherodox Perspective
ISBN 3-89821-407-9

Stephanie Solowyda
Biography of Semen Frank
ISBN 3-89821-457-5

Margaret Dikovitskaya
Arguing with the Photographs
Russian Imperial Colonial Attitudes in Visual Culture
ISBN 3-89821-462-1

Stefan Ihrig
Welche Nation in welcher Geschichte?
Eigen- und Fremdbilder der nationalen Diskurse in der Historiographie und den Geschichtsbüchern in der Republik
Moldova, 1991-2003
ISBN 3-89821-466-4

Sergei M. Plekhanov
Russian Nationalism in the Age of Globalization
ISBN 3-89821-484-2

Михаил Лукянов
Российский консерватизм и реформа, 1905-1917
ISBN 3-89821-503-2

Robert Pyrah
Cultural Memory and Identity
Literature, Criticism and the Theatre in Lviv - Lwow - Lemberg, 1918-1939 and in post-Soviet Ukraine
ISBN 3-89821-505-9

Dmitrij Chmelnizki
Die Architektur Stalins
Ideologie und Stil 1929-1960
ISBN 3-89821-515-6

Andrei Rogatchevski
The National-Bolshevik Party
ISBN 3-89821-532-6

Zenon Victor Wasyliw
Soviet Culture in the Ukrainian Village
The Transformation of Everyday Life and Values, 1921-1928
ISBN 3-89821-536-9

Nele Sass
Das gegenkulturelle Milieu im postsowjetischen Russland
ISBN 3-89821-543-1

Josette Baer
Preparing Modernity in Central Europe
Political Thought and the Independent Nation State
ISBN 3-89821-546-6

Ivan Katchanovski
Cleft Countries
Regional Political Divisions and Cultures in Post-Soviet Ukraine and Moldova
ISBN 3-89821-558-X

Julie Elkner
Maternalism versus Militarism
The Russian Soldiers' Mothers Committee
ISBN 3-89821-575-X

Maryna Romanets
Displaced Subjects, Anamorphosic Texts, Reconfigured Visions
Improvised Traditions in Contemporary Ukrainian and Irish Literature
ISBN 3-89821-576-8

Alexandra Kamarowsky
Russia's Post-crisis Growth
ISBN 3-89821-580-6

Martin Friessnegg
Das Problem der Medienfreiheit in Russland seit dem Ende der Sowjetunion
ISBN 3-89821-588-1

Florian Mühlfried
Postsowjetische Feiern
Das Georgische Bankett im Wandel
ISBN 3-89821-601-2

Nikolaj Nikiforowitsch Borobow
Führende Persönlichkeiten in Russland vom 12. bis 20 Jhd.: Ein Lexikon
Aus dem Russischen übersetzt und herausgegeben von Eberhard Schneider
ISBN 3-89821-638-1

Anton Burkov
The Impact of the European Convention for the Protection of Human Rights and Fundamental
Freedoms on Russian Law
ISBN 3-89821-639-X

Katsiaryna Yafimava
The Role of Gas Transit Routes in Belarus' Relations with Russia and the EU
ISBN 3-89821-655-1

Christopher Ford
Borotbism: A Chapter in the History of Ukrainian Communism
ISBN 3-89821-697-7

Series Subscription

Please enter my subscription to the series *Soviet and Post-Soviet Politics and Society*, ISSN 1614-3515, as follows:

❑ complete series   OR   ❑ English-language titles

                                                    ❑ German-language titles

                                                    ❑ Russian-language titles

starting with

❑ volume # 1

❑ volume # ___

     ❑ please also include the following volumes: #___, ___, ___, ___, ___, ___, ___

❑ the next volume being published

     ❑ please also include the following volumes: #___, ___, ___, ___, ___, ___, ___

❑ 1 copy per volume   OR   ❑ ___ copies per volume

Subscription within Germany:

You will receive every volume at 1st publication at the regular bookseller's price – incl. s & h and VAT.

Payment:

❑ Please bill me for every volume.

❑ Lastschriftverfahren: Ich/wir ermächtige(n) Sie hiermit widerruflich, den Rechnungsbetrag je Band von meinem/unserem folgendem Konto einzuziehen.

Kontoinhaber: _____ Kreditinstitut: _____

Kontonummer: _____ Bankleitzahl:_____

International Subscription:

Payment (incl. s & h and VAT) in advance for

❑ 10 volumes/copies (€ 319,80)   ❑ 20 volumes/copies (€ 599,80)

❑ 40 volumes/copies (€ 1.099,80)

Please send my books to:

NAME_____ DEPARTMENT_____

ADDRESS _____

POST/ZIP CODE_____ COUNTRY _____

TELEPHONE _____ EMAIL_____

date/signature_____

A hint for librarians in the former Soviet Union: Your academic library might be eligible to receive free-of-cost scholarly literature from Germany via the German Research Foundation. For Russian-language information on this program, see
       http://www.dfg.de/forschungsfoerderung/formulare/download/12_54.pdf.

Please fax to: **0511 / 262 2201 (+49 511 262 2201)**
or mail to: *ibidem*-Verlag, Julius-Leber-Weg 11, D-30457 Hannover, Germany
or send an e-mail: ibidem@ibidem-verlag.de

ibidem-Verlag

Melchiorstr. 15

D-70439 Stuttgart

info@ibidem-verlag.de

www.ibidem-verlag.de
www.edition-noema.de
www.autorenbetreuung.de

Malet Street, London WC1E 7HX
020-7631 6239
Items should be returned or renewed by the latest date stamped below.
Please pick up a Library guide or visit the Library website
http://www.bbk.ac.uk/lib/
for information about online renewals.

ONE WEEK LOAN

Printed in the United Kingdom
by Lightning Source UK Ltd.
127629UK00001B/62/A

9 783898 214131